World System History

This book is the fundamental starting point for the study of continuity and change in the global social, economic and political system over the longest historical term. Bringing together eminent interdisciplinary scholars, *World System History* considers the nature of social continuity back through history, resulting in a book which cuts across boundaries in social science and deals with at least 5,000 years of the human past in a truly global perspective.

No other volume offers so coordinated a picture of the issues or the prospects for the unified study of world system history. The kind of transdisciplinary cooperation needed to make sense of our complex world is made clear through a range of carefully coordinated interactive contributions from archaeologists, anthropologists, economists, historians, political scientists and sociologists. This controversial book shows that in order to understand contemporary issues we must study the long-term history of the world system. It will be a vital overview of perspectives on the history of the world system for all graduates and researchers in a variety of fields such as international political economy, world history and sociology.

Robert A. Denemark is Associate Professor of Political Science at the University of Delaware. **Jonathan Friedman** is Directeur d'études, Centre d'anthropologie des mondes contemporains at the Ecole des Hautes Etudes en Sciences Sociales, Paris and Professor in the Department of Social Anthropology at the University of Lund, Sweden. **Barry K. Gills** is Senior Lecturer in International Politics at the University of Newcastle upon Tyne. **George Modelski** is Professor Emeritus of Political Science at the University of Washington, Seattle.

World System History

The social science of long-term change

Edited by
**Robert A. Denemark,
Jonathan Friedman, Barry K. Gills,
and George Modelski**

London and New York

First published 2000
by Routledge
11 New Fetter Lane, London EC4P 4EE

Simultaneously published in the USA and Canada
by Routledge
29 West 35th Street, New York, NY 10001

Routledge is an imprint of the Taylor & Francis Group

Typeset in Baskerville by RefineCatch Ltd, Bungay, Suffolk
Printed and bound in Great Britain by
Biddles Ltd, Guildford and King's Lynn

British Library Cataloguing in Publication Data
A catalogue record for this book is available from the British Library

Library of Congress Cataloging in Publication Data
World system history : the social science of long-term change / edited by
Robert A. Denemark . . . [et al.]
        p. cm.
    Includes bibliographical references and index.
        1. Social history. 2. World history. 3. Social change. I. Denemark,
Robert Allen.
        HN8 . W67 2000   99-087145
        303.4–dc21

ISBN 0–415–23276–7 (hbk)
ISBN 0–415–23277–5 (pbk)

**This book is dedicated
to all those who ask
difficult questions.**

Contents

Figures

Map

Tables

Contributors

Andrew Bosworth received his Ph.D. in political science at the University of Washington, Seattle.

Christopher Chase-Dunn is Professor of Sociology at the Johns Hopkins University, Baltimore, Maryland.

Sing C. Chew is Professor of Sociology at Humboldt State University, Arcata, California.

Claudio Cioffi-Revilla is Professor of Political Science at the University of Colorado, Boulder.

Robert A. Denemark is Associate Professor of Political Science at the University of Delaware, Newark.

Kajsa Ekholm-Friedman is Professor of Social Anthropology at the University of Lund.

Andre Gunder Frank is Professor Emeritus of Economics at the University of Amsterdam and Visiting Professor of International Relations at the University of Miami and at Florida International University.

Jonathan Friedman is Directeur d'études, Centre d'anthropologie des mondes contemporains at the Ecole des Hautes Etudes en Sciences Sociales, Paris, and Professor of Social Anthropology at the University of Lund.

Barry K. Gills is Senior Lecturer in International Politics in the Department of Politics at the University of Newcastle-upon-Tyne.

Thomas D. Hall is Lester Jones Professor of Sociology at DePauw University, Greencastle, Indiana, and in 1999–2000 was visiting as A. Lindsay O'Connor Professor of American Institutions at Colgate University, Hamilton, New York.

Alf Hornborg is Professor of Human Ecology at the University of Lund.

William H. McNeill is Professor Emeritus of History at the University of Chicago.

George Modelski is Professor Emeritus of Political Science in the University of Washington, Seattle.

Stephen K. Sanderson is Professor of Sociology at Indiana University of Pennsylvania in Indiana, Pennsylvania.

Andrew Sherratt is Reader in European Prehistory and Senior Assistant Keeper in the Ashmolean Museum, Oxford University.

William R. Thompson is Professor of Political Science at Indiana University, Bloomington, Indiana.

David Warburton is Research Assistant in the Department of Biblical Studies at the University of Aarhus.

David Wilkinson is Professor of Political Science at the University of California, Los Angeles.

An introduction to world system history

Toward a social science of long-term change

Robert A. Denemark, Jonathan Friedman,
Barry K. Gills and George Modelski

This volume is designed as a fundamental starting point for the transdisciplinary study of continuity and change in the global social, economic, and political system over the longest of historical terms. Scholars from a variety of fields have long sought to acquire knowledge of this scope. Attempts to frame such a perspective face several significant challenges.

World history in its proper context

The first challenge is epistemological. What is it that can be known about such broad sweeps of the human experience? The work in this volume is predicated on the belief that there are real themes, continuities, perhaps even patterns that emerge over the long sweep of world history. These may be explicated, though this must be accomplished with careful attention to relevant context. Our goal is not to frame inviolate historical laws, but to explore continuities, consistent patterns, and recognizable behavioral repertoires, and understand their genesis and development over time.

The first section of this volume includes four major papers on the nature and dynamics of world system history by scholars from different disciplines and perspectives. Each deals in an explicit manner with a number of critical concepts and the processes that are linked to them. These include:

The world system

While in some sense fundamental to each of the perspectives in this volume, the term 'world system' continues to draw criticism, particularly for its lack of specificity. What constitutes a world system? What are to be considered its legitimate parameters? By what processes is such a world system defined? Does world systemic logic undergo fundamental transformations? Is the world system always basically the same? Has there been a single (evolving) world system, have there been areas external to it, or have separate systems existed side by side? If the latter, how can different world systems be compared?

Hegemonies, leadership and zones of innovation

The nature of global leadership is among the most hotly contested issues in contemporary political science, and plays a fundamental role in each of the four principal perspectives, regardless of the home discipline of the authors. The rise and decline of various powers or areas, and the implications of that process, are given concerted attention by several contributors, who each see such processes as central to world system history.

Center–periphery relations

By what processes are centers and peripheries created? Do all intersocietal systems have center–periphery hierarchies? Do center–periphery relations work in basically the same ways in all systems, or are there fundamental differences that emerge by context? Have center–periphery relations been a constant structural feature of world system history?

The world economy

Questions about the definition and parameters of the world economy mirror those regarding the world system. The term is not always consistently defined, nor are the nature of its units and the processes which link them always consistently identified. Is there one world economy or many world economies in world system history? Evolutionary conceptions of the world economy, understood as a complex adaptive system, also need to be explored.

Such an agenda places us at odds with a variety of influential contemporary positions in the social sciences. Behavioralists may find the definitions too fuzzy, the hypotheses too complex, and the data that long-term, historically contextual studies produce, too problematic. The authors of this volume are open to criticism that may help us frame our understandings in a more rigorous manner. We also welcome all those who would help us gather data from the historical record, which this volume illustrates is richer, deeper, and more amenable to review than some might suspect. We also believe, however, that the ransacking of history in search of decontextualized data bits adds little to our understanding of long-term social processes. The mass of 'results' that such a perspective has created remains unfocused or contradictory. This is true largely because of the lack of a sufficient framework from within which to understand social processes over the historical long term. We seek to construct such a framework.

Social constructivists and adherents to various post-modern or post-structuralist positions may consider our efforts to be naive because we generally believe that there may be real structural impediments to agents' action. We welcome such criticisms to the extent that they help us recognize certain pitfalls of social research designed to reconstruct complex societies. Our position nonetheless remains one of cautious methodological realism. While our history may well be socially constructed, there would seem to be at least as much re-creation of patterns of social interaction as there is creation. The repetitive nature of the historical process is one of its most disturbing properties. Structural sanctions and other limitations may await those who stray too far from existing social patterns. Structural incentives may be provided to those who follow established paths. We recognize the contestable nature of all social reality, but we also recognize that most individuals in most periods largely conform to the norms, roles and patterns expected of them. The very content of people's strategies are emergent in definite historical conditions. We need, then, to problematize the sources of intentionality in social life.

Critical theorists may show concern because we appear to fail to suggest an explicit program for emancipation. The scholars in this volume do not lack commitment to the betterment of the human condition, but they share a certain concern with the nature of social intervention. Social experiments are expensive in human terms, and policies rarely have their desired effects. Plans and manifestoes can be of more use to those who oppose them than to those they are meant to mobilize.

We do not wish to engage in open-ended methodological debates. Instead we invite our critics to join us in the attempt to examine world system history and show us where we have erred, or where such knowledge construction can be improved. We conceive of this project as a long-term endeavor. Positions are likely to alter with new information and new insights.

Holism and the agent-structure problem

A second challenge, that of the most appropriate 'level' at which to begin, is more practically methodological. Our position is holistic. Large-scale social systems provide the environment within which individuals make choices. Those choices, most of them consistent with the re-creation of the social systems involved, are the frameworks against which social actions are understood. Consistent behaviors presuppose consistent social conditions. Hence our concern is primarily with the system itself, and not with its individual human actors.

This puts us at odds with some current trends in the critical social sciences. The post-Cold War 'triumph of capitalism' appears to have vaulted various forms of methodological individualism and rational choice analysis to the fore. The fundamental argument appears to be that since only individuals act, individual behavior must rest at the heart of any legitimate social analysis. While we do not deny the utility of individual level analysis, we do question its claims to primacy.

Any attempt to understand broad-scale social processes by starting with the study of individuals must assume both the dominance of intentional action and the rather seamless translation of that intentional action through its various individual and institutional manifestations and on to the social environment which constitutes the context against which individual choices are made. Both the dominance of intentionality and such unproblematic translation are questionable.

The ability of individuals to apprehend the full extent of the implications of their behavior seems tenuous. When aggregated in markets or corporations or bureaucracies or states, individual behavior gives rise to the creation of institutions that have effects beyond the intentional range of their creators. We do not intend to impoverish foreign garment workers when we purchase inexpensive, as opposed to expensive, clothing. We do not intend to create conflict when through our actions we create institutions with inconsistent goals. Nonetheless, these outcomes may result. Giddens recognizes this in his work on structuration when he poses three levels of social interaction. Habermas acknowledges the same thing in his consideration of the tension between 'blocks of norm free sociality' like the global economy, and the more local 'lifeworld' (cited in Bohman 1991:168). Our actions do not automatically become disembodied 'systems' beyond the control of individuals, but as a result of this potential complexity they are unlikely to be apprehended by methods that begin by positing the primacy of individual intentional action.

The nature of rationality and the content of intentional actions designed to elicit certain outcomes are both dependent on a stable social structure. When social structures change rapidly, preferences are altered. We see the ephemeral nature of rationality as it mutates across a range of time horizons. Individuals also learn. As they learn, their behaviors may change to take into account new information or patterns of expectations. This reflectivity is often found at the base of criticisms of structural analyses. But it seems even more destructive of any attempts at understanding human behavior outside its specifically historical and experiential context.

Another way of conceiving the problem of the micro is to focus on the way subjects and their strategies are constituted. Rather than accept the common notion of the universal rational actor, one might instead study the way in which motivations and intentionalities are constructed and transformed. This may beg the question of free choice on the surface, but in fact it situates the problem in concrete historical contexts in what is perhaps a more productive way.

Though microfoundations are unsuitable starting points for a social science of long-term change, they do offer a good deal of methodological utility. One of the problems faced by structural analyses is that they are incomplete. They do not usually trace the microfoundations of macro-level activities. This can be problematic. Macro-level analyses may provide different explanations for the same outcome. There is little basis upon which to choose the superior analysis. Attention to the microfoundations of macro outcomes would provide such a basis, making competing structural explanations amenable to critical comparison and also more complete.

We are sensitive to critics concerned with what they perceive as a lack of attention to agency in our work, but we maintain that any attempt to apprehend long-term social change must begin at the structural level. The individual is not defined away in doing so. Considerations of the manner in which individuals act, come to understand their environments, and change or re-create their milieu, can only sharpen our analyses. Likewise we recognize the ability of individuals to learn and respond to cues in a strategic manner, tempered by experience and designed to alter conditions. Our approaches are compatible with, and do not preclude attention to, activities and intentions of individual agents, particularly those acting on behalf of states, other organizations and collectivities. Several contributors employ evolutionary concepts, and those accord a key role to innovation (mutation), hence to innovations in such areas as institutions, leading sectors or social movements. We welcome those who would help us extend our analyses to the micro level, while we seek to understand the structural level processes that animate human behavior by providing the context that makes social action intelligible.

The historical long term

A third fundamental challenge is the temporal one. When do we begin? By association, the question of 'when' also speaks to the question of 'where' we begin. There is no shortage of historical stage theories. Food gathering techniques, political styles, astronomical configurations, forms of transportation, habits of mind, and modes of production are but a few of the foundations upon which we have created developmental typologies. Many of these debates have grown old, restating core principles instead of moving to provide new answers to new questions.

The participants in this work sought to push the analysis of world systemic interaction as far back as they could, noting continuities and trends along the way. Though various participants disagree on the proportion of that past which may be relevant to understanding current conditions, the collection deals in a serious manner with at least the past 5,000 years of the historical record. We provide a basis upon which to reconsider some of the fundamental issues relevant to historical 'transitions' and long-term change.

Critics of macro-historical treatments have long sought to marginalize long-term analyses as hopelessly esoteric. Even some proponents of longer term social analyses avoid such broad sweeps. Marxists, for example, have long held that we cannot use information from social orders that existed before the transition to the capitalist mode of production in our attempts to understand current conditions. For Samir Amin (1991) and others, conditions were fundamentally different in the days when power yielded wealth than they are now that wealth yields power. It is, of course, important to try to identify fundamental discontinuities and focus on issues of contemporary import. We suggest, however, that temporal schemes based on such fragile distinctions as power yielding wealth as opposed to wealth yielding power ought to be re-considered. Our position is that empirical, not doctrinal, grounds must provide the foundation for any temporal self-imposed limits on social analysis. This volume calls for the reopening of such debates. We invite such critics to illustrate for us the error of our ways, not by mere assertion but by concrete example, evidence and argument.

As noted above, the question of when to begin is intimately related to the question of where to begin. Historical understandings are all too vulnerable to conditions and issues in the localities in which they are conceived. Both 'geo-centric' and 'unit-centric' tendencies can be identified.

Our current problems with Eurocentrism derive from the development of scholarship in a European dominated world system. As Abu-Lughod (1989) suggests, Eurocentric analysis framed a world system that systematically ignored its predecessors, their achievements, and the nature of the system that existed before European hegemony. Both familiar developmental paths, and discontinuities of world system history, go unrecognized as a result. However, the solution to this problem does not rest with the creation of various new counter-centrisms. Instead of calling attention to areas that are ignored, such a strategy would only concretize their compartmentalization. In this work, the authors attempt to focus instead on the extent of human interactions across political boundaries. The similar or differential effects of various processes in different spaces over time promises a more coherent picture of social interaction than do fractured sets of competing centrisms.

Attention may be focused not just on places, but on various units that inhabit those spaces. Historian Frederick Teggart laments that

> academic history has not succeeded in liberating itself from the influence of the Romantic period, during which, in every country of Europe, the spirit of nationality demanded the rewriting of history in terms of a new sense of national existence and a new enthusiasm for national achievements in the past . . . The division of history . . . into 'ancient,' 'medieval,' and 'modern' obscures the fact that these terms have reference, not to the world at large, but to a relatively small part of the earth's surface.
>
> (Teggart 1925:40–1)

The resulting state-centric analysis is narrow, particularistic, and makes it easy for us to ignore social processes that are not so conveniently packaged. The deleterious effects of acute state-centrism are well understood in the field of political science.

Thus, the contributors to this volume reject both geographic and unit based centrisms, though taking this position may generate criticism. We invite those with particular geographic or organizational interests to add their specialized knowledge and understanding to this broader project of constructing a new world history.

Intellectual breadth

A fourth challenge concerns the locus of research on long-term social interactions. The analysis of social reality and history has been parceled up among denizens of various disciplines and subdisciplines. Divisions of labor have their place. Attempting to understand continuity and change over the long historical term is a daunting task. Scholars may be quickly overwhelmed. The division of history and the various social sciences, with their attendant vocabularies, methodologies, separate time horizons and theoretical strains, facilitated the expansion of specialized knowledge. But this knowledge has been purchased at a cost. Real synthesis has been rendered terribly difficult. Students of society have more to teach one another than ever before, and are less likely to be able to do so. Our specialization, our institutionalized separation, and our exclusive literatures, make it harder for us to share our stores of knowledge and construct a history of the world for all of humanity.

Solutions to this problem do not rest with the simple assertion of the need to do 'interdisciplinary' work, or to edit volumes that mix 'theory' with 'cases.' Disciplinary boundaries must be broken down. We must become understandable to one another. We count our attack on traditional disciplinary boundaries as one of the most significant contributions of this volume. It is not an interdisciplinary dialogue, but a transdisciplinary social science we seek. This collection includes works by scholars who have taken their degrees in history, sociology, political science, anthropology and economics. All address the same general issues. All show concern for the manner in which concepts are developed. No regimentation is required, just an agreement to work toward common understandings, if not common concepts and languages.

We are prepared for criticisms of our attempts at transdisciplinary synthesis. Specialists will no doubt complain that we have ignored crucial phenomena, misunderstood critical events, or given short-shrift to important processes. Still others will warn that our desire to dilute disciplinary boundaries will give rise to vague social philosophies better suited to abuse than understanding. We do not eschew specific knowledge. Empirical falsification or support for the hypotheses proposed here must be the basis for this kind of research. But we must work continuously to overcome the incompatible ways students in different disciplines seek to categorize the phenomena we jointly deal with. This can be especially difficult in highly specialized fields. The use of different definitions for the same concepts, the use of impenetrable jargon, and the failure to communicate about problems of mutual interest, are needless hindrances to understanding. It is necessary to overcome these differences in order to establish successful and productive communication and cooperation, and the meeting that gave rise to these papers proved important in this respect. Our experience suggests that specialists in some areas marshal evidence that allows them to take very much for granted issues that remain problematic for other scholars, not for lack of agreement but for lack of access.

Our commitment to breaking down disciplinary boundaries is also reflected in our refusal to allow 'theory' and 'cases' to play carefully circumscribed roles. The four major theoretical statements in this volume were all crafted with careful attention to a transdisciplinary body of specific case analysis. Some of the more specialized chapters emerged in response to these structuring principles, while others continue along independent paths and may lead to new theory. Sometimes the fit is good, sometimes not. We take anomalies seriously. Our hope is for a dynamic synthesis of method, theory and case.

Appraisal

A final challenge concerns appraisal. How do scholars know when a research program is productive and when it is not? In our case this is especially important.

There are no clear signposts in transdisciplinary work. Progress is slow when faced with so vast and underspecified a set of questions, and so tremendous a literature. Nor is there much agreement yet on what would constitute progress. This is perhaps our most difficult challenge. Chapters which assess the state of cumulation of knowledge, clarify the possibilities for convergence, and identify areas for future research and collaboration, conclude the volume. To the extent that we create new understanding we believe we are successful. The point is to generate more light than heat. As our project matures, these are the criteria we shall apply.

Plan of the book

Our volume has four parts. Part I presents four principle perspectives. Each of the four was designed around a similar set of questions and was charged with taking the positions of their colleagues into consideration. In Part II we introduce a transdisciplinary set of regional and temporal studies that illustrate important instances of the key processes discussed in Part I. Part III considers a set of global historical macroprocesses, including the environment, the flow of information, the evolution of war, and urban development and decline. Part IV concerns itself with the problems of comparison, cumulation, and the future development of this field of inquiry.

These papers were originally presented at a special conference that took place in 1995 at the University of Lund in Sweden. They were subsequently refined in light of the interaction made possible by that meeting. We gratefully acknowledge the support of the Swedish Council for Planning and Coordination of Research, the Swedish Research Council for Social Sciences and Humanities, and the Wenner-Gren Foundation, without whose assistance this work would not have been possible.

Part I

General perspectives on world system history

1 The five thousand year world system in theory and praxis

Andre Gunder Frank and Barry K. Gills

We posit a world system continuity thesis. Our purpose is to help replace Eurocentric history and social science by a more humanocentric and eventually also ecocentric approach. Our guiding idea is the continuous history and development of a single world system in Afro-Eurasia for at least 5,000 years. This world historical-social scientific approach challenges received studies that attribute 'the rise of the West' to European exceptionalism. In our view, the rise to dominance of the West is only a recent, and perhaps a passing event.

Our approach is unabashedly historical materialist. Its main theoretical premises are: (1) the existence and development of the world system stretches back not just five hundred but some five thousand years; (2) the world economy and its long-distance trade relations form a centerpiece of this world system; (3) the process of capital accumulation is the motor force of world system history; (4) the center-periphery structure is one of the characteristics of the world system; (5) alternation between hegemony and rivalry is depictive of the world system, although system wide hegemony has been rare or non-existent; and (6) long economic cycles of ascending and descending phases underlie economic growth in the world system.

Theoretical categories and operational definitions

The world system

Per contra Wallerstein (1974a), we believe that the existence and development of the same world system in which we live stretches back five thousand years or more. According to Wallerstein and unlike our world system (without a hyphen), world-systems (with hyphen and sometimes plural) need not be even world wide. Braudel and Wallerstein both stress the difference between world economy/ system and world-economy/system. 'The world economy is an expression applied to the whole world . . . A world-economy only concerns a fragment of the world, an economically autonomous section' (Braudel 1984:20–1). 'Immanuel Wallerstein tells us that he arrived at the theory of the world-economy while looking for the largest units of measurement which would still be coherent' (Braudel 1984:70).

In our view, shared by Wilkinson, this largest unit has long been much larger and older than the European-centered 'world-economy/system' of Braudel and Wallerstein. Wilkinson (1987a, 1993c) emphasizes political coherence and sees 'Central Civilization' as starting in 1500 BC and expanding more slowly than its earlier and more far-flung economic connections. We use the latter as a major criterion for the identification of the world system since at least 3000 BC and see its spread as having been more rapid.

The debate between 500 and 5,000 years of world system history is really about how to write world system history. It is a debate about continuity versus dis-continuity. One position is that the mode of production or social formation in world history makes a sharp break about 1500. This position is dominant among historians and world-system theorists, including Wallerstein and Amin. The other position is that capital accumulation did not begin or become 'ceaseless' only after 1500 AD, but has been the motor force of the historical process throughout world system history. There was no such sharp break between different 'world-systems' or even 'modes of production' around 1500.

The real disagreement revolves around the question of what structures consti-tute a 'system' or a 'world(-)system' in particular. We contend that a hierarchy of center-periphery (and hinterland) complexes within the world system, in which surplus is being transferred between zones of the hierarchy, necessarily implies the existence of some form of an 'international' (at best a misleading term) division of labor. A criterion of systemic participation in a single world system is that no part of this system would be as it is or was if other parts were not as they are or were. The interaction from one part of the system to another may be only indirectly chain-linked. A weaker systemic link would be that the various parts may also have reacted to, and on, the same global ecological constraints. In Gills and Frank (1990/1) we suggest:

> The capture by elite A here ... of part of the economic surplus extracted by elite B there means that there is 'inter-penetrating accumulation' between A and B. This transfer or exchange of surplus connects not only the two elites, but also their 'societies'' economic, social, political, and ideological organization ... This inter-penetrating accumulation thus creates a causal inter-dependence between structures of accumulation and between political entities ... That is 'society' A here could and would not be the same as it was in the absence of its contact with B there, and vice versa.

Despite our emphasis on 'economic' connections to cement the world system, we also accept the world system connections established and maintained through recurrent 'political' conflict among 'societies' as emphasized by Wilkinson (1987a). The recognition of such conflict as a mark of participation in the same world system is all the more important insofar as much of the conflict has been over economic resources and control of trade routes. Conversely, trade in metals and/or weapons could increase military capacity and enhance control over sources of economic resources, including trade itself. Political conflict has also been the expression of the alternation between hegemony and rivalry within the world system and/or its regional parts.

Summarizing, then, we can list the following among the criteria of participation in the same world system: (1) extensive and persistent trade connections; (2) persistent or recurrent political relations with particular regions or peoples, including especially center–periphery–hinterland relations and hegemony/rivalry relations and processes; and (3) sharing economic, political, and perhaps also cultural cycles. The identification of these cycles and their bearing on the extent of the world system play a crucial role in our inquiry.

Indeed, the identification of the geographical extent of near-simultaneity of these cycles may serve as an important operational definition of the extent of the world system. If distant parts of Afro-Eurasia experience economic expansions and contractions nearly simultaneously, that would be evidence that they participate in the same world system.

George Modelski once counseled that if we want to study cycles, we should first define the system in which we want to look for them. Operationally it may be the other way around: the cycles can define the extent of the system!

The world economy

We may distinguish two related issues about the role and place of 'economy' in the world and its history. One refers to the existence and significance of production for exchange and capital accumulation. The other is whether the division of labor and competitive accumulation were played out at long distance so as to tie distant areas into a single 'world' economy. Both propositions are controversial, but we believe that both are also supported by historical evidence.

The first proposition has been the subject of debate in anthropology between substantivists and formalists. Weber, Polanyi and Finley are prominent among the former, but their findings are challenged by recent scholarship. One focus of the debate has been the Athenian economy. A lecture on the character of the ancient political economy by Millett (1990) argues for a political economy approach in which the 'primacy of exchange' is central. Millett's approach rests on an important criticism of Polanyi (1944/1957), who unfortunately regarded the forms of exchange (e.g. redistributive, reciprocal, and market) in an evolutionary way, and hence incompatible with one another. Millett throws doubt on Polanyi's thesis of the 'invention' of the market economy in fourth-century Athens by pointing to recent work by anthropologists on the complexity of exchange in 'non-capitalist' societies. Millett contends that the primitivist approach, which minimizes the role of capital, 'is apparently contradicted by sheer volume of credit transactions in Athenian sources' as credit was 'everywhere' in antiquity. For evidence of the market/credit economy as far back as Assyria note Larsen (1967, 1976); Adams (1974); Silver (1985); and Rowlands, Larsen, and Kristiansen (1987).

In our definition of the world system, regular exchange of surplus also affects the 'internal' character of each of the parts of the world system. Some scholars, like Wallerstein (1991), reject our definition because they do not believe that 'mere' trade makes a system. We do. We not only believe that regular and signifi- cant trade is a sufficient ground for speaking of a 'system' or of a real 'world economy,' but also that trade integrates social formations into something that should be called the 'international division of labor,' even in the ancient Eurasian world economy. This takes place because trade and production are not (falsely) separated. The nature of trade directly affects the character of production, as the history of the early modern world system so clearly illustrates, but which is also true much earlier. These effects are a consequence of specialization if nothing else, but we contend they are intimately related to the system of the regular transfer of surplus as well.

A related question then is how extensive was this division of labor and trade network. By our criteria it included Egypt, Mesopotamia, the Arabian Peninsula, the Levant, Anatolia, Iran, the Indus Valley, Transcaucasia, and parts of Central Asia, in the third millennium BC. All of these are south of the mountain ranges that ran across Asia from east to west. Chernykh's work (1993:302) leads to the inclusion in this world system of 'a whole chain from the Atlantic to the Pacific: the European, Eurasian, Caucasian and Central Asian provinces, along with others outside the USSR' all of which are north of these mountains. He also suggests in his foreword (xxi) that 'from at least the fifth millennium BC until the third millennium BC, the peoples of the EMA cultural zone seem to have shared the same developmental cycle: the formation and decline of cultures at various levels generally coincided.'

At least two kinds of evidence support the claim that the southern and northern regions were part of one world system emcompassing much of Afro-Eurasia by the Bronze Age. There were extensive and recurrent trade, migration and inva- sion, as well as cultural/technological diffusion, and north–south contacts across and/or around the mountains in various regions from Anatolia eastward. There was also substantial coincidence in the timing of long economic cycle phases identified independently for the north by Chernykh and for the south. This temporal coincidence may be traceable to ecological and/or other systemic commonalities. Therefore there is evidence for the existence of one immense Afro-Eurasian wide world system by the early Bronze Age. Therefore also, one of the important tasks of research and analysis is to inquire into its earliest develop- ment and explore its (cyclical?) expansion and transformation over time. We find that this world system was formed in the third millennium BC or earlier, and proceeds today.

Although preciosities did play a significant role in these trade and political relations, it is well to stress that there also were significant amounts of economic- ally vital trade in bulky necessities: metals, timber, grain, animals and other raw materials and foodstuffs, and of manufactures such as textiles and ceramics. For instance, southern Mesopotamia lacked metals and timber and was dependent on their import from Anatolia and the Levant, while it exported grains and textiles.

Like Blaut (1993) we argue that the most important European impact was the injection of new supplies of American bullion, and thereby themselves, into the already well established Eurasian economy. The Europeans did not in any sense 'create' either the world economic system or 'capitalism.' What the injection of new liquidity into the world economy actually seems to have done was to make important, though also limited, changes in financial flows, trade and production patterns, and to permit the Europeans to participate more actively in the same. They specialized in exploiting global differences in resources, production and prices to maximize their profits as middlemen, and where convenient they used force to assure their own participation in this exchange.

Thus long before the birth of the putative 'European world-economy' and still long after its advent, the real world economy had a far-flung division of labor and an intricate trade system, which was preponderantly Asian. Its major producers/ exporters of silver were Latin America and Japan, and of gold, Latin America, Southeast Asia, and Africa. South, East and West Africa had been major sources of gold for centuries, but parts of Africa also exported slaves westward and eastward.

The major importer and re-exporter of both silver and gold bullion was western and southern Europe, to cover its own perpetual massive structural balance of trade deficit with all other regions, except (perhaps) with the Americas and Africa, although the Europeans received African and especially American bullion without giving much in return. Western Europe had a balance of trade deficit with and re-exported much silver and some gold to the Baltics and eastern Europe, to West Asia, to India directly and via West Asia, to Southeast Asia directly and via India, and to China via all of the above. China also received silver from Japan.

West Asia had a balance of trade surplus with Europe, but a deficit with South, Southeast, East, and possibly Central Asia. West Asia covered its balance of trade deficits to the East with the re-export of bullion derived from its balance of trade surplus with Europe, the Maghreb and via it with West Africa, and gold from East Africa, as well as some of its own production of both gold and silver, especially in Persia.

India had a massive balance of trade surplus with Europe and some with West Asia, based mostly on its low cost cotton textile production and export. These went westwards to Africa, West Asia, Europe, and from there on across the Atlantic to the Caribbean and the Americas. In return, India received massive amounts of silver and some gold from the West, directly around the Cape or via West Africa. Since India produced little silver of its own, it used the imported silver mostly for coinage or re-export, and the gold for coinage (of so-called 'pagodas') and jewelry. India also exported cotton textiles to and imported spices from Southeast Asia, and also via the same exchanged cotton textiles for silk and porcelain and other ceramics from China. However, India had a balance of trade deficit with Southeast Asia and especially with China, and so was obliged to re-export especially silver to the east.

Southeast Asia exported spices and tin of its own production to Europe, West Asia, India and re-exported imports from India to China, which were its major customers, some eight times more than Europe. Additionally, Southeast Asia exported gold from its own production to India, China, and Japan, although it received silver from India, some of which it also re-exported to China via Malacca. Southeast Asia seems to have had a balance of trade surplus with India, but a deficit with China.

China had a balance of trade surplus with everybody (making it a 'super-accumulator?') based on its unrivaled manufacturing efficiency and export of silks and porcelain and other ceramics. Therefore, China, which like India had a perpetual silver shortage, was the major net importer of silver and met much of its need for currency out of imports of American silver which arrived via Europe, West Asia, India, Southeast Asia and with the Manila galleons directly from the Americas. China also received massive amounts of silver and copper from Japan and some through the overland caravan trade across Central Asia.

Japan, like Latin America, was a major producer and exporter of silver to China and Southeast Asia, but also of some gold and considerable copper as far as India and West Asia. Gold was both imported to and exported from China, depending on changing gold/silver/copper price ratios. Silver moved generally eastward (except westward from Japan and Acapulco via Manila), and gold moved westward (except eastward from Africa) via overland and maritime routes. Some eastward moving gold even reached Europe.

The complexity of the international division of labor and the network of world trade was of course vastly greater than this. However, even this mere summary should suffice to indicate how, contrary to Braudel and Wallerstein, all of these world regions were integral parts of a single world economic system between about 1400 and 1800 AD. The injection of American bullion provided new liquidity that facilitated an important increase in world-wide production, which rose to meet the new monetary demand. This 'pull' factor encouraged further development in China, India, Southeast Asia, and West Asia, including Persia. Even so, the Europeans were able to sell very few manufactures to the East, and instead profited substantially from inserting themselves into the inter-Asian country trade.

Capital accumulation

We regard the process of accumulation as the motor force of (world system) history. Wallerstein and others regard continuous capital accumulation as the *differentia specifica* of the 'modern world-system.' We have argued elsewhere that in this regard the 'modern' world system is not so different and that this same process of capital accumulation has played a, if not the, central role in the world system for several millennia (Frank 1991b; Gills and Frank 1990/1; Frank and Gills 1993). Amin (1991) and Wallerstein (1991) disagree. They argue that previous world-systems were what Amin and Wolf (1982) call 'tributary' or Wallerstein 'world empires.' In these, Amin claims that politics and ideology were in command, not the economic law of value in the accumulation of capital. Wallerstein seems to agree.

It is particularly important to clarify our controversial suggestion that 'ceaseless accumulation' is a feature of the world system throughout its development.

Though there can be no real doubt that industrialization played a crucial role in bringing about a quantitative change in the rate of ceaseless accumulation, in our view this change is essentially a matter of degree. This debate turns on the definition of 'ceaseless.'

We contend, following Marx (up to a point), that 'ceaseless' accumulation implies that capital is constantly reinvested into the circuits of production in order to sustain capital accumulation. This ceaselessness is imperative given competition. The historical evidence suggests to us that capital accumulation has normally been 'competitive' and has involved a continuous reinvestment in the means of production, and indeed in a whole social and political ensemble of sectors, including infrastructure. This investment process is carried out both by private capital and by the state, which is the case even today.

Then, as now, states lived partly on a 'rent' from this international commerce, through direct taxation on trade; from 'profits' generated by 'national' merchants, manufacturers, and money-men; and partly from taxing the national product or income of the general population. Imperialism provided an additional source of revenue to powerful states in the form of 'tribute,' meaning extortion or loot acquired through conquest. Indeed the logic of conquest often followed the logic of the trade routes and the sources of materials, especially the precious metal means of payment (Gills and Frank 1990/1; Frank and Gills 1993).

There has been a fundamental misconception of the character of the 'premodern' economy, particularly of Eurasia, based on the mistaken generalization of the 'command economy' or as Anderson (1974b) would have it, the role of 'coercion' and determination by the 'political instance' rather than by 'economics' (Gills 1993; 1995). In our view, what Amin (1991) and Wolf (1982) call the 'tributary mode' is, more often than not, merely taxation by another name. The fact that all historical states have lived by some form of taxation is hardly a revelation, nor is it incompatible with the idea that more often than not these premodern states coexisted with a vibrant commercial sector directed by private merchants and bankers and conducted on a vast international scale. The sheer volume of evidence from specialist histories of Eurasia corroborates the contention of the centrality of this world economic commerce again and again. (For the earlier period see Adams 1974; Ekholm and Friedman 1982, 1993; and Frank 1993a.)

The center–periphery structure

This structure is familiar to analysts of dependence in the 'modern' world system, and especially in Latin America, since 1492. It includes, but is not limited to, the transfer of surplus between zones of the world system. We now find that this analytical category is also applicable to the world system before that. However, the structure of this world system does not conform to the 'unipolar' model of center–periphery relations common in most dependency approaches. We now see more 'multipolar' center–periphery relations. The world system is not viewed as having always been composed of a single core and single periphery, but rather of an interlinked set of center–periphery complexes (including 'hinterlands') as discussed in Gills and Frank 1990/1 and Frank and Gills 1993. This approach to structuralist analysis allows greater flexibility, since distinct regional, imperial, or market mediated center–periphery complexes are accepted and yet are all seen as part of a single whole with systemic links to one another. Yet this multicentricity does not mean equality among the various centers or between different center–periphery complexes. There is a very complex hierarchical chain of metropole–satellite relations of extraction and transfer of surplus throughout the whole world system.

Hegemony–rivalry

We have defined 'hegemony' as a hierarchical structure of accumulation between classes and states, mediated by force. In this sense, the center–periphery structure of the world system is simultaneously an economic and a political hierarchy. Hegemony embodies both.

World system and international relations literature has recently produced many good analyses of alternation between hegemonic leadership and rivalry for hegemony in the world system since 1492 (Wallerstein 1984; Modelski 1987; Modelski and Thompson 1988). We find that hegemony and rivalry also mark world system history long before that (Gills and Frank 1992).

However, just as the world economy/system never entirely 'falls' but only changes, hegemonic ascent and descent are usually quite gradual and do not occur in a unipolar framework, but rather in a multipolar one. This world historical process 'favors some at a particular time while discriminating against others, and so on through time' (Gills 1993:121). Indeed, it is integral to our structural theory of world development that areas once peripheral may ascend to hegemonic or core status, while areas once in the core may descend into the periphery. We particularly emphasize how economic rhythms common to the entire world system, such as long cycles of expansion and contraction, affect the relative position of all of the 'parts' of the system. The schema of the structure of the world system should perhaps be akin to a truncated pyramid, at the apex of which there is not usually one sole hegemonic center of political power and capital accumulation, but rather several. Our position is distinguished by the argument that these ascents and declines occur within the same world system.

We have serious reservations about received theories of hegemony, be they Modelski and Thompson's 'political leadership' or Wallerstein's 'economic hegemony.' To begin with, the claims that Portugal, the Netherlands, England (twice) and the United States have successively been hegemonic refer to their dominance in an essentially Western-based and centered 'world-system.' If however we recognize that in the sixteenth to eighteenth centuries the world system was much larger than the European world-system, then the claim to hegemony of little Venice, Portugal and the Netherlands within the whole Afro-Eurasian and American world economy becomes doubtful if not ludicrous. All of these economies were much too small to exercise any kind of hegemony in, let alone over, the world system. Moreover, they certainly were not the centers of world

economic accumulation. By comparison and instead, Ming/Qin China and
Moghul India, as well as Ottoman Turkey and perhaps Safavid Persia politically
and economically far outranked any of the individual West European economies
and states, and probably all the European ones put together.

We find that hegemony at the scale of the entire world system, when conventionally defined as a unipolar hegemony, is extremely rare, self defeating, and
perhaps non-existent. Rather, the norm is a situation we have called 'interlinked
hegemonies' (Gills and Frank 1992; Frank and Gills 1993). In this regard we
follow Abu-Lughod (1989), i.e. we do not see hegemonic ascent and descent so
much as a process of absolute rise and decline by particular states, but rather as a
situation wherein some states, or groups of states, temporarily gain relative power
vis-à-vis others. On this basis they can set the terms of their interactions with
subordinates as they ascend but gradually lose this capacity as they descend. We
focus not so much on breakdowns of hegemonic power/s and still less on any
supposed breakdown/s of the world system or its continuity, which so far have not
occurred in the Central World System, but on world system cycles, which have
characterized its continuous but cyclical development over the last five thousand
years.

Long and short economic cycles

We have already noted the apparent existence of alternating ascending ('A')
phases of economic and political expansion, and descending ('B') phases of political economic crises. An important characteristic of the modern world system is
that the processes of capital accumulation, changes in center-periphery position
within it, and world system hegemony and rivalry are all cyclical and occur in
tandem with each other. We now believe that we can identify a cyclical pattern of
long A and B phases in the same world system back through the third millennium
BC. We have already noted that a most revealing operational criterion of the
extent of the world system is the participation or not in the same about 500-year-
long economic cycle and the interregional near-synchronization of its about 250-
year-long A and B phases. World economic synchronization of shorter cycles and
their phases are even more revealing.

Our suggested datings of the A and B phases for the Bronze Age world system
are BC: A: 3000–28/2700, B: 2700–26/2500, A: 2600–2400, B: 24/2300–2000,
A: 2000–18/1750, B: 18/1750–16/1500, A: 16/1500–1200, B: 1200–1000,
which was the Bronze 'Dark Age' Crisis (Frank 1993a). Tentative Iron Age dates
are: A: 1000–800?, B: 800–550?, A: 600/550–450/400?, B: 450–350?, A: 350–
250/200? B: 250/200–100/50, A: 200/100 BC–200 AD, B: 150/200–500, A:
500–750/800, B: 750/800–1000/1050, A: 1000/1050–1250/1300, B: 1250/
1300–1450, A: 1450–1600 (Gills and Frank 1992).

Wilkinson (1992b) and Bosworth (1995b) independently tested the existence
and timing of our cycles using data from Chandler's (1987) census of growth and
decline in city sizes. Both confirmed the existence and most but not all of the
timing of our cycles, especially during the second half of the first millennium AD,

where we ourselves expressed doubt about our findings. The dating of periods during the Bronze Age first millennium BC by the Sherratts (1991) coincided almost exactly with ours. Kristiansen (1992) has similar datings, as does Randsborg (1991). Chase-Dunn and Willard's (1993) analysis, again using Chandler's data, lends less corroboration to our precise datings, but does confirm the simultaneity of cycle phases between East and West Asia since the mid-first millennium BC.

Other world systemic cyclical characteristics complicate this pattern. Expansion and contraction seems to begin in one part of the world system, usually in its core, and then to diffuse from there to other parts, including core competitors and the periphery. Dales (1976) observed and Frank (1993a) pursued an apparent eastward displacement of cycle phases through West, Central and South Asia in the third millennium BC. Today cyclical expansion and especially contraction begins in the United States and spreads out from there. Cyclical decline tends to spell the relative or even absolute decline of the principal core power.

This decline offers opportunities to some core rivals, or even some peripheral parts of the system. Some of them advance both absolutely and relatively, perhaps even to replace the previous central core. Today, we witness this process in Japan and the East Asian NICs relative to the United States. While trying to identify cycles in *World Accumulation 1492–1789*, Frank (1978a) made the empirical generalization that incipient exploratory expansions of the world system occurred during B phases, like seventeenth century European settlement in North America. These new areas then offered the basis of subsequent major investment and expansion during the next A phase. These phase-displacement and/or out-of-phase characteristics in and of economic cycles, of course, complicate the identification of system-wide cycles in the past, and all the more so in the distant Bronze Age. However, the existence of such complicating factors does not mean that there are, or were, no systemic cycles with distinguishable expansive A and contractive B phases. (Our more complete discussion of these cycles appears in Frank and Gills 1993 and Frank 1993a,b.)

We also inquire into the possible continuation after 1450 of our long world system cycle. We seek evidence for the continuation (or not) of this cycle and patterns of hegemonic rise and decline into the modern period. So far, our reading of the evidence is still very tentative. There seems to be evidence for its continuation far beyond the 'long sixteenth century' well into the eighteenth century. Apparently even over this much longer A phase, the world economy expanded, with the creation of vast new liquidity, capital formation, growth in population, urbanization, production, trade, and the simultaneous expansion of the imperial Ming, Jin, Mughal, Safavid, Ottoman and Hapsburg empires, up to the mid-eighteenth century. During this period the world economy was on a silver standard. The Ottomans, Ming and India coined huge quantities of silver to support their currency systems, ultimately sustained by the production of American and Japanese mines.

Of related concern are the shorter, approximately fifty-year 'Kondratieff' cycles, and both how and whether they fit into our longer cycle. How far back these Kondratieff cycles go is still in dispute. Modelski and Thompson (1996a) have identified nineteen 'K-waves' beginning in 930 AD. But can any of these cycles be said to have been world system wide? Modelski and Thompson say so; but after the first four in China they see hegemony moving to Europe. We would have to find evidence for K-waves that include large parts of the still dominant Asia.

We also propose to inquire to what extent we can identify shorter economic cycles, and especially financial crises and recessions, that were simultaneous in many far-flung parts of the world economy. The recessions of the early 1760s, 1770s and again 1780s were world-wide economic downturns, each of which had simultaneous repercussions in India, Russia, Western Europe, and the Americas, including the American and French revolutions (Frank 1978a, 1994a). Other such cases can surely be identified and should be analyzed from a world economic perspective. We contend that the simultaneity of such economic events in distant parts of the world is *prima facie* evidence of their participation in a single world economic system, rather than in several different and distinct 'world-economies' as per Braudel and Wallerstein. Both claim, for instance, that Russia was 'obviously' in a 'remote' or 'autonomous' 'world-economy.' However, the three declines in Russia's balance of trade in the early years of the three decades mentioned above were, on closer inspection, connected to simultaneous and related events in many parts of continental Western Europe, Britain, North America, and far away India. All of these occurred during three important recessions in what should be termed a world system wide Kondratieff B phase crisis from 1762 to 1790 (Frank 1978a, 1994a). Other world system wide short cycles in modern history could surely be identified and analyzed, if only economic historians were willing to try.

In summary and comparison, we find that the principal systemic features of the 'modern world system' can also be identified earlier than 1500. Wallerstein and Amin argue that our world system emerged about 1500 and was essentially different from previous times and places. However, Modelski (1987) includes some leadership before 1500 in his analysis, and Modelski and Thompson (1996a) now trace nineteen Kondratieff cycles back to 930 AD. Chase-Dunn (1992) and others find parallels in 'other' and prior world systems. Wilkinson (1989) discovers at least some of these features also in his 'Central Civilization' and elsewhere. He sees historical continuity, but no world system. Abu-Lughod (1989) sees a 'thirteenth century world system,' but she regards it as different from the world system before or since. We combine all of the above into an analysis, or at least an identification, of the principal features of this world system over several thousand years.

Putting Europe in its Afro-Eurasian place

Seeing the origin of the world system five thousand years ago in Asia instead of five hundred years ago in Europe adds further dimensions to the critique of Eurocentrism. Firstly, a longer real-world-historically-based more humanocentric alternative, and secondly, a real basis for denying three related presumptions: (1) that the world system began in Europe; (2) that the 'Rise of the West' was based on European exceptionalism, which is shared by Weberian and Marxist social science; and (3) that the Europeans 'incorporated' the rest of the world into their own 'capitalist modern world-system' after 1500.

Almost all modern and economic world history since 1500 has been written as though it began in Europe and then spread out to incorporate and modernize the Americas, Africa and 'traditional' Asia. The ancient roots of this 'modernizing' process are sought within Europe itself and earlier on in Rome and Greece, while the (Orientalizing) influence of Egypt and Mesopotamia upon Greece and Rome is ignored. Afro-Asian history is disregarded other than to note the Asian origins of such 'items' as numbers, compass, gun powder, etc., but omitting even printing, which originated in China centuries before Gutenberg was born!

Economic history is even more confined to the West. *The Study of Economic History* (Harte 1971) collects lectures by twenty-one eminent English speaking economic historians who review the literature of the century past. Almost every word is about Europe and the United States. The *Europe and the People Without History* (Wolf 1982) appear to have even less economic history.

A particularly Eurocentric example is *The Rise of the Western World: A New Economic History* by the 1993 Nobel laureate in economics Douglass C. North and Robert Paul Thomas (1973). It merits note not only for the recognition given one author but also because of its explicitness. On the very first page they state 'the development of an efficient economic organization in Western Europe accounts for the rise of the West.' They then trace this institutional change, especially the development of property rights, to increased economic scarcity generated by a demographic upturn in Western Europe. The rest of the world was not there for them. Moreover, as North and Thomas (1973:vii) emphasize, their history is 'consistent with and complementary to standard neo-classical economic theory,' which we may suppose influenced the award of the Nobel prize.

Marxist economic history seems different in using concepts like 'mode of production' and 'class struggle,' but it is equally Eurocentric. Both of these concepts have been interpreted within a framework of a single society or social formation. Thus, Marxist economic historians look for the sources of 'the rise of the West' and 'the development of capitalism' within Europe and are equally or even more Eurocentric than their 'bourgeois' opponents. Examples include the nefarious concept of 'the Asiatic Mode of Production,' of which there was nary a trace anywhere in Asia. This concept bequeathed Marxism with a bias against Asian development, which it regarded as traditional, backward and stagnant.

In recent years, Fernand Braudel's (1984) *Perspective of the World* and Immanuel Wallerstein's (1974a) *Modern World-System* try to break away from some of this Eurocentrism. So did Frank's (1978a) *World Accumulation 1492–1789* and the work of Samir Amin. Yet the last three (Frank even in the title!) still mark 1492 or thereabouts as a breaking point, and read all succeeding history as having been centered on Europe and its westward and eastward expansion. Only Braudel (1984:57) writes that 'I do not share Immanuel Wallerstein's fascination with the sixteenth century' as the time the modern world-system emerged in Europe. Braudel is 'inclined to see the European world-economy as having taken shape very early on.' Nonetheless, he also concentrates on the emergence and expansion of a supposed autonomous 'European world-economy' even though his book is replete with evidence that Europe was part and parcel of a wider world economy centered in Asia through the eighteenth century.

Indeed a whole library full of books and articles has been devoted to explaining 'the rise of the West' in terms of its own supposed exceptionalism. Jones (1981) revealingly entitles his book *The European Miracle* and many others do the same implicitly (e.g. White 1962; Hall 1985; Baechler, Hall and Mann 1988). They all find the rest of the world deficient or defective in some crucial historical, economic, social, political, ideological, or cultural respect. These authors then revert to an internal explanation of the presumed superiority of the West to explain its ascendance over the rest of the world.

Important critiques also emerge. William McNeill (1963), the dean of world historians who used *The Rise of the West* as the title for his pathbreaking book, is among the few Western historians to take exception to this exceptionalism. Islamicist and world historian Marshall Hodgson writes:

All attempts that I have yet seen to invoke pre-Modern seminal traits in the Occident can be shown to fail under close historical analysis, once other societies begin to be known as intimately as the Occident. This also applies to the great master, Max Weber, who tried to show that the Occident inherited a unique combination of rationality and activism.

(Hodgson 1993:86)

Blaut (1992) exposes the 'myth of the European miracle' in its various versions based on biology (race and demography), environment, (Weberian) rationality, technology, and society (state, church, family) and demolishes the theory of European exceptionalism on all these counts.

Hodgson (1993) and Blaut (1992, 1993) derisorally call Eurocentric history 'tunnel history' derived from tunnel vision, which sees only exceptional intra-European causes and consequences and is blind to all extra-European contributions to modern European and world history.

Eurocentrism has also come under attack in Bernal's (1987) *Black Athena* and Amin's (1989) *Eurocentrism*, and more popularly by Afro-, Islamo-, and other 'centrisms' and 'multiculturality' (Voll 1994; Hamashita 1988, 1994). Some of these otherwise welcome critiques seek to replace one centrism by another and do so on a largely cultural/ideological level. We see no good theoretical or historical/factual reason to make it Islamo- or Sino- (let alone Afro-!) centric. We believe that our work both on the pre- and post-1500 period can demonstrate the existence of a wider world system, which in fact does and theoretically can encompass the Islamic, Chinese-centered, and other supposedly independent 'world-systems,' all of which were connected with each other in a single world system.

A less biased reading of modern and economic world history would give Asia its historical due. Two recent departures stand out: Abu-Lughod (1989) describing a thirteenth-century Eurasian world system *Before European Hegemony*, and

Chaudhuri (1990) analyzing *Asia Before Europe*. As their titles imply, these writers recognize the significance of Asia before European hegemony. Chaudhuri also recognizes that Asian economic life prospered long after the supposed sixteenth century 'rise of the West.'

Although he was not a close 'relative' of this group, another important precursor in this recognition was Marshall Hodgson. His *Venture of Islam* (1974) not only claimed the central place in world history for Islam from the seventh through the ninth centuries, he also argued that Islam still or again merited this place through its expansion (again) in the fourteenth to sixteenth centuries. The recent posthumous compilation of some of Hodgson's still earlier articles and manuscripts underscores the importance of *Rethinking World History* (1993). Hodgson wrote:

> A Westernist image of world history, if not disciplined by a more adequate perspective, can do untold harm; in fact it is now doing untold harm. That is why I lay so much stress on not assuming 'decadence' in Islamic society before the 18th century unless one has really good evidence . . . One of the most important tasks of world history, as I see it, is to give people a sense of the pattern of time periods and geographical areas which is free of the multifarious Westernist presuppositions.
>
> (Hodgson 1993:94)

Even the master Europeanist Braudel (1984:496) finds that 'it was only because the accessible markets of the Far East formed a series of coherent economies linked together in a fully operational world-economy, that the merchant capitalism of Europe was able to lay siege to them and to use their own vitality.' Or as Abu-Lughod (1989:388) put it, 'the decline of the East preceded the rise of the West.'

Capitalism?

Braudel and Wallerstein address the question of whether the European world-system was or is 'capitalist' and whether this term clarifies more than it obscures. The answer, and indeed even the question, has important ideological/political consequences. They have been the subject of intense debate about the 'transition from feudalism to capitalism' (Hilton 1976), the 'Brenner debate' (Aston and Philpin 1985), and the 'European Miracle' (Jones 1981; Hall 1985), and others. All these debates have been Eurocentric. Even Blaut's (1992, 1993) anti-Eurocentric formulation remains limited by his attachment to the idea of transition, of a break between 'feudalism' and 'capitalism.' Even Metzler (1994) and Sanderson (1992) seem similarly obsessed by the ideas of feudalism and transition at the same time that they research the advanced commercialization of Tokugawa Japan.

However, as Tibebu (1990:50) suggests, the fundamental justification among almost all Marxists for the term 'bourgeois revolution' is an argument based on an analogy to the long awaited proletarian revolution. He argues that both revolutions are 'imaginary.' So are, we submit, both 'transitions.'

Palat and Wallerstein (1990) insist that the European-centered 'modern world-system' is distinguished by its unique capitalist mode of production. Yet according to Braudel (1984:57) 'capitalism did not wait for the sixteenth century to make its appearance.' Braudel sees the commercialization, expansion and Renaissance of the European world-economy since the eleventh century. Braudel (1984:91) suggests that 'The merchant cities of the Middle Ages all strained to make profits and were shaped by the strain . . . Contemporary capitalism has invented nothing.'

> By at least the twelfth century . . . everything seems to have been there in embryo . . . bills of exchange, credit, minted coins, banks, forward selling, public finance, loans, capitalism, colonialism – as well as social disturbances, a sophisticated labor force, class struggles, social oppression, political atrocities.
>
> (Braudel 1984:91)

But was this past limited to, and 'capitalism' invented in, only one world-economy centered in Western Europe, which then exported it to others in Asia? No.

> Everywhere, from Egypt to Japan, we shall find genuine capitalists, whole-salers, the rentiers of trade, and their thousands of auxiliaries – the commission agents, brokers, money-changers and bankers. As for the techniques, possi-bilities or guarantees of exchange, any of these groups of merchants would stand comparisons with its western equivalents
>
> (Braudel 1984:486)

Braudel and even Wallerstein concede that there was no dramatic, or even gradual, change in mode/s of production. There was no such noticeable change, not to mention any succession, from other mode/s to a 'capitalist' one, and certainly none beginning in the sixteenth century or in Asia after centuries of European re/incorporation into the Asian world-economy.

So, these Eurocentric and (anti-) historical categories of 'feudalism,' 'capitalism,' and the alleged 'transition' between them merit criticism from an alternative world economic perspective. We agree with Chaudhuri (1990:84) that 'The cease-less quest of modern historians looking for the "origins" and roots of capitalism is not much better than the alchemist's search for the philosopher's stone that trans-forms base metal into gold.' Better, as we have argued, to abandon the chimera of a unique 'capitalist' mode of production, not to mention its supposedly West European origin (Frank 1991b, Frank and Gills 1992, 1993). All these 'world-economies' in the 'west' and 'east' were only parts of a single age-old world system, within which this change took place, like all else, only temporarily!

Thus we believe, as Chase-Dunn and Hall also seem to, that the modes of production are not the key to understanding the 'transitions' in the history of world development. Rather, the developmental dynamic of the world system as a whole is far more important. Furthermore, 'transitions' seem to be more a consequence of larger competitive patterns in the world system than of changes in modes of production. Above all, 'transitions' seem to be a matter of the role and position a particular entity fills in the world accumulation process.

Clarifying some misunderstandings

The most common misperception is that the term 'world system' means that there has only ever been one single world system throughout all of world history. Herein we find no difficulty in joining Chase-Dunn and Hall in their reference to 'world-system*s*.' Not only do we find a largely separate development of the political economies of pre-Columbian America vis-à-vis those of Eurasia, but even for Eurasia it would not be correct to conclude that there has only ever been one giant all-encompassing world system. Rather there were several streams of regional development, that at earlier periods in their development may have constituted separate systems. We hold however, with Wilkinson, that one world system gradually came to 'incorporate' (if only by merger) all others, first in Eurasia, and then after 1492 over the entire globe. It is this Afro-Eurasian born and then overarching world economy that we have called 'the world system.' This argument cuts against the grain of so much received theory and so many compartmentalized branches of knowledge and so many specialized histories (and historians), that it is very controversial even when properly understood. In hindsight it may have been an error to adopt the term 'world system' since it has facilitated misunderstandings of our theses on world development.

We are also unashamedly (historical) materialist. We define the world system on the basis of regular trade which embodies a transfer of surplus, implies a 'division of labor' and brings in its train systemic political, social, ideological, cultural, and even religious rhythms as well. However we are not simply 'economic determinists' because we insist that the 'economic' is also 'political.' This is why, in our own defense, we chose the term 'world system' for our concept of the world political economy, because we also argue that an integral aspect of the world system's development process is its hegemonic rhythm, i.e. a 'political' pattern. We reject sterile debates about causality based on a false separation of the 'infrastructural' from the 'superstructural' or of the 'economic' from the 'political' or that the economic rhythms automatically determine the hegemonic/political rhythms. In our formulation, economic and political power are inseparable, as are economic and political means to desired ends.

Another implication that has been wrongly attributed to the idea of the five thousand year world system is that capitalism is five thousand years old. We argue instead that the concepts of feudalism, capitalism, and socialism are transitional ideological modes (Frank 1991b) and are best abandoned for their lack of real or 'scientific' basis. They obscure more of the fundamental continuity of the underlying world system than the historical differences and transitions that these terms supposedly clarify.

Misunderstanding has led to the unfounded charge that in our view nothing ever changes, and there is nothing to be done about it. No. We do live in the same world system that began to develop more than five thousand years ago; but the system is not the same, or not everything is the same in the system. There have been many changes. Indeed, some of the structural features of the world system (inequality, cycles, etc.) seem endogenously to generate processual and evolutionary changes in the system.

Thus, we do not deny qualitative changes and secular trends in world development. Rather we emphasize the essential continuity of fundamentally embedded patterns of overall systemic dynamics. This does not require a strict determinism whereby everything that happens 'on the ground' at a 'lower' level is simply a mechanical expression of determining overall patterns. Indeed, we think that the specific characteristics of each area of the world system at any particular time should be taken into account in order to understand the specific responses each makes to stimuli that come from the systemic rhythm as a whole. The structure of the system imposes limitation to voluntaristic action and policy to transform it into 'another system' (e.g. from 'feudalism' to 'capitalism' to 'socialism' to 'communism'). Nonetheless, some (policy?) alternatives are possible and many popular struggles are necessary, and will continue to be, against the exploitation, oppression, inequities and polarization, which the system itself generates. As the people struggling against Portuguese colonialism said, and as we will also conclude, 'A Luta Continua' – The Struggle Continues!

Possibilities for collaborative research

We are gratified that our continuous five thousand year world system scheme is gaining increasing acceptance from Wilkinson (1993c); that Modelski and Thompson are pushing their own empirical work beyond their previous 1494 divide; and that Chase-Dunn and Hall (1994) are moving in our direction, as we are moving in theirs! They (1994:22) refer to 'the general idea of a single Afro-Eurasian world-system with nearly synchronous phases of growth and decline.' They ask whether that is correct; answer that they hesitate to so conclude; but end up with 'what are the alternatives?' The only one they offer is that an East Asian world-system may have developed independently of the West Asian one, but that interaction between them, and of both of them on Central Asia, created a dynamic which then affected both simultaneously, at least since the middle of the first millennium BC. Chase-Dunn and Hall agree that climatic changes need further study in this connection, and suggest that our five thousand year world system perspective can also 'be used to tease out the real structural and processural differences as well as the similarities across time and across different systems.' We are happy to cooperate with them, although perhaps a division of labor in which they concentrate more on the differences and we more on the communalities would be fruitful.

World system history scholars increasingly try to extend studies farther and farther back through history and prehistory. This procedure conjures up the question of how alike or different the early world system was from the modern and contemporary one. The 'continuationists,' like Wilkinson and ourselves and increasingly

Chase-Dunn and Hall (who like us eschew modes of production and prefer modes of accumulation) and Modelski and Thompson, emphasize the commonalities. The 'transformationists,' especially Wallerstein and Amin, focus on, or only see, the differences. Yet what both lack most, as per Sanderson (1990), is a systematic theory of social or historical evolution. In our case, if as Gills puts it, it is the same system but it is not the same, then what has made the same system different?

We do not have many answers to that question, except the very general, albeit we think important, ones that the unequal social (including center–periphery) structure and uneven temporal (cyclical) processes of the world system generates change within it and thus its transformation. These days it is increasingly fashionable at least among the more materially inclined to look at ecology, demography and technology as major factors in the generation of the social/historical 'evolutionary' dynamic. Our own work has given these factors too short shrift. We could benefit from the technological propositions of Chase-Dunn and Hall (1994); the ecological propositions of Chew (1995); and the demographic propositions of Goldstone (1991). Nonetheless, though we are not monetarists, we are inclined also to recognize a decisive role in monetary factors, such as changes (even if not autonomous ones) in bullion supplies.

Chase-Dunn and Hall (1994:6) also suggest that 'all world-systems pulsate in the sense that the spatial scale of integration, especially by trade, gets larger and then smaller again' and that 'all systems experience the rise and fall of hierarchies' (Chase-Dunn and Hall 1997:204). We agree and have found large regions which seem to 'drop out' of the world system for long periods of time as evidenced by the lack of evidence for continued cyclical up-swings. Examples include India, which apparently dropped out from 1900 to 900 BC, as well as Western Europe between 500 and 1000 AD. However, if a region was an integral part of the world system and was marginalized during (and by?) a major world crisis, then we should not regard that region as being separate from the world system even, or precisely, during the time when it is not or less active within it. Paradoxically, it was the very participation in the world system that generated the non- or reduced-participation. This is a process that we can observe today, particularly in Africa. The extent of the world system cannot be read from the amount of interaction within it at any particular time. The cyclical rhythms or pulsations of the system itself generate greater or lesser scales of integration, especially by trade.

A related issue is that of 'internal' vs. 'external' influence or determination. Weberians and Marxists privilege 'internal' ones. World system theory stresses influences that are 'external' to a particular 'society' or 'economy.' However, world systemic influences may be more important at some times than at others. Expansive cyclical A phases in the world system, like the rising tide, can raise most individual political and economic boats, as it also strengthens the economic relations among them. The onset of a receding tide B phase crisis also affects most boats. We see the breakdown of these closer economic relations and a turning-inward-on-itself involution of some or even many parts of the world. This makes 'internal' processes seem more preponderant. Further empirical testing of these propositions would be a useful cooperative endeavor.

This understanding of world system cyclical expansion and contraction could also help bridge the differences between our larger world system and Wilkinson's smaller 'Central Civilization,' while at the same time allowing us to benefit from his detailed analysis of the rise and decline of polities within the same. Wilkinson (1987a, 1993c:235,240–1) concurs in the importance of Central Asia, finds that 'civilizations follow oikumenes and "the flag follows trade" and not the reverse,' stresses that no endogenous crisis has ever made the central world economy itself collapse, and regards our apparent differences as 'not in principle unresolvable,' especially with data on city sizes below those recorded by Chandler. These could resolve our chronological disagreements by demonstrating more world systemic economic connections than Wilkinson has found.

There is also the problem of refining the calibration of the overall world systemic cycles across all of the regions. The clearest working hypothesis seems to be that world systemic cycles are probably more sequential than simultaneous, though there is also a causal link in the sequentialization. Following Dales (1976), Frank found a sequential eastward shift through West and South Asia of the Bronze Age world system cycle in the third millennium BC. The process is also uneven. Even in a general world economic crisis not all core or peripheral areas are equally affected.

Most importantly, the world system approach must be extended by research into the causality of the cycles, both the economic and the hegemonic, and their mutual relations. In this regard and even if they may not be causative, the intervention of climatic, ecological, and demographic change, and their relations with each other and in turn with social structural ones have received far less attention than they merit. This problematique also invites further research into how local conditions interact with systemic level impulses and stimuli. Specifically, there should also be further research into how local responses affect ascent and decline in the 'interlinked hegemonies' hierarchy.

Modelski and Thompson's (1996a) temporal and spatial expansion of their empirically grounded work overlaps with ours in several respects and offers opportunities for mutual enrichment and cooperation. They now also refer to five thousand years of world history, but refer only to stages of its 'evolution' before 1000 AD and do not carry their cyclical analysis farther back. We do, and perhaps they could join us, or use some of our findings in their own work, and then let us benefit from their sophistication to improve our own work. They already offer an analysis of Kondratieff cycles centered in China and the Mongol Empire from 930 to 1350 AD, and from then in Egypt and Venice until 1500. Their data for this period are welcome grist for our mill, and we will have to see if and how their long leadership cycles and our 'long' cycles fit together. The same is true for the later period, for which we seek to investigate possible relations between K-waves, 'hegemonic transition' and our long/er cycles.

Despite our welcome, we also have some serious reservations about their work. We could grant them that the 'lead economies are the spark plugs of the world economy' and that as McNeill (1982) already claimed, the lead economy in the eleventh and twelfth centuries was in China. But in their schema the shift to

European dominance occurs in the fifth Kondratieff beginning in 1190, which they see as centered on the Champagne fairs, the sixth on Black Sea trade, the seventh on Venice after 1300, from 1350 on the pepper trade, from 1430 on Guinea gold, from 1494 on Indian spices, 1540 the Baltic and Atlantic trade, and 1580 Asian trade. Yet most of these relate to Asia more than to Europe! For Modelski and Thompson 'The principal structural change experienced by the global economy in the fifteenth to eighteenth centuries was the construction of an oceanic trading system . . . [and] innovations in long-distance trade after 1500 . . . centered around the pioneering of new trading routes . . . [in] new phases of European imperialism' (1996a:70–8). True for Europe, but only for Europe and its new American colonies. For Asians these same 'innovations' were age old.

How, and through what cause or at least mechanism, does the Modelski–Thompson center of gravity in the world economy shift from Song China westward allegedly all the way to Portugal? We need more explanation of this crucial process of transition, if it took place at all, which we deny.

We invite Modelski and Thompson to continue bringing their analytic sophistication and empirical knowledge to bear on economic and political cycles, and to carry it back as far as the historical evidence permits, perhaps well beyond the 1000 AD date that they now view as the beginning of the 'global economy process.' We would be honored to be permitted to join them in such a common enterprise.

Chase-Dunn and Hall valiantly come out for comparative analysis, which is exactly why they insist on studying world-systems. Indeed, they are so anxious to do comparative work that they categorize not only all or parts of Eurasia, but also the Wintu Indians in California or 'indigenous' Hawaii as 'world-systems.' We agree that the more comparison we can manage, the better; but we prefer to use the term 'world system' for as much of Afro-Eurasia and later the 'New World' as can legitimately be viewed as sufficiently interconnected to have been parts of a single world system. The point of Chase-Dunn and Hall's project is to undertake comparative analysis, where the units of analysis being compared are 'world-systems,' including even the putative 'mini-systems.' This worthy and potentially fruitful project could generate useful abstractions about similar (and different) large-scale, long-term processes of social change and especially about the transformational logic in world system evolution, particularly if the comparisons were among long-lasting large-scale historical world systems. We see three possible problems with the inclusion of 'mini-systems': (1) the vast amount of historical data that must first be gathered and analyzed before meaningful comparisons become possible; (2) the resulting temptation to simplify the processes too much, particularly if this takes the form of some kind of economic reductionism, as pointed out by McNeill in his recent comments on Chase-Dunn and Hall at the 1995 International Studies Association meetings; and (3) the tendency to emphasize evolutionism too much to the detriment of other types of change, e.g. conjunctural, retrogression, crisis, etc. In so doing they risk losing the parsimonious elegance and the comparative potential of their original project.

Of course we welcome all useful comparisons promoted by Chase-Dunn and

Hall both within this 'central' world system and between it or any part of it and other places.

Conclusion

We believe that a humanocentric history of the world can form the intellectual basis for a new cosmopolitan praxis. Since we reject essentialist views on ethnicity and civilization in favor of our structuralist approach to ever-changing political economic configurations, our humanocentrism speaks directly to the present era of conflicting nationalisms, localisms, religious identities, and fragmentation. From our perspective humanity truly is one, having a true common heritage and sharing a common destiny. We do not propose to return us to the cause of universalism(s), and especially not of the Western-based universalism of 'development' or 'modernization' now being sold in the guise of the equation 'democracy = free market' (Gills, Rocamora and Wilson 1993; Frank 1993b). This modern 'universalism' has been inextricably linked with imperialism, and perhaps all universalism must be so to some extent. Modern European colonialism and imperialism, it must be said, was not the first or only attempt to impose universal values.

However, one can and we believe we should propose a defense of cosmopolitanism in the face of a growing chorus for particularism, methodological individualism, fundamentalism and emotive nationalism. A cosmopolitan praxis, based on a humanocentric understanding of the common historical development of humanity, could serve to rechannel the impulses of rebellion so prevalent in the present world crisis situation in a more positive direction. The present situation breeds new construction of new separate historical narratives and emphasizes separation, distance, and otherness. Such historiography, if that is what it can be called, can have little other effect than encouraging conflict and mutual suspicion, even hatred and contempt. If humanity is truly to have a common future on this planet, it is most imperative that the intellectual underpinnings of a new cosmopolitan praxis be established, and the sooner it is translated into practice the better. We must learn to accept our differences while recognizing our common history and working toward our common future. Those who have rejected our world system approach because they believed that it denied all agency and practice in favor of some ahistorical view of unchanging world history have been totally mistaken. On the contrary, our perspective has been intended from the outset to rethink the fundamentals of political economy, world history, and world development precisely in order to try to find a broader and better basis for progressive, cosmopolitan praxis.

2 World system evolution

George Modelski

If the question is: what explains world system change over the past five thousand years of its trajectory? Our answer is: such change is the product of an evolutionary process, or better still, of an array of evolutionary processes.[1]

We therefore propose that world system history be examined in the first place as an incident in the evolution of the human species, for world system is one form of social organization humankind can assume, and our task is to flesh out the characteristics of that concept and its real world references. Secondly, we intend to examine the structural components of the world system, such as economic or political, as well as global and national, each of which might be expected to be subject to evolutionary process, of a distinct character but subject to the same mechanism. We assume finally that evolutionary processes are not randomly scattered but rather exhibit synchronization of a coevolutionary character.

Such a social science-based conception yields a number of conjectures about the shape and timing of world system change, hence about some crucial developments in world history. It is a conception that is especially fruitful for contemplating the big picture of the fate of the human species; it yields a periodization of world history viewed as a phased evolution of the world system; it serves as a way of ordering the growth of the world economy, and of world politics, and accretion of a world community; and for the last millennium of our experience it affords a finer-grained depiction of structural change at the global level, with an explicit role for agents of change, leading sectors and world powers. As though miraculously, all these separate processes appear interdependent, and well-synchronized.

All of this adds up to an extended theoretical conjecture. At its heart, it consists of the spinning out of a few basic rules of evolutionary processes. But unlike nineteenth-century schemes of evolutionism, it also purports to be testable in accord with contemporary methods of the social sciences and with full attention to systematic historical data, and has in parts already been tested. Correspondences between predictions derived from these conjectures and standard accounts of world history will also be discussed. But our principal purpose here is to lay out the basic logic of this argument and to demonstrate how all of it forms an interrelated, symmetric, and mutually supportive structure that derives its strength from being grounded in evolutionary theory.

World system evolution is the story of humans learning to be human: learning to live with each other, and doing so on a large scale and in global settings. It is the story not of a movement guided either solely by instinct or directed toward a preordained end or design, but rather that of a continual and continuing search and selection among variety generated by evolutionary processes.

The concept of world system

World system as process

Let us begin by establishing a definition of our basic term, world system, and show how it accommodates a 'process' conception. As already noted, we define world system as the social organization of the human species. That means that world system is an attribute of the human species viewed as one population. That also implies that such a population might at any time be in either one of at least two states: either unorganized, or more or less organized; and having in common basic institutions such as cities or writing, states or state systems, technologies or trading networks.

World system therefore is, in the first place, a form of species organization. A species is a population of individuals that interbreed, and that share common attributes and a common fate. Such a population forms a complex system and represents a collection of organisms that is subject to evolutionary process. Biologists inform us that the number of animal species on this planet is in the order of one million (Lumsden and Wilson 1981:4) and about each of these the questions might be asked: is that species organized, and how well is it organized? For by the condition of interbreeding alone, they are intimately related, and share important symbioses that include forms of social organization. They signal in order to establish mutual recognition as members of the same species; they cooperate if only in the process of reproduction; they experience competition and conflict as selective mechanisms; and they depend on certain resources in order to survive and continue breeding.[2]

The species concept thus implies interdependence among its members. That interdependence is initially a matter of quite close common origin. It is now thought that all modern humans might derive from a small population of maybe 2,000 individuals 400,000 years ago whose descendants then populated the earth, spreading to various parts of the globe over routes that have remained significant to this day, such as those of Central Asia north of the Himalayas, and the maritime ones of South and Southeast Asia. Common origin, as well as mobility (search for independence), seem to be the characteristic features of human behavior from early on.

Thus in their distribution, modern humans have settled worldwide, probably as a result of superior communication skills, expanding from Africa to every continent by, at the latest, 15,000 years ago (Asia, 60,000 years ago, Europe 35,000, Australia 40,000, the Americas 35–15,000 (Cavalli-Sforza *et al.* 1994: 112,154–7). But this was clearly not a coordinated movement; the numbers were quite small, and long-range communication let alone organization was lacking, and did not satisfy the minimum conditions of world system: common identity, solidarity, collective action, and a resource base. Yet in our view the first steps toward such a world system seem to have been undertaken not too long after the spread of modern humans worldwide, some 5–6,000 years ago.

If interdependence is a characteristic of the human species, then various kinds of linkages are part of its experience, and basically unsurprising, even though unevenly distributed. That is why we do not make the existence of networks of interdependence as the primary research question facing students of world systems. Networks of interdependence are important parts of a world system but pointing to, for example, certain trade or migration routes of modern humans is not enough to show that a world system exists. To demonstrate the existence of a world system we need to show institutions that potentially or actually are of species-wide impact and significance.

The first basic real-world referent for the concept of world system is the population of humans. Table 2.1 is a summary of the salient figures of world population over the time span relevant to this analysis.

If we ask: has the human species, as depicted in the long perspective of Table 2.1, formed a stationary system, a condition in which social processes merely reproduce themselves, without any changes? Or has it been a dynamic one, undergoing substantial, and even dramatic change? The answer is obvious: the human species, as indexed by world population, has been, throughout historical experience, not just reproducing itself but expanding at a rapid rate. It is therefore to be presumed that its social organization, too, must have been changing with comparable rapidity.

We might wonder about the direction of the causal arrow between population growth and social organization. Is it the rise in population that caused changes in the social organization and the emergence of world system potential? Or is it that new forms of social organization, epochal innovations such as the rise of cities, or industrial revolutions, made possible the rise of populations? We would tend to argue that both types of causation are in fact relevant, at different points of human social experience.

Even at this preliminary stage it is easy to see that world system history is not about a stationary world system that keeps reproducing itself but about human social organization undergoing a sustained process of long-term change. That is why the appropriate stance for such an undertaking is not a reduction of the

Table 2.1 World population

Year	World population (millions)	of which in major regions of Asia
4000 BC	7	60 p.c.
2000	27	62
1 AD	170	70
2000	6000	58

Source: After McEvedy and Jones 1978:344, 349.

system to a number of static entities such as societies or civilizations but a process conception that allows us to capture variability of structures and movement in time. We do not hold the world system to have emerged fully fledged and perfectly connected some five millennia ago. Rather we are attempting to model the rise of the world system from a condition of potential, over some preliminary stages, toward a more fully developed status, and a future condition yet to be determined.

A 'singular' world system

All this presupposes what we might call the 'singular' conception of the world system. Such a conception maintains that the human species has exhibited, and will continue to exhibit, important regularities and common behavioral patterns not only at the level of individuals but also at the collective level of institutions, and organizations for humankind. It stands for the idea that behavioral uniformities of humanity viewed as an interacting whole – uniformities such as urbanization, or war – are worth knowing about, and that the changes in those characteristics are a most important subject of study.

There are some interesting parallels here with interdisciplinary debates about the origin of modern humans. On the plural (or polycentric) view, *homo sapiens* emerged separately but by parallel evolution to form distinct races in the world's major regions. The 'singular' view, supported by contemporary genetic research, sees to-day's world population as the product of a single expansion of 'anatomically modern humans' from Africa over the past one hundred thousand years (Cavalli-Sforza *et al.* 1994:62).

The singular conception of world system is exemplified also in the work of A. Gunder Frank and Barry Gills (1993, also this volume) and might be contrasted with the 'plural' one, that proceeds from the existence of a number of world systems (as in Chase-Dunn and Hall 1997, also in this volume). These are called world systems not because they extended potentially or actually to the human species as a whole or because they covered the entire planet, but because they are deemed to have been self-contained, or regarded by their members as 'worlds-in-themselves.' In the plural conception, the major questions become those of system identity and differences among systems, of relations among world systems, and of mergers of world systems into 'super' world systems.[3]

Our own preference would be to use terms such as 'regional' or 'local' for systems that may seem to have been self-sufficient over some periods, or whose distinctive traits appear to confer a special identity, and reserve the term 'world-system' to that one whose operations, potentially or actually are coextensive with humanity. The distinction is not unimportant. It is not merely an idiosyncratic choice between 'lumpers' who see things writ large, and 'splitters' who see reality, in the first place, only in the microcosm. It is also a choice between the sort of question one deems important: a broad-gauged inquiry into the behavior of the human species, or the detailed accounting of the fates of some individual societies as compared with others, each interesting in their own right, and that, in the aggregate, might add up to the story of humanity. The difference is not a new one, with merit on both sides, and it reflects contemporary debates in the study of world history.

For Condorcet, in his pioneering account of human progress, or for Kant, in his concept of 'universal history,' the story of the world was, in the first place, the story of humanity. For them, there was only one (evolving) world system, and one world civilization. Contrast this with influential conceptions of 'multiple' (or plural) civilizations viewed, in Toynbee's (1934:51) words as 'the intelligible field' of history conceived as the 'comparative study of civilizations.' For the British historian, as for Oswald Spengler, 'civilizations' were the societies that had a 'greater extension, both in Space and in Time, than national states or city states' but none of which embraced 'the whole of Mankind' (ibid., p.45). The story of mankind was for them an account of the life cycle of these distinct civilizations, of which more than twenty were identified by name.[4]

This 'plural' perspective, of a number of separate civilizations pursuing essentially independent careers may be contrasted with William McNeill's (1963/1991) position that the cultures of mankind have experienced a significant degree of interaction with other cultures at every stage of their history, and never more so than when great transformations were underway in the world system. For McNeill, the present state of world organization is the consummation of a single continuous process that he recently (1991:xxii) described as 'ecumenical.'

World system evolution

The explicandum: structural change

A process conception of the world system naturally focuses upon sequences of change in the social organization of humanity. But which, specifically, are those changes that need to be explained?

It is the strength of this approach that it allows for asking questions both about structure, and about agency. World System Evolution, in its broad sweep, is about structural change of planetary scope, and it proposes questions at two principal levels of structure: about major institutional change, such as the rise of the market economy, and second, about organizational change, such as the emergence of global organizations in tandem with the nation state. But it does not ignore either the role of agents. For social change is driven, at the grass-roots level, by innovation, and it is the innovators who are the agents of change. The long cycles of global politics that drive global political evolution, and Kondratieff (K-) waves that motivate their economic counterparts, are propelled by important innovations, and often well-known innovators.

What changes need to be well explained in the world system?

1   Eras of world system history, which reflect the conventional periodization of the story of the human community. We shall conceive of them as a sequence of major changes in world institutional arrangements.

2   World social, political, and economic change. This too can be represented as a sequence of major institutional changes of a more specialized kind.
3   Global change in the modern era that might be seen as organizational change, in turn driven by the world powers of the long cycle, and by leading industrial sectors of the global economy.
4   What is the broad context of world system change? What is human evolution and what constitutes civilization?

These are, at different levels of analysis, four sets of questions about key aspects of the clearly expanding world system of the past five millennia. The first looks upon the world system as a whole. The second distinguishes between the several components that make it up, while the third highlights prominent vertical structures of the modern era, the global system, and its product, globalization. The last concerns the evolution of modern humans. All four pose large questions and demand solid explanations. Together, they compose a scaffolding for the exploration of world system evolution.

The explanations: evolutionary logic

To answer these large questions about the fate and vicissitudes of the social organization of the human species we employ an evolutionary explanation. What are the elements of an evolutionary explanation applicable to world system processes (see also Modelski 1991, 1994, 1996, 1999a, Andersen 1994:14ff)?

Let us propose that an evolutionary explanation of a 'social fact' requires reference to previous such facts as well as a causal link that includes the following four mechanisms: those of (1) variety-creation; (2) cooperation (and segregation); (3) selection; and (4) preservation and transmission. In turn, these four mechanisms, taken together in that sequence, constitute a social learning algorithm.

We also propose that world system processes might be seen, at their several levels of analysis, at the institutional and organizational levels, and in respect of agency, as propensities for major social learning processes. At a very rough approximation, we might say that the first of the mechanisms is cultural, the second primarily social, the third political, and the fourth, economic. Since such a synthesis has to be an ordered one, all world system processes have a time-structure that allows for successive optimizations of these mechanisms in a formal-logical learning sequence, in the order in which the mechanisms were presented in the previous paragraph. World system processes can therefore be seen as possessing the make-up of four-phase temporal learning experiments.

The underlying premise is that evolution is proportional to time. That is the hypothesis of a 'social evolutionary' clock, not unlike that of a 'molecular clock' timing genetic mutations over long time periods, and helping to chart the time elapsed in the separation of two species. Cavalli-Sforza *et al.* (1994:33) use that same postulate to study the history and geography of human genes. They define the rate of evolution as the amount of evolutionary change – measured as the genetic distance between an ancestor and a descendant – divided by the time in which it occurred, and they report to have found that the hypothesis yields good results when used for comparing major population changes. A directly analogous procedure, known as 'glottochronology' (Swadesh 1971:271), has also been employed in linguistic analysis and is used to date the origin of languages by assuming a 'relatively constant rhythm of substitution' in a basic vocabulary, with an average retention rate of some 86 per cent per one thousand years. Results from linguistic work tend to reinforce genetic studies even though the rate of genetic change is much slower than that of languages.

This leads to the following postulates:

1   World system processes, both at the level of major institutions, and of major organizations, as well as agents, are evolutionary in make-up. They are self-similar in that the same explanatory logic applies at each level, implying that the system has a fractal structure. Self-similarity is 'symmetry across scale' a 'repetition of structure at finer and finer scales' (Gleick 1987:103,100).
2   World system processes each undergo change at their own rate that is proportional to time, and they each have a time-structure that integrates the four evolutionary mechanisms of variety creation, cooperation, selection, and reinforcement. Each period of a world system process consists of four such learning phases.
3   World system processes flourish in conditions of high evolutionary potential conducive to innovation.
4   World system processes are nested and synchronized (they coevolve). Nesting means that large-scale processes enfold, and are in turn animated by, smaller scale processes of determinate proportion in conditions of synchronization.

In other words, we do not search for a distinct logic for each era or structure of the world system because 'one system' requires 'one process.' We propose one common logic (or algorithm), an evolutionary learning one, to explain each world system process we identify.

Sources for evolutionary explanation

The classical source of nineteenth century philosophies of history is Immanuel Kant's *Idea for a Universal History* (1784/1991). Kant himself was not an evolutionist but his basic ideas might be thought of as foundational for evolutionary explanations. He raised the question whether it is possible to discover, among free-willed human actions considered on a large scale, a 'regular progression,' 'in accordance with natural laws,' in the 'history of the entire species,' such that it might be recognized as a 'steadily advancing but slow development of man's original capacities.' He also advanced nine propositions as guidelines for such a history, the fourth of which identifies 'antagonisms in society' as the long-run source of a 'law-governed social order' and comes close to portraying them as mechanisms of selection. We cannot but take heart in the ninth proposition, that 'a philosophical attempt to work out a universal history of the world in accordance with a plan of nature . . . must be regarded as possible,' and read it as a prescription of a search for a better theory of world system change, though we also need to debate in what sense and to what degree such a 'plan of nature' might be thought to be 'aimed at a perfect civil union of mankind.'

Nineteenth century evolutionary thought assumed two main forms. The founders of sociology, Auguste Comte and Herbert Spencer, put forward bold new conceptions of the development of humanity. While aspects of their ideas, of a phased advance toward industrial society, remain influential to this day, they are on the whole regarded as dated. Marxist thought developed along similar lines. This broad 'evolutionist' strand of thought might be contrasted with the 'selectionist' approach of Charles Darwin, whose innovative contribution was the identification of natural selection and variation as the mechanisms of species development. Darwin also launched the grand idea of a 'tree of life,' mapping the common origins of life on earth, thus in effect laying the foundations for a macro-history of biology; but he avoided any large claims to explaining patterns of human social evolution.

Social evolutionary thought experienced a revival in the mid-twentieth century, just as Darwinian biology was reinvigorated through the 'modern synthesis' founded on genetics. In economics, the work of Joseph Schumpeter, or Friedrich von Hayek, is now regarded as evolutionary, and viewed as offering an important alternative to neoclassical analysis. In sociology, Talcott Parsons was, in his later work, a significant contributor to social evolutionary theory. Karl Popper and Donald Campbell advanced evolutionary epistemology as a methodological foundation for the natural and social sciences.[5]

More recent social thought has been less hospitable to 'big picture' theorizing. Anthony Giddens (1984:243,236–9) for example, compounds evolutionary theory with historical materialism, and argues that it is necessary to deconstruct them both. 'In explaining social change, no single or sovereign mechanism can be specified. There are no keys that will unlock the mysteries of human social development.' 'Human history does not have an evolutionary shape' because 'history is not a "world-growth story"'; 'the relatively short period since the emergence of civilization in Mesopotamia is not marked by the continuing ascent of civilization; it conforms more to Toynbee's picture of the rise and fall of civilizations.'

We disagree with that position. The task of social scientists is to unlock the mysteries of social development, and to discern its shape, evolutionary or not. We need to attempt a synthesis of 'evolutionism' of the Big Picture, with the rich detail of Darwinian mechanisms of selectionism. We aim to explain large-scale social change, but seek to do it by carefully tracing the processes that propel such change, and the mechanisms, selection being crucial but not the only one among them.

In social theory, we need to contrast the evolutionary explanation with both rational choice, and functionalism. Rational choice (Elster 1989), whose paradigm is neoclassical economic analysis, is an elaboration of what Alfred Weber called the ends-means schema. That approach takes opportunities and resources (and constraints) as well as preferences (or interests) as given, and generates from them a stream of intended outcomes. By contrast, selectionist and evolutionary models do not depend upon intentions; they focus on actual outcomes, and they make changes in constraints and interests as part of the model. Design, the ideal product of rational choice, is not part of selection, that plays upon trial-and-error. Speed of response is the glory of rational choice; evolutionary change is the tortoise that moves slowly but surely over the long haul.

Selectionist models therefore appear preferable for studying evolutionary processes and macro-level phenomena such as world system change. They are not to be confused with functionalism. At the heart of functionalism is the sound idea that structures have consequences for wider systems. But classical functionalism asked: what maintains social systems? And answered, practices that respond to (postulated) social need. Critics (such as Little 1991:101–20) were right in arguing that this did not get us very far, and that it implied an excessively optimistic, 'Panglossian' meta-theory, that 'societies will produce practices that satisfy their long-term needs.' Evolutionary explanations, by contrast, do not seek to explain persistence, but rather social change and the processes that transform social structures.

Eras of the world system

Periodization of world history

One way into the macro-analysis of world systems is through the established field of periodization of world history. McNeill's (1963) divisions of world time (shown in Table 2.2, first column) might be regarded as an example of standard specification of epochal divisions over the past several millennia (subject to his comments in 1991:xvii-xix). That periodization conforms quite comfortably under the familiar headings of ancient, classical, and modern. It is also based on the additional criterion of 'dominance,' in that it relies, in that sense, on changes in macro-political organization. In doing so, it illuminates just one facet of the world system process, but there is no reason to suppose that facet to be unimportant or unrelated to other principal components. Indeed, there are grounds for thinking of political periodicity as a kind of 'clock' timing the entire social system.

On McNeill's account, the political organization of the world system has now passed through three stages. In the first, starting well before 3000 BC, the Middle East was the center of world development. In the second, no one region occupied a similarly striking position, and the situation was one of 'cultural balance' in which 'each of the four major civilizations developed more or less freely along its own lines' (1963:253). The third stages might be thought of as a return to 'dominance,' and this time, 'Western dominance.' The long-term vision of the future, hence also possibly the fourth stage, is indicated by a reference, in the book's closing pages, to the 'establishment of a world-wide cosmopolitanism' (a Kantian term) that 'would enjoy vastly greater stability' (ibid.:806–7).

McNeill's shifts in the pattern of dominance suggest a world system tendency toward long-term alternation between equal and unequal structures, but imply a

Table 2.2 Eras of the world system

McNeill's categories and dates	Conventional designations	Phases of world system process
Middle Eastern dominance −3000 to −500	Ancient	Learning-infrastructural −3400 to −1200
Eurasian cultural balance −500 to 1500	Classical	Community-building −1200 to 930
Western dominance 1500 to 'World wide cosmopolitanism'	Modern	Collective (species-wide) organization 930 to 3000
	Postmodern	Stabilization 3000 to 5000

long-term tendency toward equalization, in the Kantian spirit. We might also note that the overall phase structure, of ancient, classical, modern, dovetails nicely with the general trend portrayed in the summary of population growth present earlier in Table 2.1. We observe in that earlier tabulation not only the striking pattern of growth but also its patterning in line with conventional periods of world history. With population measured roughly at mid-point, to each of the well-known stages corresponds a new order of demographic magnitude. Throughout this 'history,' the expanding population also maintains a fairly even distribution in space, with the major regions of Asia invariably accounting for more than one half of the world total. We have here a vast expansion in the numbers of the human species as a whole, hence a systemic process, but one that is also clearly patterned, roughly in line with historical periodization.

Explaining world system phases

What we have is a process with a strong phase structure, both political and social (demographic), that is also suggestively cumulative and in a sense progressive. We propose an evolutionary explanation. We argue that the process is one of the emergence and consolidation of the world system. Or else we say that the process is one of launching the world system as a major institutional complex for the human species, hence an epochal innovation. The standard periodization reflects the political phasing of that process, and the cumulative demography indicates successively more effective conditions of world organization. Each phase of that process, broadly corresponding to the conventional eras is also marked by the optimization of one of the four evolutionary mechanisms.

Our model therefore proposes that the world system has now nearly passed through three (out of four) evolutionary phases: the learning-infrastructural phase (laying down the cultural base for the entire process); the community-building phase (foundational for enterprises of large-scale cooperation); and collective organization (selection of forms of worldwide organization); the fourth phase being that of consolidation (reinforcement and replication). These would represent successive optimizations of evolutionary mechanisms of variety-generation, cooperation, selection, and reinforcement.[6]

If structural change, that is social learning viewed as problem-solving, is to occur these phases must be passed in the sequence just presented. The completion of one phase depends on the conditions created by the preceding phase, and becomes a necessary condition for the phase that follows. Each of these phases represents the principal theme of the social universe in the major epochs of its functioning; it reflects major social priorities but does not imply neglect of other domains of social organization.

The first phase (in Table 2.2, column three) labeled 'learning-infrastructural' might be understood as generating the variety for building the world system, and does so by drawing upon the resources developed in the preceding era (in this case, during the agricultural revolution, that preceded it by up to 8,000 years). That variety arises by means of city-building and gradually spreads, in a system of interconnected – and partly preexisting – networks of intercontinental propor-tions: cities being by definition cultural constructions that are oriented to, and closely connected with, other cities, coming to form the center of an emerging world system. Cities are the hardware, the invention of writing supplies the software of the infrastructure of world system learning. Writing records and stores information, and it organizes social life both to the past and to the future; it lends continuity to social organization and makes systematic structural changes possible. It leads to the emergence of professional classes, such as scribes or teachers; centered on temples it helps, as do cities, in differentiating culture from the social system. Writing means the start of systematic learning, and science (astronomy, calendars), makes possible intensive agriculture, and is essential in disseminating the elements of bureaucracy.

Proceeding from this learning-infrastructural foundation thus understood, the next major phase of the world system goes on to community-building on a scale going beyond tribe and city. This is the time that innovates the structures of wider cooperation implicit in the world system, because in principle such cooperation must extend to all humanity. We propose that in this second phase such coopera-tive potential is actuated via universal religions. Religion, in turn, forms the basis for solidarity and cooperation, enhances education and communication, large-scale political organization, and long-distance trade. Each in their own way, the great religions are in turn forms of differentiating populations and building larger regional ensembles.

Given a set of major communities, the stage is set for organizational selection. Competitive pressures of several kinds (economic competition, political conflict, ideological confrontation, scholarly debates) select the organizational forms best attuned to the emerging complexities of the world system. The collective man-agement of human affairs becomes the operative problem, both at the new national, and new global levels. Such collective organization finally gives way to adaptation, a stabilization comprising an adaptive adjustment to the environ-ment, preparing the stage for yet other evolutionary developments.

A test

How does such a model square with the conventional understanding of the unfolding of the human story? Let us look once again at Table 2.2, and note some differences between the conventional, and the analytic account. Both start before 3000 BC, in Sumer. But the first column consists of periods of unequal length that nevertheless average out to a little over 2,000 years; the right-hand column shows world system phases as of roughly uniform length, and only in the first two cases is that evidently so, at just over 2,000 years; the duration of the modern and post-modern phases remains to be determined. The postulated four-phased world system process would thus extend over a total of 8,000 years; the possibility of verifying that extends to no more than five millennia.

Can the era of 'Middle Eastern dominance' be convincingly labeled as pre-eminently cultural, or 'learning-infrastructural,' as predicted by the model? We observe that the Middle East was not then dominant in the sense that it might have controlled say China, or Europe, but only in so far as it was the location of the period's major institutional innovations. For this was where cities emerged, at first mainly in Sumer, and cities were the first great human artifacts that mani-fested cultural achievement and laid the foundations for an entirely new form of social organization. This is, too, where writing first appeared, another major breakthrough toward social organization. Indeed, all evidence suggests that these two developments first occurred in one Sumer city, in Uruk, that around 3000 BC was the largest city of the world system (Modelski 1999b). Cities, and writing, in turn stimulated new departures in society, sparked technological and scientific innovation, as in transportation, civil engineering or astronomy, creating a set of conditions in the absence of which a world system could not emerge, and on the basis of which the great religions rose in the next era. The course of the period saw both cities and writing spread to other world regions, including China and Europe.

At the start of the classical era, that of Eurasian cultural balance, 'there existed four distinct regions of high culture in Eurasia,' and 'two thousand years later the physiognomy of Eurasia was recognizably the same' (McNeill 1963:249) and, we might add, persists to this day. As balance replaced dominance, conditions were established not just of relative autonomy but also, more importantly, in which each major world region contributed its share to world development, and shared in its evolution. What was the nature of that contribution?

Our model proposes that in this 'classical' era the major priority, and critical innovations, lay in 'community-building.' This was the era of institutional innov-ation of universal religions. The Eastern Chou (Zhou) era of Chinese history brought forth Confucius, whose ideas 'catalyzed the institutional and intellectual definition of Chinese civilization' (McNeill 1963:232), and in due course began to mould the cadres of its scholar-officials. The teachings of Buddha first came to be institutionalized in the Indian subcontinent, but then spread far and wide along the Silk Roads, powerfully influencing not just West and Southeast Asia but also China, Korea, and Japan. Buddhism was organized around the practice of monastic communities. Christianity formed in the Hellenistic culture of the Mediterranean and then under Roman rule, but also outlived it. Islam first arose among the city states of Arabia but then shaped the Ummayad and Abbasid Caliphates as its framework, which resolved the issue as to how 'the community of the faithful should be led and by what principles it should be governed' (ibid.: 429). Accounting for 'much of the institutional pattern' that gave Islam its strength was 'the strategic position of the mercantile class' (Hodgson 1993:107).

We observe that all four of these cases have in common the creation of a new basis for an extended, overarching community, even potentially world system-wide. None fully succeeded, but each served to lay the foundations for a more inclusive world and each in turn contributed some important strains to the enterprise of community-building. We observe, though, a contrast with Karl Jaspers' concept of the 'axial age' of Confucius, Buddha, and Socrates (800 BC to 200 BC), that he regarded as having witnessed the creation of all fundamental cultural constructs simultaneously all across Eurasia. Our own 'learning' conception is resolutely sequential, as can be demonstrated in a study of the world cities of the classical age (Modelski 1999c) that can be shown to have become first importantly Buddhist, then Christian, and between 700 the majority Moslem, with a strong continuing Buddhist participation.

If the classical era was, in its basic thrust, Eurasian, then the modern age might more appropriately be labeled 'global,' and we might wish to suspend judgment on the question whether this should be called the era of 'Western dominance.' If, as McNeill (1982) has more recently argued, we see the modern world system to take off in Sung (Song) China, just before the turn of the first millennium, then its complexion must be a mixed one, with the Chinese Renaissance being followed by the Italian, and Atlantic Europe only taking a lead after 1500. Maybe it is too early to give a final definition to that era whose likely reach might extend for some more centuries but also possibly into space.

But we might be entitled to assert that, propelled by a powerful 'organizational revolution,' those dominating the social landscape in the modern age are the prominent forms of collective (species-wide) action, not old-fashioned empires, but nation-states, armies and navies, corporate business entities, universities and other non-governmental and governmental organizations, not forgetting either the growing network of global institutions. That is how we would define the most striking social innovations of the modern era, and it is these new powerful organizational creations that give substance to the term 'world system.'

We have now traced these through five millennia but might also observe that only in the last millennium has the world system begun to assume concrete shape through organizations and institutions of worldwide impact: in the Mongol's bid for world empire around 1250; in Portugal's global network of fleets and bases after 1515; and most recently, in the growing array of global organizations since the middle of the nineteenth century. Does that mean that no world system existed prior to the modern era, and are we indeed justified in labeling those earlier ages as world system evolution?

The answer is: world system is not built in a day, or even a millennium. It is an epochal learning project for the entire species that starts slowly at first, then gathers up nuclei of cooperation, and only in good time, after some false starts, reaches the possibility of crystallization (or punctuation, as in punctuated equilibrium), at the selection phase of that process. For the world system, that would be the stage of collective (species-wide) organization that has been underway for the past millennium, which is about the time when the fact of world organization first started to become a reality.

World system processes

What have we learnt so far about world system evolution? That a gross ordering scheme cast in evolutionary terms is at least conceivable, and that a rough characterization of the eras of world history in terms of modalities of a learning process, and the innovations punctuating that process, is not inherently implausible. Such a model cannot be rejected as glaringly at variance with the conventional scheme of things, and is in fact better than might be expected from an exceedingly macromodel. It is equally clear we are still far from a full explanation, and must make this ordering more convincing by reducing the extended time-span between cause and effect, and by introducing additional mechanisms of less-grandiose temporal dimensions.

We have treated the conventional periodization as applying across the board to the world system process. But we noticed too that the basis of such periodizations is in the first place expressed along one dimension, the political, or the geopolitical one, because it invites us to view world system development through the lens of such concepts as Middle Eastern 'dominance,' or Eurasian 'balance.' Clearly political evolution constitutes one aspect of world system process, meaningfully related to other processes. How might political evolution be explained, and how might the political process be related to the main currents of economic or social change in the world system?

The world system, at least in its more developed form, exhibits along its horizontal dimension, not only political but also economic, social, and cultural (or learning) structures.[7] It has states and intergovernmental organizations, financial markets, humanitarian projects, and the worlds of media and scholarship. These are, by now, conventional distinctions but we do note that they broadly match the array of evolutionary mechanisms discussed earlier on. If the world system has 'structural potential' then we should also be able to trace the evolution of these structures over time.

What is more, we assume these four structures to be self-similar. That is, we view each one of them as subject to an evolutionary process of the same logical make-up, but the process proceeds at different time scales in each case. The economy is expected to change at a faster rate than political structures, and so on. Because the time scales of these processes differ, some of them might be thought of as nesting within others of longer periods, and in that sense economic change might be thought of as proceeding with the political framework. Nesting, in turn, calls for synchronization, and that might be the reason why the time scales of the four evolutionary processes here discussed must stand in a determinate relationship to each other. The set of these forms a spectrum of interlocking periodicities. We hypothesize a set of relationships in Table 2.3.

In other words, we propose that the constituent processes of the world system interlock in a determinate manner. While all four of them undergo change at a rate that is constant in respect of a particular process, the periods of these differ in a determinate ratio. Four periods of the world economy process are equal to two periods of the (political) active zone process, and one period of the (social) center-hinterland process. The relationship, at the world level, is thus regulated by the relative scale of these event sequences, in a manner that reflects a 'cybernetic hierarchy' according to which 'the longer the time perspective, and the broader the system involved, the greater is the *relative* importance of higher, rather than lower factors in the control hierarchy' (Parsons 1966:9,24,113). In such terms, the overall process of world system evolution that we reviewed in the previous section might, for some purposes, be analyzed (or refracted) into four distinct evolutionary processes whose temporal dimensions stand to each other in a relationship of 1:2:4:8, each in turn composed of four phases.

World system process   We hypothesize that this is the process that gives overall shape to the world system, programs it, orders its priorities, and times the major phases we discussed. It takes its cue from the world information networks and, giving a distinct texture to major eras, is at bottom cultural.

World socialization   The evolution of the human community and the growth of human solidarity is not a process of linear expansion but one of persistent tension between the pressures for innovation that are the consequences of evolutionary processes, and a necessary outcome of learning, and the demands for equality that is the operative condition of every community. Innovations produce concentrations of metropolitan power, and peaks of prestige, often centered on opulent cities and brilliant empires. Forming in opposition to them are the hinterlands, or the margins of civilized society, that from time to time organize themselves to effect a system leveling (or dependency reversal). It is hypothesized that major phases of concentration, a millennium in length, alternate with equally significant intervals of hinterland assertiveness and that this alternation constitutes the process of world socialization.

Table 2.3 Interlocking periodicities

Structure (horizontal)	Evolutionary process	Period (yrs) (equal to four phases)
World system	World system process	8000
Community	World socialization	4000
Collective organization	Active zone process	2000
Production/Commerce	World economy process	1000

We borrow this pair of terms 'center/hinterland' from Frank's studies in the 1990s. It parallels the conceptual pair of 'core-periphery' but needs to be distinguished from it because the latter proceeds from a differential division of labor while the former refers to a social relationship that might also be grounded in a differential access to political power, social prestige, or claims to innovation.

Active zone process   Let us define an active zone as the spatial locus of innovation in the world system. Social and cultural evolution proceeds by means of innovation and its diffusion, and it flourishes in conditions that favor the generation of variety and, more generally, of high evolutionary potential. The political seedbeds of such variety are not powerful empires that tend to attract the attention of historians but zones of autonomous entities, such as state systems, and intermediate political networks, and more broadly, regimes and domains in which individuals, and communities enjoy openness, freedom and autonomy that foster creativity.

Thus conceived, the active zone becomes the center of the world system but only as long as it generates the innovations that respond to world problems. The active zone process is the political process that in each period of 2,000 years focuses upon a broad geopolitical zone (such as the Middle East), but in each of its phases of about 500 years moves along spatially to a new region. Standard eras of world history might be seen as periods of the active zone process.

Production/commerce   The hypothesized world economy process defines changes in the major modes of organization of production and exchange, in agriculture, mining, and industry. Periods of productive development, and surges of new technologies, such as bronze, or iron, alternate with others that expand networks of interchange, pioneer new trade routes, and generally disperse innovations.

Model presented

Table 2.4 presents this model for visual inspection, to show how the processes coevolve. It adds detail, and adduces some other information that puts flesh on the bare bones of this structural argument. The second column shows the three eras of the *world system*, reviewed earlier. In addition to bearing a conventional designation (ancient, etc.), each of them also defines a major theme of cultural development.

The next column of Table 2.4 is a schematic outline of *world socialization*. We know that the center-building that produced the flowering of civilization in Sumer, and then in the Nile and Indus Valleys, did not continue in a straight line upward. If the growth of major cities is the right indicator then we observe a rise in their numbers until about 2300 BC, after which the growth abates. The number of hinterland migrations and incursions rises, and Sumer in particular experiences a drastic decline. By 1200 BC only Egypt remains secure in the line of 'barbarian' onslaughts but loses its drive and falls behind. While the Indus Valley civilization collapses, the qualities that made Mesopotamia and Egypt special now diffuse more widely in Eurasia, to Europe, China, and later India (Modelski and Thompson 1996a; Modelski 1999b).

Table 2.4 World system processes

From about (year)	World system process (eras)	World socialization	Active zone process	World economy process
3400 BC	Ancient	**ROUGH WORLD** (center-building)	**MID-EASTERN** (Uruk) (Sumer)	**COMMAND ECONOMY:** BRONZE
2300		(dispersal)	(Mesopotamian) (Egyptian)	FERTILE CRESENT
1200	Classical	(concentration)	**EURASIAN** (East Asian) Indian	IRON
100		(dispersal)	(Mediterranean) (Mid-eastern)	SILK ROADS
930 AD	Modern	**NICER WORLD** (reconcentration)	**OCEANIC** (Eurasian transition) (Atlantic Europe)	**MARKET ECONOMY:** NATIONAL MARKET
1850		democratic base	(Atlantic-Pacific)	WORLD MARKET

The dispersion affected by this process served to consolidate the central portions of four civilizations, East Asian, South Asian, Mid-Eastern, and European that came to constitute the 'balance of Eurasia' in the classical era. Within that balance, each of these made its own contribution to the major process of community-building previously reviewed. Each of these civilizational regions served as the basis of a major religion. But within that process, the pulse of center–hinterland interaction was also palpable. After about the year 100, the new social structures in the several regions came under pressures of new invaders, and urban growth abated once again. The movements of Germanic tribes that broke up the Roman empire were part of the same great migration as the barbarian occupation of North China, and the Ephthalite invasions of India. The eruptions of the tribes of Arabia upon the Mediterranean world after 632 completed what appeared to be another sustained process of systemic leveling (Modelski and Thompson 1999; Modelski 1999c).

In the early modern era it appeared for a moment as though, under Mongol rule, China might become the center of the world system. But attempts at world empire collapsed, and the active zone moved first to the Mediterranean. We are familiar with the thought that after 1500 the center shifted to Atlantic Europe, in a manner such that various parts of the world became increasingly dependent upon it, in colonial and semi-colonial situations. Our analysis leads to the prediction that, once again, this extensive period of systemic concentration that culminated with the Industrial Revolution might be due for a reversal: for the world system might have entered, after 1850, onto a movement of systemic leveling, though hopefully at a higher level of organization. This leveling is taking the form of democratization, in which an initially small nucleus of democratic societies (about 10 per cent of world population at the end of the nineteenth century) is gradually bringing into the fold of a future democratic community an increasingly larger portion of the world's peoples (about 50 per cent of a much larger population at the turn to the twenty-first century).

How might this be so? On the present analysis, world socialization is now in its second period (of 4,000 years each). The first, labeled here 'Rough World' was, in a sense unsurprising, for in the course of it the splendor of civilization was regularly, albeit at long intervals, balanced by the excesses of those who attacked it, order to share in it, and sometimes to destroy it. While this was indeed a rough world, maybe there was also in it an element of rough justice.

Can the rough edges be taken off the world system, while increasing its civilizational quotient? Axelrod (1984) argues that even in a 'nasty' world, 'nice' strategies can arise as mutations of established operating procedures, and in certain situations, namely those of clustering, might not just survive but also prosper. Let us therefore entertain the proposition that the second period of center/hinterland interaction might be experiencing a move toward a 'nicer world.'

At first, we would once again expect a stage of reconcentration, powered by prodigious innovation of various kinds, giving rise to much dependency. But the same process would also be responsible for setting off mutant forms, say in Sung

China, or in Renaissance Italy, launching experiments, reformist, republican and liberal that build up potential for social and political development. It is from those mutant forms that cooperative arrangements could arise and lift the raw conflict among center and hinterland to a higher level of performance. The diffusion of democracy since the nineteenth century to i.e. Japan, India, East Europe, and parts of South America is beginning to create conditions in which demands for greater equality might find expression in forms that are 'nicer.'

The sequence of 'active zones' (column 4 of Table 2.4) has been neither arbitrary nor unsystematic. The progression described by that sequence has been along zones of spatial contiguity, and has successively lent priority to cultural, social, political and economic factors. Thus for instance in Confucianism, emphasis rests on scholarship and learning; in Buddhism, on the creation of monastic communities; in Christianity, on individuals and on church organizational factors; and in Islam, on the evolution of long-range communications based on pilgrimages and trade routes facilitated by that community.

The active zone process can be documented with the help of data on urban population growth, cities in the active zone being seedbeds of innovations. Andrew Bosworth (1995a:198ff) has shown that the process appears to capture 'those regions whose population growth outpaced those of the rest of the world, with each active zone building upon the foundations of its forerunner.' For each of the zones identified in column four after 1000 BC, that is for all those for which such data were available, its share of the population of the world's top twenty-five cities exceeded that of every other region in the relevant time period.

As expected, the active zone is shown to have been, in most cases, an area occupied by autonomous political systems, from the city states of Mesopotamia, to the interstate systems of the Middle East, the Eastern Chou, and India at the time of the Buddha. The Roman Empire splintered not long after its emperor embraced Christianity, and the Islamic Caliphates were noted for the flexibility of their political organization. The city states of classical Greece might appear as an omission from that list but it was in their shaping of the Hellenized civilization of the Mediterranean in which Christianity arose that Greek culture found its enduring place.

At about 1000 it appeared as though Sung China, then the most conspicuous country of East Asia, might take the lead in the world system, and for a while the most salient feature of that system appeared to be Chinese predominance. But the Sung first lost the North, and then fell, in the South, before the onslaught of the Mongols. It is the Mongols' design for a world empire at the center of the Eurasian landmass and the dominance of their cavalry armies that defined the age as one of 'Eurasian transition,' a transition that moved the wellspring of innovation of the system from East Asia toward Europe. The Mongols' project extended from China over most of the Eurasian landmass, but it never materialized completely, nor did that of Timur a century later, and imposing though both were, they soon collapsed under their own weight just as the last European attempts at medieval empire (those of Charles d'Anjou) crumbled before even getting properly underway. The republican regimes of Genoa, and Venice, were the initial beneficiaries of that transition, took up the challenge and became the springboards from which the power of Atlantic Europe was projected upon the world after 1500.

The last column in Table 2.4 suggests the outlines of *the evolution of the world economy* (see also Modelski and Thompson 1996a, ch.8). The world economy process begins with bronze as a basic new technology and source of productive organization, with implications for tool-making, construction, and weaponry in particular. That technology encouraged urbanization, helped to raise levels of production, and increased trade. The age of bronze is rounded off with the broadening of what initially was a Sumerian center area to the entire Fertile Crescent becoming the basis of economic organization, extending from the Persian Gulf to the Mediterranean.

Between 1200 BC and 1000 BC in the Middle East and Europe, (though in China not until 600 BC), iron begins to assume general importance, gradually replacing bronze as the more cost-effective primary metal for tools and weapons. The 'closure of the Eurasian ecumene' in turn provides the opportunity for an expansion of long-distance trade, chiefly by land but also by sea, with the Silk Roads (including the maritime Spice Roads) assuming a key role in that process in the fourth period in particular.

The overall movement in the world economy over this long period has been from command to market economy. That is how the modern period is at first notable for the emergence of more flexible and productive market economies at the national and regional level, in the sense of an increasing differentiation between economy and polity, the consolidation of the economy as a potentially and substantively a self-organizing system, and the increasing role of autonomous, and increasingly corporate, business organizations. The groundwork for that development was laid over the past millennium, and more recently, say after 1850, conditions began to ripen for the emergence of world markets as the framework of exchange in a now significantly productive economy. But the world market still has a long way to go.

Globalization

So far so good. World system evolution has now assumed a fuller-bodied complexion and presents a more rounded picture. The resolution of its analysis, represented by the shortest phase interval, is now reduced from 2,000 to about 250 years, but it does remain quite a wholesale view of the human experience, and especially so for the modern times, and the role of human agency in innovation remains essentially dim.

What is it precisely that we are trying to explain? We are trying to explain the finer texture of evolution, no longer as a sequence of major institutional changes, but this time in the grainier detail of organizational developments principally at the global level, and most importantly, by tracing the agents of innovation who propel these movements.

Let us define evolution at the global level as globalization. It consists of the emergence of organizations that actually or potentially operate in planetary scope. Globalization thus comprises a set of processes: global economic evolution (of trading systems and world markets); global political evolution (of nation-state systems, world power competitions, and international organization); democratization (forming a potential democratic community); and the creation of a world public opinion (via media, and learning).

And who are the agents of globalization? They are individuals and organizations advancing and sponsoring innovation that results in strengthening the global layer of interactions. Among these we would name business firms that work transnationally, world financial markets, nation-states in positions of global leadership, non-governmental organizations of an humanitarian character or individuals who fund such projects, leaders of social movements, Nobel prize winners.

Agency is most clearly apparent when we study processes that actually drive globalization: the rise and fall of leading industrial sectors, in the rise and decline of world powers, the course of the democratic lineage, and the long movements of world opinion. That is where agents of innovation can be seen at their most active.

Global processes

Let us make more fine-grained the analysis for the modern era. Some treatments of this subject set the start of modernity, or of the modern world system, at about 1500, give or take some decades, and it is admittedly clear that a 'birth' of sorts did indeed occur at that time. But students of evolutionary processes would tend to go beyond mere birth, to the actual sources of such an event and ask: when and in what conditions did 'inception' (or conception?) take place? Our model suggests that it happened earlier, as early as maybe 930 (if we focus on the Chinese context), and accordingly we shall assign the onset of global processes, and of globalization, to that date.

Second, our model takes account of the increased organizational complexity of modernity because its main institutional emphasis is one of 'collective (species-wide) organization.' We know that the premodern world was, organizationally-speaking, fairly simple, basically a two-tier arrangement, one that combined the world of the 'great tradition' based on imperial courts, cities and temples, with a multitude of little traditions of the village peasantry (Modelski 1987:24–6). We hypothesize that the modern era produced, along the vertical dimension, a division of this two-tier set-up into a potentially four-fold structure ideally comprised of local, national, regional, and global layers of organization. The inception of that process of vertical differentiation coincides with the modern era, and its unfolding has produced, and continues to produce, two processes of major consequence: the rise of nation-states and the nation-state system, and the formation of organizations of global scope. We focus our attention on the second, the global system process.

Globalization, or global system process, might be decomposed (or refracted) into four nested sequences of cultural, social, political, and economic elements, each subject, just as the institutional movement was, to self-similarity, and bringing forth new organizational structures. These processes are labeled in Table 2.5.

Globalization might again be defined as the formation of a planetary organizational framework and might best be viewed as a spectrum of four processes. We observe that the period of each of these structure-building processes at the global level equals one phase (that is one-quarter) of the overarching world system periods previously discussed, on the ground that its scope is that much more limited. Once again, we postulate that the four processes stand in the 8:4:2:1 relationship we showed for the larger process. In the paragraphs that follow we briefly review this model, and then support it with some data.

'Global system process' might be expected to program the global system, much in the same way that we have observed the world system process to do earlier. Its working depends on the more detailed specification of the world system priority of 'collective (species-wide) organization,' and its phases represent the steps by which such organization framework might be thought of as emerging at the global level, via Preconditions, Global Nucleus, Global Organization, Consolidation.

'Democratic community process' traces the evolution of community at the global level, and embodies the premise that such community can only be built upon democratic foundations. It does so by tracing the antecedents, and then the members of the 'democratic lineage,' defined as the 'line or succession of societies that have shaped world democratization' (Modelski 1999d:154). Two periods of that process will be distinguished: that of 'experiments,' and of 'democracy.' The terms are inspired by Robert Axelrod's (1984) analysis of the evolution of cooperation, previously mentioned, that shows that even in a 'nasty' world, mutant cooperative forms might arise in an experimental exploration of the potential for cooperative (that is, higher-yielding) undertakings. We propose that reform movements in Sung China (ca. 1100), and republican experiments in the city states of northern Italy (ca. 1300) constituted two sets of such trials, but that it was the religious turmoil of the European Reformation, centering upon the Dutch Republic that laid the foundations for the cumulative growth of a nucleus of a global system, embodied in particular in the 'liberal-maritime alliance,' with England. That is how some of these experiments succeeded in conditions of clustering, and we propose further that conditions particularly favorable to such clustering have prevailed since the mid-nineteenth century, laying the groundwork

Table 2.5 Global system processes

Global system processes	Period (years)	Driven by
Global system	2000	
Democratic community	1000	four D-waves
Global political evolution	500	four long cycles of global politics
Global economic evolution	250	four K-waves

for a future democratic community, in a process first anticipated by Immanuel Kant, and then by Alexis de Tocqueville who in 1835 postulated the ultimate success of democratization on the basis of his American experience. Why not call the successive periods of democratic community formation D-waves (for Democracy)?

'Global Political Evolution' has a period of some 500 years that corresponds to one phase of the active zone process. Each such period therefore tends to center upon one region of the world system, and we name these periods provisionally after the periods of the active zone process. The first is 'Eurasian transition,' followed by 'Atlantic-Europe,' and 'Atlantic-Pacific,' the names tending to suggest the shift in the geopolitical center of the global system. The phases of each period are activated by successive instances of the rise and decline of world powers, in their learning cycles, this being the mechanism whereby some nation-states have been selected to the role of leadership at the global level, and have been able by that means to shape global organization.

'Global Economic Evolution' describes structural change in worldwide commercial and industrial arrangements, and has a period of some 225 to 250 years. Within each of these periods nest four K-waves. These changes reflect movements in the world economy process previously discussed, from 'National' to 'World' market, and spell out the finer structure of that transformation, as a sequence that leads in the now familiar path from Sung China, through Italy, to an oceanic trade system that generates an 'industrial take-off.' In other words, the famed industrial revolution of the eighteenth and nineteenth centuries is but one, albeit dramatic, incident along a long path of growth for the global economy, that is now being followed by the 'Information Economy.'

A discussion

Table 2.6 presents a model of global evolutionary processes derived from the considerations just discussed. It also adduces some data that lend it greater validity. We note that the resolution of these processes is now down to 50–60 years, the average length of a K-wave, in the last column. (For reasons of clarity of presentation, only the last three K-waves are shown in the last column; for a complete list see Modelski and Thompson 1996a.)[8] But we do need to emphasize that the K-wave, the surge of a leading industrial sector (currently the information industries) and its effect upon the global economy is another instance where agency conspicuously enters the evolutionary process.

There is no reason to suppose that the breakthrough to a global system could have occurred at only one place or in one time interval. Table 2.6 presents a concept of an 'Eurasian inception' of the global system, namely that such a breakthrough occurred, in Eurasia, at about 1000, both in China, and soon afterwards in Mediterranean Europe. The developments in China looked, for a while, more substantial and promising, and it was there that the technologies first developed that animated that breakthrough. There was a surge of sea power and a notable expansion of water-borne trade. Society moved in a 'bourgeois' direction.

Table 2.6 Processes of globalization (930–2080)

From about (year)	Global system process	Global community process	Global political evolution (long cycles)	Global economic evolution
930	preconditions	**EXPERIMENTS** Reforming	**EURASIAN TRANSITION** North Sung South Sung	**SUNG BREAKTHROUGH**
1190		Republican	Genoa Venice	**COMMERCIAL/ NAUTICAL REVOLUTION**
1430	global nucleus	Calvinist	**ATLANTIC EUROPE** Portugal Dutch Republic	**OCEANIC TRADE**
1640		Liberal	Britain I Britain II	**INDUSTRIAL TAKE-OFF**
1850	global organization	**DEMOCRACY** Democratic groundwork	**ATLANTIC-PACIFIC** USA	**INFORMATION** K17 Electric, steel K18 Electronics K19 Information industries K20
2080				

But Sung China faltered and failed to carry through at the global level. The Sung saw themselves as the bearers of China's classical tradition (recently reinforced through the printing of Confucian classics), but they had to contend with aggressive Sinicized dynasties of Inner Asian origin that came to rule much of North China. In 1004 they reached a stand-off with the Khitans (Chinese dynasty name of Liao). But the Liao dynasty was destroyed with Sung help, in 1125, by the Jurchen who took the dynastic name of Chin (Jin). By 1224 Chin rule in turn succumbed to the Mongols under Genghiz Khan who then took on the southern Sung and, under Kublai Khan, completed the conquest of China in 1279 (dynastic name of Yuan) whereby the Mongol world empire reached its greatest extension. The Sung paid much attention to seafaring and maritime affairs, especially in their southern phase, but the nomadic threat from the North never allowed full energy to be devoted to activities of truly global scope.

Structural politics in China 930–1420 could be presented as a sequence of four dynastic cycles, each of about 100 to 120 years in length, and each composed of the four phases of a political learning process (see Table 2.7). China's structural evolution was timed by four macrodecisions: the war with Liao, the war with Chin that forced a shift of the capital from Kaifeng to Hangchow and launched the Southern Sung; the Sung's conquest by the Mongols, who established themselves at Peking; and the Ming rebellion that expelled the Mongols and coincided with a system-wide collapse of Mongol power, also under the attack of Timur (1405). Ming rule was first founded at Nanking, with a potentially maritime orientation, but despite the great expeditions to the Indian Ocean, China soon turned inward, and the move to Peking in 1421 put a seal on that fateful shift.

The rule of the Mongols extended not only to China, but also through major parts of the Eurasian mass, in an imposing structure that embodied a bid for world empire. But that bid soon crashed, in just the way similar imperial bids, though on a more vast scale, also collapsed in the Far West at the same time. The same model we just used to outline the evolution of East Asia could also be employed, with an identical time grid, to depict the salient developments in Mediterranean Europe, whose original center was then Byzantium. The first three cycles had the same imperial bent as those of the Chinese system: an attempt at Byzantine recovery that collapsed after the disaster at Manzikert (1054); the Holy Roman Empire and the Hohenstauffen bid to rule the Mediterranean; and the French (Anjou) and Papal try for universal monarchy, launched at the peak of Mongol power. All three were carried through to a macrodecision. But they all failed to make good on execution.

Running parallel to these imperial gestures was a series of bids for commercial supremacy by prominent Italian city states (Braudel 1984:106–11), beginning with Amalfi, a dependency of Byzantium, followed by Pisa, in league with the Holy Roman Emperors, and then Genoa, working with the Popes and the French and indirectly coordinate, via Black Sea trade and alliances with the Mongol Empire. Each city was in turn routed by its successor, synchronous with the macrodecision of the imperial bids: Pisa sacked Amalfi; Genoa crushed Pisa. And

Venice defeated Genoa after much bitter fighting and for a time profited on its own from the victories of Timur.

But it was only Venice that stood on its own, dominated its golden *quattrocento*, and served as the regional prototype of a global power and a bridge to the next phase of global politics. These are the circumstances that inform the earlier parts of the Matrix of Evolutionary World Politics shown in Table 2.7.

In global political evolution, depicted in Table 2.7 as a series of long cycles (LC1–11) the Chinese antecedents, and the Italian prototypes, were inchoate, proto-global political sequences, laying at the regional level the foundations of future global enterprises. With Portugal, we move beyond laying the foundations, to building, in Atlantic Europe, the nucleus of the global system, and then adding to it with each successive cycle, with the successive world powers being the principal agents of leadership that they did or might not exercise. We note, too, that the four-phase evolutionary structure, observable both at the level of organizational structure (A,B,C), and at the agency level of long cycles (LC), remains the same but in contrast to its fumbling beginnings is, in the later cycles, more steady and, from the Dutch case onward, noticeably cumulative. In the 'Atlantic-Pacific' period we see the beginnings of international organization of a complex kind.

That makes it clear that the long cycle which depicts the sequence of world powers, is in fact a mechanism of global political evolution, wherein powerful nation-states, pursuing their own goals and interests, also forwarded the tasks of political construction. What Table 2.7 also shows is that each world power passed through its own learning and selection process as it was reaching a position of global leadership. What is more, the leaders of the world powers, interacting with the challengers they confronted, were the principal agents of international change. We note that the resolution of the analysis is down to 25–30 years (one phase of the long cycle, such as coalition-building – consult Table 2.7), that is to what is usually considered to be the generational period (the time it takes a generation to replace itself). This period of one generation is the basic time unit of this analysis.

The key elements of the political process are now well understood, and explored. In particular the way in which global leadership was presented, in their own words, by those who exercised it, and how leadership was transferred among them (Modelski and Modelski 1988), and how sea power distributions can be measured over five centuries to determine empirically who wielded global power (Modelski and Thompson 1988). Its basis in world economic evolution is explored in Modelski and Thompson 1996a. The recognition of the special role of the United States, Britain, and the Netherlands, in global arrangements, is now quite widely shared (Thompson 1988); the present study (and others) extend the reach of that process to the onset of modernity.

World system and the evolution of modern humans

We have now shown world system evolution to be an array of major and lesser processes, all of which though do 'hang together.' But we also know that the world

Table 2.7 Matrix of modern evolutionary world politics

Agenda-setting (global problems) PERIOD	Coalition-building	Macrodecision (major warfare)	Execution After 1500: WORLD POWER next challenger	
A. EURASIAN TRANSITION				
930 information	960 Sung founded	990 war with Liao	1020 Northern Sung	LC1
1060 integration	1090 reform parties	1120 war with Chin	1160 Southern Sung	LC2
1190 world empire?	1220 Mongol confederacy	1250 Mongols conquer China	1280 Genoa Mongol empire	LC3
1300 trade	1320 shipping links	1350 Genoa, Mongols routed	1380 Venice Timur	LC4
B. ATLANTIC-EUROPEAN				
1430 discovery	1460 Burgundian connection	1494 Wars of Italy and Indian Ocean	1516 **PORTUGAL** Spain	LC5
1540 integration	1560 Calvinist International	1580 Dutch–Spanish wars	1609 **DUTCH REPUB.** France	LC6

C. ATLANTIC-PACIFIC

1640 political framework	1660 Anglo-Dutch alliance	1688 Wars of Grand Alliance	1714 **BRITAIN I** France	LC7
1740 industrial revolution	1760 trading community	1792 Revolutionary/Napoleonic wars	1815 **BRITAIN II** Germany	LC8
1850 knowledge revolution	1878 Anglo-American special relationship	1914 World Wars I, II	1945 **USA**	LC9
1973 integration	2000 democratic transition	2026	2050	LC10
2080 political framework	2110		....	LC11

Note: LC long cycle of global politics (numbered).

system is not a free-standing or autonomously self-propagating process. It is likely to be, in a nesting fashion, and extending the postulate of self-similarity, part of some larger-scale arrangement of the learning variety. That larger process, too, is likely to be of the logical form of the evolutionary processes we have just studied. What might that be?

These are complex but intriguing questions, possibly insoluble in the light of present knowledge. Is there a larger process of which world system evolution (with a period of 8,000 years) is a part? How might world system evolution place in that larger scheme of the evolution of modern humans? How do we explain the origins, or the inception of the world system, and what is the larger framework in which that system must be situated?

'Good questions.' Could it be that, at first, human evolution wrought the differentiation of humanity from nature? Could that prehistorical period, extending for over 30,000 years, be thought of as having comprised four major phases of some 8,000 years each? It might have begun with the adoption of a fully efficient human language, that included the use of syntax. Such a cultural breakthrough, we might suppose, would in turn promote, in the next phase, kinship linkages and extended family groups. Then, at the peak of the last ice age, humans might have been driven into caves and other permanent settlements. Finally, some 10,000 years ago, agriculture might have begun, slowly at first in today's Middle East, and then elsewhere. This celebrated 'Agricultural Revolution,' and the networks of exchange that it might have promoted, would lay down the preconditions for the next step in human evolution, the rise of civilization on the basis of sociality.

What is not in doubt is that the centuries between 4000 and 3000 BC mark a strategic turning point, towards sociality, and the onset of world system evolution, and of all that we have reviewed as making up our major social institutions. They also signaled the beginnings of civilization, a deeper change that extended not only to society but also to culture, human nature, and to the humans' relation to their environment. We might define (singular) civilization (a word whose root is the same as that for city) as a condition of humanity characterized by a culture of urbane living, contrasting with barbarism in a condition of nature. The city, made possible by agricultural surpluses, is itself a large-scale cultural artifact and makes possible the differentiation of culture from society, and its more autonomous development. Human evolution entered civilization (and history proper) with cities and writing, and that is the stage that we are still living through, and are likely to continue well into the future.

Conclusion

This has been an exposition of the logical structure and some indication of the range of supporting evidence that suggest the initial plausibility of an evolutionary world system analysis. Species-wide evolutionary processes have been identified at three major levels of analysis: institutional, organizational, and agency; and a four-phased learning process could then be observed. Surprisingly, the logic is the same at each of the levels, while the period of the learning is in each case proportional to the scope of the process, in a manner that preserves symmetry, nestedness, and synchronization in coevolution. Even more encouraging is the thought that important processes including the rise and decline of world powers, as well as that of the rise and decline of leading sectors, might in each case be seen to be incidents in an unfolding panorama of world system history.

Notes

1   This is a reworking of the paper 'World System Evolution: A Learning Model' first presented at the thirty-second annual convention of the International Studies Association, Vancouver BC, March 1991.

2   But Lumsden and Wilson (ibid.:3–7) also argue that the human species is unique in the magnitude of its enculturation process. 'Mankind has attained' the 'complete' or 'true' cultural state because its repertoire includes not only simple learning and imitation, but also complex learning: teaching linked to socialization of the young, and the employ-ment of symbols by human agents. This creates the potential for the creation of more advanced forms of organization via species-wide learning processes. But the focus of the present analysis is social organization and social structure, not culture as a complex of meanings and the codes that govern it, changes in the make-up of personalities, or the adaptations in the biological organism that mediate between its physical existence and human action.

3   For full comparative treatment of the principal approaches see contribution by William Thompson to this volume.

4   Another, recent, example is Samuel Huntington's *The Clash of Civilizations* (1996).

5   Jane Azevedo's *Mapping Reality: Evolutionary Realist Epistemology for the Natural and Social Sciences* (1997) is an excellent recent exposition of the current state of that field.

6   They could also be seen as phases of a learning process that Parsons and his associates described in 1950 as the LIGA sequence (Modelski 1987:104ff).

7   Along the vertical dimension, we distinguish global from regional, national, and local structures.

8   The outline of global economic evolution comes close to what Fernand Braudel (1984: 76–88) identified as the secular trends in the European (world) economy, each linked to four K-waves. We place less emphasis than Braudel on the ups and downs of the economy, and on its price trends, than on ongoing transformations in economic structure at the global level via lead sectors.

3 Civilizations, world systems and hegemonies

David Wilkinson

Fundamentals of a civilizations-as-world-systems approach

What constitutes a world system?

Civilizations are world systems. (Non-urban world systems, as studied by Chase-Dunn, do exist; but I shall not discuss them further in this expository context.)

What then are civilizations? Civilizations are societies with cities (settlements of or above the order of $10^4 = 10,000$). Their spatial limits are located by the limits of regular transactional interaction, especially politico-military-diplomatic interaction. Contrary to the common ('Parsonian'?) assumptions that a society has a polity, an economy, and a culture, civilizations are social systems *with* a coextensive polity (usually a system of territorial states). But they usually nest *within* the more spatially extensive penumbra of an *oikumene* (world economy) which links them economically to other civilizations and to non-civilized (i.e. non-urban) but populated space. And they exist *without* coherent cultures or cultural systems; instead they usually, probably always, are *polycultures*.

Civilizations have customarily been distinguished from non-civilized societies by such criteria as cities (my criterion), writing, surplus, accumulation, non-producing classes, and from each other by criteria of *coherence* (cultural homogeneity, unity, uniformity) and *connectedness* or *closure* (transactional unity and wholeness; internal interdependence and external independence). However the criteria of coherence and connectedness are in application incompatible: one must be relaxed or abandoned. Most civilizationists have preferred to maintain the coherence criterion; I have argued the desirability of the alternative, and studied as 'civilizations' large, strongly interconnected, but culturally heterogeneous and incoherent social systems. Network maps of politico-military-diplomatic transactions between cities will show clusterings different from those shown by trade route maps or maps of cultural (religious, linguistic) interaction: I use the politico-military-diplomatic criterion.

Examining civilizationists' competing rosters of civilizations on the assumption that the spatio-temporal boundaries of civilizations would coincide with spaces and times of low or no regular intercity politico-military-diplomatic transaction (invasions, alliances, embassies, commands, demands, requests) produced a roster in which about half of the traditional 'civilizations' remained, while the other half reappeared as regions (or even as epochs) of a single, larger, and hitherto unrecognized network entity. In particular, the traditional 'Western,' 'Classical,' 'Islamic,' 'Medieval,' 'Byzantine,' 'Russian,' etc. appeared to be regions or phases in a single, larger, longer-lived multiurban network which I labeled 'Central Civilization.'

Central Civilization also appeared to be the sole contemporary survivor of the species, having expanded to global scope and engulfed all competitors. This process was advanced by but was not identical with the 'Western' conquests and colonizations of the 'modern' era, and was not in the least reversed by the dissolution of the various empires with West European – or East European – metropoles (Wilkinson 1982; 1987a).

In its contemporary period, Central Civilization is indistinguishable from the modern global world system. I contend that in its previous, less-than-global condition, Central Civilization was also inescapably a world system, as were all its competitors.

The roster of world systems would include the following:

1 *Mesopotamian*, or – more accurate for its later period – Southwest Asian, including areas and/or epochs customarily labeled Sumerian, Akkadian, Elamite, Gutian, Amorite, Babylonian, Syrian, Assyrian, Hittite. Its largest cities, using Chandler's (1974, 1987) data and dates, but my taxonomy, are: 2250 BC, Agade; 2000 BC, Ur; 1800 BC, Isin; 1600 BC, Babylon. As a reminder that this is a polyculture, its cities include Ebla (Syria), Hazor (Canaan), Assur (Assyria), Susa (Elam), Khattushash (Anatolia)

2 *Egyptian*, or Northeast African, including Kush and Nubia. Its largest cities, per Chandler's data, are: 2250 BC and 2000 BC, Memphis; 1800 BC, Thebes; 1600 BC, Avaris. Avaris is Hyksos; again to keep attention on the polycultural character of these civilizations/world systems, this one includes Kerma (Nubia).

These two are conventional entries on rosters of civilizations. The next is not.

3 *Central civilization*. About 1500 BC, the expanding Mesopotamian and Egyptian civilizations collided and fused into a single, of course polycultural, sociopolitical entity. This civilization never fell; this world system exists today, now grown to global scope, as the sole survivor of its ilk. Its successive largest cities, using Chandler's data and dates, are: 1360 BC, Thebes (Egypt); 1200 BC Memphis (Egypt); 1000 and 800 BC, Thebes again; 650 BC, Nineveh; 430 BC, Babylon; 200 BC, Alexandria; AD 100, Rome; AD 361 and 500, Constantinople; AD 622, Ctesiphon; AD 800 and 900, Baghdad; AD 1000, Cordova; AD 1100, Constantinople again; AD 1200, Fez; AD 1300, 1400 and 1500, Cairo; AD 1600 and 1700, Constantinople again; AD 1800 and 1900, London. This list is evidently polycultural.

The next four are, again, generally agreed on by civilizationists, with some differences as to labels and datings.

4   *Indic.* Largest cities, using Chandler's data and my taxonomy: 1800 BC, Mohenjo-Daro; 1200 BC, Ayodhya; 1000 BC and 800 BC, Hastinapura; 650 BC, Kausambi; 430 BC and 200 BC, Patna; AD 100, Anuradhapura (Ceylon); AD 361, Patna again; AD 500, Sialkot (Ephthalites); AD 622 and 800, Kanauj; AD 900, Manyakheta; AD 1000, Anhilvada; AD 1100, Kalyan the Later; AD 1200, Polonnaruwa; AD 1300, Delhi; AD 1400 and 1500, Vijayanagar. By about AD 1600, the Indic world system had been engulfed by the Central.

5   *Far Eastern*; more 'Sinocentric' than 'Chinese.' Largest cities, per Chandler, as above: 1360 BC, Ao; 1200 BC, Anyang; 1000 BC and 800 BC, Changan-=Sian; 650 BC, Lintzu (Chi); 430 BC, Yenhsiatsu (Yen); 200 BC, Changan again; AD 100, Loyang; AD 361, Nanking; AD 500, Loyang again; AD 800 and 900, Changan again; AD 1000 and 1100, Kaifeng; AD 1200 and 1300, Hangchow; AD 1400, Nanking again; AD 1500, 1600, 1700, 1800, and (if applicable) 1900, Peking. To underline the polyculturality of this world system, note its cities would include Tonggoo (Korea), Kashiwara (Japan), Prome (Burma), Indrapura (Cambodia), Ye (Hunnic Anyang), Tatung (of the Toba Wei), Kashgar (Turkestan), Lhasa (Tibet), Tali (Nanchao), Silow (Khitan), Ninghsia (Tangut), Sukotai (Siam), Hanoi (Vietnam). Between the Opium Wars and World War I, the Far Eastern world system was engulfed by, and became part of, the Central world system.

6   *Mexican*, or Mesoamerican. Largest cities, per Chandler: 430 BC and 200 BC, Cuicuilco; AD 100, 361, 500 and 622, Teotihuacan; AD 800, Copan (Mayas); AD 900 and 1000, Tollan (Tula); AD 1100, Cholula; AD 1200, Tenayuca; AD 1300, Texcoco; AD 1400, Azcapotzalco; AD 1500, Tenochtit-lan. In the first half of the sixteenth century, the Mexican world system was engulfed by, and became part of, the Central world system.

7   *Peruvian*, or Middle Andean. Largest city, AD 1400, Riobamba; AD 1500, Cuzco. The Peruvian world system was engulfed by the Central world system in the course of the sixteenth century.

The next four are familiar to all civilizationists, but accepted as separate civilizations only by some.

8   *Aegean.* Largest cities, per Chandler: 1600 BC, Knossos; 1360 BC and 1200 BC, Mycenae; 650 BC, Miletus.

9   *West African.* Largest cities, per Chandler: AD 800, Gao; AD 1300, Njimiye; AD 1400, Mali; AD 1500, Gao again. Toward the end of the sixteenth century, the West African world system was engulfed by, and became part of, the Central world system.

10   *Indonesian.* Largest cities, per Chandler: AD 800, 900, and 1000, Prambanan; AD 1300, Majapahit. The Indonesian civilization/world system was engulfed by the Central in the course of the sixteenth century.

11 *Japanese*. Split off from Far Eastern. Largest cities: AD 800, 900, 1000, 1100, Kyoto; AD 1200 and 1300, Kamakura; AD 1400, Kyoto again; AD 1600, Osaka; AD 1700 and 1800, Yedo (Tokyo); AD 1900 (if applicable), Tokyo by that name. Within the period from the 1854 Perry mission to World War I, the Japanese world system was engulfed by, and enrolled in, the Central world system. Of the various civilizations, only the Japanese may possibly have been monocultural, at least at some periods.

The last five members on this list are treated by most civilizationists as too small, too brief, or too poorly documented to make their rosters. Only recently (Wilkinson 1993a) did accumulating evidence persuade me to add the last two.

12 *Mississippian*. Largest city, AD 1100, Cahokia. Apparently the only civilization on the list to have collapsed endogenously.
13 *Irish*. Largest city, AD 1100, Dublin.
14 *Chibchan*. Largest city, AD 1500, Bacata.
15 *East African*, or Swahili. Extant, fourteenth (possibly twelfth) and fifteenth century AD. Largest city, AD 1400 and 1500, Kilwa. Engulfed by Central civilization early sixteenth century.
16 *West Central African*, or Kongo/Tio. Extant, fifteenth century AD, possibly earlier. Largest city, AD 1400, Ambessi/Mbanza Kongo (Sao Salvador); AD 1500, Sao Salvador. Engulfed by Central civilization early sixteenth century.

(For this roster of civilizations/world systems, and a large number of candidates not so classified, see Wilkinson 1982, and 1993/1994.)

A chronogram of the fusion of these civilizations (except Mississippian, which fell rather than fused) into Central Civilization is given as Figure 3.1.

I have attempted a more precise mapping of the first fourteen members of the above list, by assigning to them the largest world cities at various moments in time (Wilkinson 1992a, 1993a).

What are to be considered legitimate parameters?

I take this to be the question 'how much variation can entities display and still be considered world systems?' rather than the equally legitimate (but logically posterior) 'what are the numerical characteristics of the collection of all world systems taken together?' or 'what aspects of any given world system are constant for that system over time, though varying as between world systems?'

Civilizations/world systems (I use the terms interchangeably, subject to Chase-Dunn's reservation) may vary enormously in size. The minimum: one marginally qualifying city and its politico-military hinterland. The maximum thus far: the half-urbanized global world system of the late twentieth century AD. The theoretical upper bound is arguable: could there be an interplanetary civilization? Logistic difficulties would be enormous; I'd rule it out under current or reasonably predictable technologies and treat the whole Earth as a practical upper-bound domain.

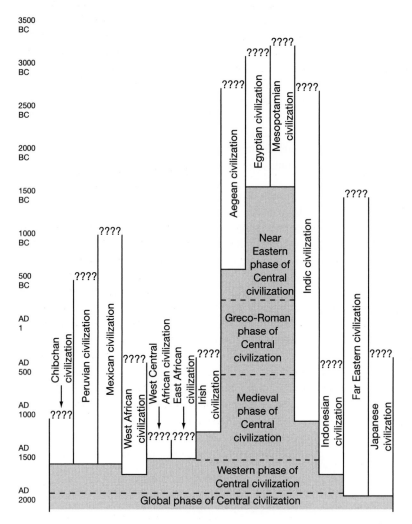

Figure 3.1 The incorporation of fourteen civilizations into one 'Central civilization.'

Note: This figure illustrates the successive incorporation of autonomous civilizations into a larger, composite 'Central civilization' in gray. ???? = transitions to civilization took place no later than this date for this case.

The spatial and demographic parameters of world systems thus allow a size range of five or six orders of magnitude at least; still, whale and flea are both 'animals' despite some scale differences, and the size range of civilizations is paltry when compared to that of the systems observed by physicists.

The temporal parameters are even more flexible. I would probably treat a city that lasted only about a generation before being destroyed by its neighbors (Dithakong) or evaporating through lineage fission (Kaditshwena) as a 'protocivilization' or, to borrow and refurbish Toynbee's term, an 'abortive civilization,' to be studied mostly to learn about startup failures, which must have been very numerous, and the failure process (Wilkinson 1993/4). However, the current world system/civilization I regard as having an unbroken continuity of 3,500 years to its formation in the Middle East by the fusion of two root civilizations (Mesopotamian and Egyptian), whose continuity adds at least another 1,500 years and probably rather more. Despite many vicissitudes, and crises in proportion to the number of analysts, it shows no signs of imminent demise.

Has there been a single evolving world system, have there been areas external to it, or have alternative systems existed side by side?

In the past, from whenever Mesopotamian and Egyptian world systems began to coexist, until the end of the historical autonomy of the Sinocentric Far Eastern world system, and of the Japanese world system, several civilizations/world systems have coexisted on the global surface. By the late nineteenth or early twentieth century, only one survived, which I would treat as the effective date of the globalization of society and politics. By the late twentieth century, probably no non-urban world systems remained. The basic point is: once there were several world systems; now there is only one.

The same point, incidentally, holds – mutatis mutandis – for oikumenes/world economies, of which there were several on the globe until the nineteenth century 'opening' of Japan incorporated its isolated world economy, the last such, into the much larger one, the current sole survivor, which I have labeled the 'Old Oikumene.' (See Wilkinson 1992a,b, 1993a,c.)

By what processes is such a system defined?

It is as yet premature to use process-based definitions for world systems. Definition is itself an evolving process: we are still looking for the full set of processes characteristic of a world system. There can be located at least the following: a *political process* of fluctuation between states systems (the empirical norm) and world state/universal empire (often an ideological norm); a more finely specified *political process* of fluctuation among nonpolar, multipolar, tripolar, bipolar, unipolar-nonhegemonic, unipolar-hegemonic, and world-imperial orders; a *war-peace process* that generates and terminates deadly quarrels, with frequency, magnitude, duration, complexity and other characteristics; economic-demographic *growth-decline* processes at several spatial and temporal scales; several processes surrounding the rise, decline and shift of civilizational/world-systemic *cores*; and some processes that maintain a *polyculture* or cultural pluralism, with fluctuations, involving the generation and fission (balancing the termination and fusion) of religions, languages, styles, nations, ethnicities, tribes, regionalities, etc. There is a *turnover process* in which cities, states, nations, etc. come into and go out of existence within world systems which continue. There may also be a *general war–general peace* process that operates at a very large scale.

Incidental findings on civilizations/world systems

There are some propositions which, though not of major concern to the participants in this particular debate, should be noted briefly.

Political forms of world systems: states systems and universal empires

The political structure of civilizations has ordinarily approximated one of two types: 'universal empire' or 'states system.' About twenty-three universal empires and about twenty-eight states systems may be identified: the states systems seem more durable.

The contemporary states system can be traced back to the decline of Rome in the face of the rise of Sassanid Persia, and is of unparalleled longevity, more than half a millennium older (with a span 40 per cent longer than) its nearest competitor (the post-Maurya pre-engulfment Indic system). Over time the post-Roman states system has expanded geographically; has lost old members and gained new ones; has shifted its power core; has had different kinds of member states, different great powers, and different would-be hegemons from century to century. But it remains a single system, extending from the days of Ardashir I and Shapur I of Persia to our own (Wilkinson 1983).

Martin Wight once posed this problem:

> Most states-systems have ended in a universal empire, which has swallowed all the states of the system. Is there any states-system which has *not* led fairly directly to the establishment of a world empire? Does the evidence rather suggest that we should expect a states-system to culminate in this way?
>
> (1977:43–4)

The empirical answer is that most states systems have ended in universal empires; that most universal empires have ended in states systems; that the contemporary states system has *not* led fairly directly to the establishment of a world state, but rather has proven the most durable member of its species, not to mention having outlasted any world state ever recorded (Wilkinson 1986).

By comparison to states systems, universal empires are peaceable, repressive, stagnant – and short-lived. Their collapses, and the consequent re-emergences of states systems, display a variety of motifs. Satraps usurp; provinces rebel; barbarians invade; border states arise; sects partition; classes struggle; enemies combine; and troubles multiply. These themes recur with different frequencies, but none seems universal. On the other hand, crisis in the real, functioning monarchic office of the universal empire political structure is very characteristic of the fall of universal empire (Wilkinson 1988).

Political forms of world systems: polarity

Students of power structures who examine only the modern world system from 1648 to 1939 are commonly led to assume that multipolarity is the normal political form for a system of states, and treat bipolarity as deviant, unipolarity as imaginary, tripolarity as implausible, nonpolarity as inconceivable.

However, a study of power structures in the Indic world system from 550 BC to its incorporation into the Central world system produces a rather discrepant picture. Unipolarity (non-hegemonic, hegemonic, or universal-state) was the most frequent form, and a stable (durable) one; bipolarity was next most frequent, and relatively stable; tripolar and nonpolar forms were more frequent than multipolar (Wilkinson 1993b). Multipolarity cannot then be treated as a transhistorical and transcultural norm for states systems: it becomes a condition to be interrogated, not assumed.

Cultural forms of world systems: polyculture

A civilization is not identical to a culture, a language, a religion, a 'race,' a class, a state or a nation. It is a macrosociety whose boundaries ordinarily include many national, state, economic, linguistic, cultural and religious groups. The various civilizations are not necessarily based upon any major premise, nor do they necessarily articulate, develop and realize such, nor are they necessarily logically or aesthetically consistent or complementary – on the contrary, they are actually highly and evolvingly contradictory, conflicted, dialectical (Wilkinson 1995d).

Civilizations expand faster than civilization diffuses, but civilization diffuses faster than it is discovered or invented. Out of tens of thousands to millions of precivilizational social groups that have existed in human history only very few have evolved historically autonomous civilizations; an enormous number have been absorbed by expanding civilizations evolved elsewhere. Of the tens of historically autonomous and identifiable civilizations, most were engulfed by one of their members. But this engulfment is macrosocial and macropolitical: it has usually been preceded by economic penetration, and it has not usually been accompanied or followed by (mere) cultural assimilation.

Our time is unique in that only one civilization now exists on Earth, of global scope, without a periphery into which to expand further. It is, evidently, a polyculture, a mixing pot of coexisting contiguous cultures, interacting intensely, slowly exchanging memes and genes and persons and traits, yet maintaining some distinctive characteristics even over many generations. What is evident today was also true for the civilizations/world systems of the past – probably even for Japan with its established monocultural ideology, certainly for the rest.

Furthermore, in all probability world systems were polycultures at the time of their first urbanization, i.e. we hypothesize a polycultural precivilizational or proto civilizational matrix will be found to have preceded the settlement condensation, as will a local increase in population density and social pressure (Iberall and Wilkinson 1993).

62   *David Wilkinson*

Incidental to the assessment of systemwide monoculturalism as an ideology or ideal rather than a systemic characteristic, is the same assessment for actors and subsystems. In particular, contrary to the assumption that there today exists a world of nation-states, it is the case, in the modern world system as before and elsewhere, that the (normal) multistate polity never matches the multinational polyculture, but is only weakly coupled thereto, on account of transhistorical and transcultural phenomena such as imperialism and empires, colonization and colonies, diasporas and occupational ethnicism, slave-trading and slavery (Iberall and Wilkinson 1993).

Cores and peripheries

Do all world systems have core–periphery hierarchies?

Yes; but not at all times; but usually. Civilizations usually possess a *core* (central, older, advanced, wealthy, powerful); a *semiperiphery* strongly thereto connected (younger, fringeward, remote, more recently attached, weaker, poorer, more backward); and a weakly connected *periphery* (nomads; settled subsistence producers; other civilizations in the same oikumene, connected by trade but not by fighting or alliance). Civilizational cores may take any of several political forms, e.g.: a single hegemonic state; a great power oligarchy; the metropolitan region of a universal empire. Core areas expand and contract, the latter especially during hegemonic and universal-state epochs. Civilizations usually have a semiperiphery, especially during such periods, but need not; during states-system periods they sometimes do not have a core.

Cores move over a long time span, sometimes in a single prevailing direction, sometimes shuttling back and forth. Old cores return, and new areas rise, to core status, with no marked propensity either way. Core areas of a civilization may partition functionally, with different areas serving as politico-military, economic and cultural cores, though there is some tendency for the functions to go together or drift together. Recent arrivals to core status have some advantages in competitions to destroy states systems.

By what processes are cores and peripheries created? City-making; economic innovation; military conquest; god-creation; political manipulation; cultural creativity and fascination; evasions of Malthus; rent-getting. Do core–periphery relations work in basically the same ways in all systems, or are there fundamental differences that emerge by context? Similarities seem more fundamental than contextualized differences (Wilkinson 1991).

Hegemony and its cognates

An important theme in the world-systems literature, as well as that of international political economy, and one of increased interest to civilizationists such as Matthew Melko (1995), is that of 'hegemony.' The researchers represented at Lund 1995 take varyingly reserved and critical approaches to such common theses as that: world systems usually have hegemons; Britain was hegemon in the world system of the nineteenth century; America became the hegemon after World War II. I reject all these theses unreservedly, while accepting that they are sufficiently widespread and deep-rooted to warrant an extensive and intensive critique. Not only critique: reconstruction. Hegemony is a genuine issue in the study of civilizations/world systems; there have been some few historic hegemons, more near-hegemons, and many hegemonic aspirations; failed and successful hegemonic (and anti-hegemonic) careers are worth studying; and there are intriguing cognates or analogues to hegemony equally worth attending to.

The issue of hegemony in the context of the discussion of world system history brings to mind the extensive arguments of Immanuel Wallerstein on the subject: these arguments provide a useful point of entry.

Nature and ambiguity of Wallersteinian hegemony

The idea of 'hegemony' assumes a remarkable significance in Wallerstein's theory. It is distinguished from world-empire (Wallerstein 1984:38). It has political, economic and politico-economic features, by definition or by hypothesis. Whatever its character otherwise, it is brief, rare, and peculiarly related to war, sea-power and free trade, and to the Netherlands, Britain, and America.

Wallersteinian hegemony defined

At times, Wallerstein defines hegemony *politically*, in 'power' terms. Given that there exists an interstate system with several great powers, hegemony exists when one of them has unquestioned supremacy (1984:58), is truly first among equals, with a really great power margin or differential (1984:38–9), can largely impose its rules and its wishes in the economic, political, military, diplomatic, and even cultural arenas (1984:38), has an edge so significant that allied major power are *de facto* client states and opposed major powers feel highly defensive (1984:39).

At times, hegemony is defined by Wallerstein in a completely different way, *economically*, as great and general competitive advantage. When 'no second power or combination of second powers seems capable of challenging the *economic* supremacy of the strongest core power' the situation is called 'hegemony' (Hopkins, Wallerstein *et al.* 1982a:52). What has occurred in each historic instance of hegemony was that

> enterprises domiciled in the given power in question achieved their edge first in agro-industrial production, then in commerce, and then in finance. I believe they lost their edge in this sequence as well . . . Hegemony thus refers to that short interval in which there is *simultaneous* advantage in all three economic domains
>
> (Wallerstein 1984:40–1).

The pattern of hegemony seems marvelously simple. Marked superiority in agro-industrial productive efficiency leads to dominance of the spheres of commercial distribution of world trade ... Commercial primacy leads in turn to control of the financial sectors of banking (exchange, deposit, and credit) and of investment (direct and portfolio). These superiorities are successive, but they overlap in time. Similarly, the *loss* of advantage seems to be in the same order (from productive to commercial to financial), and also largely successive. It follows that there is probably only a short moment when a given core power can manifest *simultaneously* productive, commercial and financial superiority *over all other core powers*. This momentary summit is what we call hegemony.

(Wallerstein 1980:38–9)

Finally, at times hegemony is defined in a combined, *politico-economic* sense.

If we assume a number of core states, we can assume 'rivalry' as a normal state of affairs, with exceptional periods in which one core power exceeds all others in the efficiency of its productive, commercial, and financial activities, and in military strength. We can call this latter 'hegemony.'

(Hopkins, Wallerstein *et al.* 1982b:116)

When the political and economic forms of hegemony are not treated as if related by definition, they seem in Wallerstein to be *causally* connected. Having economic advantage depends on political power:

Hegemony involves more than core status. It may be defined as a situation wherein the products of a given core state are produced so efficiently that they are by and large competitive even in other core states, and therefore the given core state will be the beneficiary of a maximally fee market. Obviously, to take advantage of this productive superiority, such a state must be strong enough to prevent or minimize the erection of internal and external political barriers to the free flow of the factors of production.

(Wallerstein 1980:38)

Having economic advantage leads to political power:

When producers located within a given state can undersell producers located in other core states in the latter's 'home market,' they can transform this production advantage over time into one in the commercial arena and then into one in the financial arena. The combined advantages may be said to constitute hegemony and are reflected as well in a political-military advantage in the interstate system.

(Wallerstein 1984:17)

Or having economic advantage may be independent of having political power: economic supremacy is to be distinguished from 'imperium,' the characteristic of world-empire, 'in that it operates primarily through the market' (Hopkins, Wallerstein *et al.* 1982a:52).

Free-market policy of the Wallersteinian hegemon

Wallerstein argues that it would be rational for a hegemon (presumably in the economic or politico-economic senses only) to promote free trade. The material base of hegemonic power

> lies in the ability of enterprises domiciled in that power to operate more efficiently in all three major economic arenas – agro-industrial production, commerce, and finance. The edge in efficiency of which we are speaking is one so great that these enterprises can not only outbid enterprises domiciled in other great powers in the world market in general, but quite specifically in very many instances within the home markets of the rival powers themselves.
>
> (Wallerstein 1984:38–40)

> If hegemony is defined as a situation in which a single core power has demonstrable advantages of efficiency *simultaneously* in production, commerce, and finance, it follows that a maximally free market would be likely to ensure maximal profit to the enterprises located in such a hegemonic power.
>
> (Wallerstein 1984:5)

War-origin and seapower-basis of Wallersteinian hegemony

According to Wallerstein, the United Provinces (the Netherlands), Great Britain, and the United States have each held hegemony in the modern capitalist world-system. Each hegemony followed a world war (Thirty Years War 1618–48; Napoleonic Wars 1792–1815; the single long 'world war' 1914–45) in which a previously maritime power transformed itself into a land power to defeat a historically strong land power (the Hapsburgs, France, Germany) which seemed to be trying to transform the world-economy into a world-empire (Wallerstein 1983:58–9). The basis for the victory was the – momentarily greater – economic efficiency of the capital accumulators in these states in 'agro-industrial production, commerce and finance' (1983:59).

> In each case, the hegemony was secured by a thirty-year long world war. By a world war, I shall mean . . . a land-based war that involves (not necessarily continuously) almost all the major military powers of the epoch in warfare that is very destructive of land and population.
>
> (Wallerstein 1984:41)

Hegemonic powers were primarily sea (now sea/air) powers. In the long ascent to hegemony, they seemed very reluctant to develop their armies, discussing openly the potentially weakening drain on state revenues and manpower of becoming tied down in long land wars. Yet each found finally that it had to develop a strong land army as well as face up to a major land-based rival which seemed to be trying to transform the world-economy into a world-empire.

(Wallerstein 1984:41)

Rarity and brevity of Wallersteinian hegemony

For Wallerstein, hegemony is a rare and unstable situation; the statistically normal situation of rivalry within the interstate system is one in which 'many powers exist, grouped more or less into two camps, but with several neutral or swing elements, and with neither side (nor *a fortiori* any single state) being able to impose its will on others' (1984:39).

The hegemonies were brief because: the production advantages could not be sustained indefinitely (1984:17) – indeed, other states could copy the productive efficiencies without paying the same amortization costs of obsolete equipment; the hegemonic powers brought labor peace with internal redistribution; and the high military costs of hegemonic responsibilities were economically burdensome (1983:59–60); and 'the mechanisms of the balance of power intrude to reduce the political advantage of the single most powerful state' (1984:17).

Wallersteinian hegemonic succession

In the long period following the era of hegemony, two powers seemed eventually to emerge as the 'contenders for the succession' – England and France after Dutch hegemony; the US and Germany after British; and now Japan and western Europe after US. Furthermore, the eventual winner of the contending pair seemed to use as a conscious part of its strategy the gentle turning of the old hegemonic power into its 'junior partner' – the English vis-à-vis the Dutch, the US vis-à-vis Great Britain . . . and now?

(Wallerstein 1984:42–3)

Disambiguating hegemony

A critique of the theory of hegemony is obstructed by the confusing multiplication of definitions of 'hegemony.' We can best escape that confusion by remembering that 'hegemony' is a term that predates the confusion, and had (and has, if we wish) a reasonably unambiguous usage. For example, Herz (1951): 'When Wilson led the United States into the war at the side of the Entente, he did it in order to save Europe – and the world – from the danger of German *hegemony* [emphasis added]' (p.213); 'The balance of power system of the last centuries has not prevented wars and injustice, nor has it been a safeguard against exploitation and imperialism. But it has preserved a world of nations against the threat of *hegemony* [emphasis added] and domination by one super-power' (pp.220–1).

Going farther back provides further illustration of the political-influence sense of hegemony. *The Oxford English Dictionary* tells us that hegemony is 'Leadership, predominance, preponderance, esp. the leadership or predominant authority of one state of a confederacy or union over the others.' Historians from the nineteenth century use the term with respect to Athens in the Delian League, Macedon in the Hellenic League, and Prussia in the North Germanic confederation. Hegemony was in all these cases the step just before empire, i.e. the abolition of the independent existence of the states. Thus, in the Delian League, founded (478 BC) at the instance of the smaller states, those who sought to pull out (Naxos 467, Samos 440) found their walls razed, their fleets seized, their once-voluntary tribute made compulsory, their islands colonized or garrisoned; those who stayed in found their forces under Athenian command and the League treasury moved to Athens. The Hellenic League, founded 338 at the instance of Macedon after it defeated Athens and Thebes, was a perpetual alliance (of those states, and the rest of the Greeks save Sparta), under Philip's headship and military command; when the Greeks tried to escape (335), Thebes was destroyed and its population enslaved, which persuaded the rest to be quiet; when Athens again tried to withdraw (323), and was defeated (322), it was garrisoned and its constitution remade by Macedon. What Prussia had wanted in the Germanic Confederation (1815–66) it got from the North German Confederation (1867–71): the presidency and commandership-in-chief; this hegemony was shortly replaced (1871) by an empire organized around Prussia.

One can go even farther back, inasmuch as 'hegemony' is an ancient term of political theory. In its classical context, its sense is once more clearly political (vs. economic or cultural) (Wilkinson 1994b). Systemwide hegemony is a distinct, meaningful and useful politico-military concept: a condition of overwhelming strength such that all other states in a certain group follow the hegemon, voluntarily, or through fear, or through applied force. This distinct concept is historically and politically important. No useful purpose is served by watering it down, or by turning it into an economic concept, or by weighting it down with economic provisos, stipulations or preconditions. Henceforward I shall therefore normally use 'hegemony' in its fundamental politico-military sense, to denote a systemwide unipolar influence structure in a system of states, including but something more than a unipolar coercive-capability structure, but something less than universal empire: unquestioned supremacy, a really great margin of power over other states, the ability (unequivocally demonstrable only by the act) to impose rules and desires throughout the system.

It then becomes necessary to find a replacement term to fit Wallerstein's economic of 'hegemon': a state characterized by great productive, commercial, and financial competitive edge, profitability, wealth and prosperity relative to the other states in a system. Modelski would prefer 'leader,' a term with which I am uncomfortable because the 'followers' of these 'leaders' are pursuers, perhaps disciples, but by no means associates, retainers, dependents or adherents. 'Fountainhead' might convey the sense of the principal source of innovation in the system, 'apex' the sense of being at the top of a structure without controlling it, 'leadingwheel' the sense of being the first part of a system to get where the whole system is going. I have used the nautical 'forereacher,' one who gains an advantage and goes ahead of others in a competition. This being an election year, I'll try 'frontrunner.' The unhistorical economic definition of hegemony could then be replaced by a falsifiable economic hypothesis of hegemony: i.e. 'all world-system frontrunners (and only they) become world-system hegemons.' This hypothesis can then be scrutinized by inspecting the careers of the Wallersteinian hegemons, on the assumption that these states are correctly described as 'frontrunners,' greatly advantaged economically, but that evidence of their (politico-military) 'hegemony' remains to be sought. Wallerstein names three hegemons: the United Provinces, the Netherlands, in the mid-seventeenth century, Great Britain in the mid-nineteenth, the United States in the mid-twentieth (1983:58). In two cases there are perplexities in the dating of the alleged hegemonies.

The alleged Dutch hegemony   In trying to date and comprehend the Dutch 'hegemony,' it seems necessary to set aside two anomalies in its treatment by Wallerstein. On one occasion the Dutch hegemony is alleged to have begun as early as 1608, presumably because otherwise the hegemon's free-trade ideology would have appeared prematurely (when 'at the moment of Dutch accession to hegemony in the seventeenth century, Hugo Grotius published that "classic" on international law, Mare Librium . . .') (Wallerstein 1984:5). On another occasion, 1651–78 is seen as 'the height of Dutch hegemony' (1980:65); this dating fits the theory only in that it follows the Thirty Years War. Most often, however, the Dutch hegemony is seen as beginning 1620 (1984:17,40; Hopkins, Wallerstein *et al.* 1982b:116–18 – at latest 1625, as in Wallerstein 1980:39 and Hopkins, Wallerstein *et al.* 1982a:62) and ending 1650, followed by hegemonic decline and acute conflict with successors 1650–72 (Wallerstein 1984:58). Let us therefore examine the proposition that the United Provinces had hegemony in the world-system from 1620 to 1650.

Poles, whom Wallerstein includes within the modern world-system at this time, fought Russians (outside); Poles and Venetians (inside) fought, and Hungarians (inside) worked loose of, Turks (outside); Turks fought Persians, Persians fought Moguls, Moguls threatened to fight English. Wallerstein excludes, and I cannot countenance excluding, Russia, the Ottoman Empire, Persia, and perhaps India from the world-system in the mid-seventeenth century. If one counts them in, as I believe we must, there can be no question of a Dutch hegemony, which these actors surely never felt. Even if we include only western and central Europe and Iberian America in the world-system at this time, Dutch hegemony is by no means evident. One must grant that by this period the Dutch had become a naval power of the first rank: though humiliated by the Spanish fleet at Bahia as late as 1625, the Dutch were able to defeat the Spanish invasion fleet at the Slaak 1631, and even to gain an apparent naval primacy (by defeating Spain at the battle of the Downs in 1639) during the last third of their 'hegemony.' It is however also true that this primacy could be viewed, in the light of later events, as quite nominal, since it lasted only until the first time it was challenged (by the English – first Anglo-Dutch War, 1652–4). One must also concede to the case in favor of Dutch hegemony that, while Portugal was a dependency chafing under Spanish rule, the Dutch were able to take away many of her (sub)-colonies; still, once having re-established de facto independence 1640–4, the Portuguese were strong enough to take back Brazil, 1645–54. Having granted this much to the Dutch case, which remains far from overwhelming, one must then note what lies in the other pan of the scales.

1   During most of the Thirty Years War (1618–48), far from behaving or being treated as a hegemon intervening to impose their rules throughout the world-system, the United Provinces were glad to hold their own, since they were fighting to preserve their de facto independence from Spain, and to persuade it to recognize them as de jure independent, and therefore to stop trying to reconquer them.
2   In this battle, Spain was quite able to invade the Netherlands (and held Breda 1624–37), while the Netherlands was never able to invade Spain (though others did).
3   The Dutch aspired to liberate the Spanish-occupied southern Netherlands, and did manage to counterinvade them, but failed to liberate them (except Maastricht), so that the 'Spanish Netherlands' they remained. When Spain at long last conceded Dutch independence by the Treaty of Munster (January 1648 – twenty-eight years after the Dutch attained 'hegemony'!), the Dutch had less of the Netherlands than in 1577, never having been able to regain Brussels, Tournai, Bruges, Ghent or Antwerp (lost to Don John of Austria and Alexander Farnese in the late-sixteenth century) nor Ostend (lost to Spinola in the early seventeenth).
4   When Spain made peace with the Dutch, it did so not because it was defeated in the field, but in order to fight on unhindered against what it apparently viewed as a more powerful, more threatening, more dangerous enemy, a state which had invaded metropolitan Spain (aid to Catalan insurgents 1641, occupation of Roussillon 1642) and had annihilated the Spanish field army (at Rocroi, May 1643): France. Apparently Spain was correct in its judgment, since, fighting on without Dutch assistance, France nonetheless proceeded to defeat Spain again (Battle of the Dunes, June 1658) and even forced it to cede much of Flanders (Peace of the Pyrenees, 1659), in the same Spanish Nether-lands which the Dutch had been too weak to pry from the hands of Spain.

Leaving aside the obvious inference that France surely was, and Spain probably was, on balance more powerful than the Dutch, it would be well to remember that during the Thirty Years War, other participants also raised large armies, fought longer, and/or collected more winnings, than the Dutch. It was Sweden, not Holland, which was able to demand and receive concessions in territory, money and intra-German influence to purchase peace. The Austrian Hapsburgs kept larger armies in the field longer and operated at longer distances from home than the Dutch, and when they were defeated, it was the French, Swedes and German states that did the crucial fighting. As for other states, Bavaria, Brandenburg, Denmark, England, Poland, Saxony, Scotland, Switzerland and Transylvania all seem to have fought (or abstained), gained (or lost) with very little reference to or notice taken of their Dutch 'hegemon.' A more traditional reading of history contends that the Thirty Years War marks a shift from the Hapsburgs to France as the first-ranking, but not hegemonic, power in the states system. On the whole the traditional interpretation remains more persuasive than the Wallersteinian. It is hard to maintain the idea that the Dutch were a hegemonic power 1620–50, or at any other time. In that period, there was no hegemon. The Dutch were frontrunners, marvelously competitive and prosperous. Never did they have hegemony, never did they approach hegemony.

The alleged British hegemony   Again the time-boudaries of this 'hegemony' flex more than is desirable. It may run from 1815–50 with a decline 1850–73 (Hopkins, Wallerstein *et al.* 1982a:62, by analogy with Netherlands dates), or 1815–73 maximally (Wallerstein 1984:17,40), or from 1850–73 (Hopkins, Wallerstein *et al.* 1982b:116,118), with 1815–50 then a period in which the new hegemon bypasses an old one in decline and 1873–96 (Wallerstein 1984:58) a period of declining hegemony with acute conflicts with successors. The most frequently cited dates for British hegemony are 1850–73.

In the British case (as in the American) there is no longer a difficulty caused by world-systems' analysts excluding some notable members of the states system of Central Civilization from the hegemonic accounting. Britain, too, was during the period of its putative hegemony accepted by all powers as an independent state, and avoided the indignity of having any part of its metropolitan territory occupied by a foreign power. Thus far the case is easier to make than that for the Dutch.

Choosing 1850–73 as the hegemonic period, and again assuming that Britain was indeed the world-system's frontrunner (and the Crystal Palace exhibition of 1851 surely asserted a flagrant prosperity), the case for Britain's political hegemony can at least be made more credibly than for the Dutch.

Even skeptics must concede that Britain in this period did blockade Greece (1850) to compel interest and compensation payments; did block Siamese attempts (1850–63) to expand southward into Malaya; did (or the East India Company did) end friction with Burmese interests by a war (1851–3) in which south Burma was annexed; did drive Persian occupiers out of Afghanistan (1856–7); did put down the Great Mutiny in the armies of the East India Company, and take the government of India from it (1857–8); did fight the second Maori War in New Zealand (1860–70) to a settlement satisfactory to Britain; did bombard Kagoshima (1863) to punish Japan's Satsuma clan for a murder; did conduct a successful punitive expedition against Bhutan (1865) over frontier disorders, and another, even more successful against Abyssinia (Ethiopia; 1867–8) over the imprisonment and murder of consular officials; did put down Louis Riel's first rebellion in Canada (1869–70). These were indubitably hegemonic acts, even in some cases imperial acts, *with respect to these countries.*

To prove the systemwide hegemony of the hegemon such a listing is of some value, but certainly not sufficient, for those who felt the British yoke were not the crucial actors in the system, the great powers. On the other hand, to deny that Britain had hegemony, it is of some value, but again not sufficient, to point out that most events in the Americas, North and West Africa, Southwest Asia, Indochina, Indonesia, interior China, Japan and Korea went on without reference to the rules, desires or permission of Britain: conceivably the small powers were controlled by the great, and the great by the Greatest.

What is critical to the case for and against British hegemony is to examine the other 'great powers' – in this period, France, Russia, Austria-Hungary, Prussia/ Germany. One might also look closely at the conduct of the United States, given that hegemony theorists have named it as Britain's successor. In this period 1850– 73, it is not easy to make a case that Britain's hegemony was regularly felt by all these powers; nor regularly felt by any; nor, indeed, that it was felt.

Was Britain hegemonic over France? Britain tamely observed the coup of Napoleon III in 1850, and the revolution of 1871, and did nothing to assure that either new regime would subserve its desires. The Franco-British expedition in the Crimean War (1853–6) was largely an egalitarian collaboration, but if either led the way it was France; to balance this (and preserve us from believing in *French* hegemony) the British may then be seen senior partners with the French in the Second Opium War against China (1856–60). When France and Piedmont combined (1859) to despoil Austria of northern Italy (1859–70), Britain's objections to a war were ignored, and ignored with impunity. When the British, French and Spanish jointly occupied Vera Cruz (1861) to compel payment of the Mexican debt, it was France which attempted to create a puppet empire under Maximilian, Britain (and Spain) which responded by withdrawing (1862), the Mexicans who balked France, and ultimately the US which, mobilizing 50,000 men on the Rio Grande and threatening military intervention (1865–6) persuaded France to withdraw its troops. When France was ultimately defeated, and Napoleon III's career ended, it was not accomplished by Britain, but by Germany, 1870–1. Where was British hegemony over France? Invisible, and nonexistent.

Was Britain hegemonic to America? While Britain did intervene, indirectly and delicately, in the American Civil War – by building raiders (*Florida*, *Alabama*, *Shenandoah*) for the Confederacy, the side toward which Britain's economic interests predisposed it – not only was that side not saved by the 'hegemon,' but the British even accepted an arbitration (1871) which awarded the US damages (1872) for the cruisers' depredations. American pressure, not British, opened Japan (1853–4); the US participated (with Britain, France and the Dutch) in bombarding Shimonoseki (1864) to end the anti-foreign activity of the Choshu clan. Where was hegemony over America? Not in evidence.

Was Britain hegemonic over Russia? One might as plausibly ask, was Russia hegemonic over Britain? If Britain behaved hegemonically in its sphere, so did Russia in its. Russia put down the rebellious Poles (1863–4) despite British protests. Russia advanced its frontiers in Central Asia toward India (1860–8), Tashkent, Samarkand and the Oxus, despite Britain's fears and objections. Russia outpaced Britain into China; indeed, it was the Russians who truly won the Second Opium War against China – without even having fought it! – by acquiring (in the 1858 Treaty of Aigun) the left bank of the Amur, and (in the 1860 Treaty of Peking) the Ussuri region. Russia unilaterally abrogated its obligation (Treaty of Paris, 1856) to leave the Black Sea neutral, unfortified, and without a navy – and despite British protests Russia compelled the London conference (1871) to accept the abrogation as a *fait accompli*. Indeed, it would be easier to make the case for Russian than for British hegemony in this period: after all, when Napoleon III prepared to advance against Austria in Italy, it was Russia's acquiescence France sought, not Britain's. And in the Crimean War (1853–6) it took the combined forces of Britain, France, Turkey, and Piedmont, repeated Austrian threats of war, and a defensive alliance of Prussia and Austria, to bring weight enough against Russia to frustrate her attempt to extend her influence in the Balkans, the Black Sea and Turkey: the implication is that Russia would have been more than a match for any one of the allies (say Britain) alone; such strength is a characteristic usually attributed to hegemons, and a combination of great powers to bring low one of their number is frequently treated as implying that the victim is seen as near-hegemonic in attainments and hegemonistic in ambition.

If Britain was the hegemon, and Russia too, surely Austria was also the hegemon. While Britain and France fought the battles and took the casualties, Austria's first Crimean War ultimatum to Russia (June 1854) ended the Russian occupation (from July 1853) of the Danubian Principalities (Wallachia and Moldavia); Austria's second ultimatum (December 1855) ended the war on terms very unfavorable to Russia (Vienna Four Points, rejected by Russia 1854, medicine made even more unpleasant, swallowed at the Congress of Paris, 1856). Surely this is how hegemons behave.

Was Britain at least hegemonic to Prussia? Here at last one sees a single genuine instance of quasi-hegemonic behavior. Swedish troops, backed by British naval threats, caused Prussia to settle its 1848–50 war with Denmark over Schleswig–Holstein on unfavorable terms. Thereafter, however, the story is different. In the better-known Schleswig–Holstein war of 1864, Prussia, carrying Austria in its train, effaced the humiliation and reversed the verdict of the prior war, and despoiled Denmark of these provinces in the teeth of British attempts to bring about peace and save the Danes. In the Austro-Prussian war (1866), Prussia (and Italy) defeated Austria and most German states; France, cowed by Prussia, mediated a settlement on Prussian terms which reduced Austria and aggrandized Prussia; Prussia did not move until its relations with Russia were excellent; Britain's feelings were not consulted. In the Franco-Prussian War (1870–1), Prussia's purpose was to bring the south German states into a Prussian-ruled Germany; France was defeated, Germany united as an empire on Prussian terms; Britain's concern was to preserve Belgian neutrality; that guaranteed, Britain counted for nothing. Was this British hegemony? Surely not.

In 1850–73, Britain was rich, powerful, and controlled a great empire. Nonetheless, it was not hegemonic to the world-system, which had no hegemon.

The alleged American hegemony In the American case, time-boundaries are more consistently asserted: 1945 to 1967 (Wallerstein 1984:17,40; 1979a:95; Hopkins, Wallerstein *et al.*, 1982b:116,118 and 1982a:62). At the end of the World War II, 'the US emerged as the uncontested hegemonic power' (1984:71); 'the United States was unquestionably the strongest power in the world' (1984:69). 'The only significant constraint on US power was the USSR' (1984:135); 'Although the USSR was not as strong, either economically or militarily, as anyone pretended, it was just strong enough to create world-systemic space for various anti-hegemonic and antisystemic forces' (1984:135). 'Until 1967 the United States dominated the world military arena and political economy – including the markets of other industrialized countries – and western Europe and Japan followed US leadership willingly and completely. By 1990 the former allies will have parted company with the United States' (1984:58). 'The heyday of US world hegemony is over. This means that at no level – economic production and productivity, political cohesiveness and influence, cultural self-assurance and productivity, military strength – will the US ever again match its unquestioned primacy of the period 1945–67. However . . . the US is still today the most powerful state in the world and will remain so for some time' (1979:95). 'I expect the emergence of two new *de facto* blocs, that of Washington–Tokyo–Beijing on the one hand . . . and that of Bonn–Paris–Moscow on the other' (1984:141). 'I have argued elsewhere that the *de facto* Washington–Beijing–Tokyo axis which developed in the 1970s will be matched in the 1980s by a *de facto* Paris–Bonn–Moscow axis' (1984:183).

The case for an American hegemony having existed is easier to make than for a British (and far easier than a Dutch): the US was a superpower after World War II, one of only two; unlike the British it sought and got a voice in the resolution of virtually every major world issue in the years in question. Since the US surely did emerge from World War II as the 'frontrunner' of the world-economy, it conceivably represents a (lone) confirming case of the path from frontrunners to hegemon.

Furthermore, there are numerous events of the period 1945–67 which could indeed be interpreted within a framework of global hegemony: the reconstruction of Japan and Western Germany, and the politico-economic structures and world roles of those states; the Marshall Plan economic reconstruction, and NATO politico-military reconstruction, of Western Europe; the maintenance of the status quo in the Greek–Turkish events of 1946–8 and the Berlin blockade of July 1948; the mobilization of a winning military coalition in the early Korean War, June–October 1950; the settlement of the Suez Crisis of 1956 and the Congo Crisis of the 1960s. Let us therefore examine the 1945–67 period, assume 'American hegemony' as of 1945, and look for its termination. The procedure here adopted will be to explore history from 1967 backward to look for events which might be seen as terminators to a hegemony which presumably began in 1945. We are seeking, for instance, a stalemated outcome which might evince global bipolarity or multipolarity; seeking also cases in which the hegemon's 'hegemony' is flouted or ignored, and it responds with passive acceptance or impotent frustration (rather than enforced obedience or condign and deterrent punishment). Hegemony, if real, will be flaunted, not flouted.

Perhaps then the American hegemony ends in October 1964 rather than 1967, when China explodes a nuclear weapon and blasts its way into the nuclear club, and is not expelled. Or in April 1963, when France begins to pull out of the naval side of NATO, and is not prevented. Or in October 1962, when the USSR by making and reversing a nuclear-missile initiative extracts a US promise not to invade Cuba, which is kept. Or in August 1961, when East Germany reinterprets Berlin border-control rights in its own favor by the *fait accompli* of the Berlin Wall, which remains standing. Or in April 1961, when the US-sponsored exile invasion of Cuba gives new meaning to the word 'fiasco,' and defeat is accepted. Or in February 1960, when France explodes a nuclear weapon, while the US stolidly looks on.

Perhaps the first hegemonic failure could be dated in March–April 1959, when China puts down the Tibetans despite US unhappiness. Perhaps the first failure of hegemony comes in October–November 1956, when Russia puts down the Hungarians with similar unconcern. Or does hegemony end in April 1955, when the Bandung Conference launches a 'nonaligned' movement of states at a time when the US is vigorously promoting alignment, and succeeds while American diplomacy fails? Or in 1954–5, when India refuses US military assistance and arranges Soviet economic assistance as a substitute? Or in August 1954, when France rejects the European Defence Community? Or in June 1953, when the USSR puts down the East Berlin rising? Or in 1950–3, when China fights US-led forces to a stalemate in Korea, preventing the annihilation of the North Korean state? Or in February 1952, when Britain explodes a nuclear device? Or in November 1950, when China invades Tibet?

Perhaps the end of American hegemony should be dated to June–December 1950, when India refuses to cooperate with US policy in Korea and goes its own way. Or to February 1950, when China allies with the USSR in open defiance of vigorous US efforts at dissuasion. Or to the undisturbed slicing of the Hungarian salami 1947–50. Or to September 1949, when the USSR explodes a nuclear device. Or to 1947–9, when the Republic of China collapses and a Communist revolution is victorious despite US objections. Or to 1946–8, when the British Labour government embarks on massive socialist experiments at nationalization, not to be reversed until the days of Thatcher, and then not at America's behest. Or to July–August 1948, when the USSR excludes the US, Britain and France from the new Danubian Basin regime. Or to February 1948, the intensely resented but unimpeded Communist coup in Czechoslovakia. Or to July 1947, when the USSR rejects the Marshall Plan. Or to March 1947, when the USSR rejects the US–UN atomic energy control plan. Or to January 1947, when the US charges that the USSR has violated the Yalta Agreement for free elections in Poland.

The hegemon's collapse may be earlier still: December 1945–January 1947, when Marshall's mission to stop the Chinese civil war fails because neither of the Chinese parties will comply with US wishes. Indeed, one could see American hegemony as having vanished as early as April–June 1945, when the US acceded to a United Nations Charter which gave it a Security Council role no greater than that of Russia, Britain, France or China, in no way comparable to that of Athens, Macedon or Prussia in their respective leagues. If so, American hegemony was born dead.

Are these episodes of self-restraint (or perhaps of impotence, or prudence, or unredeemed frustration), proper tests of American hegemony? We can best judge by asking another question: what if each of these events had occurred differently? What if in each case US pretensions, demands and achievements had been greater, and US desires willingly complied with (as in the Western European Marshall Plan), or complied with under fear or threat (as in the Suez Crisis), or recalcitrants occupied militarily and reconstructed (as were the powers just defeated in World War II) or attacked by force and harshly punished (as was North Korea). Suppose the US had demanded, and secured, the permanent presidency and only right of veto on the Security Council, and the perpetual high command of all UN military forces; had imposed a free-market free-election settlement of the Chinese Civil War against the will of both parties; had canceled the tainted elections in Poland, and conducted new ones; had imposed unilateral nuclear (and perhaps conventional) disarmament on the USSR; had demanded and obtained a reversal of Britain's socialist experiment. Would not such impositions be treated by any hegemonist historian as first-class evidence that the US possessed hegemony over the states thereby victimized, and, if these were all the other great powers, over the world-system as well? Surely then the consistent *absence* of such impositions must be consistently treated as evidence that there was no US hegemony over the USSR; nor China; nor India; nor many Third World states; nor, at some time, France nor Britain. These states, however, account for most of the world-system. Only if we define the 'globe' to omit the Soviet Union, Eastern Europe, China, India, the Third World after 1954, Cuba under Castro, and France under Gaullist influence, can the case for American hegemony become more plausible. Unfortunately for the proposition we are examining, it would remain plausible long after 1967.

The conclusion is inescapable. America was remarkably prosperous and a politico-military superpower 1945–67, one of two, in a bipolar system in which it occasionally exercised a regional hegemony, but no more. In the world-system as a whole, there was no hegemon; and there was no American hegemony.

Do frontrunners achieve hegemony?

Apparently they do not. There have been economic frontrunners. The frontrunners have been more inclined than most states to free trade, have been seapowers, have been great powers, have prospered in great wars that have punished their rivals. But they were never hegemons. Hegemonic research ought to be redirected to finding out why not. Did they even *seek* hegemony? Could they have had it if they had sought it? Perhaps the fact that they were not hegemons, probably never sought hegemony, and possibly were never seriously suspected of seeking hegemony, is evidence of common sense, and helps explain why they prospered while others were brought low by the costs and counteralliances that afflict hegemonist imperialism.

In any case, the hypothesis that frontrunners become hegemons is nonviable. The evidence contradicts it, and actually suggests the contrary proposition. The comparative study of civilizations may enlarge the contrary proposition, for there exist world systems that, having become universal empires, almost certainly passed through some prior stage of hegemony. If we can show, as perhaps we probably can show, that genuine hegemons like Ch'in, Assyria, Persia, Rome, were not only geographic fringe states but economically uncompetitive states when their ascent began, and even during much of it, the contrary proposition can become part of the theory of world systems.

Economics of parahegemony

Despite the fact that they did not have hegemony in common, there remains something similar about the economies of those states which have been mislabeled 'hegemons,' something of historic privilege which all sense and some misattribute to mere power. What is it?

'Parahegemony' is a term which I have coined, somewhat in contrast to Frank and Gills' 'superhegemony.' 'Parahegemony' is a position in an oikumene in which the parahegemon derives economic benefits similar to those which a true hegemon is able to extract by the use or threat of force. But the parahegemon does so without the need to spend on force, because it has the economic advantage of being a highly privileged frontrunner (a center of invention and technology, and/or saving and investment, and/or entrepreneurship) and/or rentier (monopolizing geoeconomic control of a scarce resource, a trade-route intersection or choke point, an enormous market, etc.); and because it has the geopolitico-military advantage of being strong enough to defend its centers and monopolies against predatory or hegemonic attack, or of being outside the politico-military striking range of its rivals and/or victims (Wilkinson 1993a:67–70).

The Netherlands (which may barely make this list), Britain and America have indeed shared certain features that make them studiable as a set. They have been frontrunners; they have been 'parahegemons'; they have also been 'antihegemons.' They are 'parahegemonic' in the sense that they were able to find or make and defend a place (geopolitical and geostrategic as well as technical and innovative) which allowed them to extract great benefits from the world economy without paying the very high coercive costs that hegemony entails.

The Netherlands, Britain and America also shared with each other an 'antihegemonic' character: these states seemed to have defined their conscious interest, what others would say was their rational interest, as neither to seek, nor to accept, nor to permit any others to achieve, hegemony.

General queries

World systems and world economy

For me, two types of issues exist here: the relations between world systems and oikumenes; and the relations, within world systems, between economic and other phenomena.

Data on city sizes for the last four millennia are consistent with the proposition that civilizations/world systems show long-term phases of alternating economic growth and stagnation or decline. However such phases come against the background of a strong secular uptrend; their durations are somewhat irregular; inter-civilizational collisional effects interrupt, interact with, and obscure them; some such phenomena appear attributable to intracivilizational regions, or to supracivi-lizational oikumenes (world economies) without world politics, integrated by trade but not by war and diplomacy. Nonetheless, macrosocial decline phases do exist, and their causes are accordingly of theoretical interest (Wilkinson 1995a).

In the Indic world system, there was some sign of a loose coupling between bipolar power structures and A; phases of economic growth, and between uni-polarity (and tripolarity) and B; phases of economic decline. Periods of economic decline also appear to have been associated with stability of system power structure and of major-power elite membership, relative to periods of economic growth (Wilkinson 1993b).

There is a great deal of interesting work in the comparative and evolutionary study of world economies that can be done on many lines: analyses by system, by phase, by commodity, by technology, by factor of production, by mode of production (loosely defined), by statist/marketive structure. The competing approaches are not yet fully enough developed to make interaction more fruitful than independent pursuit of independent paradigms and research programs; but some interfaces exist, that can be worked at with mutual benefit.

World systems theory and political praxis

There may have been some faint penetration of actual policymaking by civilizational/world systems theory, which raises intriguing and disturbing issues. The noted comparative civilizationist Carroll Quigley, whose theorizing rested on the whole span from Mesopotamia to the 1960s, was a teacher well-remembered by his student Bill Clinton. Quigley, by an intensive process of reduction or rather idealization of masses of historical data, derived a procedure for the diagnosis and therapy of ailing civilizations, notably that which he thought he inhabited. Some coherent, recurrent, personal motifs in the policy discourses and peculiar variant initiatives of his student, the President, bear more than a passing resemblance to the hopeful, idealistic, voluntaristic, intellectual, scientistic, economistic, demi-materialistic propensities of the civilizationist-teacher (Wilkinson 1995c). Despite the fact that Quigley sought lucidity, brevity, and political effectiveness, and that Clinton was intelligent, absorbent, and favorably disposed to Quigley and his ideas, the maximum estimate of the actual impact of Quigleyan theory on Clintonic praxis would have to be that it was residual (surfacing when Clinton was not yielding to immediate pressures), small (since Clinton usually was thus yielding), primarily rhetorical (affecting words more than deeds, hopes more than laws or budgets), and simplified (even beyond Quigley's formulas).

Setting aside irrelevant feelings about Clinton per se or Quigley per se, we might instead contemplate the prospect that if world systems theory were ever to seek and achieve practical application, it might do so by inserting and valorizing as little as *one single word* into political discourse and decision. (With Clinton, Quigley perhaps managed two words; but probably this was a tour de force, a tribute to student and teacher alike.) Given that such a *word* would be partly misunderstood, and, to the extent it was not, understood only in its least subtle meaning – what's the good word?

Does systemic logic undergo fundamental transformations, or are all systems basically the same?

I cannot assume a systemic 'logic,' whether Platonic, Hegelian, Marxian, Sorokinian, Spenglerian, Toynbeean or Hordian. I suspect empirical inquiry will locate pluralities of 'logics,' perhaps to be labeled 'dialectics,' but not in the Platonic, Hegelian, or Marxian senses; Heraclitean fluxes of logics that will show Hordian fissions, may show Sorokinian fluctuations, may conceivably show a Toynbeean spiral, seem more likely.

Can different world systems be compared?

They can be compared and contrasted, certainly; equated, certainly not. The comparative study of civilizations/world systems is a necessary part of their study, drawing from and questioning case studies. The number of civilizations in human social history has been small, but there are several, with distinctive histories and contents. They consequently lend themselves more to comparative-historical than to statistical study. The small number of cases means that comparative analysis is likely to remain viable indefinitely, to be duly supplemented but never superseded by quantitative or formal approaches of counting and modeling. Since only one world system currently exists, comparative analysis must be comparative-historical.

The present solitude of the global civilization defines the limits of applicability of comparative-historical study to the present world system: studies of encounters between civilizations, or of geographic expansion into a cityless periphery, are less engineeringly or predictively relevant than studies of endogenous problems, phases and sequences.

Are our concepts adequate?

Barely. We were asked to assess the adequacy of the existing conceptual equipment for dealing with the 5,000 years of world system history: its evolution, its transformations, and the regularities underlying these processes. A brief answer: (1) the concepts 'world,' 'system,' 'civilization,' 'world system,' 'states system,' 'world state,' 'city,' 'oikumene,' 'core,' 'semiperiphery,' 'periphery,' 'hegemony,' 'dominant power,' 'general war,' 'balance of power,' 'decline phase,' 'unipolarity,' 'bipolarity,' 'tripolarity,' 'multipolarity,' 'nonpolarity,' and some others, can be just about adequately specified to permit empirical, comparative-historical research and theorizing; (2) no unambiguous or precise specification is as yet feasible, but nor is such urgently necessary; (3) no consensus specifications are now feasible nor foreseeable, but there could well be consensus on what the competing specifications are, which would allow for substantial translations of findings between researchers.

Is convergence in sight?

Not generally, but in some significant respects. More precisely, we were also asked to clarify the possibilities of convergence among extant approaches on substantive and methodological issues, and as regards data collection. With respect to convergence between the approach I employ and those of others:

(1) There is a very high degree of compatibility between my approach and that of Frank and Gills. We have to clarify between us the status they give to civilizations/world systems other than the one I label Central Civilization. We have also to discuss among ourselves the issue of what I call 'parahegemony.' I see no currently insuperable barriers to substantive concurrence, though our terms may remain somewhat divergent.

For my own purposes, I prefer Quigley's nexus savings-investment-invention to Frank and Gills' focus on capital accumulation. Furthermore, I believe an element of analytical neo-Malthusianism or Ricardianism needs to be juxtaposed to the Frank–Gills emphasis on capital accumulation, which emphasizes material accumulation. At least as fundamental, as a datum, as a strategy for the poor, and as a strategy for statist economics (especially rent-seeking and hegemonistic) has been the multiplication of people. This is not an independent variable; and much depends on it. If elites value a large and increasing flow of rents (rather than an accumulation of capital), and masses value a marginal increase in wages (via child labor), then maps of populations (rather than material accumulations) will best display the growth of wealth. Granted that maps of demographic growth will no doubt largely match those of capital accumulation, still there will be discrepancies, which would be missed by too strong a 'materialistic' focus.

We ought indeed nonetheless to support research into the relations between hegemony and surplus-accumulation. I would hypothesize, however, that the relationship between hegemons, hegemonic candidates, and the hegemonic project, on the one hand, and surplus-accumulation, on the other, is by and large predatory and dissipative: the hegemonic project targets existing surplus-accumulations, but tends to dissipate them in war damage, armaments costs, and grandiose monuments (Wilkinson 1994a:375).

We ought also to research the characteristic economics of hegemonistic states. My counterpoint to Gills' proposal that 'mercantilism' is associated with hegemonistic imperialism, and 'openness' with a hegemon's attempts to maintain the stability of the hegemonic status-quo is: 'mercantilism' or perhaps better 'Colbertism' is indeed the characteristic economics of hegemonistic states; hegemonic states have tributary and imperial-redistributive economies; openness is the characteristic strategy of parahegemonic and antihegemonic states.

The concept of super-accumulation, though it will need considerable dialectical refinement, is likely to provide the impetus for some fruitful empirical research, which will be reflected in century-by-century maps of capital accumulation.

Many of the research proposals of Frank and Gills are important to all approaches to world systems. We must do Central Asia; we must trace spatio-temporal boundaries and route structures; we must chronogram the interregional balance of trade within civilizations, and the intercivilizational balance within oikumenes.

(2) There is also a very high degree of compatibility between my approach and that of Chase-Dunn and Hall. We have a bone or two to pick, those of Plato and Heraclitus among others: where they see logics I see at best dialectics. Rather than single organizing principles, I see coexisting organizational polycultures. Like Frank, I believe that 'tribute' is also understandable as 'taxation,' but with states not individuals as its targets. I also stand with the classical pessimists Ricardo and Malthus, and the classical optimist Henry George, in holding that rent, not profit, was and remains the fundamental form of extraction: the nineteenth century overstated the role of profit, for polemical and utopian reasons.

A point for argument with Chase-Dunn concerns the cause of the failure of the hegemonic projects of Napoleonic France and the Second and Third German Reichs, which I believe he attributes to the 'capitalistic' structure either of the world system or of the hegemonistic states (1994:362), while I attribute it to antihegemonic parahegemons (1994a:375). This probably is researchable.

The most productive interaction I see with Chase-Dunn and Hall lies at the origins of civilizations, the first proto-urban world systems. By our polycultural hypothesis (Iberall and Wilkinson 1993), these should be found to be descendants of polycultural non-urban world systems of the type they particularly study. The most recent such transitions appear to have occurred in Africa (1993/4) there could be some cooperative research planning on African world systems, urban, proto-urban, non-urban.

(3) I observe with great interest Modelski and Thompson's working backward in time in search of earlier long cycles. We are likely to have some discussion of spatio-temporal boundaries of the system they are studying, with whose earlier manifestations I have some problems.

Talcott Parsons' learning process sequence is a powerful analytical construct, and I am glad to see his late work on civilizations being extended and built on by Modelski and Thompson. I remain skeptical that the degree of global process integration that is necessary for the scheme to be successfully applied globally over a multi-thousand year time scale did exist; and I would like to see some physical foundation for the evolution of the teleology implicit in their sequential-functionalist version of evolutionary selectionism. It is clear that there were some very early global or near-global demographic processes, as we have argued elsewhere (Iberall and Wilkinson 1984a), and technology and/or commodities when studied will surely reveal oikumenical processes of some sort. I would be more inclined to see a less purposive, less agent-like global process, with global social pressure and local agent-like exchange processes. The search for process time scales is a strategy that can effectively precede, and permit, a firm definition of the systems and boundaries within which those processes operate, a point already made indirectly by Sorokin (Wilkinson 1995d).

In this connection, some phraseology I would flag for discussion includes, in Modelski (this volume), the concepts of 'search'; 'advancing,' 'advanced'; 'learning sequence,' 'learning program'; 'phases . . . of roughly uniform length,' 'the time-scale of the several evolutionary processes must stand in a determinate relationship to each other'; 'the task of global political construction.'

It is prudent to insist on the use of Darwinist selectionism and Axelrodian evolution-of-cooperation to provide mechanisms for the development of social *telos.* That a retrospectively directional-seeming process (the 'global polity process' should have 'fumbling beginnings' but then become 'more steady' and then 'cumulative' is also reassuring.

Despite the desirability of a fuller examination of the concepts and assumptions of this approach, Thompson (1995) is probably right to give priority to his school's current effort to integrate 'its 'modern' findings with 'premodern' history.'

These competing approaches are all worthwhile undertakings. They are not fully integrable. I see little prospect of a common consensus on terminology, assumptions, hypotheses, or program of data collection. Established researchers in this field seem by and large to possess no resources to deploy but themselves, and they do so in the manner they see as most likely to develop their own work along the lines of most interest to themselves. Younger researchers show the same propensities.

Prospects for research: cooperative

Is it possible to conceive of 'service research,' i.e. data collection priorities designed to serve the entire set of those who research world systems, rather than an individual researcher? We might try. To my mind the most obvious candidate areas for identification of such 'service research' are continuations of (1) the heroic collection of city population data of Tertius Chandler, who would get my Miltiades-vote if we were collectively allocating research-assistant resources somehow miraculously provided; and (2) the cartographic initiatives of Colin McEvedy. I would also support (3) a systematic collection from archaeological field reports of a database of areas of settlements at various moments in time. (4) A qualitative data collection – an HRAF-like file – on premodern trade routes and commodities traded would also be of value. I suspect Chase-Dunn will agree with me about the priority of item (1) at least, and Gills and Frank about item (4). On the other hand, we may inspire some archaeologist to undertake effort (3).

Prospects for research: independent

An element of the comparative study of world systems/civilizations that is still in need of much work is their comparative geopolitics. The geopolitics of Spykman, for instance, with its characteristic anti-exceptionalism, interventionism, globalism, anti-hegemonism, and containment, was clearly a 'modern,' global, central-civilizational, twentieth-century and American conception (Wilkinson 1985). Not only the technology but the geography of non-global world systems was bound to produce different conceptions of actually different 'worlds.' A particularly interesting comparative study would involve the geopolitical constraints and conceptions of two potential globalizers – Mongol/Yuan and Ming dynasties – vis-à-vis two actual globalizers – Portugal and Spain.

Can dissertation topics be descried in our emerging subfield? I have unsubtly hinted to one student who is interested in the Ming dynasty naval expeditions that a comparative study of failed and successful globalizers would include the Mongol/Yuan dynasty and the Iberians; he agrees, in principle. But in practice, most interesting topics look like life-works rather than dissertations, and there is, regrettably, something to be said for entering this effort only after one is well established at some institution known to tolerate what Mattei Dogan and Robert Pahre (1990) have labeled 'Creative Marginality.'

Prospects for research: challenging

The latter reference leads more or less naturally to my next argument: there is a benefit to be gained from studying world systems according to physical principles. The physics of complex systems deals with entities that have boundaries, that transform and dissipate energy, that act and produce in self-serving ways that support their existence, form and function and delay their dissolution into the environment: that expend energy over time to persist. The behavior of all ensembles of interacting atomisms may be described in terms of a very limited number of quantities that are conserved in, during and despite their interactions, varying only over a longer time scale and larger space scale than such local interactions. Complex systems, within the time scales and space scales at which they survive, repetitively and periodically go through certain performance repertoires at measurable energy-time costs in order to maintain themselves, and are to be known by their repertoires.

All complex physical systems display 'long' cycles: action cycles, factory days, lifetimes, population turnover times, species turnover times. Complex systems in general are observed spatially by finding interior–exterior boundaries (hence forms, patterns, morphology) and temporally by tracking their actions, energy budgets, activity spectra – their process spectroscopies. Sorokinian two-phase fluctuations; three-phase dialectics; Toynbee's three-dimensional spiral process, with oscillatory motion in each of two dimensions (or revolutionary motion in both together) and unilinear progress in the third; Parsonian four-phase social system maintenance; Kaplan's six-plus phase system structure: all represent empirically-based, partly competing hypotheses for complex human social system spectroscopies (Wilkinson and Iberall 1986).

One entree for systems physics into the study of world historical systems would be via Gibbsian phase space mappings. A Gibbsian phase space plots a variable against its rate of change. Thus one axis of such a space represents high vs. low value for the chosen variable, the other axis represents increasing vs. decreasing variable values. For instance, one might plot, for uniform intervals of time, system population vs. the rate of system population growth; or system surplus accumulated value-in-exchange vs. its rate of accumulation; or system energy throughput vs. its rate of growth. Watching a temporal sequence of such plottings would provide a picture of a system dynamically unfolding through time. Observing the density of occupation per region of phase space would provide some sense of the probability that a system would on the average be expected to be found in each such region during a particular portion of its career. Engineeringly, it would provide some sense of the accessibility ease of certain phase-space regions for the contemporary world system (Iberall and Wilkinson 1986).

Civilizations are not geographically or demographically either fundamentally stable or (except perhaps at very small scales) cyclic. They have shown strong propensities to expand, which underlie their cyclic fluctuations. By a general application of Zipf's Law, it would seem that there ought to have been many more small civilizations than are now recorded. We have accordingly collected data on city sizes and graphed them to sharpen up a story told by many others who have found evidence of small, brief, failed civilizations. The story suggests that there remain to be found a considerable number of civilizations; that these will tend to be small (e.g. one small city) and early or distant from the cores and even the semiperipheries of the better known, longer lived civilizations; and that they will be found to have terminated less often through engulfment by Central civilization, and more often through destruction (war, famine, pestilence), than has been typical for the larger, later and better known civilizations that figure on most extant rosters (Wilkinson and Iberall 1994).

Conclusion

Recognizing civilizations as world systems, and (most) world systems as civilizations, permits some fruitful interplay between the cultural focus of many civilizationists and the economic focus of many world-systems analysts, at some cost. Plurality of past world systems/civilizations, long term global evolutionary change, the singularity of the present soliton world system/civilization, ubiquitous polyculturality in world systems/civilizations, inequality of momentum as between world systems/civilizations, are the chief fruitful, and costly, theoretical propositions involved. The differences among the four approaches to world systems (Modelski and Thompson; Chase-Dunn and Hall; Frank and Gills;

Wilkinson) herein noted often seem to involve fundamental definitions and assumptions, and are probably irresolvable either through dialogue or through empirical work, so that research must proceed on separate tracks; though the results of such research can be rendered mutually comprehensible, translation will be required. There are however some resolvable issues, and some research projects likely to be of equal value to several or all approaches. And there is infinite scope for the satisfaction of curiosity.

4 Comparing world-systems to explain social evolution

Christopher Chase-Dunn and Thomas D. Hall

In this chapter we do several things. We begin by summarizing the conceptual apparatus we have developed for a theoretical research program that compares world-systems. A more extended treatment may be found in our *Rise and Demise: Comparing World-Systems* (1997). We describe our approach to the problem of spatially bounding world-systems, summarizing what we think is one of our more important contributions: conceiving of world-systems as having four, typically nested, networks of interaction. We also outline our approach to core/periphery relations. Then we discuss three recurrent processes: incorporation of new areas or peoples; merging of formerly autonomous world-systems; and the phenomenon of the upward mobility and transformational innovations by semiperipheral actors. Then we briefly sketch our explanation for the evolution of small-scale egalitarian world-systems into the single hierarchical global system of today.

The remainder of the chapter is largely devoted to analyzing the cyclical processes of world-systems: the pulsation of interaction networks, and the rise and fall of central polities. We report on a puzzling empirical finding: the synchronicity of urban and empire growth and decline phases at the two ends of the Eurasian landmass over the last two millennia. We conclude with a reprise on the issue of transformation of world-systems, a summary of the findings in *Rise and Demise*, raise more unanswered questions, and speculate about the future of the world-system.

Our main conclusion is that world-systems, properly conceptualized and bounded, are the fundamental unit of analysis of social change. Put simply, it is not possible to understand how humans got, in a mere 12,000 years, from living in small groups of 50 to 100 individuals to today's global system composed of states of up to a billion (1,000,000,000) individuals without attending closely to *inter-societal* interactions. Studies that look only at single groups, societies, or states are doomed to misunderstand social change, because much of it originates in the interactive and structured relations among these units.

Such structural arguments often raise questions about where are the actors? What about agency in this structure? To paraphrase Marx's old chestnut, humans make their own history, but not any way they please. In short, they are constrained by existing structures. We also note that macro structures and processes have emergent relations to more localized processes and structures. We argue that it is only by understanding how and why structures change, that we can determine where human action can have the greatest effect in transforming those structures. Bluntly, structural analysis does not obviate human action. Rather, it makes it possible. We return to this issue in our concluding speculations about the future of the world-system. Thus, our analysis does not ignore human action. Rather, we seek to understand structural processes in order to know better precisely where, when and how human action can most fruitfully be employed to build a more humane world (see Boswell and Chase-Dunn 2000; Chase-Dunn 1996).

We have described elsewhere (Chase-Dunn 1992; Hall and Chase-Dunn 1993, 1994) how those who study precapitalist world-systems fall along two continua. First is the *transformationist–continuationist* continuum. At one pole are those who see essentially the same processes repeating through time with no major qualitative breaks. At the other pole, where we place ourselves, are those who see major transformations in the way world-systems function. Many scholars have argued that the world is currently experiencing another major transformation. To save the suspense, we do not think so, although we do see the possibility of a major transformation in the next century or two.

The second continuum is one we inelegantly call *lumpers vs. splitters* – those who see large systems with similar features versus those who see small systems that are qualitatively different. Lumpers are often also continuationists, while splitters are more likely to be transformationists, but these categories are by no means totally overlapping. We are, not surprisingly, closer to the splitter pole than the lumper pole.

Our concepts

Because we wish to study transformations, we maximize the range of possible cases by including all sedentary human groups that have existed on Earth over the last twelve thousand years.[1] To facilitate broad comparisons we define *world-systems* as intersocietal networks in which the interactions (e.g. trade, warfare, intermarriage, information) are important for the reproduction of the internal structures of the composite units and importantly affect changes that occur in these local structures. Because the boundaries of non-state social groups (e.g. 'bands' or 'tribes') are often empirically fuzzy, and because the term 'society' can too easily imply a clearly bounded social group, we use the term 'composite units' in our definition.

Because the ability to produce more than is needed for immediate consumption plays important roles in *social* reproduction and *social* change[2] in all human groups, we take the 'mode of accumulation' as a fundamental characteristic of any world-system. Even so-called egalitarian (classless) groups organized accumulation by storing foodstuffs and socially regulating the use of resources. We define *mode of accumulation* as the deep structural logic of production, distribution, exchange, and accumulation. That is, the reproduction of social structures and cyclical processes occurs by means of certain typical forms of integration and control for any specific mode of accumulation. These constitute a *logic of development*. While our position is avowedly materialist, we do leave open the possibility that non-material factors may sometimes initiate social change. We prefer 'mode of accumulation' to 'mode of production' because we do not want to restrict our focus solely to the analysis of production. Instead, we want to focus on the institutional mechanisms by which labor is mobilized and social reproduction is accomplished.

We begin with a heuristic typology drawn from the works of Amin (1980, 1991) and Wolf (1982), supplemented by Polanyi (1944, 1977).[3] We distinguish among four classes of systemic logics:

1   *Kin-based modes of accumulation*, in which social labor, distribution, and collective accumulation is mobilized by means of normative integration based on consensual definitions of value, obligations, affective ties, kinship networks, and rules of conduct – a moral order.
2   *Tributary modes*, in which accumulation of surplus product is mobilized by means of politically institutionalized coercion based on formally organized military power and codified law.
3   *Capitalist modes*, in which land, labor, wealth, and goods are commodified and strongly exposed to the forces of price-setting markets and accumulation occurs primarily through the production of commodities using commodified labor.
4   *Socialist modes*, an hypothetical class of logics in which major policy, investment and allocation decisions are controlled democratically by the people they affect according to a logic of collective rationality.

The main features of modes of accumulation that can be used as empirical indicators are forms of exchange (gift-giving, state-administered exchange, market trade) and forms of control that are employed to mobilize social labor and/or to extract surplus product (normative regulation, serfdom, slavery, taxation, tribute, wage-labor). Different modes of accumulation are often present within the same system. Furthermore, some forms of exchange and control have elements of more than one mode.

We do not claim that modes of accumulation are features that permeate entire world-systems. Rather, they may exist at any level of a system (see Chase-Dunn 1998:335–7). For instance, the broad category of tributary mode includes both centralized and decentralized political forms that rely on coercion to mobilize labor and extract taxation, tribute, or rent. Thus, feudalism is a sub-type of the tributary mode, one of its most decentralized forms. Similarly, the so-called 'Asiatic' form, in which the state owns the land, is one of the most centralized forms of the tributary mode.

Different modes may coexist within the same system. Some forms of organization are best understood as transitional or mixed. For example, class-stratified but stateless systems in which kinship metaphors are used to legitimate the exploitation of commoners by a noble class (e.g. precontact complex chiefdoms in Hawaii or early Thai 'chiefdoms' in Southeast Asia) constitute a mix of kin-based and state-based (coercive) systems. The 'Germanic mode of production' or

88   *Christopher Chase-Dunn and Thomas D. Hall*

'decentralized stratified society' (Kristiansen 1991:19), various forms of slavery, and 'market socialism,' are other mixed modes.

While transitional and mixed forms complicate the analysis of transformations, we contend that there have been qualitatively distinct logics of accumulation. We do *not* assume a theory of unilinear evolution, but seek to discover empirically the patterns, possibilities, probabilities of past and future transformations. We further argue that it is possible, if difficult, to use knowledge of past transitions to help humans choose among more desirable future alternatives. We emphasize trans-formations of modes of accumulation more strongly than most of the other scholars who study precapitalist world-systems.

Spatial boundaries: a multicriteria approach

Since we are interested in connections, we propose to study interaction networks rather than various types of trait distributions. The types of interactions that are important should be studied empirically, rather than assumed. This allows us to investigate any variations in the relative importance of different types of interaction.

We note that different kinds of interaction often have distinct spatial character-istics and degrees of importance in different sorts of systems. We hold that the question of the nature and degree of systemic interaction between two locales is prior to the question of core/periphery relations. Indeed we make the existence of core/periphery relations an empirical question rather than an assumed characteristic of all world-systems.

Spatially bounding world-systems necessarily must proceed from a locale-centric beginning rather than from a whole-system focus. This is because all human societies, even nomadic hunter-gatherers, interact importantly with neighboring societies. Thus if we consider *all* indirect interactions to be of sys-temic importance (even very indirect ones) then there has been a single global world-system since humankind spread to all the continents. But we note that interaction networks, while they were always intersocietal, have not always been global in the sense that actions in one region had major and relatively quick effects on distant regions. When transportation and communications were over short distances the world-systems that affected people were small. Obviously, the spatial range of consequences of all kinds of action increases as transport and communications costs decrease.

We use the notion of 'fall-off' of effects over space to bound the networks of interaction that importantly impinge upon any focal locale. The world-system of which any locality is a part includes those peoples whose actions in production, communication, warfare, alliance and trade have a large and interactive impact on that locality. It is also important to distinguish between endogenous systemic interaction processes and exogenous impacts that may importantly change a sys-tem but are not part of that system. Maize diffused from Mesoamerica to eastern North America, but that need not mean the two areas were part of the same world-system. A virulent microparasite might contact a population with no developed immunity and ravage it. Such an event does not necessarily mean that the region from which the microparasite came and the region it penetrated are parts of a single interactive system. Interactions must be *two-way and regularized* to be systemic. One shot deals do not a system make.

Clearly, economic forms of interaction are important in all world-systems. Of these, bulk-goods exchanges are constitutive forms of interconnection (Wallerstein 1974a, 1974b, 1979a). However, we also agree with Jane Schneider (1977) that luxury goods, especially when they are used in a prestige-goods economy (Friedman and Rowlands 1977; Peregrine 1996), are very important for the reproduction of power structures. Since there is considerable ethnographic and archaeological evidence that even nomadic foragers can pass goods over great distances, we expect that the prestige goods net may be several orders of magnitude larger than the other nets.

Intermarriage networks are also central institutions of interconnectedness in many systems, but especially in kin-based systems where they are a fundamental basis of geopolitics and geoeconomics (Collins 1992). Furthermore, marriage exchanges in kin-based systems are almost always associated with exchanges of bulk and prestige goods.

For political interconnections we use regularized political/military conflict interaction (Wilkinson 1987a, 1987b; Tilly 1984:62). Typically, this network will differ from the bulk or prestige goods networks. Finally, we note that networks of information including, but not limited to, ideology, religion, technical information, and culture must also be included as a bounding mechanism. We do not expect the information network to spatially coincide with any of the other networks.[4]

Thus, we propose four sets of bounding criteria:

- bulk-goods exchange network (BGN)
- prestige-goods exchange network (PGN)
- political/military exchange network (PMN)
- information exchange network (IN).

All regularized material and social exchanges should be included as criteria for bounding systems. Often these networks will define a set of nested boundaries. Generally, bulk goods will compose the smallest regional interaction net. Political/military interaction will compose a larger net which may include more than one bulk-goods net, and prestige-goods exchanges will link even larger regions which may contain one or more political/military nets. We expect the information net to be larger than the prestige goods net, sometimes far larger. Nonetheless it may also be smaller (see Figure 4.1).

At first it may seem counterintuitive to have the information boundary inside the prestige goods exchange, since exchange of goods typically implies some exchange of information. There are, however, well known mechanisms by which goods can be exchanged beyond the range of information. When trade goes from partner to partner the physical objects may travel much further than information.

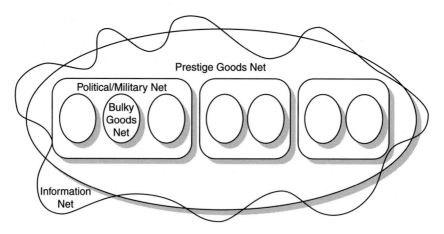

Figure 4.1 Boundaries of the four world system networks.

When warfare is severe the political/military boundary may cut the flow of information even while prestige goods cross the boundary via circuitous down-the-line exchanges.

A few other comments on Figure 4.1 are in order. First, other nets are shown as regular geometric shapes for clarity of presentation. Second, the numbers of nested nets are illustrative only. Any actual world-system could be either simpler, or more complex than Figure 4.1 suggests. Third, we do not expect each net to be of the same scale. Rather, we seek only to convey *relative sizes*. Rather than *a priori* privileging one of these networks, we propose that world-systems may be constituted by any or all these linkages.

We do not claim that the networks will always be nested in the fashion described. Occasionally, as in both the modern global world-system and some earlier geographically isolated systems (e.g. the Hawaiian Islands), these four networks converge. Such convergence may be an important characteristic which differentiates some world-systems from others.

We do, however, expect that the relative sizes of the nested networks may change through time. Figure 4.2 shows one possible sequence. Reading Figure 4.2 from left to right as an historical sequence, we note that the bulk goods and political/military nets increase in size relative to the prestige goods and information nets. Second, the information net shifts through time. These shifts suggest significant changes in intersocietal relations and in the conditions and costs of travel and transportation. Again, the figure is suggestive of the types of changes we might find. Once we have bounded a system we can discuss how it might change.

The first question for any focal locale is about the nature and spatial characteristics of its links with the above four interaction nets. This is prior to any consideration of core/periphery position because one region must be linked to another by systemic interaction in order for consideration of core/periphery relations to be

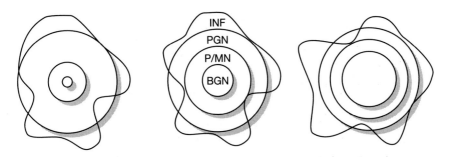

Figure 4.2 Hypothetical evolutionary sequence of world system boundaries.
Key: BGN: Bulk Goods Net.   P/MN: Political/Military Net.   PGN: Prestige Goods Net.
INF: Information Net.

relevant. We divide the conceptualization of core/periphery relations into two analytically separate aspects: core/periphery *differentiation*, and core/periphery *hierarchy*.

Core/periphery differentiation exists when two societies systemically interact and one has higher population density and/or greater complexity than the other. The second aspect, *core/periphery hierarchy*, exists when one society dominates or exploits another. These two aspects often go together because a society with greater population density/complexity usually has more power, and so can effectively dominate/exploit the less powerful neighbor. But there are important instances of reversal (e.g. the less dense, less complex Central Asian steppe nomads exploited agrarian China) and so we want to make this analytical separation so that the actual relations can be determined in each case. We also note that the question of core/periphery relations *needs to be asked at each level of interaction* designated above. It is more difficult to project power over long distances and so we should not expect to find strong core/periphery hierarchies at the level of Information or Prestige Goods Networks.

To test hypotheses about how core/periphery relations shape intersocietal relations and processes of social change we distinguish between two types of interaction (following Myrdal 1971). First are *spread effects*, akin to diffusion, in which core/periphery interactions cause peripheral areas to become more core-like. Second are *backwash effects* in which core–periphery interactions cause peripheral areas to become less core-like. This is familiarly called the 'development of underdevelopment.'[5] The circumstances that promote one over the other, their relative frequencies and, most importantly, their roles in the degree of intersocietal inequality and the stability of core/periphery relations are fundamental issues for empirical investigation.

We intentionally omit consideration of the nature of what is produced and traded between cores and peripheries in our definition of these concepts. The idea that core areas specialize in manufacturing and peripheral areas in raw materials remains controversial even for the modern world-system (Chase-Dunn 1998:ch. 10; Martin 1994a). Phil Kohl (1987a, 1987b) argues that in the ancient Mesopotamian world-system steatite (soapstone) bowls were manufactured on the peripheral Iranian plateau and traded to the core cities of the Mesopotamian lowland in exchange for food, reversing the division of labor typical of the modern world-system. This reversal is readily explained: in the absence of cheap bulk transportation it is easier to move already manufactured goods to the core than to move the raw materials there.

Core/periphery relations can be even more complex. Mitchell Allen (1997:ch. 1) has developed the concept of a 'contested periphery,' for which one or more core regions compete. Based on a study of Philistia and its relations to the Neo-Assyrian and Egyptian world-systems, he finds that once an area has been incorporated into one world-system it can more easily be moved into another world-system than if it were being incorporated for the first time. Not surprisingly, contested peripheries have more leverage in responding to core demands. Furthermore, what is a periphery in one world-system can become a semiperiphery in another. If such a region provides access to valuable resources or other core regions, it can often leverage this control into semiperipheral relationships.

Allen's analysis is one impetus to rethinking our conceptualization of the semiperiphery. We argue that semiperipheral regions:

1   may mix both core and peripheral forms of organization;
2   may be spatially located between core and peripheral regions;
3   may be spatially located between two or more competing core regions;[6]
4   may be the locus of activities between core and peripheral areas; and
5   may be one in which institutional features are in some ways intermediate between those forms found in core and periphery.

Without more detailed empirical studies, it is premature to define the semiperiphery more narrowly. Indeed, we should not assume *a priori* that all world-systems have semiperipheries.[7]

Finally, we see historical social change as open-ended and path dependent. That is, it occurs in any existing social structure within the context of a specific historical legacy and specific current conditions. Important bifurcations and discontinuities of development, rapid transformations, and instances of devolution are normal characteristics of social change (see Sanderson 1990, 1999).

Our argument that world-systems are the primary unit of analysis for understanding these processes does not vitiate the importance of processes that operate within societies or other social groups. A world-system is composed, not only of intersocietal interactions, but of the *totality* of interactions that constitute the whole social, economic, and political system. Good world-systems analysis in modern or precapitalist settings always attends to the complex dialectic between social change within any of its composite units and the entire system.

Toward a theory of transformations

If our hypothesized typology of modes of accumulation is correct, we have only two transformations to study: the transition from kin-based to state-based or tributary logics and the transition from tributary to capitalist logic. A transition to whatever follows capitalism would constitute a third transformation.

We propose the following four research strategies:

1   Hierarchy should be approached as an empirical issue, not as a theoretical assumption. Degrees of hierarchy, the units which are hierarchically related, the forms of exploitation and domination, rates of mobility, rates of expansion, peripheralization vs. more egalitarian interaction, the development of underdevelopment vs. coevolution, are matters to be investigated in each case.
2   Commodification should be conceptualized as a variable process. It should be broken down into the sub-components of land, labor, wealth, and goods. Forms of commodification should be analyzed. The extent and importance of commodification should be determined in comparative perspective. Types of goods, forms of production, nature of payment, importance of price-setting, competitive market forces, and the timing of spread of these should be determined by careful studies.
3   World-system interaction networks should be studied empirically in terms of densities, types of contact, and relationships between the four interaction nets. Future studies may require the refinement of these categories or the development of new ones.
4   The concrete study of transformation should attend to the historical particularities of the systems being studied. While patterns and general principles may emerge from comparative analysis, they must be grounded in historical details.

We also suggest inventorying of large numbers of world-systems to facilitate formal comparative studies that can address issues regarding what is typical and what is exceptional. The assembly of a data set containing large numbers of world-systems will enable us to separate some of the more conjunctural aspects of the transformation problem from its more systemic aspects.

Incorporation, merger, and semiperipheral development

World-systems tend to grow. Societies have gotten larger, in terms of population size, population density, territorial extent, absolute and relative productivity. Growth entails absorption of formerly external areas, the incorporation of new peoples and territories and/or the merger of formerly autonomous world-systems. Throughout these processes no core area remains a core area indefinitely. Development is uneven. Old cores are replaced, often by formerly semiperipheral societies.

Incorporation

Incorporation involves the absorption of territory and population into a larger world-system. While mergers occur when systems with comparable levels of complexity unite, we use the term incorporation to refer to cases in which a large world-system engulfs a small one.

We argue that incorporations or mergers can occur at each network level. Two separate systems are first likely to interact through the information network. If one or both are expanding they will later become part of a single prestige goods network, and still later they will join into a single political/military network, and then a single bulk goods network. This sequence is likely to be the same regardless of the relative levels of complexity of the two systems. But their relative levels of complexity will often be an important element in the nature of the interactions that occur.

We conceptualize incorporation as a continuum that ranges from weak to strong. We argue that to label the entire continuum of incorporated areas 'peripheral' masks important variations and makes it difficult to understand the boundary processes of world-systems (see Figure 4.3 and Hall 1986, 1989, 1999; Chase-Dunn and Hall 1997:ch. 4).

At the weak pole are areas external to a world-system; next are areas where contact has been slight. We call these *external arenas* and *contact peripheries* respectively. In the middle range are *'marginal peripheries,'* or *'regions of refuge.'*[8] At the strong pole are 'full-blown,' or *dependent peripheries*.

Key points of Hall's critiques (1986, 1989) of conventional world-system analyses of incorporation are: (1) that even at very weak levels, incorporation can

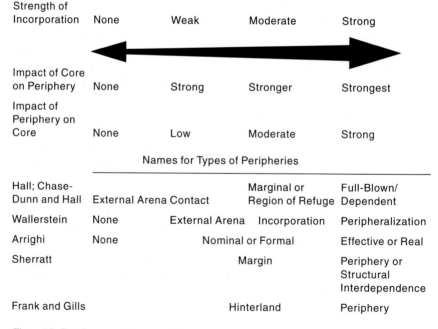

Strength of Incorporation	None	Weak	Moderate	Strong
Impact of Core on Periphery	None	Strong	Stronger	Strongest
Impact of Periphery on Core	None	Low	Moderate	Strong

Names for Types of Peripheries

Hall; Chase-Dunn and Hall	External Arena	Contact	Marginal or Region of Refuge	Full-Blown/ Dependent
Wallerstein	None	External Arena	Incorporation	Peripheralization
Arrighi	None	Nominal or Formal		Effective or Real
Sherratt			Margin	Periphery or Structural Interdependence
Frank and Gills			Hinterland	Periphery

Figure 4.3 Continuum of incorporation.

Source: From Chase-Dunn and Hall 1997.

have dramatic effects; (2) that while somewhat reversible, incorporation is 'sticky' or 'grainy,' tending in general toward stronger levels and very seldom returns to the *status quo ante* (contra Arrighi 1979); (3) that even at very weak levels of incorporation, peoples in newly peripheralized areas attempt to control and shape the process, often with a modicum of success; and (4) that conventional world-systems analysis has examined only strong levels of incorporation where backwash effects have been very strong, and as a result they misunderstand the overall process.

For instance, North American furs were not vital to European economies, yet the fur trade produced major social and economic changes in indigenous world-systems (Wolf 1982:ch. 6; Kardulias 1990; Abler 1992; Dunaway 1994, 1996a, 1996b).

Similarly, plunder is a form of incorporation within the PMN. Thus, West Africa was incorporated into the PMN of the Central system when slave raiding became regularized, rather than, as Wallerstein (1989:ch. 3) would have it, after the development of colonial agriculture.

Even weak incorporation can lead to major transformations of incorporated groups. When Cherokees became extensively involved in 'a putting-out system financed by foreign merchant-entrepreneurs' (Dunaway 1994:237), not only was their culture transformed, but techniques of production changed. The spread of horses from New Mexico to foraging groups living on the fringes of the Great Plains transformed erstwhile sedentary (or sometimes semisedentary) horti-culturalists into full-time nomadic hunters (Secoy 1953; Mishkin 1940).

Wolf (1982) and Ferguson and Whitehead (1992) present other examples, all of which point to the dramatic consequences and limited reversibility of the effects of incorporation of nonstate peoples into state systems: precapitalist, mercantile, or capitalist. Because the effects often spread far beyond the zone of contact, many so-called 'pristine' ethnographic examples are actually the products of dramatic transformations.

Sherratt described quite similar effects in Bronze Age Europe (1993a, b, c; Sherratt and Sherratt 1993): 'The characteristic of the margin is that it is domin-ated by time-lag phenomena – 'escapes' – rather than structural interdependence with the core' (Sherratt 1993a:43). His 'margin' corresponds approximately to our contact or marginal peripheries.[9]

Thus, incorporation creates frontier zones where 'mixed' and hybrid social forms are found. Our main point is that 'frontiers' are formed and transformed by world-systemic processes, and cannot be fully understood by examining only the frontier itself (see Hall 2000 for more details).

The process of incorporation also varies with differences *both* in the type of world-system doing the incorporating *and* the type of group being incorporated. Our heuristic typology suggests that there are many possible combinations. As we have noted, large differences are likely to lead to incorporation, whereas smaller differences led to merger.

One very important difference is between state and nonstate societies. While all stateless societies are kin-ordered, tributary and capitalist systems are state-based.

Their organizing principles are fundamentally different. State-based world-systems typically try to impose some degree of political centralization on nonstate peoples.

Sometimes the strategy can backfire, and a powerful enemy can be created. This almost happened with Comanches in eighteenth century New Mexico (Hall 1989). It definitely happened with the Mongols (Barfield 1989).

Analogously, severance of core domination, typically due to collapse of a core state, can produce opposite effects on weak versus moderately incorporated peripheries. If the core is extracting some local resource, such as human captives, the loosening or severing of that connection would typically allow a return of local prosperity. If, however, the core supplied some resource for which there was no local substitute, such as guns, any consequential prosperity would typically collapse with its loss.

Mergers

Mergers are somewhat different. First, the incorporation or merger of states is a costly process because states are capable of powerful resistance. Second, following the 'no intervening heartland' rule (Collins 1978, 1981, 1986), expansion that entails passing through the heartland of another state is likely to fail. This is why most successful expansion is typically into contiguous territories. Third, tributary empires more often engage in pure plunder, whereas capitalist states are more likely to follow initial plunder with an effort to set up commodity production based on coerced labor.

Mergers of world-systems are sufficiently different that they should not be subsumed under the topic of 'incorporation.' A merger of world-systems seldom results in the peripheralization of one by the other, whereas incorporation most often does. Rather, it constitutes a new, larger world-system in which the two formerly separate systems play more or less equal parts. The two most well-known instances are the merger of the Mesopotamian and Egyptian systems and the merger of Afro-Eurasia.[10] Obviously, throughout human history many small systems must have merged to make larger ones. These processes need to be studied comparatively in order to discover: (1) whether world-system mergers differ across types of world-systems; and (2) the differences in merger or incorporation at the information, prestige goods, political/military, and bulk goods nets levels.

Semiperipheral development

We argue (1997:ch. 5) that the semiperiphery is fertile ground for social, organizational, and technical innovation and is an advantageous location for the establishment of new centers of power. In particular, secondary state-formation on the marches of empires has frequently been recognized as a semiperipheral phenomenon that is related to the rise and fall of empires and the shift of hegemony within interstate systems (e.g. Mann 1986). A broadly similar phenomenon occurs among chiefdoms (e.g. Kirch 1984:204). Semiperipheral capitalist city states in the tributary world-systems and some semiperipheral national states in the modern world-system have been upwardly mobile and played transformative roles.

Sargon at Akkad, the first unifier of the Mesopotamian city states, combined elements of a peripheral kin-based mode with those of the core tributary mode to conquer the Sumerian core and establish a more centralized, more exploitative, purer form of the tributary mode of production than had ever existed before.[11]

The ability to generate new and effective institutional forms also occurred very often in capitalist city-states, which typically existed in the semiperipheral interstices of empires dominated by the tributary mode of accumulation. The city-states of antiquity were semiperipheral because they were on the edges of, or the boundaries between, large territorial empires. They were often located such that they could easily mediate trade between the core empires and peripheral regions. They could sometimes manipulate this position to maintain considerable political and economic autonomy, although they were not infrequently swallowed up by imperial expansion (Frankenstein 1979). The important cases were formally sovereign: e.g. Dilmun, Byblos, Tyre, Sidon, Carthage, Malacca, Venice, Florence, Genoa, Antwerp, and the cities of the Hanseatic League.

Most of these cities specialized in maritime trade. Coastal or island locations made them defensible with naval forces from would-be conquerors. Easy access to water lowers transport costs. These cities often engaged in manufacturing goods that facilitated their trade-based strategy of accumulation. They were powerful agents of commodification and commercialization in the still predominantly tributary world-systems. We argue that the 'rise of the West' is best understood as another instance of semiperipheral development, an upwardly mobile semiperipheral region within the larger Afro-Eurasian system that eventually succeeded in dominating the entire globe.

World-systems evolution

Our explanation of world-systems evolution is composed of three elements:

1   semiperipheral development;
2   an 'iteration' model that involves demographic and ecological variables as causes of hierarchy formation and economic intensification; and
3   transformations of modes of accumulation.

We have already outlined the phenomenon of semiperipheral development above. The iteration model (Figure 4.4), a synthesis of the approaches developed by anthropologists Harris (1977, 1979), Cohen (1977) and Carneiro (1970), shows what we think are the main sources of causation in the development of more hierarchical and complex social structures. It is an 'iteration model' because the variables both cause and are caused by the main processes.[12] This is a positive

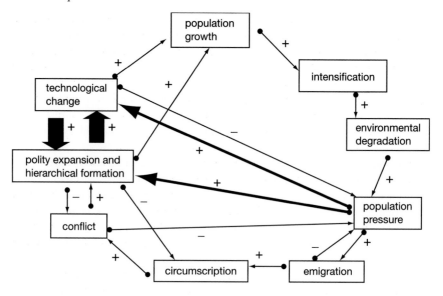

Figure 4.4 The iteration model with temporary direct effects.

feedback model in which systemic expansion, hierarchy formation, and technological development are explained as consequences of population pressure. In
turn these changes intensify population growth. The process repeats cyclically.
With each 'iteration' the process repeats on an expanding scale. This is a world-
systems model because it necessarily involves processes that occur among societies
as well as within them. The main forces are population growth, ecological degradation and population pressure. Population pressure results when scarcities
cause people to increase the effort necessary to meet their needs. This often results
in emigration, if new regions are available. Circumscription occurs when new
locations do not geographically exist or are already filled with other populations
who resist. Thus population pressure causes competition among societies for
land and other resources and this is necessarily an intersocietal phenomenon.
One possible outcome is increased conflict, especially warfare, as groups contend for scarce resources. In some systems, endemic warfare functions as a
demographic regulator by reducing the population density and alleviating
(temporarily) population pressure. But in other cases new hierarchies or larger
polities emerge to regulate the use of resources, and/or new technologies of
production develop that allow larger numbers of people to live within a given
area. The world-system insight here is that the newly emergent elites often come
from regions that have been semiperipheral. This is because semiperipheral
actors are usually able to assemble effective campaigns for erecting new levels
of hierarchy.

The institutional inventions made and spread by semiperipheral actors often
led to qualitative transformations in the logic of accumulation, and thus significant alterations in the operation of variables in the iteration model. Still, these

qualitative changes are themselves the consequences of people trying to solve the basic problems produced by those forces and constraints depicted in the model. Figure 4.5 illustrates in a general way what happens with the emergence of new modes of accumulation, especially states and capitalism. The new modes allow some of the effects of population pressure to have more direct effects on changes in hierarchies and technologies of production. This short-cuts the path that leads through migration, circumscription, and conflict. How can the emergence of states allow population pressure to have a more direct effect on hierarchy formation and technological change? Population pressure in outlying semiperipheral areas combines with the threats and opportunities presented by interaction with the existing states to promote the formation of new states. Thus, secondary state formation becomes common. This is the main way state formation short-cuts the processes. This does not mean that conflict disappears. Rather that it does not need to reach the same levels of intensity in order to provoke the formation of new states once states are already present in a region.

State formation also articulates the rising costs of intensification with changes in technology. The specialized organizations that states create (bureaucracies and armies) sometimes use their powers and organizational capabilities to invent new kinds of productive efficiency and to implement new kinds of production. Governing elites sometimes mobilize resources and labor for irrigation projects, clearing new land for agriculture, developing transportation facilities, and so forth (e.g. the oft noted superiority of Roman roads). In this scheme semiperipheral marcher states and semiperipheral capitalist city states were the most important transformational actors in the rise of larger and larger empires, the

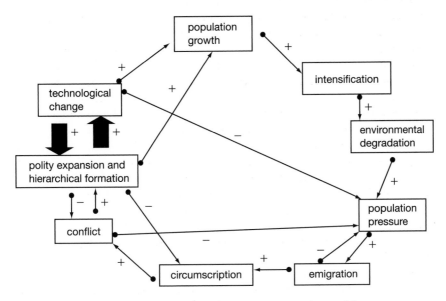

Figure 4.5 Population pressure/intensification hierarchy formation model.

increasing scale of markets and the eventual emergence of predominant capitalism.

World-system dynamics: pulsations and rise and fall

Here we construct a spatio-temporal chronograph based on our approach to spatially bounding world-systems. The sequence runs from small networks of nomadic foraging bands, to larger systems of mesolithic sedentary foragers, to even larger systems of sedentary horticulturalists, to still larger systems in which core regions included the first cities and early states, to yet larger systems of agrarian empires, and eventually to today's single global capitalist political economy. Please note Figure 3.1 on p.58. Here Wilkinson used the PMN (political/military network) to bound major systems, following his earlier work (1987b). Figure 3.1 shows how a 'Central' PMN composed of the merging of the Mesopotamian and Egyptian PMNs in about 1500 BCE eventually incorporated all the other PMNs into itself. Figure 3.1 shows only those PMNs with cities larger than 10,000. Many cityless PMNs were also incorporated.

Figure 3.1 does not show what happened to the other interaction nets. If we were to consider the expanding boundaries of PGNs, the result would look much the same except that the time scale on the left margin would be shifted. For example, the Mesopotamian and Egyptian PGNs became linked probably as early as 3000 BCE, while the PMNs did not merge until 1500 BCE.

We have found that all hierarchical world-systems exhibit cyclical processes of:

- pulsations in the spatial extent of interaction networks;
- sequences of rise and fall of large polities; and
- oscillations between state-based and private forms of accumulation suggested by Ekholm and Friedman (1982).

We have found that all systems we have studied, *including even very small and egalitarian ones*, exhibit cyclical expansions and contractions in the spatial extent of interaction networks. Based on this, we posit that all four networks (BGNs, PMNs, PGNs, and INs) 'pulsate.' By 'pulsate' we mean that the spatial scale and intensity of interaction increases and then decreases at each of these network levels. When interaction increases, there are more exchanges with consequences over a greater distance.

We call cycles of centralization/decentralization of political/military power among a set of polities '*rise and fall.*' Again, we observe that for all *hierarchical* world-systems (whether they are composed of chiefdoms, states, empires, or capitalist states) the larger polities experience cycles of growth and decline in size and power.[13] However, very egalitarian and small-scale systems such as the sedentary foragers of northern California (Chase-Dunn and Hall 1997:ch. 7) do not display this kind of cycle. According to Ekholm and Friedman (1982), Frank (1993a), and Frank and Gills (1993) all world-systems for the last 5,000 years also oscillate between private and state-based forms of capital accumulation.

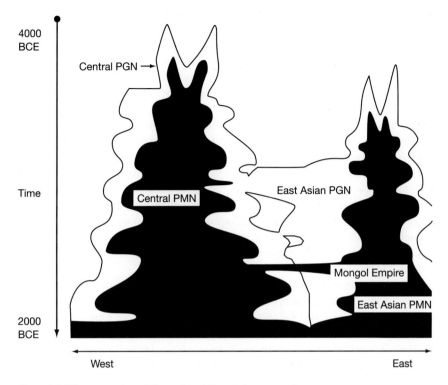

Figure 4.6 The expansion of Central and East Asian networks.

That these cyclical processes – pulsation, rise-and-fall, and oscillation – occur in very different kinds of systems raises several questions. Are the underlying mechanisms that generate these sequences the same or similar in all systems? What are the temporal and causal relations among these different cycles? What is the relationship between the rise and fall of large polities and changes in the degree of inequality within polities? Are these relationships similar across different kinds of world-systems? What is the relationship between the rise and fall of large polities and oscillations between state-based and private forms of accumulation? How are political rise-and-fall and network pulsations related to the general 200 year phases of expansion and contraction posited by Gills and Frank (1992; Frank 1993a)? Are these cycles really synchronous in regions connected only by very long-distance trade in prestige goods? We can only begin to address some of these questions here.

Qualitative differences in rise and fall

Some cyclical processes have different characteristics and different causes in distinct types of world-systems. Even though the rise and fall of chiefdoms is analytically similar to the rise and fall of empires and of hegemonic core powers, and even though all are related to the stability of institutions for extracting resources from distant regions, there are tremendous differences in scale and process.

Anderson (1994) summarizes the anthropological and sociological literature on 'cycling' in his study of the rise and fall of Mississippian chiefdoms. These 'cyclings' are processes by which a chiefly polity extended control over adjacent chiefdoms and developed a two-tiered hierarchy of administration above local communities. Later these regionally-centralized chiefly polities disintegrated back toward a system of smaller and less hierarchical polities.

Chiefs typically relied more completely on hierarchical kinship relations, control of ritual hierarchies, and control of prestige goods imports than have the rulers of states. States have specialized organizations for extracting resources that chiefdoms lack. In turn, states and empires have been more dependent on the projection of armed force over great distances than modern hegemonic core states have been. The development of commodity production and mechanisms of financial control, as well as further development of bureaucratic 'techniques of power' (Mann 1986) have allowed modern hegemons to extract resources from faraway places at less cost.

The development of techniques of power have made core/periphery relations ever more important in competition among core powers and have altered the ways in which the rise-and-fall process works in other respects. One of these is the degree of centralization achieved within the core areas of the modern capitalist world-system as compared to tributary world-systems. Tributary systems alternate between a structure of multiple, competing core states and core-wide (or nearly core-wide) empires. The modern interstate system experiences the rise and fall of hegemons, but the hegemonic core state *never* even attempts to conquer the other core states to form a core-wide empire. This is because modern hegemons are pursuing a capitalist, rather than a territorialist, form of accumulation. Thus, even omitting non-state, chiefdom world-systems, there is a significant difference between capitalist and tributary systems.

The simplest hypothesis regarding the temporal relationships between rise and fall and pulsation is that they occur in tandem. Whether or not this is so, and how it might differ in distinct types of world-systems, are questions amenable to empirical research. The spatial relationship between PMNs and PGNs expand and contract synchronically across Eurasia over the past 6000 years (Chase-Dunn and Hall 1997:ch. 10; see Figure 4.6).

Figure 4.6 is a hypothetical depiction of the temporal relationship between PMN and PGN pulsation in the Central and East Asian systems as they expanded, intermittently touched each other, and eventually merged to form the global system. This is the old issue about whether the flag follows trade or trade follows the flag. In our version, prestige goods trade leads the flag, but both expand more or less concurrently. While this portrayal is hypothetical, it would be possible to use actual temporal changes in the spatial extent of PMNs and PGNs to examine the synchronicity of expansion and contraction.

What about the relationship between rise-and-fall and PMN expansion and contraction? It would seem that this also would be temporally synchronized.

When core regions are more centralized (during 'rise') they contain larger polities with presumably greater spatial reach. This would extend the boundaries of the PMN. Thus, we should be able to use a measure of the centralization of political power within a core as a proxy for the expansion and contraction of the PMN.

At this point we do not have a direct measure of trade expansion and contraction. What we do have are estimates of the population sizes of cities. It may be reasonable to assume that cities grow larger during periods of economic growth and the expansion of trade, and that they decrease in size (or grow more slowly) during periods of decline.

Based on this tenuous assumption we have examined the relationships between changes in the population size of the largest city and changes in territorial size of the largest empire within several different PMNs. The correlations of the relationships between these measures for the Central and Far Eastern PMNs over the last 4,000 years are positive, but neither large, nor statistically significant (Chase-Dunn and Hall 1995:130–1). This weak support for simultaneous trade and political/military pulsations might be due to poor measures. Clearly, further research is needed.

The same study found little support for the hypothesized expansion and contraction phases specified by Gills and Frank (1992; also Frank 1993a). Neither urban growth nor empire size correspond very well with the Gills/Frank phases in either the Central or the East Asian PMNs (see Figure 4.7).

Synchronization of PMNs within the same PGN

While examining the relationships within PMNs of urban and empire growth/decline we discovered that city growth and empire growth seem to occur synchronously in the Central (West Asian and Mediterranean) and the East Asian PMNs (Chase-Dunn and Willard 1993). Some relevant evidence is contained in Figure 4.7 which shows the territorial sizes of the largest empires in the Central and East Asian PMNs from 1500 BCE to 1750 CE.

Figure 4.7 presents strong evidence that growth and decline phases are synchronized in PMNs that are linked within a larger PGN. However, we also found that the intermediate Indic PMN did not experience a similar sequence of growth and decline phases (Chase-Dunn and Hall 1997:fig. 10.11).[14]

What are the causes of this synchronization? Does this kind of relationship hold in other PGNs? To answer the second question we have examined the relationships between urban and empire growth in the Mesopotamian and Egyptian PMNs during the period in which they were linked into a larger PGN. Figures 4.8 and 4.9 show these results. Figure 4.8 displays the population sizes of the largest cities in the Mesopotamian and Egyptian PMNs between 2250 and 600 BCE. In 1500 BCE the Mesopotamian and Egyptian PMNs merged to become a single larger PMN that we call the Central PMN. Nevertheless, changes in the sizes of the largest cities in these regions do not seem to be synchronous.

Figure 4.9 shows the changes in the territorial sizes of the largest empires in Egypt and Mesopotamia from 3000 BCE to 1450 BCE. Clearly, the empire sizes

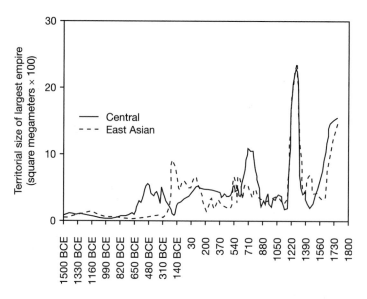

Figure 4.7 Central and East Asian empire sizes, 1500 BCE–1800 CE.
Note: Pearson's 4 = .90, n = 60, p < .0001.

are uncorrelated across fourteen time points (Pearson's r correlation coefficient is −.17 [n = 14]). The Egyptian/Mesopotamian comparison does not support the idea that all PMNs within larger PGNs have synchronous processes of growth.

The synchronicity of the growth of cities and empires in the Central and East Asian PMNs remains a puzzle. One possibility is northern Eurasian-wide climatic fluctuations. India, at a more equatorial latitude across the Himalayas, may have experienced very different climatic fluctuations. Climate change can affect urban growth and empire-formation through its affects on agricultural productivity (Nix 1985). Periods of flooding may disrupt irrigation systems, and drought may negatively affect agriculture. Recent evidence indicates that the collapse of Mayan states may have been caused by a period of extended drought. Weiss *et al.* (1993) contend that both the expansion and collapse of the Akkadian empire were spurred by climate changes.

If we found significant relationships between indicators of climate change and the urban and empire growth/decline sequences we would want to examine the direction of causality. Does climate change cause urban change, or does the expansion of agriculture associated with urban growth cause climate change? It is possible that expanded agricultural activity, and/or deforestation due to human exploitation, may have affected local and regional rainfall patterns and ground water levels. (See Chew in this volume.) Thus, population density, mediated by intense agriculture and forest exploitation, and thus urbanization, may have affected climactic fluctuations. There is a developing literature on the anthropogenic causes of climate change. It is well known that the intensification of

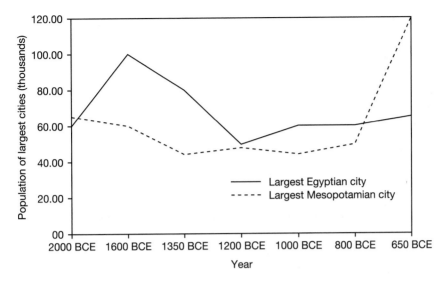

Figure 4.8 Largest cities in Egypt and Mesopotamia.
Source: Chandler 1987; Wilkinson 1992a.

productive activities causes environmental degradation. This, in turn, has affected the development of human societies for millennia. If urban growth episodes precede climate change or changes in water levels then causality in the direction of human effects on climate will be supported. But as it stands research on climate change in the relevant areas has not been combined with our measures of urban and empire growth to see if these are empirically related.

Microparasites, mediated through trade networks, could also affect city and empire growth and decline. As trade increases in density and volume, formerly isolated disease pools come into contact, unleashing 'virgin soil epidemics' (Crosby 1972, 1986). These epidemics can produce massive disruptions, and following Goldstone's (1991) argument, can unleash social, economic, and political changes. As pathogens and hosts adapt to each other, diseases become less lethal and populations recover. Trade resumes, and the cycle can repeat as other, formerly isolated disease pools come into contact, or as new diseases spread along trade networks. This might account for some regularity in such cycles since humans have only been able to intervene in the biological processes of mutual adaptation in the late twentieth century.

A more interesting explanation from the world-systems perspective is Frank's (1992) hypothesis of the 'centrality of Central Asia' as a peripheral region linking both ends of the Eurasian continent. The Mongol Empire briefly linked Western Asia and China into a single polity in the thirteenth century CE. Barfield (1989) built on Lattimore's (1940) observations to trace the long-term linkage of the rise and fall of steppe empires with the rise and fall of agrarian empires in China. Citing this and other evidence, Frank (1992) contends that processes of peripheral

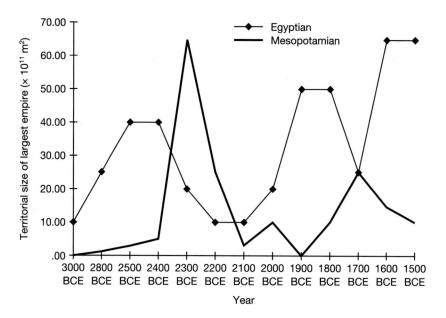

Figure 4.9 Egyptian and Mesopotamian empire sizes.
Source: Taagepera (1978a,b).
Note: Pearson's r correlation = −.17, n = 14.

migration and steppe-empire formation and their affects on the long-distance trade carried along the Silk Roads are the explanation of the linkages between Rome and China first reported by Teggart (1939). Figure 4.7 (and others in Chase-Dunn and Hall 1997:ch. 10) show similar synchronization.

Perhaps it is Frank's Central Asian linkage that accounts for this. But in order to accept his explanation we need to rule out the climatic fluctuations hypothesis and explain why India was not affected in the same way. The same caveat holds for disease linkages (McNeill 1976). One explanation for the South Asian exception – but a none too satisfactory one – might be that the tropical and semi-tropical climates there were subject to a different disease regime. It is also conceivable, given the Himalayan barrier, that climatic cycles in South Asia differed significantly from northern Eurasia. The monsoons certainly follow a different rhythm from the weather in northern regions.

Since warfare affects both urban growth and the territorial size of empires, steppe-empire formation and the attendant fighting and migration of pastoral nomads may well be the cause of the simultaneous rise and fall of empires at both ends of the Eurasian landmass. If so, warfare between steppe nomads and agrarian states in both western Asia and East Asia should be correlated. Barfield's (1989) *Perilous Frontier* provides information for the East Asian region. For western Asian, data on warfare obtained by the LORANOW project (Cioffi-Revilla 1991; 1996) could be used.

The way in which South Asia was connected into Afro-Eurasian trading patterns may account for the South Asian exception. India had multiple connections overland. Maritime links go back at least two millennia. At first they consisted of coastal trade. Later, as sailors mastered the monsoons, they crossed the Arabian Sea and the Bay of Bengal (see maps in Chaudhuri 1985 and Abu-Lughod 1989:172–3, 202, 252). Thus, at any given time, South Asian states had multiple routes of access into trade, so disruption of any one route – for whatever reason – could be compensated for by means of alternate routes.

Beyond the multiple routes, South Asia had extensive relations with Southeast Asia which opened up even further routes.[15] At times when conditions through the straits of Malacca and/or Sunda made sea trade very risky, portages across the Malay Peninsula or overland through northern Southeast Asia (what today is northern Myanmar (Burma), Thailand, Laos, and Vietnam, were possible. Thus, while a large state (e.g. Funan, Khmer Empire, Srivijaya [Java], and later Siam or the city-state Malacca) could block one or more paths, no one of these states could control all the paths from India to China.

Indian connections to, and trade with, various Southeast Asian states itself buffered India from blockages on other routes. Southeast Asia supplied aromatic woods, spices, and especially gold. When access to northern sources of gold were severed by Bactria in Central Asia, and the Romans sought to curb the export of gold to the east in the first centuries of the current era, India turned to Southeast Asia to fill the gap. As Coedès notes (1968:19ff) the region was known as 'the land of gold.' However, unlike the Central Asia steppe federations which rose and fell with Chinese empires (Barfield 1989, 1991), the states of Southeast Asia seemed to wax and wane counterpuntally to Chinese and Indian empires.

Thus, for the Mongol era at least, an elaborated version of Frank's Central Asian thesis seems to make more sense of the coordination of events in West and East Asia, and the exceptionalism of South Asia than any other explanation. While not ruling out a role of climatic fluctuations and/or spread of pathogens, it suggests that they were key factors.

Conclusion

On some issues the differences between ourselves (as probably the most extreme transformationists) and the most extreme continuationists (Frank and Gills) are of a rather mild order. Frank and Gills, like Ekholm-Friedman and Friedman, see a continuous coexistence of capitalism and geopolitics for five thousand years since the emergence of states in Mesopotamia. We see a slow and uneven rise of commodification and capitalism over the same period, culminating in a watershed of capitalist predominance that occurred first in the European regional system in the seventeenth century. We emphasize comparison of different systems while Frank and Gills concentrate on the Eurasian World System. We agree that there are important similarities between different systems and that there are many structural and processual continuities that link the Eurasian world-system with the contemporary global system. While we see the value of very long-term studies of single large systems, we argue that a comparative approach is important because it allows us to study both differences and transformations as well as similarities and continuities. Our case studies support the notion that there are important differences and qualitative transformations.

Our first conclusion is that there have indeed been transformations in the basic logic of accumulation. Our study of the Wintu and their neighbors revealed a small world-system in which social labor was primarily mobilized by means of kinship structures based on cultural agreements about obligations. Accumulation was not accomplished by means of market exchanges or political taxation or tribute. These forms of accumulation did not exist. We contend that this very small world-system of sedentary foragers was similar to the first sedentary systems of mesolithic western Asia and the Levant twelve thousand years ago. If true, major qualitative transformations must have occurred to produce world-systems in which tributary and capitalist accumulation became predominant. We also identify important qualitative changes in the operation of cycles of rise and fall as they occur in tributary and capitalist world-systems. This supports the transformationist approach.

Regarding our multilevel approach to spatially bounding world-systems (the four nets) our survey leads us to conclude that the degree of systemness is typically greatest in the bulk goods net and lessens as we move to the larger nets. This does not mean that the larger nets are unsystemic. Political/military and prestige goods nets are frequently important for both reproduction and structural change. We do not assert that this is always the case, but it is a plausible generalization. This conclusion provides a new slant on the debate about which are the most important types of interaction. Wallerstein's emphasis on bulk goods networks is the most conservative, because bulk goods are always important.

World-system evolution involves three interlinked processes: semiperipheral development, iterations of population pressure and hierarchy-formation, and transformations of modes of accumulation. These three processes account for the evolution of human societies from a hundred thousand or so nomadic foraging bands to the single complex global system of today. Semiperipheral development linked core/periphery structures to institutional innovations that expanded and transformed social networks. Iterations of population pressure, intensification, and hierarchy-formation provided the engines of development and the dynamics of political rise and fall that are visible in all systems. Transformations of modes of accumulation altered the nature and dynamics of production, distribution, and accumulation. This, in turn, changed the way the processes of rise and fall and expansion operated.

World-systems composed of unhierarchical groups do not have stable core/periphery structures. Core/periphery relations become more unequal as societies develop the 'techniques of power' that allow distant groups to be dominated and exploited. Core/periphery relations are very important for world-systems evolution both because of the role of semiperipheral development and because competition among core societies revolves around how well they can exploit and dominate peripheral regions. The modern world-system is an extension of this trend toward the increasing stability and importance of core/periphery relations. Geopolitically structured capitalist commodity production is the most efficient and stable exploiter of peripheral regions. But semiperipheral development continues to operate in the global world-system, and so new transformations are possible.

We have seen that throughout the process of world-system evolution new areas and new peoples have continually been incorporated or merged into expanding systems. Incorporation and merger often drastically transform individual groups, underscoring the need to study social change in a context of intergroup interaction. Pristine conditions seldom exist, although we argue we have found one such case (Chase-Dunn and Hall 1997:ch.7). The study of incorporation further emphasizes a point McNeill made in *Polyethnicity* (1986), that multiethnic states and ethnogenesis are ancient social processes (see also Hall 1998).

Questions

Answering the many questions we have raised will require a combination of detailed case studies of single systems and formal comparisons of large numbers of systems. No one has yet proposed a chronograph of the expansion of the Central information net or the Central bulk goods net. Both of these face the problem of fall-off. This does not mean that systemic consequences of changes (e.g. shortages or surpluses) extend indefinitely. The range of systemic interaction is a function of transportation and communications costs, and these change greatly across systems. Studies of these relations are sorely needed. We also need studies of the boundaries of kin-based systems.

The existence of pulsation, rise and fall, and oscillation need much more precise documentation. Are the cycles of pulsation of each of the four kinds of interaction temporally related to each other in regular ways in most systems? What are the relations among the three types of cycles? What is driving these cyclical processes and how are their causes related?

Part of the answer may be embedded in our model of demographic intensification and hierarchical iterations. The pulsation and rise and fall cycles interact with demographic and epidemiological processes to shape long-term sociocultural evolution. The ways in which these processes interact appear to vary across different types of world-systems, and yet the hypothesized regularities suggest some underlying basic mechanisms that operate in all systems.

Speculations

Many authors contend that the contemporary system has undergone fundamental changes in the last decade. We argue that most of the visible changes in technology, globalization of investment and trade, the demise of the Soviet Union, and the appearance of 'world culture' are not fundamental. Rather, the systemic trends and cycles that have been characteristic features of the modern system for hundreds of years are continuing. Fundamental change has not yet occurred. However, fundamental change (systemic transformation) is likely to occur within the next two hundred years as global capitalism runs into planetary boundaries (Meadows *et al.* 1992).

There are several possible scenarios for future transformation. World-systemic cycles and trends could continue much as they have in the past and the whole system could be destroyed in the 2020s by a global war among core powers. Another possibility is the emergence of a world state. This would involve another round of the iteration cycle in which a global state emerges to deal with global problems. However, the iteration model has usually operated through long phases of conflict and centralization by conquest. These mechanisms would likely be fatal given current military technology. The transformation of the rise and fall sequence from empire-formation to hegemonic rise and fall involves an increase in the importance of economic competition over political/military competition, though it did not eliminate warfare. But this long-run evolutionary trend may presage the eventual elimination of warfare as a method of choosing global 'leadership.' The problem is to find an alternative mechanism to conquest for allowing global political integration. It is obvious that democratic political institutions at the global level could serve several purposes – the legitimation of a global collective security provider; a mechanism to address global environmental problems; and an opening for democratizing and balancing the processes of economic development.

We also speculate on a possible future transformation to democratic socialism. We suggest that further experiments with socialism are likely to emerge in the contemporary semiperiphery. Any rise to predominance of socialism as a mode of accumulation will also require global-level organizations.

While our main purpose has been to construct a scaffolding for the comparative study of world-systems, our eventual goal is to use this apparatus to address the real problems and possibilities of the contemporary system. This requires further research and more refined theorizing. Our speculations are meant to prod others to join the effort by demonstrating these are not mere idle, if interesting, inquiries into our past, but vital questions to understanding, and we hope, shaping a humane future.

Acknowledgment

We thank the editors of this volume and the participants in the Lund conference for many suggestions, corrections, and stimulating ideas that contributed to the development of our thinking. Over the intervening years many others have contributed to sharpening our ideas at many conferences where we have presented these and other ideas derivative of them. Figures 4.3 through 4.6 are copyright © 1997 Westview Press, and are reprinted here by permission.

Notes

1 The earliest known sedantary foragers are the Natufians of the Levant circa 10,000 BCE.

2 In sociology 'social change' is a 'covering term' which subsumes cultural, political, and economic change.

3 Typologies developed by most evolutionary thinkers are broadly convergent, even while differing in the details. Moseley and Wallerstein (1978) present a useful concordance. These typologies are rooted in considerable empirical investigation.

4 We added the information network to take into account the important insights of Schortman and Urban (1987), and Bentley's (1993) masterful survey of cross-cultural encounters in Eurasia. Discussions with William McNeill at the 1995 International Studies Association meetings and the Lund Conference prompted us to include the systemic aspects of information flows.

5 The phrase, 'the development of underdevelopment' was coined by Gunder Frank (1966) to describe the process in which core countries extract resources from the periphery. This core/periphery exploitation not only blocks development in the periphery, but also systematically distorts development in harmful ways, producing 'underdevelopment.'

6 Berquist (1995) brought this to our attention in his discussion of the Achaemenid empire's treatment of its various western colonies. Allen (1997) discusses this in detail.

7 Woolf (1990) argues that there was no semiperiphery in the Roman world-system.

8 The term 'region of refuge' (Aguirre Beltran 1979) describes areas only partially incorporated into a state system. Partial incorporation has the consequence of freezing social change. This 'preserves' the area by setting it aside for future development. Hence it is a 'refuge' for older, 'traditional' social forms that have been destroyed elsewhere in the system.

9 The concept of 'hinterland' used by Frank and Gills (1993), Gills and Frank (1991) and Collins (1978, 1981) also corresponds to the weaker ranges of incorporation.

10 For discussion of the former see Chase-Dunn and Hall (1997:ch.5); for the latter (ch. 8). Also note Amin (1991).

11 Collins (1978) contends that the advantages of states in the marchlands is primarily geomilitary. Because they are near the edge of the core 'heartland' they do not need to defend several borders at once. They can pursue a strategy of conquest that adds territory sequentially without threats from the rear. The disadvantage of older core powers is that they must defend themselves from many sides and their resources are spread thinly.

12 This discussion goes beyond that in *Rise and Demise* (1997), but draws heavily on it. We have respecified our model in order to clarify the distinction between intensification and technological change.

13 For the modern world-system, rise and fall cycles involve national states that perform the role of hegemons (e.g. Britain, the US) but do not conquer the whole core. This phenomenon is termed the hegemonic sequence (Chase-Dunn 1998:ch.9).

14 Further testing with somewhat refined data further strengthens these findings (Chase-Dunn, Manning and Hall forthcoming).

15 See Cady 1966; Coedès 1966, 1968; Glover *et al.* 1992; Marr and Milner, 1986; and Wyatt 1984, 1994.

Part II

From regional and sectoral to a global perspective

5 Envisioning global change

A long-term perspective

Andrew Sherratt

Understanding the past

Each generation has a fresh opportunity to understand the past, by perceiving it from a unique standpoint: that of the present. Since this standpoint constantly shifts, so also do views of the past. This common-sense assertion does not imply a retreat into relativism – that there can be no common description of phenomena, only an infinite choice of attitudes – because it is true of all our cognitive processes: out of the uniqueness of personal experience, common perceptions emerge. It does, however, help to make sense of why certain views of the world are espoused at certain times, and why our perceptions differ from those of our predecessors (and, not unusually, many of our contemporaries). What contemporary conditions do is foreground certain properties of the world around us, because of their current relevance. They direct our attention to comparable conditions in the past. To a previous generation these particular properties were unimportant or even invisible, because they had no pressing relevance. They were not within the visual field of the backward-looking gaze. It is only by accumulating the insights of successive generations, and observations made from a diversity of standpoints, that a fully three-dimensional view of the past can be obtained. That is why intellectual history is one of the most fundamental disciplines of the social sciences: it explains why opinions differ, and why our colleagues can be blind to what seem to be self-evident truths.

The current, minority, interest in world-systems[1] perspectives falls squarely within this formulation. The institutional structure of academic life contains a multiplicity of barriers which insulate disciplines and shield them from the implications of a global view. World-systems approaches differ, in this respect, from other contemporary shifts in perception such as those achieved by feminism. When gender roles are in flux, it is easier to see them as culturally constructed rather than god-given or determined by nature. Although globalization is a phenomenon which affects us all, it does so in ways which are less direct, and are interpretable in a multiplicity of different paradigms. World-systems viewpoints are also easily mis-represented as the revival of nineteenth century conceptions when 'globalization' was essentially colonialism. Since many 'subjects' in the humanities are set within subject areas whose definition implies a cultural genealogy ('classics,' 'oriental studies'), models which imply that these entities are misleading are likely to be stoutly resisted by established interests who are happy to rule within their own (shrinking) domains.

Nevertheless, the time is propitious for a global academic view, and the experimental formulations now surfacing are a foretaste of what is likely to become the common coin of discussion in the social and historical sciences – until such obvious truths, hardened into unimaginative dogma, are themselves attacked and re-formed. Symptomatic of these changes is the way in which certain phrases and metaphors have an instinctive appeal. One of these is the idea of the network. It is hardly coincidental that many of the contributors to this volume have communicated with each other via the Internet. It may be hoped that the immanence of this concept will lead to a more ready acceptance of Eric Wolf's classic appeal (1982: 1–7) for an emphasis on connections rather than on entities, since an entity-by-entity approach renders invisible many of the most significant features of human history. Bounded structures are secondary phenomena arising from the properties of networks: only the crude convenience of national history and national accounting have given these transitory entities a disproportionate role in the social sciences (including anthropology, where illusory equivalents of nation-states have been sought in the mysterious entities called 'tribes'). Networks have no logical boundaries, save at the global scale; all social systems are 'world systems.'

One other current re-envisioning of the world is of relevance to the world-systems challenge: consumerism. In a world of shopping malls and competing brand images, it is not surprising that there has been a rash of books with titles such as 'Consuming culture.' It is easy to dismiss such interests; but I argue that they reflect a more fundamental rediscovery of the importance of culture, and more particularly the simultaneous meaningfulness and materiality of material culture. This is not to resurrect a reductive materialism, but to assert the power of ideologico-material phenomena, whether these be recent features of the world scene, such as 'coca-colanization,' or earlier phenomena such as 'farming,' which has traditionally been treated as a set of subsistence arrangements but must now be seen as a socio-subsistence system embodying powerful ideological elements. This approach would see the world as being made up, not of cellular units of culture, but of growing arenas for competing regimes of value. The propensity of certain ways of life (such as 'farming' or 'civilization') to spread at the expense of others is fundamental to the study of world systems, while scarcely apprehensible within the conventional disciplines.

Beyond specialization

What is required to take advantage of these intellectual opportunities is a new kind of discipline. Neither the conventional comparativism of the social sciences, nor the inherent insulation of the classical humanistic disciplines, is equipped to deal with the connectivity of the real world. What is necessary is a larger, structural approach. Aspects of this approach can be found scattered through subjects which have already obtained intellectual respectability. One is anthropology, which has resolutely opposed the rigid forms of categorization (for instance into economic, religious or social aspects) which form the basis of the conventional academic division of labor; but its concentration on small-scale, face to face interaction – which gave it this comprehensiveness of outlook in the first place – has directed disciplinary attention more to on-the-ground manifestations than toward larger, structural properties.[2] Another is human geography, which – had its recent history been different – might constitute just the discipline that is required; but its lack of a time dimension (for historical geography rarely penetrates beyond the medieval period in Europe), and successive concerns with urban planning and cognitive topography, have largely inhibited the more comprehensive formulation that is now needed.[3] History, of course, should be the answer: but the longitudinal view of the development of past societies over a timescale of millennia is interrupted by a differently constituted domain of 'ancient history,' which is subject to the pressures of its own peer community in ways which inhibit its contribution.

The cumulative effect of disciplinary divisions is a disabling fissivity which disguises the common aspects of their enterprises. An academic division of labor which partitions spatial aspects as 'geography' and temporal aspects as 'history' calls for the satirical skills of a latter-day Jonathan Swift in imagining how a university might set about measuring a cube, when this involved an inter-faculty committee to coordinate the departments needed for the different horizontal and vertical measurements. Academia is constituted in such a way as to obfuscate recognition of large-scale spatio-temporal structures, and to deny advancement to those that do recognize them. That is why the field is studded with the names of intellectual mavericks whose works defy disciplinary attribution, and are the bane of librarians forced to work within the conventional categories.[4]

One field of inquiry ought to have the relevant credentials, and that is archaeology. With methods applicable irrespective of social complexity or cultural specificity, its perspective can encompass the broad sweep of prehistory and track the flow of items which moved around the world in historical times, whether or not the bills of lading have survived. In practice, however, archaeology offers a microcosm of the problems which beset the wider academic community. Its few practitioners are haphazardly deployed across a trivial fraction of the evidence, and subject to the same forces which beset their colleagues in other historical disciplines. Nevertheless archaeology commands an increasing body of observations, over vast expanses of time and space; and its relative freedom from the constraints of linguistic specialization, together with its comprehensive approach, make it a natural seed-bed for large-scale interpretations. It might even be argued that archaeology manifested this propensity too soon, in the set of doctrines known as diffusionism, and that the contemporary effort to re-introduce world-system ideas is made more difficult by the taint of association with these now unfashionable ideas. In this respect it parallels the cycle of interpretations in ancient history from the nineteenth century on, between primitivists and modernizers,[5] which was both a debate about whether the economy of ancient Greece was simple or complex, and about the role of the Near East in relation to Europe. At the same time as the 'primitivist' (substantivist) interpretation of the ancient economy was being forcefully restated in the post-World War II period by Karl Polanyi (1958) and Moses Finley (1973), prehistorians were at the furthest extent of their reaction to the diffusionism of Gordon Childe, so that an emphasis on local autonomy has recently prevailed both in prehistory and in the study of the ancient world.

These attitudes are currently in course of change; and it seems a propitious moment to attempt to develop a common conceptualization with those world-system theorists (e.g. Frank and Gills 1993) who have broken out of Weberian constraints and are attempting to extend an interactionist framework back from the sixteenth century to the beginnings of urban life in the fourth millennium BCE. This chapter is offered as an archaeologist's view of what a common description of global processes might look like, using insights from a variety of disciplines, but with a terminology taken directly from none. It is based on a simple premise: that time and space are the dimensions of the process to be studied, and are not, therefore, a useful basis for long-term academic specialization. History and geography must fuse.

Conceptualizing global change

If the continuity of temporal development (and thus the common properties of social systems through time) has been lost in the proliferation of specialist disciplines, it is the specificity of spatial processes which has been partly abandoned by geographers. Seduced by mathematical elegance, a generation of 1960s ('New') geographers gave up the inductive approach in favor of attempts to specify fundamental properties of spatial organization on an isotropic surface. But the world is not isotropic, and important developments have taken place in topologically complex and atypical parts of the Earth's surface. It might even be argued that change itself is closely related to the existence of such singularities. A unified spatio-temporal approach must balance comparability and specificity.

Competing conceptualizations: 'layer-cake' and 'calyx'

Informing such a methodology must be a sound grasp of the shape of the structures being sought. Two competing visions of the dominant processes of world development have alternated in the minds of theorists. One might be called the 'layer-cake,' the other the 'calyx.' The former is based on stratigraphic succession, and gives the impression of a set of common phases or stages through which populations progress. Development theory in economics (Rostow 1960), is a recent example, paralleled by the still-powerful school of regional autonomism in prehistoric archaeology or the candelabra model of human origins in biological anthropology (early dispersal of a common stock, followed by the parallel development of different regional populations towards modern humanity). These were all, in their different contexts, elaborated in rhetorical opposition to diffusionist models, such as colonialism. While contagious processes such as diffusionism largely lack such an explicit theoretical description, there is a clear kinship between the kinds of models which have recently tended to succeed 'layer-cake' models in a variety of disciplines: core-periphery models of economic development, both in historical and prehistoric times; or the 'out of Africa' models which have recently become the new orthodoxy of human evolution. By comparison with the horizontal stratification through time which characterized the layer-cake, these latter attempts at visualization describe structures which are the shape of inverted cones, beginning in specific areas and growing upwards through time and outwards in space like a bush or flower, hence the image of a flower-calyx.

Both images are 'true.' Each metaphor describes one aspect of the temporal process, and the two images have continuously alternated in popularity in biological and social theory – Darwin and Spencer being notable nineteenth century exemplars of the genealogical bush and the stadial sequence respectively. The more organic metaphor appeals to the Romantic imagination, the regular succession accords better with the Enlightenment sense of order. It is not accidental that one image is based on an individual life, the other on impersonal sedimentary accumulation. Such metaphors have alternately risen to prominence in both science and literature as they have reflected dominant aspects of their contemporary economic, social and political environments (Sherratt 1992; 1997).[6] Each has a measure of validity, and it would be wrong to emphasize their mutual exclusiveness or to claim that one is more 'scientific' than the other. After all, the growth of an organism is as scientifically describable a process as is sedimentary deposition, but there are undoubtedly times when the usefulness of one image needs to be asserted against the dominance of its alternate. This would seem to be the case today: organic growth needs to be seen as an important property of human social systems, as opposed to neoevolutionary stadial descriptions. Long-lasting structures which expand through time (the calyx image) seem to be a better representation of important phenomena as they can be reconstructed over long periods than does the more passive image of successive layers.

Such growing and expanding structures are not unique to human society. They are a fundamental feature of biological evolution also, describing how new species emerge. Improved palaeo-environmental reconstructions not only provide a more realistic background to biological evolution, but also form a significant mechanism of change itself. This has led to a new conception of 'punctuated' change, produced by episodes of rapid environmental forcing. What has been less emphasized, however, is that this temporal punctuation has a spatial dimension in that the specific conditions which give rise to change are limited to particular places or regions, from which successful innovations then spread (Sherratt 1997). Nowhere is this better exemplified than in the rift valleys of East Africa where human populations had their ancestry. Successive generations of human ancestors emerged in the environmentally diverse conditions of this geologically unusual setting; and from here successive waves of more advanced hominids spread out to replace or overtake earlier generations who either survived unchanged, or (like the Neanderthals) underwent physical specialization as they adapted to the cold northern margin. It is only the speed with which successful innovations spread over large areas that gives the impression of a common, stadial or layer-like sequence.

The calyx structure of spatial expansion, and the center/edge processes that have given rise to it, are seen as fundamental even to biological evolution, and not peculiar to human societies and phenomena such as the emergence of capitalism. Such structures underlie the entirety of human history. What is striking about the last 10,000 years is the multicentric pattern of such structures: several regions stand out as the foci of fast-spreading contagious processes. Whereas biological change had been uni-centric, the cultural changes made possible by the emergence of modern behavioral complexity have been notably multicentric, including foci in both the eastern and western parts of the Old World, and the central and Andean parts of the New World. During the last 10,000 years, in the warm conditions of the Holocene interglacial period in which we are still living, successive developments have consistently arisen within the same focal areas of change – notably the geographically unusual conditions at plate boundaries in sub-tropical environments where narrow montane belts are surrounded by sea and desert. These foci or 'nuclear areas' have fundamentally affected their surrounding regions, in large-scale center/edge processes; it was these macro-structures which gave rise to the idea of 'diffusionism.'[7] This formulation has been unpopular during the last half-century, and the term is no longer used in a respectable sense, but it is vital that the idea should be revived since it correctly expresses essential properties of the process. Whereas biological changes such as the spread of successive human species involved the emergence of a new genotype and its spread by migration and replacement, Holocene changes came about as much by the adoption of new practices by existing populations as by migratory spread. 'Nuclear' areas are a property of behaviorally modern humans, capable of forming networks of trade and exchange, transmitting complex messages and learning new practices by imitation.

The emergence of nuclearity

The appearance of consistent foci of change was closely related to the domestication of a set of high-yielding but labor-intensive cereal grasses, together with certain legumes. These annual plants, adapted to strong seasonal stress, formed parts of vegetational communities which expanded in certain areas in interglacials. Although modern humans had probably experimented with plant propagation and cultivation during the last glacial period, it was only with warmer and wetter conditions that cereals came to be present in sufficient numbers to justify special attention. It is likely that they were only taken into cultivation as a result of climatic changes which forced the use of all available resources, however labor intensive. Initial cultivation systems were essentially horticultural, and involved little forest clearance. The principal form of labor input was the back-breaking process of grinding the seeds, undertaken by women. Since cereals and beans could supply protein as well as carbohydrate, their cultivation led to population growth; since cultivation could be extended to new areas, population growth could be sustained. This was expressed both in increasing local densities and in a propensity for farming to spread. The spread was so rapid that they overtook more slowly developing forms of cultivation (e.g. tending root-crops); though local crops might be integrated into an expanding complex, and even take over the role of principal cultigen as farming spread to new climatic zones (as with temperate millets in North China or tropical millets in sub-Saharan Africa). The date at which such explosive processes began, and the area which they affected, depended on local vegetation and climate. The western Old World focus, with winter rainfall crops, began right at the onset of the Holocene. New World developments, in tropical (summer rainfall) settings, began much later (Sherratt 1997). The seasonality of crops affected the area to which their cultivation could spread: western Old World crops spread rapidly into a temperate (winter-rainfall) hinterland, while New World crops spread more widely in adjacent tropical areas and penetrated only slowly into temperate North America. The availability of potentially domesticable ungulates also affected the character of farming. The New World provided fewer candidates than the Old, and only in the Andes was animal raising more important than hunting. For these reasons, Old World societies evolved faster than New World ones. The following discussion deals principally with the western Old World.

Farming systems were characterized by a tendency to increasing sociocultural complexity and a tendency to spread. Once farming was in existence, the process of cultural change was reinforced by features which accompanied it: larger communities, increased sedentism and the associated arts of architecture, pottery, textile production, and stone-working. This horticultural complex spread westward over Mediterranean and temperate Europe, and eastward through Iran to western India. Within the new village communities, patterns of private consumption grew up by which certain families and villages came to control a larger portion of consumable and durable commodities than others; ostentatious display became an increasingly prominent part of village life. The more complex forms of material production associated with this way of life were important in the transmission of farming and associated practices to indigenous foraging groups. Elaboration of material culture was further promoted by technological innovations. Copper became a widely desirable commodity and medium of exchange, promoting liquidity. In temperate Europe, this accompanied an enhanced role for cattle-raising. In the ecologically more diverse environments of the nuclear region it permitted a degree of specialization in the production of products such as cheese, wool and fruit. These gave rise to more specialized forms of husbandry, such as pastoral livestock rearing or arboriculture. They were matched by more intensive techniques of cereal production: irrigation, the use of animal traction, and the development of a simple plough. These innovations remained largely restricted to the nuclear area where farming began. In temperate Europe these more advanced forms of agriculture and pastoralism did not appear until urbanism had begun in the Near East, perhaps as a consequence of increasing long-distance links.

The processes by which farming spread can be summarized as a nuclear/ margin system. Innovations, including primary farming ('founder crops' and meat-animals) and secondary farming (commodity crops including animal products and tree fruits), occurred primarily within the nuclear area. New forms of food-getting were accompanied by technological innovations (pottery, metal) and social changes. Some of these spread ('diffused,' whether by migration or adoption) out of the nuclear region, but this extension had little effect upon the nuclear area itself: the process of spread did not create an outer sustaining area, and the term 'margin' reflects this lack of two-way linkage. What the existence of a margin did was to provide an external arena of farming and simple metal-working societies, which might be tapped by long-distance routes for particularly desirable commodities. This, however, was a feature of the next phase.

The emergence of cores and peripheries

The process by which more differentiated structures arose may again be followed in the Old World: but once more it stands for three or four independent regions. The model proposed here is based on an interpretation of urban centers as locations of manufacturing activity: more precisely, of added-value production. This definition does not exclude administrative or religious functions; indeed, it is formulated so as to encompass them. Urban centers import raw materials and add value, exporting some of their products: the difference pays for the materials and other consumables. The value created in the manufacturing process is ideological as much as material. It is the desirability of the products which keeps the cycle in existence (cf. Hornborg, this volume). The outward growth of an urban system can be described as the expansion of a hegemonic regime of value, in which new consumption practices are promoted.[8] Its typical commodities are metalwork, textiles and psychotropic consumables such as alcoholic drinks, packaged within a system of beliefs and practices within which they have a coherent ideological role. These practices are the prerogative of a minority, and societies characterized by these forms of specialized elite consumption have traditionally been termed 'civilizations.' These form a special category of high-consumption societies, whose needs have to be supplied through the transport of large volumes of goods, far beyond the requirements of subsistence. Ideological and material aspects are thus intimately related: missionaries tell the natives they are naked, and traders sell them clothes! Flows of ideas are as important as the flows of products. Nevertheless the process has a definable economic base, which is the asymmetrical division between suppliers of raw materials and providers of manufactures. The emergence of elites is therefore not a local process, but always takes place within a larger structural setting (Sherratt 1995). An important element in the continuing expansion of such a system is import substitution: peripheral areas acquire the skills to undertake their own manufacturing processes, becoming parts of an expanding core region, and generate their own external supply area which becomes the new periphery. Some innovations spread further, as easily transferable skills spread among surrounding populations, though without entailing a continuing economic articulation. This outer area, culturally affected by the existence of urban communities but not actively participating in their economy, forms a margin in the same sense as the spread of farming created a penumbra of farming societies around the original nuclear region.

In many respects, therefore, the formation of urban systems can be seen as a continuation of the structures and processes created by farming. Instead of a nuclear/margin system there was now a core/periphery/margin system, with the nucleus functionally differentiated into core and periphery. Whereas the relationship between nucleus and margin involved only the transmission of innovations and not any continuing interdependence, that between core and periphery involved a series of real-time interactions, where changes in one partner actively affected the fortunes of the other. This assymetrical relationship was the first regional division of labor. Such zonally specialized systems emerged within each of the areas which had previously been central to the origins of farming, and core regions with urban economies grew up at specific locations within them: typically in alluvial river valleys which were major transport arteries (the Euphrates, Nile or Indus). These were associated with improved transport systems including boats with sails and pack-animals. Such alluvial environments also provided habitats where the productivity of farming could be intensified by irrigation, and this correlation has in the past suggested explanations of urban origins in terms of the achievement of an agricultural surplus. While this provided a means of sustaining larger communities, it can no longer be seen as simply causal, since it is the new consumption patterns which demand explanation, not their calorific base.

Agricultural surpluses were not exported directly, but in the form of labor-time in the production of desirable manufactured commodities: improved farming supported sheep and people, and textiles were exported as part of a total ideological package. The process behind the emergence of a core was in fact industrialization. This is reflected in the appearance both of techniques of mass-production (like wheelmade pottery) and of advanced craftsmanship (like sheet-metal vessels or elaborate jewelery). Innovations in technology were often directed toward import substitution, as in the invention of blue glass as a substitute for lapis lazuli. The Industrial Revolution of the eighteenth century can be seen as a logical extension of this system, on a new, global scale (and with a fossil fuel subsidy), rather than a fundamental rupture with 'traditional' economies.

Although the system began within a strongly religious and theocratic framework, the proliferation of competing centers within the advanced ideological/manufacturing core created tensions which gave rise to armed conflict, and precipitated forms of social organization in which the explicit use of force was institutionalized: the state, and soon also a system of temporarily dominant regional powers which were experimental forms of empire. Such structures typically attempted to control flows of high-value products and their nodal points rather than territory as such. As the system grew in area, it altered in scale and configuration. Increases in scale were reflected both in centralization and in the emergence of competing foci of power. As new external supplies were tapped, major shifts in arterial flows could occur, which brought new centers to prominence and isolated old ones. New transport technologies could also alter the balance of advantage between land and water transport, and since sailing vessels could cope with increasingly bulky cargoes, maritime transport privileged certain coastal areas. All these processes were capable of producing rapid alterations in the wealth of particular regions, and such shifts in the topology of the system were probably more important than cyclical phenomena in explaining ups and downs in prosperity.

The spread of urban trading networks, and their extension along the Persian Gulf and eastern Mediterranean, created a complex molecular structure of regional foci so that as well as the zonation of core and periphery (originally created around Mesopotamia) there was a series of interacting civilizations: Mesopotamia, Egypt, the Indus valley; then also Syria, central Anatolia (Hittites) and the Aegean (Minoans and Mycenaeans). Beyond this was a margin which included not only temperate areas such as Europe, but the dry steppe corridor of central Asia. This was truly a world system, even if it occupied only a restricted portion of the western Old World. Whilst each civilization emphasized its ideological autonomy, all were identifiably part of a 'common-world' of interacting components. In the eastern Old World, China had only indirect contacts with the complex of western Old World civilizations through their common margin, which now extended across the forest and forest-steppe belt of Eurasia. Nevertheless, important technological innovations passed between East and West in the Old World during the Bronze Age.

Aspects of bronze-casting metallurgy reached Europe, and chariotry reached China, across the steppes. Societies on the margin were also increasingly penetrated by long-distance trade. In Europe, the Danube formed a major axis of contacts from the Black Sea to the center of the continent, succeeded (as trade spread west along the Mediterranean) by contacts across the Alps as far north as Scandinavia. These carried precious materials over long distances, such as the small quantities of amber which reached Troy and Mycenae, and were even buried in the tomb of Tutankhamun. In mirror-image of these northern routes, tropical products such as incense and spices came to Egypt from Nubia and Somalia.

Great Basins: the Mediterranean, Indian Ocean, and Atlantic

Although divided into 'civilizations' and a multiplicity of polities, the growth of urban systems is a clear example of contagious expansion (corresponding to the 'calyx' model rather than the 'layer-cake'). The concentric structure of core, periphery and margin expanded simultaneously: the nuclear area (core and periphery) because of the dynamic of competition and import substitution, and the margin because innovations which spread beyond them created new cultural possibilities (as with wheeled vehicles on the steppes, or iron-working in Africa). The system was very sensitive to transport costs, so the urban core and its peripheral supply area expanded differentially along maritime sea-lanes and tributary rivers. The network of urban links expanded first along the length of the Mediterranean and Black Seas, opening peripheral hinterlands in temperate Europe and the steppes and semi-desert regions of eastern Europe and central Asia. By the end of the first millennium BCE, both the western and eastern Old World systems had grown to such an extent that their peripheries overlapped, and trade between the cores themselves became a significant factor, increasingly in amounts which gave the advantage to transport by sea.

While maritime expansion in the Mediterranean had begun in the Bronze Age, it was interrupted by a period of system-wide crisis at the end of the second millennium BCE, which coincided with the discovery and spread of ironworking in the east Mediterranean (Sherratt 1994). Fundamental technological and social changes produced a dissolution of old forms of political organization and the emergence of a new pattern with a block of territorial empires bordered by maritime city-states, which spread all round the Mediterranean. A new order of metropolitan cities (with more than 100,000 inhabitants) appeared at nodal points within this enlarging network, and such primate cities no longer had to sit in the middle of their breadbaskets. Maritime supply allowed them to be provisioned by sea. Slaves also became a commodity to be shifted over long distances to sustain industrial and agrarian production. New external connections began to exercise an important influence. The ancient road to the east, along which lapis lazuli had flowed from Afghanistan, took on a new importance in the second half of the first millennium as it extended over the Hindu Kush to the upper Indus, and continued to the Bay of Bengal. A new generation of Iron Age civilizations developed in India, centered in the Ganges valley. This axis developed first by extending further into central Asia, and second by being to some extent superseded by the maritime monsoon route between the Red Sea or Persian Gulf and India. As the overland trade route into central Asia from the west encountered the similar long-distance route supplying China from the east (the 'horse route'), the effect was to produce the first real-time contacts between the eastern and western Old Worlds: the Silk Route (Franck and Brownstone 1986). As the name implies, it transmitted oriental luxury goods from this tropical civilization to the west, paid for largely by the export of silver. The increase of economic activity where these routes entered western Asia (i.e. in Persia) balanced the expansion of trading along the Mediterranean, and created a latitudinal corridor of civilizations within which hegemonic control could shift suddenly between east and west: from Persia to Hellenistic Greece (which linked the east Mediterranean and Silk-Route terminus) and then to Rome (which unified the Mediterranean).

Political control of the principal arena of maritime activity allowed Rome to develop its extensive European hinterland, principally along coastal and river routes; but the relative underdevelopment and dispersed pattern of resources within this vast area necessitated unparalleled provision of military forces along its margins. This relatively primitive imperial structure nevertheless lasted for many centuries, but it was undermined by a combination of forces: the economic expansion of the Indian Ocean directed attention eastwards, while the growth of 'barbarian' political units increased pressure to the north. The combination of these factors led to incursions, as Germanic-speaking groups attempted to gain access to trading activity which was increasingly oriented to western Asia, symbolized by the shift of capital from Rome to Byzantium. For the next millennium, it was the Indian Ocean that was to be the principal arena of maritime activity, paralleled by (and to some extent alternating with) contacts along the Silk Route. A gravity model of interaction between the western and eastern Old World core/

periphery/margin systems, and their effective fusion into a single common-world, correctly predicts the internal shifts which each of them experienced, together with the shifting relative advantages of the two transport systems which linked them, by land and sea respectively. Andrew Bosworth's elegant description in this volume details the economic and political implications of this evolving topology of east–west links.

These routes gave renewed importance to precisely those areas where urban civilization had begun: Mesopotamia and Egypt. Baghdad and Cairo became the largest cities of their times. The western Old World nuclear region remained the heartland of an expanded system, now with the added advantage of being situated on the narrow isthmus separating the Mediterranean and Indian Oceans, Europe and Asia (Lombard 1975). Religious ideologies, and especially Islam, gave a cultural unity to areas of interaction too vast to remain under the control of a single territorial power. Agrarian intensification (Watson 1983) and technological advance had their locus in the central area of the expanded system, in the Islamic world of south-western Eurasia and in the coastal southern as opposed to northern China. The growth of Indian Ocean traffic (Chaudhuri 1985), in the three overlapping cycles of Southeast Asia, the Bay of Bengal and the Arabian Sea, provided the motor of hemispheric growth. Yet overland contacts remained important, and just as the Roman Empire gave rise to a barbarian hinterland in temperate Europe, so the activity in southern and central Asia stimulated political development on the steppe belt and adjacent montane and desert areas, to produce a succession of steppe empires, culminating in the Mongols (Abu-Lughod 1989). Ironically, it was the very integration of this corridor and surrounding areas (and imposition of the 'Pax Mongolica,' allowing individuals to traverse the entire route for the first time) which permitted the spread of the Black Death, Eurasia's first pandemic (McNeill 1976). The overland corridor never regained its prosperity.

The most fundamental change in the topology of inter-continental connections came about from the sixteenth century onwards, marking the decisive shift to long-distance maritime routes. The exploration of the Atlantic is conventionally ascribed to the blocking of Near Eastern trans-isthmian routes by the Ottoman Empire; but this 'push' factor must be balanced by the 'pull' factor of the growing maritime competence of the European Atlantic community. Fertilized by the maritime experience of the Mediterranean and the Baltic, and stimulated by riverine feeder routes which linked the Baltic to the northern Silk Route, the North Sea trading communities of the early medieval period found themselves in a modestly advantageous position. Although links to the Mediterranean were primarily overland to northern Italy, the Alpine obstacle limited the quantities of goods that could be carried in this way. There was every incentive to develop a coastal trade linking Europe's two inland seas along the Atlantic coast, and this maritime enterprise was promoted by the development of North Atlantic fishing and by the incentive to outflank land routes across the western Sahara by sailing down the west coast of Africa. The improved ocean-going vessels that resulted led first to the discovery of the Atlantic islands (Canaries, Madeiras and Azores), and then to the great clockwise wind systems of the northern and southern Atlantic (Crosby 1986). West Europeans erupted simultaneously into the Americas and into South and East Asia; completely altering the topology of interregional connections. During the crisis years of the seventeenth century, the European center of gravity shifted from Venice to northern Italy to Amsterdam and the North Sea Basin, which now became Europe's point of articulation with the outside world (de Vries 1984). From being on the edge of a Eurasian system, western Europe suddenly occupied its center. Areas now bypassed diminished in importance, until the Ottoman Empire became the 'sick man of Europe.'

It is impossible (though some economic historians manage to do so) to divorce the economic history of modern Europe – the 'genesis of capitalism' and the Industrial Revolution – from this enlarged setting of economic activity (Blaut 1993) and the local zonation of productive activities to which it gave rise within Europe (Wallerstein 1974a; Nitz 1993). In the perspective of millennial growth adopted here, the concentration of added-value production and its associated technologies has always been most marked at the nodal points of interregional connections and the center of the system. The incorporation of all three core/periphery/margin structures into a single global system gave a unique advantage to the European maritime nations at the center of the new pattern, who reorganized the world to their advantage. The European 'Middle Ages' thus separated two phases during which the European continent rose to prominence because of its centrality: the 'Ancient,' Mediterranean-centered world, and the 'Modern,' Atlantic-centered world – down to the new middle ages which face the Atlantic world as centrality shifts to a new and larger arena of maritime activity, the Pacific.

Some regularities

This chapter has described the development of human societies in terms of evolving, long-term structures, undergoing successive transformations and acquiring new properties. These transformations have taken the form of contagious processes. They may be characterized in hierarchical terms (Figure 5.1) as processes of increasing specificity, from center/edge through nuclear/margin to core/periphery/margin systems. Successive phenomena are clearly related, and each generation of dispersals – farming, urbanism, industrialization, each 5,000 years apart – was nested within its predecessor. Farming and urbanism began within the same set of three or four nuclear regions, though industrialization began in a new central region (Wallerstein's core) which emerged rapidly. In this sense, the 'Modern' world does have a different regional focus and new properties of scale from its predecessors, though it is not fundamentally different in its motivations.

Each subsequent advance was predicated on an earlier set of changes: the dispersal of modern humans in the case of farming; the existence of agrarian populations in the case of urbanization; the existence of a city network in the case of industrialization. These nested structures were manifested geographically as a

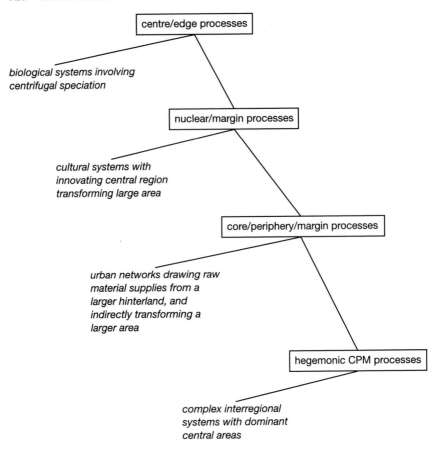

Figure 5.1 Processes of increasing specificity.

Note: Evolutionary processes with the property of centricity: a hierarchical classification. Successive subtypes are increasingly specific in their characteristics. The two uppermost levels involve contagious spread ('diffusion') processes; the two lower ones are characterized by real-time interaction. Such processes are typically nested one within another (e.g. the successive spread of modern humans, farming, urbanization and imperialism from the Mediterranean). Only the last type corresponds to Wallerstein's definition of a world-system.

set of concentric zones. The existence of a margin was a precondition for an extension of the periphery and thus of the core itself: communities which were already mobilizing useful commodities could be 'tapped' by centrally placed societies with the advantage of superior technologies and concentrations of capital. Because of this set of spatial and temporal dependencies, the analysis of 'world systems' cannot begin at any arbitrary point in the sequence, but is always faced with the problem of infinite regress. That is why an archaeological perspective is essential.

The genesis of urban systems introduced new properties into the process.

Specific routes became more important than the spread of innovations across broad fronts. Trading contacts became highly directional. Growth in the quantity of goods traded caused a general shift from land to water transport. Rivers were always important, especially in the creation of urbanism, but sea routes frequently succeeded overland routes and caused recession in the bypassed areas. Major phases of prosperity and population growth have occurred during periods of interaction around the successively larger seas of the Mediterranean, the Indian Ocean and the Atlantic, and perhaps in the future the Pacific. Indeed, the global demographic cycles identified by McEvedy and Jones (1978:343–51), ('primary,' 'medieval' and 'modernization'), can be seen as reflections of these basic geo-economic structures. At this level of abstraction, world history appears highly deterministic, in a way summarized in Figure 5.2. Cyclical upturns and downturns within this pattern (Figure 5.3) may also be related to further discontinuities encountered by expanding spatial processes. This vision of a world with a highly constrained set of macro-structures but great freedom at the level of micro-structures is one which accords well with descriptions of the world offered by complexity theory.

There is a clear zonality to the processes of contagious spread associated with urbanization, which have been crudely characterized here in terms of core, periphery and margin.[9] These must always be relative terms, for the new properties

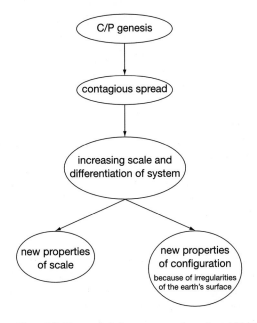

Figure 5.2 Deterministic representation of world history.

Note: The growth and transformation of a world system. As a core-periphery (C/P) area spreads, it acquires both new properties of scale (e.g. demographic mass, potential for capital concentration, etc.), and a new shape as it extends differentially over 'real space.' Either of these may cause discontinuities.

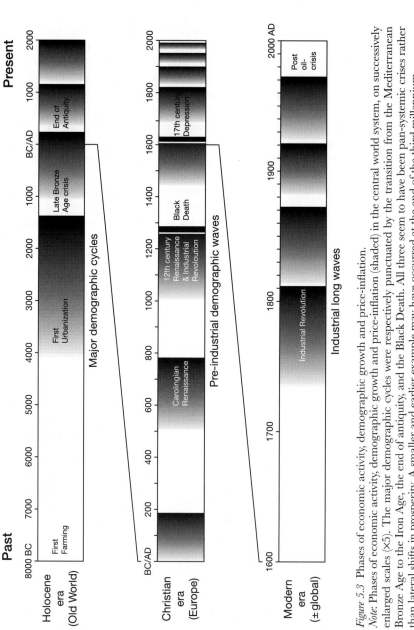

Figure 5.3 Phases of economic activity, demographic growth and price-inflation.

Note: Phases of economic activity, demographic growth and price-inflation (shaded) in the central world system, on successively enlarged scales (×5). The major demographic cycles were respectively punctuated by the transition from the Mediterranean Bronze Age to the Iron Age, the end of antiquity, and the Black Death. All three seem to have been pan-systemic crises rather than lateral shifts in prosperity. A smaller and earlier example may have occurred at the end of the third millennium.

which have appeared have altered the nature of development in each, while preserving the tripartite zonal character. Crude estimates of the relative sizes of each of these zones in successive periods (Figure 5.4) suggest that they grew more or less in ratio, though the margin reached finite limits and was increasingly eaten up by the other two. Nevertheless large parts of sub-Saharan Africa remained marginal (in this terminology) down to the nineteenth century, and the term remains a useful one until the final phase of colonialism. It is especially useful as a reminder that most of the societies described in the ethnographic record (and often, therefore, used to construct neoevolutionary, stadial narratives of change), were in large part creations of the same global processes as those which produced the literate societies whose past is recognized as history (Wolf 1982). The way of life of arctic Inuit or East African pastoralists was alike made possible by innovations that stemmed from urban cores. Similarly, the barbarians who have from time to time erupted into history must likewise be situated within the interactions of core and periphery, even though the process has been chronicled only by one side. Such incursions have often been caused by local recession and lateral shifts in hegemony within the core, often as a result of new long-distance supply routes. The histories of all human societies are more intertwined, and at a more fundamental level, than conventional accounts allow.

This contribution has stressed the importance both of antecedent conditions and of geographical realities in understanding the character of social change. It is not intended to supplant other, richer and more subtle genres of history and anthropology, dealing with events and structures on a human scale: indeed, it specifically acknowledges their priority, in insisting on the culturally constructed nature of consumption and the definition of value. In many ways it is the most

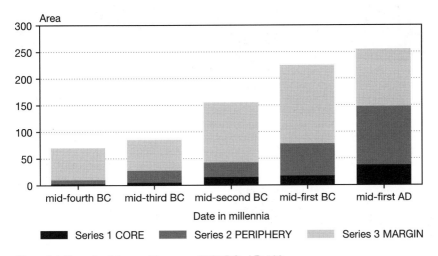

Figure 5.4 Growth of the world system, 3500 BC–AD 500.
Note: The relative sizes of the central world system and the proportions of core, periphery and margin at millennial intervals from the genesis of the system down to the end of antiquity. Core and periphery expand in tandem, increasingly absorbing the margin.

tedious and reductive form of narrative, important only because it is largely unrecognized as a coherent scale of analysis; but it is one which may nevertheless illuminate and articulate more vivid accounts of the human past. In a world in which histories are often partial and identities largely in flux, this level of description and analysis may offer some element of common orientation for different cultures and traditions.

Notes

1 The hyphen indicates an adjectival usage, not a sectarian affiliation.
2 Notable exceptions include Wolf (1982), Ekholm and Friedman (e.g. 1982).
3 Important exceptions include Vance (1970) and Blaut (1993).
4 Jacobs (1969/1984) is an excellent example.
5 Bücher versus Meyer; Weber and Hasebroek versus Rostovtzeff.
6 e.g. state-centralization, Keynesian, interventionist, welfare-state, public ownership, community responsibility, comprehensive education versus de-centralized, (Milton) Friedmanite, privatizing, individualist, Reagan–Thatcherite, etc.
7 The Near East (western Asia) has successively given rise to: behaviorally modern humans (Upper Palaeolithic), farming (Neolithic revolution), copper metallurgy, animal traction (secondary products revolution), the first cities (Urban revolution), the first empires, the first maritime states, iron metallurgy, the first metropolitan cities, and three of the major world religions. Yet in spite of this, diffusionism has for the last half-century been vilified as an interpretative framework! This argues for a very strong ideological influence in determining acceptable topics of discourse.
8 The key to this concept is the definition of added value. Value in general is a socially imposed desirability, and as such is culturally specific. There is no absolute, external standard. Rational Choice Theory cannot explain Calvin Klein underpants. Certain common features arise from the common behavioral propensities of modern humans: a delight in bright reflective materials, in methods of adorning the body, in pleasure-giving (and often psychotropic) consumables. Since humans are intensely competitive, these things must also be in short supply, so that their possession and consumption may be limited to a minority, and act as tokens of success. Besides the inherent properties of certain materials, there are also the properties conferred on materials by skilled labor. The combination of these properties has traditionally yielded the highest value, as in a finely wrought gold cup or a royal robe. Both the inherent and the added value are, however, arbitrary, in that they embody conferred meanings. With the growth of technological sophistication, there has been a long-term shift from 'primary' to 'added' value as the principal determinant of 'wealth.'
9 Other systems of nomenclature, such as those describing economic or power structures within urban networks (e.g. Wallerstein's original 'core' and 'periphery'), have described a further level of differentiation, and it may be confusing to use the same terms in different senses. The zonality described here is the most fundamental, and it may be preferable to elaborate other terms (e.g. hegemony) for the complex and rapidly changing patterns of global dominance.

6 Concretizing the continuity argument in global systems analysis

Jonathan Friedman

Probing the concrete structures of global systems

In the mid-1970s when we suggested that there were important similarities in the properties of world systems, we were met by a barrage of disbelief. This was a reflex of the times. It was not the reaction of the cultural relativists as such, but of a generation that cultivated the difference between 'the West and the Rest,' on the chasm separating modern capitalism from precapitalist societies. The idea that there was similarity, much less continuity, between the ancient and modern world systems, was considered not only false but also reactionary. Since then things have changed, especially among those who have worked extensively within the world systemic framework. Frank and Gills (1993, this volume) have recently argued for a continuity in the world system in which the major changes are geographical centers of accumulation rather than the basic structures. Chase-Dunn and Hall (1997, this volume) and others have argued that there are different world systems that can be compared with respect to a number of common variables. Frank and Gills have concentrated on what I would call commercial civilizations while Chase-Dunn and Hall have incorporated kinship based and other non-commercial systems in their analysis. Our own argument is in one respect closer to Frank and Gills insofar as we see a strong systemic continuity in world systemic history. But we also recognize that there are important structural transformations as well, even if the latter do not change the basic parameters of the system. The kind of analysis we have used is similar to that of the recent work of Arrighi (1994). The analysis of Hong Kong as a kind of Genoa of East Asia and Singapore as a kind of Venice conveys important insights into the state of the contemporary world. It focuses on differences within similarities in order to highlight precisely those issues that can be linked to the relation between systemic continuity and historical specificity. Below I offer two examples where an argument can be made for continuity where it has been systematically denied in standard discussions.

One area that has been inadequately discussed concerns similarities in economic organization. While Frank and Gills have argued for world system continuity, they have concentrated on far more abstract phenomena such as cycles of expansion and contraction. But there is more that can be said. There is source material concerning the organization of ownership, control over labor and the production process that allows a more concrete description of the actual structures of the Classical Greek economy. Phenomena related to class and ethnicity can also be elicited in varying degrees from several of the early periods.

The structures of the 'ancient' economy

In an earlier discussion (Ekholm and Friedman 1982) we suggested that much of the debate concerning the ancient economy, whether modernist versus primitivist or formalist versus substantivist, was based on a reductionist understanding of capitalism. While Weber at least tried to argue for the existence of an ancient capitalism different in character from the modern, reconciling the primitivism of Bücher (1893) with the modernism of Meyer (1910), this is not the case with the later discussions especially the total dismissal by Finley (1973) of the work of historians such as Rostovtzeff (1926, 1941). The original discussion concerned the degree to which the ancient economy was based on the self-sufficient household rather than a more integrated market. Weber argued that the household was clearly a central element in the economy of the ancient world but that there were also vast developments of a capitalist type, from commercial production to banking and international trade. He claimed that capitalism of a certain kind flourished and was even dominant in certain periods of antiquity, which he defines as including most of Old World civilizations up to the end of the Roman Empire. While insisting that some forms of production such as the *ergasterion* approached capitalist production, there were basic differences between ancient capitalism as a whole and the capitalism of today. The former he characterized as political and rentier capitalism as opposed to the modern entrepreneurial form based on rational production for the market using wage labor. While some historians such as Rostovtzeff and Frank have gone as far as to argue for the existence of large-scale industrial enterprise, there is stronger evidence for a number of smaller workshops that produced for the market. Now even real capitalists existed in Mediterranean Antiquity, but they were marginal: 'Capitalist entrepreneurs, not to be confused with gentlemen rentiers, generally enjoyed only a rather precarious social position in antiquity' (Finley 1973:43). Ancient capitalism was based on rent-taking, on tax farming, speculation, the hiring out of slaves and their sale, with phenomena such as Greek *ergasteria* and Roman *latifundia* as mere tendencies toward modern capitalism.

The differentiation of capitalism into different species is based on a model which includes many elements but is dependent on a static characterization of an ideal type nature. The capitalist is the defining specificity of capitalism. Rent-takers are not true capitalists in this argument and thus we can more fully understand the interpretation of the relation between capitalism and the Protestant ethic. The view offered here is not based on personal motivation, but on the structured conditions of existence of economic reproduction. Such conditions include a situation in which there is a commercialized world in which many important objects are commodities, in which social reproduction is dependent upon commercial transactions. Whether or not one is a true capitalist is not the issue. Marx, for example, made much of the contradictory combination within the capitalist process of fictitious versus real accumulation of capital. Modern, or perhaps, postmodern capitalism is based on rent-taking rather than real production for profit. It is estimated that world financial markets, increasing at a logarithmic rate, may be triple the size of the GDPs of the world's richest states by 2000. Does this mean that we have entered a new system, that we have gone beyond capitalism or returned to ancient capitalism? To assume that the goal of capitalists is production is an easily falsifiable proposition. In the logic of capitalist reproduction what is crucial is the transformation of money into more money and the reason for this is that the conditions of capitalist reproduction depend on the existence of credit which is the starting point of capitalist accumulation. This does not mean that there are not vast differences between the real organization of social reproductive processes in the various historical and geographical loci of Antiquity, but that there are a number of structural conditions that are at issue and not the motives of the actors involved. Dutch development of industrial textile manufacture was very much based on household production, and Donald Trump's motives are closer to the patrician than the 'true Protestant capitalist.'

The post-Polanyi generation has been more ideological in their treatment of this subject. They tend to claim that it is simply wrong, even absurd, to speak of capitalism in any other than the modern world. Love, in an interesting critique, argues that 'taxation and payment of rents in kind became far more important than market exchange as the means of wealth accumulation as Rome's economy expanded' (Love 1991:64). But there is a serious problem with the argument:

> But the question remains as to how such rents and income could have been accumulated *outside* market processes . . . There seems to be no way the bulk of the income derived directly from slave-worked *latifundia* could be valorized under the conditions obtaining in Roman times apart from market exchange.
> (Love 1991:65)

His discussion of Finley's analysis of the rationality of Roman large-scale agriculture is also important. Finley tries to demonstrate the non-capitalist nature of the Roman economy by concentrating on what he conceives as the basically non- · economic and irrational methods of calculation involved. He insists on the 'very large non-economic element in the preference . . . Investment in land in short was never in Antiquity a matter of systematic, calculated policy' (Finley 1973:116–17). Cato's discourse on agricultural economics is accused of incompetence, as if this were proof of the non-existence of capitalism. Love replies that 'even though Cato's methods of cost accounting are rudimentary, his general approach is by no means lacking rationality from an economic point of view' (Love 1991:96).

The nature of the arguments against the so-called modernist position are quite astonishing. Aside from the clearly ideological opposition involved there is a strongly reductionist characterization of the issue. This may be partly the result of the misapprehension of capitalism itself, its translation into a state of mind, a cultural essence. This seems to seriously hamper ordinary scientific discussion.

This can be illustrated by the famous issue of the so-called 'world market' for Roman terra-cotta lamps and its demise. Rostovtzeff's model of the expansion and contraction of the Roman economy is more advanced than it is often made out to be. It is one that shows the way in which central production and export centers are out-competed by their own market zones as the latter resort to import substitution. This has become a major issue in the discussion of world systems dynamics, the rise of East Asian economies, the product cycle. Roztovtzeff argued that the factories of northern Italy achieved something close to a monopoly of such lamps or at least that they were exported throughout the Mediterranean and that this monopoly was lost in the second century because the lamps were increasingly produced locally throughout the larger region. Harris (1979) argues that the evidence does not confirm this thesis although he supports the evidence for the cycle of expansion and contraction. He states this on the grounds that Italian production was not more productive, and that transport costs ought to have made such widespread trade uneconomical. The lamps might have been forgeries, but the evidence of a 'shipwreck in the Galearics which contained a hundred Bild-lampen under the mark C. Clodius' (Love 1991:126) contradicts this very weak argument which criticizes the original thesis on the grounds that it didn't have to happen that way (even if it did). This kind of argument is clearly influenced by a more general ideological positioning.

My conclusion here is that the treatment of capitalism in the critique is a reductionist position in which capitalism is a kind of behavior rather than a set of objective structures that establish conditions within which strategies can be formed. It is in this sense that one can argue for the existence of a capitalist Antiquity. Because the conditions of existence in these societies were dependent upon the control of abstract wealth which was converted into more wealth by tax farming, speculation, trade and, less often than in the contemporary world, production.

Greek capitalism

In order to illustrate the above argument I have chosen to use a well known 'modernist' historian of the Ancient World and to model some of his material into an argument for continuity. While it might be retorted that one should be using more recent material, there is to my knowledge little that can be added empirically to either refute or support this material. Indeed, some of the most recent and quite cautious discussions are most insistent on the commercial nature of the Greek economy by the fifth century BC (Descat 1995).

There is substantial evidence that Classical Attica was a heavily capitalized central place for manufacturing and commerce. By the sixth century there were permanent workshops in pottery, cheap metal goods and leather goods. These shops replaced the former household-based production that dominated previously. The pottery industry was divided into two sorts of work, pot making and pot painting. The potters were generally owners while the painters were wandering artisans who sought employment. The potters were citizens of Attica while the painters were either *metics* or slaves. Master potters were often quite wealthy. The workshops increased in size throughout the century reaching ten to twenty painters per shop, usually slaves. Production was essentially Athenian while export was controlled by Ionians. In the fifth century there is increasing differentiation of labor and forms of production. There were still independent craftsmen, small workshops and large *ergasteria*. Employment could be either full or part time.

Weaving is another activity that was freed from the domestic (feminine) sphere. There was specialized production of cheap clothes for slaves as well as production of very expensive goods. 'The population of Megara earned most of their income by producing cheap clothing for slaves' (Heichelheim 1958:99). Domestic production still accounted for most domestic clothing, but there was a movement toward market specialization.

The largest *ergasteria* of the period were those connected to the leather trade and their main source of demand was the military. The structure of production and payment is revealing of the capitalized nature of the production process which is organized as a putting-out system. Thus an *ergasteria* owner would hire a *hegemon* or supervisor who in turn might take on ten slaves all of whom were separate earners. On average the slaves got two *obols* a day and the hegemon got three. But the entire process was based on the sale of products by the producers, i.e. the slaves. The 'wage' was thus a deduction from the total earnings which were paid up the hierarchy from slaves to the owner. The structure is illustrated in Figure 6.1.

As can be seen here, the process of reproduction is entirely dependent upon the circulation of liquid income. Even slaves are not slaves in the meaning culled from the plantation variety in which owners do not pay independent wages but simply supply those goods necessary for the reproduction of the work force. Here the slaves were independent producers and sellers of their products and they kept a portion of the proceeds for themselves. That portion was predetermined by the owner of capital and was thus similar in most respects to a wage. This seems to be the main form of productive organization in Athens from the fifth century on. There are, however, interesting variations on this that demonstrate the extremes to which commoditization could be taken. In the silver mining industry some labor was contract but most was slave. The latter were either owned directly or

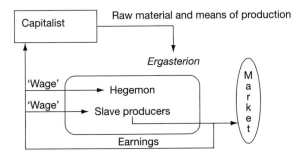

Figure 6.1. Greek capitalist structure.

rented to a third party. This arrangement was referred to as *apophora*. A mining contractor would both lease mines from the state (the sole owner of mines), and labor from private slave owners. The organization was similar to the above in the sense that the slaves were independent operators who paid their contractors and owners rather than being paid by them. Slave rental was a large and lucrative sector in this period. Some of the more wealthy senators could lease out up to one thousand slaves. Here my use of the word 'capitalist' in Figure 6.1 might be contested, since this is not the model industrial entrepreneur, and the activity is closer to the putting-out model of the preindustrial period. And even if the production process itself took place in extensions of domestic units, what is important here is the fact that it occurs within the matrix of the circulation of liquid capital. It is as such a commercialized process. The fact that slaves are rented out and that they function as independent operators who pay a rent themselves to their owners, that they themselves may rent their own slaves in the same or other activities does not contradict the existence of capitalism but, on the contrary, is evidence of an intensively capitalized social reality. Slavery is not opposed to the market but entirely enmeshed in commercial activities. And slaveowners can be seen as the major employers of the era just as *Manpower* has become the largest American employer in this period of increasing dominance of 'rent-seeking' financial capital.

There is evidence of a credit market as well as substantial speculation in Classical Athens, which reinforces the idea that money could be used as capital. This, of course, supports Weber's understanding of ancient capitalism. Aristotle reporting about Thales of Miletus in the sixth century:

> Thales used his knowledge of the weather to discover one winter that a rich oil harvest would follow that year. So he bought up all the oil mills in Miletus and Chios for very little and obtained a large profit by fixing the price for milling during harvest time, an early capitalist monopolist.
>
> (Heichelheim 1958:102)

Among the other industries of scale reported, besides pottery, are brick making, terra-cotta figurines, wood-, ivory- and stone-working, and lamps. There were dockers, shipwrights, wagon-builders, wheel-wrights, yoke-, cabinet- and coffin-makers. There were also charcoal burners and pitch producers in the forests. Demosthenes is said to have had twenty slaves in furniture workshops and thirty slaves in knife and sword production. These are described well enough to be able to understand their economic structure:

Furniture workshop:
    Twenty slaves at a cost of 200 drachmas each = 4,000 drachmas
    Income = 1,200 drachmas/year = 1 obol/man/day

The work was organized by fixed production quotas:

Cutlery workshop:
  Twenty-two to thirty-three slaves at about 500–600 drachmas each = about
  18,000 drachmas
  Income = about 3,000 drachmas/year

These workshops did not usually outlast the lives of their owners. Capital was personal for the most part, especially in the workshop sector. This argues against the establishment of abstract corporate structures that outlived those actually engaged in them.

Land ownership was a central aspect of the political and to a lesser extent the economic structure of Attica. Unlike Sparta, Thessaly and Sicily where aristocrats were large estate owners, Attica was characterized by small holdings. But it is noteworthy that by the start of the fourth century 25 per cent of the citizens did not own land and there was a development of large estates, mostly olive plantations (some with a thousand or more slaves) but also vineyards worked by a mixture of slave and free labor on the basic *ergasteria* model. Heichelheim (1958) suggests that this change is due to the commercial accumulation in the economy which leads to a distortion in land ownership. A certain Phenippos purchased more than 390 hectares which he put into the production of barley and wine. He had seven slaves, six donkeys and two spans of oxen, eighty-six ploughed fields, ten vineyards and 294 fruit trees. His investment was 215,000 drachmas. His gross income was 31,700 drachmas per year and it is estimated that his profit was nine and one half per cent. Even agriculture, then, is capitalized in this period.

Attica's most famous economic sector was silver, although there were other products such as mercury, cinnabar, ocher and lead. There were between 3,000 and 5,000 workers in this sector. The mining districts were state owned but were let out to citizens and *metics*. There were two forms of rent: a flat percentage of the proceeds, or joint venture operations with contractors. At the time of Themistocles the income from the leases totaled approximately 100 talents which was divided among the citizens, but later earmarked for construction of warships and, after 483 for other state requirements. Contracts were for three years and a twenty-fourth share of the yields of new fields also went to the state. In this area large fortunes were amassed, up to 200 talents (Heichelheim 1958:119).

The history of class structure in Attica as well as the later development of Rome display important similarities with respect to dynamics of commercial capitalism. In Attica as in Rome a former division between a state class of patricians who control much of the land and a large class of free small holders leads to a struggle in which the state is separated from the upper class and turned into a more general representative organ of the whole society, and politics intervenes directly in problems of wealth and land distribution. But the structure of upper class including large landowners and capitalists, a middle class of medium land holders and a class of poor and landless remains the general structure of these societies. Much of this is reminiscent of descriptions of early modern and modern Western industrial societies. Colonies were founded systematically with the 'Intention of bringing poorer classes of Rome to medium wealth which was the main aim of contemporary Athenian democracy also' (Heichelheim 1958:123). There was even a middle class ideal in the classical period and this class was very active in politics.

Population categories and the State

The Athenian polity had a clear sense of its own identity and a rather strong internal control over the well-being of its population, but this population was restricted to its own members, its citizens. There is a free population of foreign non-citizens from as early as the seventh century.

> This class took over much of the business in the economic sectors of trade, banking, commerce and craftsmanship wherever the local *polis* citizens were not sufficiently numerous to make competition with them unprofitable.
>
> (Heichelheim 1958:126)

The social status of this group increased from the sixth to the fifth centuries. The general term for them all was *katoikountes* and included several categories. The *metekoi* or *metics* refers only to those foreigners who had won the right to permanent settlement and thus had a legal position in the *polis*. This was achieved by paying the *metoikion* tax. The *isoteles* were an even more privileged group who had the right to buy land in Attica. To this group can be added other common freemen and ex-slaves. They formed 70 to 80 per cent of the free population dealing with trade, banking and crafts (Heichelheim 1958:127). If there was a division of occupations it can be described as follows:

Oikountes:	Agriculturalists	Katoikountes:	Trade
	Capitalists		Banking
	Mine Owners		Crafts
	State Officials		Intellectual Services
	Members of the Military		

'Only primary production, agriculture, mining, and all *polis* jobs were as a rule, protected by the *polis* . . . against intruding non-citizens' (Heichelheim 1958:127).

By the fifth century citizens were becoming a dwindling portion of the work force. This was the result of the influx of slaves. At the end of the fifth century building records at Erechtheum reveal that only twenty out of seventy-one workers were citizens (French 1964:147).

State financing is interesting in the *polis*. There is no internal income or property tax. Taxes are primarily indirect: customs, sales tax, transport tax and a tax on weights. These taxes primarily affected the *metic* professions. Instead there was the system of 'voluntary' gifts or *liturgies*. These were divided up into the following:

1 *Sitesis* – a contribution to grain and flour provisioning
2 *Choregia* – payment for seats in the Theater
3 *Gymnasiarchiai* – contributions for gymnasium festivals and expenses

4   *Lampadarchia* – contributions to torch races
5   *Hiera periodos* – payments for religious processions

There were also exceptional *liturgies*:

1   *Trierarchia* – large contributions to warship construction
2   *Proeisphora* – large contributions to public construction in Athens

Liturgy was no mere potlatch. It was required, and rich citizens were expected to bear most of the burden. The backside of generosity was the *antidosis*. 'A citizen not willing to pay liturgy had to make his property at the disposal of any citizens willing to take over and pay the liturgy' (Heichelheim 1958:135).

State finances were an enormous problem in the later period when the Athenian League was at war. Other mechanisms used were external tribute, loans from non-citizens, from foreign states or from temples. Compulsory loans from citizens were also a possibility. Most of this activity has the character of fund raising. There were special taxes levied during the Peloponnesian War and special contributions could be demanded for specific purposes. This structure is in sharp contrast to the empires to the east, but gradually a centralized system of state financing emerged first with Cimon and Demosthenes and was firmly established by the Hellenistic regimes. 'Before Alexander's time the fiscal monopoly was obviously made use of only as an occasional way out to cover deficits in the budgets of the classical *polis*' (Heichelheim 1958:142).

The welfare function, however limited, of the state exists throughout this era and is present in Athens as well as in Rome. Pericles gave jobs to the poor in state building projects and windfall profits from the mines were also distributed downward. Rome, of course, is famous for inventing the dole, subsidized food prices and free meals. These practices were much criticized and discussed as well.

The effects of long cyclical change

In the general model of the commercialized global system, there is a cyclical process leading from a highly productive center in expansion, with relatively low costs of reproduction, to a gradual reversal in which the center loses its competitive edge as a result of its own success and its social effects. The Classical Greek economy also demonstrates the typical cyclical problems of capitalism, rising prices and costs of living, the export of capital and decreasing trade advantages. From the sixth to the fourth century prices were up, interest was down and wages were stable to lower, while in Mesopotamia everything went up. In the fourth century Greece became more expensive than its surroundings. Buying power decreased from 414 to 336 by 400 per cent. In the fifth century the minimum wage at Attica was 2 *obols* per day and for steady work, 120 drachmas per year. Consumption was as follows:

Grain food – 20 drachmas per year

Other foods – 20 drachmas per year
Clothing – 10 drachmas per year

This left seventy drachmas over in ideal conditions of full-time work and is equal to a half year of employment. It was not uncommon for laborers to buy slaves with this money. But in the fourth century there was an increase in the number of *polis*, 'all too independent and small *polis* units for Greece' (Heichel-heim 1958:34), and the power of Attica declined. The minimum wage by this time was 180 drachmas per year but costs had increased:

Grain food – 45 drachmas per year
Other food – 45 drachmas per year
Clothing – 30 drachmas per year

This led to a decline in living standards, a freeing of slaves to obtain interest, and emigration/colonization, and it continued through the Hellenistic period. The famous Attic pottery was meeting heavy competition from the Black Sea. 'Not long ago the elder members of the upper classes abandoned the luxury of wearing linen garments and binding their hair in a bun held together with a golden clasp' (Thucydides in Will *et al.* 1961:159).

There is then evidence that there are similar kinds of processes at work in historical world systems. While the structures of capitalist reproduction were not identical to those of the modern capitalist world, they clearly belong to the same family of structures. And it might well be argued that they were subject to similar laws of accumulation of wealth, of crisis and decline.

Continuities in modes of cultural identification

Another area in which there are significant parallels between different eras of world system development concerns cultural identity. It has often been assumed that the kinds of ethnic integration and multiculturalism that are so ardently discussed today date from the emergence of the modern nation-state. A broader comparative approach reveals that this is not at all the case. While the modern nation-state may indeed be a historically specific kind of cultural organization, there is evidence of similar tendencies in the city states of the past. And while multiethnic empires may have been common in the past, the structures involved have their parallels in modern imperial structures as well. I am, however, not taking a universalist position, that ethnicity is the same throughout history and the world over. On the contrary there are funda-mentally different ways of organizing membership in culturally defined cat-egories in different social orders (Friedman 1994:34). The argument here is that commercial civilizations tend to produce similar modes of identification so that the historical continuity of the forms of ethnicity and multiethnicity are products of the nature of commercial world systems themselves. In order to grasp the kinds of phenomena that I wish to compare I shall focus first on cultural processes in the modern world system and then argue for historical parallels.

Multiethnicity in history

The argument that multiethnic societies have been the rule rather than the exception in history (McNeill 1986) is, of course, true, but this is because the history of the world has been the history of empires and segmentary states, and such social organizations, however multiethnic, were also ethnic *hierarchies*. It is, perhaps, the latter aspect of such societies that is the secret of their relative ethnic peace (Horowitz 1985). Significant, from our point of view, is that multiethnicity is a phenomenon that emerges and disappears and not merely a type of organization. Thus, the emergence of the Hellenistic empires was a movement from a city-state national ideology to a cosmopolitan and multiethnic ideology. The same transformation characterizes the movement from the Roman Republic to the Empire and it is clearly reflected in a whole series of changes. The emergence of the Cynics provided an entire discourse, interestingly postmodern in character, for this shift.

> disavowing all social institutions, including marriage and property. They recognized only the world as a socially relevant fact. And in the world all men were equal – whether rich or poor, Greek or barbarian, citizen or foreigner. However, since the Cynics surmised that most men were also fools, and therefore incapable of using their freedom and equality to full individual advantage, they had to conclude that only the wise could actually be cosmopolites and make the world their city.
>
> (Bozeman 1994:103)

The Ciceronian system of education based on the cultivation of Roman virtues was transformed by the time of Augustus to one more accommodating of the empire, in which all were to be citizens of Rome and where there was even a growing fear of the foreigners to which we shall return below. As communities that practice homogeneity expand into empires they also move toward a hierarchical heterogeneity. But as the latter begins to decline, the heterogeneity begins to assert itself as a political force. This takes us to the central theme of this discussion, the relation between cycles of expansion and contraction in global hegemonies and the forms of transnational or trans-state relations.

Global processes and equifinality

All of these variations, and even discontinuities, in the way in which populations can be integrated, in the way cultural differences are maintained, does not necessarily help us in accounting for the issues outlined in the title of this chapter. Part of the reason for this is that they pertain primarily to the global systemic and as such are products of a dominant commercial and urban organized central zone. While there may be vastly different forms of cultural integration in the peripheries of such situations, we have limited ourselves here to the commercialized central zones themselves. Global processes can, as we shall argue here, produce similar kinds of effects because they are of a more general nature than those of particular cultural organizations. It is for this reason that we use the verbal forms below rather than nominal forms, accentuating the processural rather than the structural aspects of the phenomena under consideration. There is no transnationalization without nation-states, it might be argued, or at least with some comparatively interesting type of organization, such as the city states and empires which date back to antiquity. But trans-polity phenomena and even social relations are comparable phenomena of a certain level of generality. Ethnification is a more serious issue, for while it may be organized in different terms, i.e. segmentary and inclusive vs. essentialist and exclusive, the practice of identification and differentiation can lead to similar violent outcomes. However, it might also be argued that it is logical for essentialization to accompany ethnification no matter what the social and cultural conditions. The claim that ethnicity is a product of modernity is only true if by ethnicity we mean a form of cultural identity that is *basically* essentialist, homogenizing and exclusive in all conditions including peace. The idea that the individual is an X because he contains the substance (blood) of X may well be typically modern, but it is also the case that stereo-typification in conditions of conflict is practically universal (Lévi-Strauss 1952). Disorder is, of course, a universal, along with many of the forms that it takes such as social fragmentation, individual crisis, new collective identifications, and what we have referred to as ethnification. When a social arena becomes disordered by crisis, its particular reactions vary as a result of its variable constitution. Among the tribal and chiefly societies of highland Burma and Assam a series of phenomena are unleashed by crisis (often endogenously generated), including headhunting, witchcraft, the appearance of were-tigers, anti-fertility–anti-chiefly movements and revolts. Such phenomena may invert the entire workings of former expansive societies in astonishing ways (Friedman 1979/1998). Phenomena such as 'cargo cults' and witchcraft epidemics (Ekholm-Friedman 1993) are widespread reactions to crisis in societies organized primarily by kinship. But cannibalism and ethnic and 'tribal' warfare are also very common and often related to the above. Now while these are surely quite specific local forms of action, there is plenty of evidence to suggest that they are not so specific as has usually been assumed. Societies in crisis are often societies in which people 'cannibalize' one another in various ways, in which hate and fear rampage through the arenas of daily life and sow the seeds for violent conflict. So rather than argue for the existence of entirely different phenomena I would rather suggest that there are interesting family resemblances at work.

The social, political and cultural parameters of decline

The decline of hegemonic zones is accompanied by a general process of regional economic decline, increasing stratification, sociocultural fragmentation, mass migration and a general increase in social disorder. It should be stressed here that disorder is not limited to the central zones themselves, but may be especially severe in those dependent peripheries that are not the targets of outward moving capital. Thus, most of Africa, parts of western and Central Asia are among the most unstable. The collapse of the Soviet empire has produced the same kind of extreme and violent disorder. It is also accompanied, as we said by increasing globalization, not just in economic terms but also in terms of the formation of global elites and elite global consciousness. I suggest how these factors are connected in a systematic way in Figure 6.2.

Disorder and fragmentation

The following discussion is based on modern conditions and is only then developed backwards in time. It is meant to suggest certain possibilities of comparative analysis rather than being their result.

The decentralization of capital accumulation creates disorder in abandoned areas. This in its turn leads to downward mobility and the economic crisis generates serious identity problems. The decline of modernism is closely related to the impossibility of maintaining a future orientation based on the liberation from the past, from tradition and an investment in the new, in change and both personal

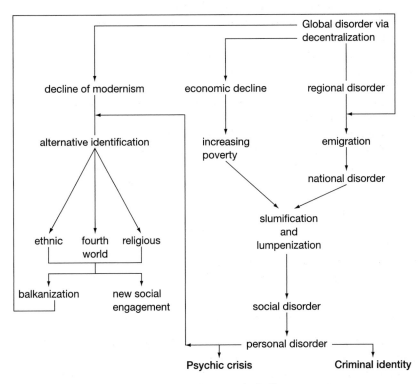

Figure 6.2 The process of disordering in hegemonic decline.

and social development. In this decline, there is a turn to roots, to ethnicity and other collective identities, whether ethnic or religious that replace the vacuum left by a receding modernist identity. This re-rooting is the resonating base of cultural politics and political fragmentation that spread throughout the hegemonic center. This takes the following forms:

Indigenization   Where there are indigenous populations within the state territories, these begin to reinstate their traditions and to claim their indigenous rights. The fourth world movements have become a global phenomenon, institutionalized via United Nations organs such as the World Council of Indigenous Peoples. The demography of this phenomenon is significant. The population of North American Indians more than doubled from 1970 to 1980. Most of this was re-identification. Five new tribes appeared during the same period.

Nationalization   The nation-states of Europe have become increasingly ethnic over the past fifteen years, moving from a formal citizenship/modernist identity to one based on historicized roots. This has been documented via the rapid increase in consumption of historical literature. In France, the Middle Ages, the Celts and everything that preceded the modern state were highest on the list from the late 1970s on. Much of this has an indigenous quality to it, especially where there is no competition from other indigenous populations. The so-called 'New Right' movements in France, Italy and Germany harbor ideologies that are similar to fourth world ideologies. They are anti-universalist, anti-imperialist, against universal religions and exceedingly multiculturalist. Thus Jean de Benoist, spokesman for the French New Right states,

> Given this situation, we see reasons for hope only in the affirmation of collective singularities, the spiritual re-appropriation of heritages, the clear awareness of roots and specific cultures . . . We are counting on the breakup of the singular model, whether this occurs in the rebirth of regional languages, the affirmation of ethnic minorities or in phenomena as diverse as decolonization . . . [whether in the] affirmation of being black, the political pluralism of Third World countries, the rebirth of a Latin American civilization, the resurgence of an Islamic culture etc.
>
> (cited in Piccone 1994)

Regionalism   Sub-national regions have been on the rise since the mid-1970s. After several decades during which it was assumed that assimilation was the general solution to ethnic problems, when social scientists calculated how many generations it would take for ethnic minority groups to disappear into larger national populations, the 1970s came as a surprise to many (Esman 1977). The weakening of the national projects of Europe became increasingly evident, Scotland, Cornwall, Brittany, Occitania, Catalonia, today supplemented by the Lega Nord and a European-wide lobby organization for the advancement of the interests of a Europe of Regions rather than nation-states. In the former empire to the east, the break-up of larger units is rampant and violent in Central Asia and southern Europe.

Immigrant ethnification   The optimism with respect to regional identities in Europe was identical to assimilationist/integrationist predictions with regard to immigrant minorities, especially in the United States. What seemed to be a trend toward integration was broken and reversed in the late 1960s when multiethnicity of Black and then Red power movements were supported at both grass roots and elite levels (the Ford Foundation was heavily involved in ethnic community local control projects). Today this has become a major state interventionist project in many Western countries at the same time as identity politics has led to what some have called 'culture wars' in which the very unity of the nation-state, its very existence is questioned. The question of the diasporization process is simply the ethnification of transnational connections, so that communication, social relations and economics become organized and even institutionalized across boundaries rather than immigrant groups becoming transformed into separate minorities. Diasporization is simply the ethnification of the immigration process. It is unlike other processes of fragmentation because it structures itself in global terms, being both subnational and transnational.

The process of fragmentation has not been a particularly peaceful one. In 1993, for example, there were fifty-two major violent conflicts in the world in forty-two countries, the most severe conflicts being in Eastern Europe, Central Asia and Africa. Half of these conflicts had been under way for more than a decade (UNRISD 1995:15). This is very different than the previous decades of the Cold War when there was a simpler division and a much stronger degree of control in the world system.

> All but five of the twenty-three wars being fought in 1994 are based on communal rivalries and ethnic challenges to states. About three-quarters of the world's refugees, estimated at nearly 27 million people, are in flight from or have been displaced by these and other ethnic conflicts.
>
> (Gurr 1994:350)

Globalization, class and elite formation

Globalization in institutional terms entails the formation of international 'communities,' however loosely knit, that share common interests. There is an interesting, and still to be researched, connection between the larger transformation of the global system and the emergence of new cosmopolitan elites. The aspect of that transformation, which seems most interesting, is the increasing portion of the world economy that is collected in the form of public and private funds, primarily based on tax moneys from Western countries. UN organizations (especially UNESCO), EU funds and other similar organizations (primarily nationally based) form what might be called global pork barrels that finance institutions, consultancies, etc. that pay enormous tax-free salaries to globalized bureaucrats and consultants and which join in the ranks of other elites, those of the international media and culture industries (we might add international sports to this, i.e. the Olympic Committee). These elites are very different from former industrial capitalist elites, not least because many of them are not owners of production but are what might be called 'pork barrel' elites. Robert Reich's (1992) characterization of this new class as 'symbolic analysts' who in Lasch's words 'live in a world of abstract concepts and symbols, ranging from stock market quotations to the images produced by Hollywood and Madison Avenue.' In Lasch's terms, 'They have more in common with their counterparts in Brussels or Hong Kong than with the masses of Americans not yet plugged into the network of global communications' (Lasch 1995:35). This is still an emergent phenomenon. In economic terms it might be part of a general shift of capital from productive to unproductive investment, to the general increase in fictitious accumulation in the old cores of the world system.

What is interesting here is that there seem to be a relatively coherent identity that has emerged in these elites. It combines a rather self-assured and superior cosmopolitanism with a model of hybridity, border-crossing and multiculturalism (even if there is much inconsistency in this). The cosmopolitanism of the elite is not modernistic, it is not devoid of cultural identification. On the contrary, it is postmodernist in its attempt to encompass the world's cultures in its own self-definition. This elitism distances itself from 'the people' who represent 'the national,' the unsophisticated, the 'racist,' and expresses loyalty to humanity rather than to its own fellow citizens, or if to its own citizens, to immigrants above nationals. This is a particular cultural structure of cosmopolitanism that has numerous historical parallels. Most recently the Free Masons harbored a similar cultural identity (Knight 1985; van der Pijl 1998). The urban upper middle class has become one of the principal focal points of this development. Sennett's 1970 *The Uses of Disorder* is an important discussion of this cosmopolitan multiculturality. The urbane, cosmopolitan and multicultural is well expressed in CNN's advertising. One well-known advertisement shows a series of images: an Australian Aborigine, a Tuareg nomad, several northern Europeans, Asians all to a nostalgic theme. All are part of the larger humanity of the CNN family. What is interesting about Sennett, as about CNN, is the normative aspect of their representations. The cosmopolitan multicultural world is a model of how things ought to be and it is part of a concerted struggle against the reactionary rural, and essentialist-nationalist 'people.' Similarly the wave of discourses on cultural hybridity (Garcia Canclini 1995; S. Hall 1996; Gilroy 1993) consist of the analysis of cultural elites and their discourses. World music may be taken up as an example of hybridization, but in spite of the name of this popular genre, a closer examination reveals that it is a metropolitan product and that it is a media industry creation rather than a street phenomenon. In other words, it can be argued that the ideology of hybridity is primarily an elitist discourse in a world that is otherwise engaged in the opposite; the drawing of boundaries to be defended, not just from land or region to land and region but from street to street. Hybridization and balkanization are two simultaneous processes of the global shift in hegemony.

The question of cultural continuity in global systems

Can the above discussion be linked backward in time? I have suggested that there are numerous general characteristics of global systems that ought to be expressed in the historical material. Taking the question of hegemonic shift as a situational type discussed at the start of this chapter we can offer the following parallels:

Ethnification In both the Hellenistic decline and the Roman decline there is an increase in ethnic and religious identification. This is complicated by the fact that the cycles of growth and decline are different in Ancient and Modern world systems. The Hellenistic expansion was part of the decline of the civilization of the city-state system. Athens and the other cities declined economically and politically, having exported a large part of its total production (producers = capital), and the emergence of Macedon (perhaps the first nation-state), led to a rapid expansion into the Middle East and Central Asia, colonization and the formation of a Greek elite diaspora that imported its goods as well as its culture in the form of Greek academies, the *Paidaiea*, and maintained a strong diasporic elite identity for the most part, at least at the start of the expansion period. Later on this dominance weakened and the Greek colonists were replaced by what appears to be a local class who practiced a kind of *mestizo* or hybrid identity. These were the so-called Hellenists who led the differentiation of the Greek expansion into a number of separate 'provinces' more or less autonomous and where the hybridization created new local traditions. They were a class who,

> in varying degrees, lived a life that straddled these two cultures and in many ways constituted the bridge between them . . . Whereas the native populations in the Near East identified themselves mainly with their traditional heritages (hence Ptolemy was regarded as a Pharaoh), and the Greek stratum identified mostly with the Greek tradition (viewing Ptolemy as a Macedonian, or a Greek god such as Dionysus), the Hellenists created something between these two worlds. Their ideas of the state were thus a mixture of eastern and western concepts of statehood and nationality. For them the Hellenistic king was neither a Greek institution nor an eastern one. They lived in a world of religious syncretism and attempted to find the equivalents for Greek gods in the various pantheons available in the ancient Near East. Thus Toth became Hermes, Osiris became Dionysus, and Melkart, Hercules. In Egypt this group was even associated with the worship of a completely new Hellenistic deity called Serapis.
>
> (Mendels 1992:22)

Now these hybridizing classes may have more in common with the rising classes in Western colonial regimes than with a postmodern phenomenon, as I have suggested. But then, it is here that we may find the continuity between the colonial and the 'postcolonial,' as the latter is expressed in the current cultural studies literature. Here we should not, of course, expect exact parallels, but the similarities may indeed be due to certain common historical structural processes. The hybrid ideologies of the present owe much to and are in dialogue with *mestizo* and similar identities in the late-colonial and 'postcolonial' world. The Hellenistic expansion produced similar processes of identification, but it is not clear in the material I have seen whether the colonial and postcolonial are related in the same way. One aspect of this relation can be found in the cosmopolitan identity of the Macedonian rulers and their successors. In the expansion period itself there was a great emphasis placed in Greek ideals, the establishment of academies:

> The Greeks, for the sake of making civilization meaningful to the majority, had clung to the polis as the cornerstone of their political existence, in the conviction that any greater political community would not adequately contain the kind of life that they had found to be most worth living.
>
> (Bozeman 1994:101)

But the formation of the Hellenistic world was the formation of a highly stratified existence in which only the elite participated in the new cosmopolitan culture and where the ideal of social unity had all but disappeared.

> The disparity between cultural and political developments in the Hellenistic Age resulted partly because the common culture, with all its glittering attractiveness, had not – in its historically most decisive period – actually reached sufficient depth in human consciousness. It was consequently unable to generate the moral forces necessary to restrain war and support peace and unity. Indeed, wars were fought more bitterly and treaties broken more frequently than during any previous period of world history. This international society was perhaps further prevented from developing the moral strength that would have enabled it to survive because it was socially divided. While theoretically accessible to individuals from all civilizations and races, the culture in all its cosmopolitan richness, was in practice open and meaningful only to the educated: the men who spoke Greek, and who liked to live the urban life that Greek culture had so eloquently advertised.
>
> (Bozeman 1994:100–1)

The Cynic philosophers, as other schools such as Epicureans that emerge in this period, have been described in terms of a reaction to the failure of the city state as a political and moral institution. The Cynics, especially, might be compared to postmodernists in their combination of cultural relativism and elitist cosmopolitanism. What is significant is that the later Hellenistic elites were no longer Greek and that the Greek homeland was in continuous decline throughout the period. Rome is a clearer parallel. Here the export of capital begins explosively with the formation of empire. The civic 'national' culture of Rome is replaced by a cosmopolitan orientation. This transition, which affected a transformation in the Roman legal code, the concept of citizenry and the entire cultural edifice of the formerly hegemonic Roman world view is a clear expression of the disintegration of hegemonic position in an empire in which the decentralization of capital occurred from the very start.

> Italy's privileged position in the commonwealth over which Augustus had watched so jealously was thus gradually weakened. It was abolished by Hadrian (A.D. 117–137) – himself a provincial from Spain – who regarded the Empire as one indivisible state, rather than a conglomeration of *civitates*, and was therefore impatient with any national or local particularism, whether expressed in Jewish uprisings in Palestine or in Roman conceit in Italy. The development culminated in 212 with Caracalla's promulgation of the *Constitutio Antonia*, under the terms of which all freeborn inhabitants of the Empire were granted Roman citizenship.
>
> (Bozeman 1994:179)

It is this kind of transformation that was so much debated in the early years of the century, when Roman history was seen as a mirror of the contemporary world:

> The immediate result of this complete revolution in the relations of nationality was certainly far from pleasing. Italy swarmed with Greeks, Syrians, Phoenicians, Jews, Egyptians, while the provinces swarmed with Romans; sharply defined national peculiarities everywhere came into mutual contact, and were visibly worn off; it seemed as if nothing was to be left behind but the general impress of utilitarianism. What the Latin character gained in diffusion it lost in freshness; especially in Rome itself, where the middle class disappeared the soonest and most entirely, and nothing was left but the grandees and the beggars, both in an equal measure cosmopolitan.
>
> (Mommsen 1911)

But this is not merely a twentieth century interpretation of the ancient world. It is also present in the increasing xenophobia of the imperial period. Seneca writing to his mother says,

> Of this crowd the greater part have no country; from their own free towns and colonies, in a word, from the whole globe, they are congregated. Some are bought by ambition, some by the call of public duty, or by reason of some mission, others by luxury which seeks a harbor rich and commodious for vices, others by the eager pursuit of liberal studies, others by shows, etc.
>
> (In Frank 1916, cited in Kagan (ed.) 1992:47)

This is a Roman empire in which there is mass immigration, where according to some studies the population of the city is substantially more than 50 per cent of foreign extraction (Frank 1916 claims over 80 per cent), in which the literature is described as 'hybrid' (Rand 1975, vol 12:571). The decentralization of the Roman economy led eventually to the transformation of Rome into a capital of imperial consumption, but not production, to a series of financial crises and to the fragmentation of the empire itself.

Conclusion

My goal here has been to try and bring global systemic analysis down to more concrete situations and processes where the argument might be accessible in almost ethnographic terms. I have suggested, following the accumulated work of ancient historians and other interested scholars, that the organization of production and exchange can be interpreted in terms of relations that are not worlds apart from the modern world system. That slavery in Classical Greece is a complex affair involving wage, interest and profit in an elaborate market system that appears to have had cyclical properties of expansion and contraction. This was, in other words, a form of capitalism that is not so different than the more obvious varieties of the modern world. The purpose of exploring this example is to balance the tendency to relegate the discussion of continuity and discontinuity to categories such as city size over time and other population statistics, evidence of expansion and contraction etc. While these macro indicators are indeed important and interesting, the ultimate goal must be to link them to the dynamics of the systems involved, i.e. to processes of social reproduction that involve relations of exchange, production, exploitation, accumulation and power. These are all strategies and relations that are culturally specific as well, which is why I find it necessary to explore the more unusual cultural aspects of the system, the forms of social integration, relations of ethnicity and ethnification and the relation between cultural politics and political economic processes. In the latter examples I think it is possible to argue for continuity as well and, in spite of obvious differences, for a strong family resemblance in the dynamics of cultural identity.

7 On the evolution of global systems, part I: the Mesopotamian heartland

Kajsa Ekholm-Friedman

An obvious problem of today's global system is the lack of political control over the globalized economy. While identifying it as a problem, we certainly also realize that this lack of political control is exactly what has made the international economy so dynamic for thousands of years. The economy operates at the highest hierarchical level of the global system, knowing no boundaries, while political control is restricted to the lower levels. Attempts at establishing political order at the global level have not, so far, been very successful. The UN is composed of states with internal autonomy and has, therefore, very limited power for intervening.

It is relatively easy to distinguish the structure of a global system from above. It is composed of center–periphery relationships thereby embracing a number of societies, in different positions and of different types. A continuous evolution of the global system has taken place during the last 5,500 years. At the same time, decentralizations of industrial production and capital accumulation have produced recurrent regional shifts, accompanied by local collapses. As we usually study situations where the global system is already at work we are able to take certain processes and mechanisms as given. I shall in this chapter go back to the very early process of social evolution in southern Mesopotamia where we can follow the primary evolution of the state within the framework of an emerging global system. Here it is possible to study the transition from 'non-coercive' to 'coercive' power (cf. Clastres 1974), the establishment and transformation of hierarchical levels, the use and extension of *rhizomes* (structures that spread horizontally between political units), and perhaps the primary separation of economy and politics as well.

A systems theory model of hierarchical levels

The systems theory model presented by Barel (1973) is a useful point of departure. A social system is conceived as a hierarchy of levels in which some form of exchange must take place between them in order for the hierarchy to be maintained. Levels must be open, but only partially so, in order to maintain its specificity.

> il n'y a pas de hiérarchie sans échanges entre les niveaux hiérarchiques et ces échanges ne peuvent intervenir que si les niveaux sont partiellement

ouverts. Inversement, un niveau ou un système ne peut être *complètement* ouvert, sans perdre sa spécificité, c'est-à-dire sa qualité de niveau ou de système. ('there is no hierarchy without exchanges between the hierarchical levels, and these exchanges can only take place when the levels are partially open. Conversely, a level or a system cannot be *entirely* open without losing its specificity, that is, its quality as a level or a system.)

(Barel 1973:168)

This also suggests that the point where output/input takes place can be controlled and monopolized. Hierarchization is a reversible process. An external/horizontal relation can be transformed into an internal/vertical relation. There can also be dissolution and a return to the former pattern.

Before trying to apply this model to the process of social evolution in Mesopotamia during the period circa 4500–2000 BCE, I shall illustrate it with reference to Central African kingdoms of the Kongo type (Ekholm-Friedman 1972, 1977, 1985).

The Kongo system is a useful starting point as it represents the simplest form of a hierarchical, social system as represented by Barel. At the top of the pyramid there was a king with monopoly over external trade. Under him we find a political hierarchy of chiefs. The village chief gave tribute to the district chief, who in turn gave to the provincial governor, who gave to the king. In the opposite direction products were transferred from the top down, which makes tribute rather look like an exchange between territorial levels. Before the arrival of the Europeans at the end of the fifteenth century, there existed external exchange between social systems of this type, the nature of which we know almost nothing about since external trade after the contact was immediately redirected toward the Europeans. Central African kings realized the importance of their monopoly over external trade for their own superordinate position, and in the early literature we can see them worrying about the fact that the Europeans refused to respect it. When the Europeans bypassed the central power and began to trade directly with chiefs at lower territorial levels, the kingdoms accordingly disintegrated.

The case of West Central Africa illustrates that external/horizontal relations ('trade') are easily transformed into internal/vertical ('tribute'). Large kingdoms initially expanded when the inflow from the top increased due to the new trade with the Europeans. It was easy for a chief to accept the status as client. It was to his own advantage because of the transfer of resources to him from above. This strengthened his internal authority. Every local unit, at every territorial level, maintained its autonomy. The kingdoms themselves were composed of long chains of interrelated local groups, or units, with a minimum of *hierarchical press*, from higher to lower levels. In this type of social system the influence from the higher level is so weak it does not even look like a hierarchy or 'vertical structure.'

In a Kongo system the hierarchy is composed of kinship-organized basic units (in principle isomorphic) plus the network that binds them together. In this way the hierarchical levels are nothing but the chain of superordinate and subordinate basic units. Their structural interrelation is, in the folk model, represented as segmentation. In the beginning, says one of the origin myths, a group of people settled in the capital. The rest of the country was empty. The original inhabitants multiplied, and as a consequence of local overpopulation there was an out-migration, or decentralization, of 'sons' to the provinces, and from there to the districts, and so on (Ekholm-Friedman 1972). It is unlikely that the kingdom of Kongo originated 'from above.' The king came last and not first. Local groups were already there, implying the emergence of a hierarchical network via *matri-lineality*, *prestige goods* and *external exchange*.

A resourceful group took wives, by bridewealth in the form of prestige goods, from client groups which thereby were transformed into 'son-groups' through avuncolocal residence. At a certain age, sons were transferred to their mother's brothers in the wife-giving groups (Ekholm-Friedman 1972, 1977). This created homogeneity with respect to language and culture. However, no aristocracy appeared. There were tendencies in this direction, as sixteenth and seventeenth century documents note that the king sent his own men to the provinces as governors. This may be interpreted as an embryo of class distinction. The process was, however, interrupted when the area was increasingly involved in slave trade and the larger political units disintegrated.

The pyramid is, in fact, nothing but a geographical surface, and its base is an open field for expansion from above. It would be more correctly represented if it was collapsed so the top is placed at the same level as the base. In this way one sees that 'hierarchical' relations rather imply horizontal alliance. The relationship between super- and subordinate group is strikingly egalitarian. The lower levels maintain much of their internal autonomy. As noted, the relationship implies exchange and resembles trade much more than tribute. The provincial governors even received more prestige goods at the king's court than he brought with him when he handed over the so-called tribute. It is in the very logic of the system that all chiefs are interested in finding their own patron, e.g. attaching themselves to someone with even greater resources. In doing so their own power is not under-mined, but strengthened both internally and relative to their subordinates in the hierarchy.

From outside it might be reasonable to question the pyramidal form, but it is unambiguously supported in the cosmology. According to precolonial religion, life-force must come to the individual from above, e.g. outside. At the highest level and furthest back in time, at maximum distance from man, there is God – as Ancestor or as a kind of Big Bang. At lower levels, closer to man, there are ancestors of various *dignities*, and at the point where the divine world enters the earthly world, the king is situated, God's representative on earth. Between the king and *Ego* there is finally a hierarchy of political/territorial chiefs, and at the bottom, Father just above *Ego* (Ekholm-Friedman 1991:145–57).

Mesopotamia: the land between the two rivers

The word 'Mesopotamia' means 'between the rivers' and refers to the land between the rivers Euphrates and Tigris, the main part of it is in today's Iraq.

The alluvial plain of southern Mesopotamia is divided into a southern-most part, known as Sumer in the third millennium, and Akkad in its northern part. Northern Mesopotamia consists of the lands east and west of the Tigris further to the north. The time interval covered here is from about 5000 to 2200 BCE, when a major crisis occurred in the area. This period is usually divided as follows:

Ubaid (4500–3500 BCE)
Uruk (3500–3000 BCE)
Early Dynastic (3000–2350 BCE)
The Akkadian empire (2350–2200 BCE)

The first two periods have traditionally been defined according to their pottery, making the temporal distinction irrelevant historically. There is a clear cultural continuity cross-cutting the periods, as well as structural breaks that do not coincide with this traditional division.

The process of social evolution in the area was by no means linear. There were disturbances at the end of Uruk, a major crisis occurred about 2200 BCE that affected a large region, including the eastern Mediterranean, Egypt and the Indus valley. In Mesopotamia the latter crisis resulted in an interruption of civilized life, where hardly any form of civil disorder was absent (Bell 1971:7). After a short period of 'anarchy and confusion' the area was invaded by a 'barbarian tribe from the Eastern mountains' (Westenholz 1979:113). A reorganization then took place about 2050 BCE with the establishment of The Third Dynasty of Ur.

Since writing did not appear until the Late Uruk period, our information about the Ubaid and most of the Uruk periods is limited to archaeological material. Archaeologists emphasize that the conditions for prehistoric investigations in the south are unfavorable due to heavy silting and a shifting pattern of lagoons and river courses (see Oates and Oates 1976:121). The first script was pictographic, on clay tablets, concerning mostly economic matters. By the very end of the fourth millennium pictograms also took on the sound value of words, an invention that made possible the identification of the language as Sumerian. From this point in time the area is called Sumer and its inhabitants Sumerians. The earliest texts come from the city of Uruk about 3100 BCE (Nissen 1986). The clear cultural continuity between Ubaid and Uruk (see Adams 1981:59) has been taken as an indication of the population being Sumerians even before Uruk. A frequently used example of this continuity is the clear resemblance between the temples at Eridu during the Ubaid and the Uruk periods. The Uruk temple is larger and more elaborate, but its general design is similar to the earlier one. The gradually higher temple-base in the later period was a result of building the new temple on the top of the old one.

Around 2350 BCE, Sumer was conquered by the Semitic-speaking north, under Sargon of Akkad, and was included in a short-lived empire. During the Akkadian period, royal officials used their own language to the exclusion of

Sumerian (Larsen 1979:78). This state of affairs was to some extent reversed in later Ur, when Sumerian was again the official language (Oates 1979:43). Around 1800 BCE Sumerian ceased to be spoken at all (Cooper 1973).

There are certain distinctive features, mainly due to ecological conditions, that remained more or less the same throughout. The southern part of the alluvium is a lowland with a nearly total lack of sufficient rainfall to ensure agricultural production. It was consistently dependent on irrigation for agriculture, a technique that was certainly introduced from outside. Irrigation farming existed in central Mesopotamia as early as 5500 BCE. The first farming settlements in the south appeared about 5000 BCE. With irrigation the river valleys provided exceptionally fertile agricultural land, enabling permanent settlement and a relatively high population density. Yields were high in relation to both land and labor inputs (Adams 1981:243). But irrigation was a tricky business. The rivers sometimes caused flooding, irrigation works could easily be damaged, they needed constant maintenance (Oates and Oates 1976:125), and the technique itself caused problems of salinization. Barley (Hordeum vulgare) and einkorn wheat (Triticum monococcum) were cultivated, and the later preference for barley can be explained by its greater resistance to salt (Algaze 1993:106; Huot 1989:26).

The presence of lagoons and marshes provided a rich and varied environment with an abundance of fish and birds. Marsh reeds were utilized as building material for huts and granaries, and the river clay for sickles, pots, plates, and jars. There is early evidence of date palm, 'without doubt one of the most useful plants known to man' (Oates and Oates 1976:121), flax, tamarisk and poplar (Hout 1989:26). Uruk texts testify to the importance of both sheep and goats, while cattle and pigs seem to have been of more importance during the Ubaid period (Hout 1989:27).

A frequently cited feature of the area is its lack of crucial raw materials. It had no metals, timber or stone. It was completely dependent on imports for many of its 'civilized' products. Its bronze metallurgy needed copper and tin and maybe even wood for fuel. The temples were mainly built of mud bricks, i.e. of local material, but to some extent of imported stone. Stone was also needed for a number of implements and for specific items, such as sculptures and cylinder seals (Larsen 1979:76).

In Sumer the monumental buildings were temples and associated administrative stuctures, not royal graves as in Egypt. The land in its entirety was conceived as belonging to a specific god, and the temple was his house. As the temples were usually built of mud-brick and not of more time-resistant stone, the remains bear, unfortunately, no resemblance to what was there in the past.

The location of the area within the larger region was certainly of great importance for its development. The two rivers, of which the Euphrates was the more navigable, were decisive communication links. Sailboats appeared at a very early time. Knapp (1988:45) notes that 'Rivers . . . and their tributaries served as trade and transport routes . . . Besides carrying imported commodities, the rivers provided for the movement of people, redistribution of goods and supplies, and transport of military contingents.' During early Ubaid, trade was mainly carried on with the north, and the area was thereby in the position as a somewhat disadvantaged hinterland. However, when trade contacts developed with central Iran and via the Persian Gulf (cf. Wright 1969:103), the area found itself in a central position within a wider regional exchange network.

When trying to understand the process of change from Ubaid until the crisis of 2200, it is essential to take both vertical and horizontal structures into account. A global system (Algaze 1993) emerged by the later half of the Uruk period, in which southern Mesopotamia occupied a position as core area. The Uruk system expanded geographically by colonization and by the establishment of control over important trade routes. Over time this global system underwent fundamental changes, as all global systems do, in both its horizontal structures and its core area. It is essential, even if it is not at all easy, to study how local/vertical processes are related to horizontal processes within the global system. The main difficulty lies in applying a holistic view, treating what happens as a unified process, in spite of the cognitive necessity of breaking it up into two different perspectives, which to some extent must be studied separately.

The hierarchization process

I shall in this section try to demonstrate that a structural change of crucial importance, the transition from a *one-level system* to a *two-level system*, occurred during Ubaid. This change provided the very basis for the cultural development that followed during Uruk.

The Ubaid period is, in both northern and southern Mesopotamia, character-ized by a homogeneous settlement pattern with small villages or hamlets scattered throughout the country. The sedentary communities were 'widely and fairly evenly dispersed sites' (Adams 1981:58; for the same pattern in the north, see Akkermans 1989:341, 349). The various Ubaid settlements also exhibit a 'remark-ably homogeneous material culture' (ibid.). The resemblance, including ceramics, burial practices and certain architectural features, suggest that close contacts existed among them. The small and dispersed sites found in northern and south-ern Mesopotamia were, in other words, linked to one another by networks of exchange. Among the widespread exchange items of the earliest period are obsid-ian, flint and bitumen. The south was the more marginalized hinterland within the regional exchange network.

The change came, however, in the south. Knapp (1988:42) notes that 'During the Ubaid period, modest farming villages began to grow into large population centers, and the temple or temple complex originated.' Some sites grew consider-ably larger. Even if most of them were still small as before, some of them were more than ten ha (Adams and Nissen 1972). The other significant feature men-tioned in the quotation above is the temple.

The first step in the process of change was the appearance of *a new form of centralization*. Instead of each local kin group managing its own businesses, a num-ber of different kin groups, probably fishermen as well as cultivators, established a *higher unity*, the function of which was cooperation and coordination to the benefit of all. This structural novelty, which emerged during the later part of Ubaid and was manifested in the appearance of the temple, showed a great potential for social evolution.

The early Ubaid social system consists of two structural elements; small local units plus an egalitarian exchange network linking them to one another. I shall call this structural form a one-level system in order to distinguish it from the two-level system that appeared later.

One-level system

The earliest Ubaid houses, mostly found in the north, are large-scale buildings where no distinction was made between domestic and sacred. At Tepe Gawra the earliest (tripartite) buildings have ovens or bins and were, as noted by Akkermans, 'intended in the first instance for living' (1989:343). There were other types of buildings as well, seemingly dedicated to serve special functions, as storage or stable. The same pattern has been reported from other excavated sites in central Iraq, e.g. Tell Abada (Jasim 1989) and Tell es-Sawwan (Margueron 1989).

The reason we know less about houses in the south is that domestic houses were constructed of perishable reed (Hole 1989:167). Ecological changes in this area have rendered prehistoric investigations exceptionally complicated. At Oueili, near Larsa, there is, however, evidence from early Ubaid of the same kind of large-scale construction found in the north. The houses exceed 200 square meters and have a 'complex multicellular plan' with evidence of communal functions (Huot 1989:32).

Some of the buildings from this period are rectangular with buttresses while others are of tripartite or bipartite design. The character of the houses reflects *an extended household economy*, centralized and coordinated but still within the borders of the local kin group, in no need of the kind of management and control that came later. The vast granaries (eighty square meters) found at Oueili 'suggests perhaps communal storage,' Hout says, and adds 'But this storage seems to func-tion without any particular means of management or control' (1989:39). This is centralization, in the form of 'communal storage,' but without the type of administration we associate with the later temple complex.

According to Akkermans (1989:349) all the settlements in northern Meso-potamia were rather small, most of them with only one or two houses. The largest, such as Tepe Gawra and Tell Adaba were not more than one ha, which would include fifty to one hundred inhabitants. Thus, in the earlier period each local unit was economically more or less autonomous, there was very little specialization, it had the form of an extended household, and the buildings had communal functions of various kinds besides being places to live.

It is worth noting that centralization existed before the temple complex. Meso-potamian agriculture, be it irrigated or not, necessitated storage and thereby a more extensive cooperation than what is found, for example, in modern West

Central African cultivation where each producer prefers to have his/her own fields controlling his/her own product. The 'communal storage' during early Ubaid may be seen as an embryo to the later *higher unity*.

True temples did not appear until the later part of Ubaid, earlier in the south than in the north. In both areas they were built according to the tripartite plan that evidently originated in the north where it was reserved exclusively for temples. In the south the earliest temple is the one at Eridu, which replaced an earlier structure consisting of a one-roomed rectangular building with interior buttresses. Opinions differ on whether the earlier structure was a true temple, or whether there was a break in the building tradition (Akkermans 1989:344f). It could as well has been a house of the type found at Oueili.

The new social system that emerged was composed of two hierarchical levels, a lower level of *local kin groups*, and a higher level represented by *the temple*. The difference between the two systems may not seem very significant. Earlier, central-ization and coordination among nuclear families belonging to one single local kin group, and now, centralization and coordination among several kin groups. But the change is crucial. As long as the point of centralization coincides with the power structure of the social group, it just underlines or preserves this structure, curbing the forces of change. What eventually alters the actual power structure is when a point of centralization is established 'outside' of the existing social groups.

Two-level system

The identified sites grew larger, and it is important to note that they only con-tained the sedentary part of the population. We should, with Adams, visualize around each center 'smaller, less sedentary groups who depended primarily on their herds or on fishing' (1981:59). There is no real evidence of these groups in the archaeological material. But we should also keep in mind that cattle and pigs predominated in Ubaid, not sheep and goats that are usually associated with herding. Herding became an important branch of the Sumerian economy only later. There are, in other words, reasons to question the role played by herdsmen in late Ubaid society. We know from the archaeological material in the north that cattle and pigs were kept in special buildings. In one such building at Abada in early Ubaid, a bitumen-lined basin has been found which was probably used to water domestic animals (Jasim 1989:83).

The new form of centralization was expressed in religious terms. As Gauchet (1977:33) demonstrated with material from contemporary primitive societies, humans tend to represent higher organizational units in religious terms, as an external point of reference. In Ubaid the political initiative must have come from below, from the power-holders at the local level, since the higher level originally was 'empty.' Their fusion in the form of a common religious center implies an alliance, aiming primarily at the maintenance of their own power and domin-ance. The relationship among the various subunits was egalitarian, which can be deduced from the lack of archaeological evidence for social stratification. David and Joan Oates relate the increasing settlement size of the period with 'an increasing need for some form of centralized control' and then remark that there is, surprisingly enough, yet no evidence for social stratification (1976:124f).

During the entire course of social evolution there are hierarchical levels in the form of a *higher unity*, devoid of any real political power, constituting more of an alliance between political power-holders at a lower level. In our contemporary world, the UN is a clear example of this type of *higher unity*. In order for a hierarchical level to take on political power, it must usually either *control external exchange or be opposed to an enemy* of the *same dignity*, or both. The world of today cannot be united politically since none of these mechanisms prevail. The only condition that could alter the situation is an encounter with aliens from outer space, cooperating with the global elites, or attacking the earth.

Social evolution often seems to take place in two steps with respect to hierarchical levels. First a *higher unity* in the form of a symbolic space is created, and then this 'empty' space can be filled with economic and political content. The process of change in southern Mesopotamia encompasses an early transformation of this type. From being nothing but a *higher unity* in the Ubaid period, this level becomes a real power center in the Uruk period. Interestingly enough, the *higher unity* does not thereby disappear. It reappears during both Uruk (Diakonoff 1973:186) and Early Dynastic, now among political units of a different kind, still as an elite strategy for maintaining power.

The temple originally represented cooperation and coordination among the various subunits in projects oriented both internally and externally. It played a decisive role in both external and internal exchange. In fact, these phenomena are aspects of one and the same system and must consequently be understood in the light of one another. We know that a point of centralization is easily transformed into something more substantial. When resources are channeled via a higher hierarchical level, it often leads to an elaboration within this special space. A rather peculiar example of this mechanism is found in modern African states where the inflow of resources from outside via the point of centralization has led to the emergence of super-wealthy state classes disconnected from the rest of the population. In ancient times the evolutionary potential of this structure was considerable. When a point of centralization was established 'above' existing social groups, it was beyond their reach and could gain enough autonomy to develop on its own. It then transformed the former power structure, giving rise to a new type of society. The possibilities lie in its capacity to use external flows for internal development.

Different forms of centralization

It is usually argued that the temple originally had only ceremonial functions. We know, however, that the temple was also a center for the collection and distribution of agricultural products, and that it was directly involved in food production. Waines (1987) points to the symbolic importance of bread as the distinctive feature of culture and civilization in medieval Iraq. The temples produced food 'for the gods whose care and feeding was a matter of daily concern' and '(a)mong the items deemed 'fit for the gods' was bread, baked in the temple ovens as special prayers were uttered at each stage of its preparation' (ibid.:259; ref. to Oppenheim 1954:191). The large quantities of fishbone found in the early temple at Eridu are interpreted as offerings (Oates 1979:124), but also as exchange. They point, according to Adams (1966:50) to 'a very early beginning of ritualized patterns of *either offerings or exchange* (emphasis added) in which at least the products of the specialized group of fishermen were made available to a considerably wider segment of the population.' There is no reason why we should expect a clear demarcation line between offerings to the gods and exchange among those involved. Cereal and fish constitute two of the most important export articles in later periods.

The temple was the god's home. It is easy to interpret the fact that it did not appear until later Ubaid as an indication of a true religious innovation, founded in a structural innovation. The city 'belonged' to the god in the sense that 'the focus of loyalty was the city,' says Joan Oates, then quoting Noah Kramer: 'People were identified as citizens of this or that city, and not with a clan or some other kin-related group' (1977:474). A god who owns the city does not belong to a kinship-organized society, as the one that preceded late Ubaid. In these types of societies the gods usually appear as ancestors, related to the living by blood and descent, in the same manner as the living are related among themselves. Here it is place and not descent that unites them. The god who owns the city belongs to a society where a *higher unity* is established among different, non-related groups of people. It is worth noting that no collections of fishbones (or anything similar) have been reported from the earlier Ubaid houses. Other categories of people were simply not involved.

When it comes to the political organization of late Ubaid, the 'primitive democracy' model suggested by Jacobsen (1957) is quite convincing, even though it is based on mythical material and can only be 'observed' with any certainty in later periods. According to this model there was a general assembly (*unken*, or 'circle of the people'), which in this context probably refers to all the free, adult men. This word occurs in the earliest texts (Oates and Oates 1976:135). There was also a more restricted group of elders, a 'council of elders.' The assembly elected among themselves an *en* ('a lord'), as a kind of chairman with administrative functions. It probably also elected a war-leader in periods of external conflict (Jacobsen 1957:103). Such a 'chairman of the assembly' is mentioned in the Uruk tablets circa 3100 BCE (Nissen 1986:328).

Jacobsen (1957:104) emphasizes the provisional nature of the assembly:

> Viewed as a whole the most characteristic element of the Primitive Democracy pattern is probably its provisional and ad-hoc character. It is called upon to function in emergencies only ... The assembly deals only with specific crisis for which it was called ... When that emergency had passed we must assume that the larger unity temporarily imposed on the community vanished with it and left the ordering of society to the numerous minor ... power structures.

The *higher unity* existed so far only as a form of cooperation and coordination among egalitarian kin groups for their common benefit. Their cooperation made them stronger than they would have been individually, externally as well as internally. The existence of a general assembly may be taken as an indication of rather egalitarian relationships within the kin groups and among free, adult men, but to the exclusion of women and unfree individuals. Initially the initiatives were entirely concentrated at the lower level and the *higher unity* seemed unequivocally to serve their common interests. However, in creating this form of centralization they let loose forces of change that soon were out of their control.

From higher unity to power center

During Uruk an amplification of the higher level took place, transforming it from an 'empty' *higher unity* into a power center, with a dominant class and its workers, and a surrounding community sector. Among the first expressions of this process are concentrations of high status goods within the temples (Knapp 1988:43). The temple grew increasingly larger and it took on both economic and political functions (Adams 1966:125). It became an encompassing organization where no distinction was made between the sacred and the secular or between political and economic activities (cf. Knapp 1988:69). It was a temple/state controlled economy, similar to modern socialism even if not so dominating. The state thus developed within the religious domain. The head of the temple had both religious and political authority. The separation between temple and palace, between 'church' and 'state,' came later, as did the separation between economy and polity.

The temple was now active and creative in a number of fields. It introduced and developed various crafts, organized agricultural production, specialized production in workshops, was in charge of storage and redistribution, and charted long-distance trading expeditions. It also managed irrigation and construction works. All the spectacular innovations of this era took place at the temple, including writing, keeping of accounts, plough, wheel, wheel-made pottery, cylinder seals, metallurgy and stone sculptures. The temple/state elite grew in size and power, usurping the functions of the lower level.

A new type of political unit emerged. A dramatic population increase occurred in both Sumer and the Susiana plain (Khuzistan) to the east, in today's Iran, which at the time was closely related to Sumer. This increase was mostly a result of the inflow of people from surrounding areas. Characteristic of the Uruk period was the clustered settlement pattern that diverged from the evenly dispersed sites in Ubaid. There is a gradual transformation from one to the other (Adams and Nissen 1972:11). Algaze describes Uruk as 'a small number of centralized cores in fierce competition,' even suggesting that the high level of conflict compelled them to form these enclaves (1993:115). The decentralized political organization of the area allowed the major sites to expand economically, giving rise to increasing competition, and likely confrontations, which eventually encouraged larger agglomerations. This picture belongs, however, to late Uruk when the general development in the area had put the various centers in 'fierce competition' with one another.

The political unit was now not only much larger but also of a very different form than the former two-level system with its 'empty' *higher unity*. The Uruk social system, found in both Sumer and the Susiana plain (see Johnson 1975), is described as a three- or four-tiered hierarchy: *cities, smaller towns, villages* and *hamlets*.

The Uruk system

The internal structure of the Uruk system has been efficiently analyzed by Johnson and Wright in a series of works (Johnson 1975; Wright and Johnson 1975:279). Their term 'local exchange' is very useful as it points to the intimate relationship between internal development and external trade. Johnson (1975:285) says explicitly that local exchange and trade are 'complementary processes' as 'long-range trade provides economic links between more or less independent settlement systems, local exchange provides similar linkage within individual systems.' This view of the combination of the two types of exchange reveals the rhizomic nature of what I have called 'vertical structure,' and offers a theoretical point of departure for the understanding of the relationship between a country's domestic economy and its export production. If the two structures are seen as complementary we may not fall into the trap of conceiving export production of minor importance just because it represents a small part of the economy as a whole. This is valid for societies in general, not just this particular area in the fourth millennium.

Johnson and Wright discuss this in terms of control hierarchy, or a hierarchy of information processing, and here they are close to the systems theory model suggested by Barel discussed earlier. The development at the temple level led to a pronounced differentiation between higher and lower levels, referring not only to the relationship between the city and the rural sector, but also to the relationship between the temple and an outer community sector within cities themselves. We must keep in mind that most of the townspeople were peasants. At the end of Uruk there was a rapid development of various types of craft production in temple workshops. In the previous period craft production was a dispersed activity. Johnson's consideration of the Susiana plain shows that craft production was now concentrated in workshops in the major settlements. We see a shift in ceramic production from 'small scattered shops to larger centralized shops' (Wright and Johnson 1975:279). Uruk ceramics are wheel-made, a technique that was invented in this area and in this period. Wheel-made ceramics were mass-produced and of superior artistic quality. Ceramic kilns have been found in the major settlements in Susiana (Middle Uruk), while 'there is no clear evidence of Uruk ceramic production at any other site in the area' (Johnson 1975:92). Something was evidently produced centrally and then distributed in mass-produced ceramic containers. Uruk pottery has been found over a very large area, an indication of Sumer's mass-production of export goods in this period. There was also a flow of other products (e.g. lithic) from large central workshops in Susiana to rural settlements (Johnson 1975:109,112).

In this process, a growing differentiation took place between the temple as such and the rest of the society, the community sector. The latter became increasingly dependent on the temple's goods and services. In exchange its members gave of their produce and labor. This new type of relationship is described as redistribution, exchange or symbiosis.

The Archaic texts of Uruk (circa 3100), the first of a series of texts, derive probably from a single large economic unit within the precinct of Eanna dedicated to the temple of the goddess Inanna (Nissen 1986:324). These texts constitute our main written source of knowledge about late Uruk society and economy. The somewhat later texts from Ur belong to the very end of Uruk or the beginning of the Early Dynastic period and can be considered as well. The texts reveal a strikingly hierarchical structure of various activities, which certainly contradicts the idea that late Uruk society would have maintained its earlier, more egalitarian spirit. In his analysis of the Uruk texts, Nissen (1986:329–30) claims that the sign *NAM* stands for 'the leader of the unit' of a given activity. If interpreted this way, there were leaders of 'the city,' 'law,' 'troops,' 'plow,' etc. The texts of Ur contain a picture of the military organization; 'a list of soldiers under sergeants (*ugula*) formed into a company (*un-sir-ra*) under colonels (*nu-banda*) one of which seems to be in supreme command' (Jacobsen 1957:107ff). There is also information on high-ranking officials, such as 'the chairman of the assembly' and different grades of priests.

Agriculture as well as fishing played a crucial role in the Uruk economy, in the form of export production to be sure, but also for internal consumption. Tyumenev (1973a:72) points to the fact that the earliest signs indicate bread-baking and brewing, which seems quite reasonable given the temple as the house of a god that needed constant feeding. The early texts also show herdsmen, hunting scenes, wild birds, and an 'abundance of pictographs of various fish testifies to the considerable role of fishing in the economy of the temple.'

As the temple complex grew larger, an increasing number of workers were employed cultivating land, in irrigation and construction, and in workshop activities. All these workers had to be fed. In one of the Uruk texts daily rations are listed of bread and beer for about fifty individuals. Another part mentions barley and fish. There is also archaeological evidence of these rations in the form of a widely dispersed, mass-produced container called 'beveled-rim bowl' that is supposed to have been a ration measure (Oates and Oates 1976:129f). Sumer could never have been a major exporter of food without advanced technology and craft production, in other words without its position as center in a global system. It has always needed the most advanced technology. In ancient times it also needed 'armies of laborers.'

Every peasant certainly owned his own tool, such as a spade, hoe and flint sickle (Crawford 1991/1997:45). But the more complicated means of production, such as plows, seed funnel and draught animals (oxen) were provided by the temple (Crawford 1991/1997:44). In the texts of Ur a 'House of the Ploughs' is mentioned (Tyumenev 1973b:74). A number of specialists are listed, such as carpenters, gardeners, cooks, bakers, coppersmiths, jewelers and potters (Nissen 1986:329; Tyumenev 1973b:74). Some of the crafts were organized in groups under the direction of a master craftsman. Copper production was carried out in Uruk, and there was a rapid increase in the amount of metal used at the end of the fourth millennium (Crawford 1991/1997:131). Harder alloys did not appear until the Early Dynastic period.

A large part of the Uruk texts deals with textiles (Nissen 1986:330). We know that early and throughout its history, Sumer was a great exporter of textiles. We have archaeological evidence for its trade with surrounding areas. There is, however, very little information in the Uruk texts referring to these foreign areas. When talking about Sumer's exports it must be kept in mind that there is no clear archaeological evidence and this lack of evidence is commonly interpreted as an indication of perishable export products as well as of perishable processing equipment (Crawford 1973:232). A way of trying to circumvent the problem is to look at later periods, assuming that Sumer exported about the same articles earlier. In this manner Algaze (1993:4) identifies the main export articles as *food*, such as cereal, dried and salted fish, oil, dates, and *industrial products*, such as textiles, leather work and in later times items of metal. Leemans (1960:114) emphasizes Mesopotamia's constant role as a producer of agricultural products, besides the production of 'industrial articles of relatively high value such as garments or articles of fine craftmanship' (Leemans 1960:115). This would be valid from Uruk until Ur III:

> Southern Mesopotamia itself was an agricultural and cattle-raising land which produced almost nothing else . . . As materials of exchange . . . the soil of southern Mesopotamia could only offer its agricultural produce such as barley, dates and sesame, or the products of cattle-raising such as butter, cheese and leather.
>
> (Leemans 1960:115)

These articles were exported in large quantities by boat north along the Euphrates and south via the Persian Gulf.

Who were the workers? There were a growing number of slaves in the economically expansive centers in the south. The population increase in the south was initially accompanied by depopulation and the abandonment of sites in surrounding areas, both in the north (Akkermans 1989:347) and to the east, (Lamborg-Karlovsky and Beale 1986:267). The temples seem to have held large numbers of slave-women, *gim*, as workers. In one of the Uruk tablets, 211 female slaves are recorded, denoted by an ideograph that is usually interpreted as 'woman from foreign mountainous country.' They were used in textile production and household activities. Female slaves are found in industrial textile production all over the Near East and eastern Mediterranean in ancient times. According to Tyumenev (1973b:73) there is no equivalent ideograph in the earliest tablets for male slaves, which, of course, does not necessarily mean that they did not exist.

Male slaves appear alongside female slaves on stone inscriptions from the end of Uruk. Chattel slaves in the form of war captives became increasingly important in the political economy of Mesopotamia in later periods (Gelb 1973), especially in large-scale irrigation and construction work. The temples could not have been built without 'armies of laborers.' It is estimated that the labor force required for the sub-structure of the Anu Ziggurat at Uruk was 7,500 man-years (Adams 1966:126). Among the workers were certainly also free and highly competent specialists, some of them from surrounding areas (cf. Kramer 1963:101). It seems probable that some of the foreign workers had to be bought or captured by force, while others may have come of their own accord.

'(I)t is towards the end of the "Uruk period" that the momentous change we have described takes place,' says Frankfort (1971:73), when discussing why it is not always useful to divide the process into Ubaid, Uruk and Early Dynastic. The most spectacular development thus seems to have taken place in late Uruk. But late Uruk embraced both an early phase of rapid development and a later phase characterized by contraction and crisis. The serious problems toward the end of Uruk appeared when Sumer's life-supporting trade network was shattered. The very end of Uruk is characterized by internal warfare and by the destruction and abandonment of sites.

War evidently played a significant role during Uruk. There are cylinder seals depicting battle scenes and fettered war captives (see Postgate 1994:241, 25; Adams 1981:63). But it is worth noting that no striking development took place in arms technology during Uruk. This came later, in the Early Dynastic period. The Uruk system was, as mentioned above, characterized by the autonomy of each major center. Even if trade and other forms of communication to some extent were effectuated between neighboring centers, they were essentially independent of one another. This means that each of them had the opportunity to encounter the surrounding world on its own, a situation that encouraged both external trade and warfare. There was a high degree of internal warfare in Susiana in late Uruk while the wars of the earlier period seem to have been primarily directed toward foreign areas (Johnson 1975:157). This pattern could be explained with the contraction of trade in late Uruk, a condition that must have led to aggravated conflicts between the various polities. In southern Mesopotamia, city walls were erected already at the end of Uruk, a clear expression of the fact that 'an epoch of wars had begun' (Diakonoff 1973:186).

External trade and warfare are decisive evolutionary dynamics. The combination of these structures gave rise to a new political strategy in southern Mesopotamia. It emerged in late Ubaid and Uruk, and was then fully developed during the Early Dynastic period. Elites belonging to a number of centers turned outwards, both toward external markets and neighboring competitors. In this process they involved themselves in a new kind of political game that was solely their own. They became the dominant actors while the rest of the population was gradually reduced to mere instruments. The state with its class structure was born. Expansion fueled by the energy generated by interstate conflicts is a mighty force in social evolution, and when conflicts of this type disappear, by the victory of one over another, or by the completion of the expansionist project, momentum is usually lost and vast empires may quickly disintegrate. Our experience as humans is somewhat odd on this point. When a satisfactory victory or level of freedom is finally reached, chaos is just around the corner.

This new political strategy made the production of weapons top priority, and from then on we have been caught in a constant and obsessive search for raw materials in order to feed the military complex. With the invention of bronze there was no return.

Toward part II

This chapter is the first half of a longer piece, to appear later. The second part deals with the evolution within the already formed city-state system itself whereas the first part deals with the emergence of this system from an earlier regional dynamic. The notion that the city-states did not emerge in a vacuum is a crucial aspect of the argument. The powerful states of Mesopotamia emerged within a larger regional organization which was the basis of city-state formation. The second part also deals extensively with the history of power relations, the differentiation of class relations, the separation of political and economic relations, the massive transformation of the labor force, the changes in representations of kinship and the emergence of imperial organization within the larger system of interregional exchange. A major aspect of this discussion concerns the spread of accumulative dynamics and productive structures from center to periphery over time, leading ultimately to shifting centers and pulsating empire formation.

8 State and economy in ancient Egypt

David Warburton

Humanity underwent three critical economic revolutions: the Neolithic agricultural revolution, the urban revolution and the industrial revolution. Although taking millennia, the Neolithic revolution was short by comparison with all previous developments in human history, and once it had taken hold, human life across the face of the earth had been changed so radically that one might be tempted to say that nothing similar has ever happened. The urban revolution which followed was dependent upon the sedentary form of life made possible by agriculture, and closely tied to state formation, and it in turn led to the creation of wealth incomparable to anything previously seen. It too has a claim to singularity. By comparison, the capitalist industrial revolution is a mere refinement of the trading habits which made the first cities preeminent.[1]

Prior to the industrial revolution, the study of economics was rudimentary and elementary principles were not consciously understood. Those studying the early period have had to overcome many difficulties before examining the period from an economic standpoint. States were undoubtedly economically significant in the early period, and the nature of the documentation preserved has tended to underline this. Scholars have tended to assume that the documentation reflects the ancient relationships, yet it does not necessarily follow that the public sector of ancient Near Eastern states was all-encompassing.

State formation accompanied the early urban revolution, but the role of the state in these developments is not well understood. Fiscal policy reflects state intervention in the economy, and may serve as a useful guide. It is argued here that ancient Egyptian fiscal policy did not involve enslaving the population to the service of the state, or signify merely an onerous system of corvée labor, but rather that the tax system and the construction of monumental architecture contributed significantly to the creation of wealth, employment, and economic growth, both private and public. Using Egyptian sources, Keynes' *General Theory* is employed to illustrate this.

Introducing Egyptian economics

While Egyptologists see scraps of papyrus as the most valuable objects in the world, evidence indicates that in New Kingdom Egypt a generous roll of papyrus cost about the same as a pair of ordinary sandals. In contrast to sandals, however, it does not appear to have been abundant. This implies either that sandals were expensive or papyrus cheap. Asserting that papyrus was cheap and yet scarce would suggest that demand and supply did not affect prices in the way we would expect them to. One of the leading experts on the economy – who explicitly denied that demand and supply influenced prices – asserted that papyrus was cheap but then concluded that it must have been abundant, unconsciously applying the law of supply and demand. Against the evidence, another denied that it was cheap, simply based on the assumption that since papyrus was reused – and thus obviously in demand – it must have been scarce and therefore that it must have been expensive. This indicates the degree to which unreflective conclusions have hitherto dominated the prevailing interpretations of the ancient Egyptian economy.

It is more profitable to explore what is known, which suggests that papyrus was at once scarce and cheap, which superficially appears to defy modern economics. In studying the ancient Egyptian economy, our object is alien to the Egyptian way of thought, since the Egyptians probably never realized that they had an economy, let alone tried to understand it. Understanding the economy is however of fundamental interest both intrinsically and because our unconscious economic thinking influences our interpretions, as evidenced above.

The father of the neoclassical synthesis, Marshall, maintained that economics studies the production and distribution of goods in an economy dominated by scarcity. Though not as important today, scarcity of goods was the primary feature of human experience since the emergence of the first hominids, and economic history is dominated by the fashion in which goods were distributed in any given society.

The largest and most important single economic entity in ancient Egypt was probably the state, and thus an examination of the fiscal policy – which represents state sponsored economic activity – may prove illuminating. Exploration of the demand which created resources in ancient Egypt is the central point of the present discussion. This reflects the fact that state activity is documented, but this state activity implies the existence of a private sector from which the surplus was acquired: it was not all produced as part of a command-economy.

Egyptian fiscal policy was based on: (1) grain (collected as 'taxes' or 'rent' and paid out as 'wages' or 'rations'), harvested on both (a) large plots belonging to king, the temples, the government and individuals and (b) small holdings; (2) governmental acquisition of labor and/or goods; and (3) exchange between private producers and official emissaries. We have no idea about the proportion of GNP consumed by government expenditures and income, nor the total GNP, so a sectoral breakdown is impossible.

The best documented of the state departments are the temples, but equally relevant is the picture of the countryside, with its hierarchical distribution of responsibility based upon exactions from the villages. While craftsmen were obliged to render services to the temples, it would appear that peasants were universally susceptible to corvée obligations, aside from the duty to render grain from their fields.

Most of our statistical information concerning wages and prices is drawn from the lives of the craftsmen civil servants at Deir el-Medineh who excavated and decorated the New Kingdom royal tombs (Janssen 1975). The materials from that village indicate a village mentality, although the residents were civil servants. The system of pricing was based on generally prevailing price levels, which is typical of peasant societies, where there is little room for real discussion. Prices were defined by the conventional rules of the economically rational market mechanism, either capitalist or precapitalist.

Economically, the distinction between the two worlds is one of scale rather than intent: the market always decides the prices, based on the principles of marginal utility analysis and other factors. In a modern economy, supply, demand and production costs as well as marketing strategies influence prices far more than they did – or could have – in ancient Egypt, yet the modern economic theory of price as reflecting the disutility of labor is the only appropriate system which can account for all varieties of price behavior in ancient Egypt and in the modern world. Disutility of labor merely implies that, for the purchaser, the price is equivalent to the toil and trouble of acquiring an object. The seller concludes that the price is sufficient to justify parting with an object. In the modern economy, time and competition affect the degree to which prices vary, while these factors may have been less significant in ancient Egypt where ordinary prices may not have been subject to much more than psychological pressures, and information about costs may have been either non-existent or difficult to acquire. These factors alone inhibit competition by discouraging entry into markets which are unfamiliar.

The craftsmen at Deir el-Medineh free-lanced and farmed in their free time, but officially they were civil servants paid by the state. It has been widely assumed that one key to understanding the economic system of ancient Egypt was the redistribution system, by means of which the workers in Deir el-Medineh were paid. The evidence indicates however that the state had considerable difficulties making regular wage payments to these civil servants, although they (1) are the only documented state employees paid on a regular long-term basis and (2) rarely numbered more than one hundred individuals.

It can thus be suggested that the principle of the system was basically the acquisition of the surplus, and that redistribution was generally carried out on an inefficient *ad hoc* basis. The private sector produced, people kept a portion of their production for themselves, and rendered a portion of their surplus or their labor time to the state authorities. The relative proportions cannot be clearly estimated, but acquisition is far better documented than redistribution. Avarice in acquiring objects and labor to ornament monuments – and to remunerate workers building them – generated the income. 'Redistribution' has been used to characterize ancient economies, and while the circulation of income as wages or as offerings at festivals did play a role, the term is misleading, as (1) it has a different ring than 'circulation,' and (2) it fails to grasp the essential economic significance of the origin of the surplus.

This surplus was created by taxation. Approaches emphasizing redistribution fail to recognize the fact that state intervention in the economy can hardly be attached to the inefficient system of expenditure, while neglecting the characteristic exactions: taxation. Just as there is a vast difference between the production of goods for the market with a view to making profits, and merely making profits by trading, there is a difference between creating wealth through taxation and acquiring wealth that already exists, although this can also be done through taxation. In ancient Egypt, it would appear that the government created wealth through taxation.

Markets

Before turning to the role of the government, it is worth noting the degree to which trading played its hitherto underestimated role in the economy. In ancient Egypt, it was absolutely essential that one's name be inscribed in all the proper spells and in all the proper places if one was to survive into eternity. The existence of Books of the Dead in which names were not filled out, and funerary figurines on which names are equally missing compels us to believe that there was production which was not intended for specific clients, i.e., production for the market. We also know that workers were remunerated for work for private individuals building tombs for themselves, and that they were paid in bread and beer, and obliged to go to the market to acquire by exchange the other articles they desired. State-employed workers also received 'rations' or 'wages.' Revenues collected in kind from fields and marshes across Egypt were turned over to the employees of the state: grain, fish, dates, firewood, pottery, etc. But even regularly employed civil servants pursued free-lance trading, and they likewise turned to the market for those things they did not receive from the state. Others may have been attached to state institutions, but acquired additional income from private trading. On the other hand, state sponsored trading missions exploited this market to circulate goods which the state had acquired, but did not require, exchanging them for goods which the state did not acquire through taxation. Individuals, civil servants and the state all participated in this market.

In the absence of a clearly defined market in which objects could be manufactured on the assumption that they would be purchased, entrepreneurial activity would be primarily oriented toward trade rather than production. As was illustrated with the seemingly anomalous price of papyrus, the inability to analyze production costs could explain some aspects of price formation. In this formative era, it was impossible to estimate the value of any given good or of labor. If traders acted on the principle of making a profit through the acquisition and sale of objects, or through hoarding in order to release products onto the market when they were scarce, this implies that they understood the effects of supply and demand, and that they would necessarily risk attracting the universal hatred of mankind as a result.

The significance of the market remains unclear, for the state appears to have been widely involved in market activities. State market activity probably did not however impinge on the private market so much as provide a large safety-net behind it, based on the assumption that with the financial and technological means available at the time, scarcity of goods prevailed but was accompanied by a scarcity of the financial means necessary to acquire more, so that the level of competition was restricted, and thus state intervention generally positive and not injurious to the private sector.

The ancient Egyptian economy could be classified a kind of nascent capitalism, for we have wage-labor, a market for land, production for the market, and state involvement. There is no evidence of rational accounting in the earliest periods or of an organized credit system, but peculiarly, banking does not appear to be regarded as an essential feature of capitalism. A case could be made for the existence of middlemen trading for a profit, but these would appear to have been primarily traders from coastal Mediterranean cities, and their relative importance in the overall economy cannot be gauged, although the quantity of wood being imported into ancient Egypt and used in private coffins indicates that they were hardly completely marginal. The following interpretation of the Egyptian economy assumes that the macroeconomic role of the Egyptian state was an essential element of a complex mixed economy, with the state generating significant economic activity.

Agriculture and the State

It is difficult to imagine prosperous rural estates existing (1) outside the security of a state system and (2) without access to trading patterns permitting them to meet wants. Rural prosperity is thus tied to urban development, and the landed aristocracy had a real interest in the political apparatus of the state which could assure security and protect merchants purveying desired products. The evidence from Egypt could be interpreted to support this origin of the state, but the evidence is not as compelling as the logic.

In ancient Egypt, it is clear that prestige did not derive from wealth but from position in the bureaucracy. Although there is no indication that wealth was necessarily derived from participation in the bureaucracy, wealth could lead to the acquisition of prestige through participation. This ability of society to gather in the capable meant that there was a constant stream of the human resources at the service of the state.

It was the job of the landowner/bureaucrat to assure the surplus agricultural production, while simultaneously reducing the number of individuals working the land. Peasants had to increase output to produce the difference. At the same time that the burdens of the peasants were increasing, the opportunities and motivation to leave the land to seek work as craftsmen and bureaucrats was increasing.

In parts of the modern third world, prices for agricultural products are kept low so as to permit an impoverished underemployed urban population to purchase foodstuffs. Low prices reduce the production incentives in agricultural areas, and production stagnates. Underemployment in both urban and rural areas rises, and foreign imports rise, so that the essential elements for stagnation are there. If demand for production is reduced to the minimum level, savings are reduced to nil, and investment fails to take place. The result is agricultural inefficiency and poverty on a vast scale.

Hobbes assumed that a government guaranteeing security was the lacking element, while in feudal China it was not the lack of authority, but the inefficiency of the system of myopic exploitation that prevented development. It is occasionally suggested that either the amount of arable land or a labor shortage were serious problems in antiquity, but the mere existence of monumental public buildings demonstrates that labor was available and that there was sufficient grain (and therefore land) available in order to maintain a population commensurate with major projects.

Parallel to the growth of state construction projects in ancient Egypt, there is a clear tendency for increased prosperity in all strata of society. Once state investment programs started to lag, the level of wealth in the country as a whole was not immediately extinguished, but merely dropped. These conditions suggest that the state investment program triggered economic growth rather than either (1) sapping it with exhaustive taxation or (2) dominating it completely.

Keynes

One key to understanding the system is demand. John Maynard Keynes pointed out that in a pure *laissez-faire* economy, in the event of a decline in demand, investment and production would sink to a level of poverty where savings would be reduced to zero, precisely the situation described by Hobbes, so that while the state is one theoretical actor in the equation, demand must be another. If the market alone is unable to correct the situation, intervention is necessary, and only the state has the power to intervene, transcending the individual microeconomic problems of the economy as a whole.

Despite all the constraints, ancient Egypt, a technologically primitive society, developed an economy sufficiently sophisticated to produce literary, philosophical, artistic and architectural wonders which still command the attention of the world. Assuming that the temples and the government were the primary factors in increasing demand in ancient Egypt, these powers will have exercised an extraordinary influence on the economy. The theoretical aspect of state intervention in an economy in order to stimulate, and thus increase, demand was carefully studied by Keynes, who showed that state intervention could call into existence demand which was hitherto not present, in order to shift the economy to a higher level of equilibrium and prosperity (Keynes 1936).

Many aspects of the Egyptian economy can be elucidated using the Keynesian approach, which enhances understanding by investigating the principle of demand. Keynes himself put it quite simply:

> Ancient Egypt was doubly fortunate, and doubtless owed to this its fabled wealth, in that it possessed two activities, namely pyramid building as well as

the search for precious metals, the fruits of which, since they could not serve the needs of man by being consumed, did not stale with abundance . . . Two pyramids . . . are twice as good as one.

(Keynes 1936:131)

This passage terminates the chapter on the 'Marginal Propensity to Consume,' discussing the difficulties of increasing demand, as there are very few products for which the demand curve is infinitely elastic. Consumption is dependent upon abstaining from investment, and thus requires liquidity. Increased consumption increases demand, which increases aggregate demand in an expanding economy, but creates competition between sectors in a stable or diminishing economy. Aggregate demand can only be increased inelastically if both liquidity and consumption are permitted to increase with competition for scarce resources excluded. On the one hand, liquidity is usually unable to sustain indefinite demand stimulation, and demand itself is usually insufficient because it flags. According to Keynes this unusual constellation was the key to growth, rather than investment as such. Put simply, an infinitely elastic demand curve is one where demand is unlimited. Normally, any product that can be consumed reaches a saturation point on the market, and demand flags, with the result that the price falls, and production and employment stagnate. Keynes thus drew upon the example of pyramid construction to illustrate the principle that if something is absolutely useless, and yet infinitely desirable, demand for it will not slacken, meaning that investment and employment will continue to increase.

In the modern capitalistic world, those investing in such products would inevitably distort the interest rate structure such that their production would continue to flourish, while other sectors declined, until a new equilibrium was reached. Keynes's theory of price formation was based not only on supply and demand, but also interest rates, so that price stability would be virtually unattainable with fluctuating interest and wage rates, which are the necessary repercussions of the massive concentration of investment and demand in one part of the market. In the modern world, state intervention would have the same – or even worse – consequences as the state is responsible for the currency as well as fiscal policy. State-financed demand would either result in (a) inflation, (b) distortion of the interest rate structure, or (c) excessive taxation. Each of these would necessarily have a negative impact on the overall economic structure, so that driving away the unemployment problem would merely create other acute difficulties. In the *General Theory*, Keynes was particularly concerned that interest can suppress demand for investment and thus the whole series of demand curves, and thus threatens to maintain a low level equilibrium unless demand can be stimulated in another way, demand being the key to increasing prosperity and employment. 'Aggregate effective demand,' the 'propensity to consume,' and the 'marginal efficiency of capital' are the decisive factors which could potentially leave an economy at an equilibrium of absolute poverty. The primary difficulty as Keynes perceived it, was to stimulate demand, while balancing off the various evils, in order to achieve an equilibrium at a higher level of prosperity.

Keynes was confronted with the depression and the inability of the capitalist system to rescue itself, as it must automatically do according to the premises of the *laissez-faire* economists who assumed that equilibrium with lower unemployment would be achieved by lowering wage rates. The neoclassical synthesis did not take account of the fact that mankind had lived for millennia with a high proportion of involuntary unemployment, and that this was the normal equilibrium. Keynes pointed out that aggregate demand would not increase by lowering wages, as effective demand had more or less peaked in any case. Thus, knocking down wage rates would not increase employment if demand was flagging, for liquidity would not be increased, and therefore effective demand would stagnate.[2] The only result would be a devastating macroeconomic blow at the economy, as poverty and unemployment spread. If effective demand did not rise, neither would invest-ment, and the economic situation would continue to be bleak (as it had been for millennia). It was thus only by external stimulation that the economy could be spurred on to a higher level. It is the 'marginal efficiency of capital' (by which the interest rate structure is meant) which thus determines the level of prosperity. If interest rates sink to zero, 'the position of equilibrium, under conditions of *laissez-faire*, will be one in which employment is low enough and the standard of living sufficiently miserable to bring savings to zero' (Keynes 1936:217–18).

It should be clear that the construction of pyramids, tombs and temples was an absolutely ideal method of increasing demand. In an agricultural economy, with-out external stimulus, production will equal consumption, with a high level of unemployment or underemployment, as overproduction would not result in an increase in consumption. Thus there is no incentive to produce above the neces-sary minimum. The price structure and investment possibilities virtually assure this. In ancient Egypt, the land itself could practically guarantee that a minimum of labor input would produce the maximum consumption level, so that demand would not increase without artificial stimulus.

In the agricultural sector the state provided the artificial stimulus by (1) obliging the farmers to overproduce, by means of fiscal measures; (2) subsidizing a class of craftsmen employed in temple and tomb construction and mainten-ance, thus withdrawing this class from significant agricultural production; (3) paying laborers on major construction projects from the surplus withdrawn from the farmers; and (4) creating a bureaucracy which also required maintenance. These measures guaranteed that demand was stimulated far beyond the subsist-ence minimum, and encouraged circulation of the agricultural surplus, as well as other goods.

If demand stimulus explains the success of the Egyptian economy via redistri-bution, this contradicts claims that the constraints were either arable land or labor. It is generally agreed that the state redistribution system collected grain (and other products) from one part of the community and turned them over to another. This was possible as grain production promised incredible yields. Since the labor input was the weak variable here, the only way to increase secondary and tertiary employment was to drastically reduce agricultural underemployment, increase the overall level of employment for individuals, take people off the land, employ them in the construction and service sectors, and maximize agricultural production with heavy rent and taxes.

Removing people from agricultural production forced those who were left to produce more per capita than before in order to pay those employed in other sectors. The investment increases employment producing temples, tombs, boats, etc.

Inflation, interest and money

The fact that the measures employed for increasing production were fiscal in nature guaranteed that state investment would not have a negative impact on private investment, because the interest rate structure was not affected, signifying that there was no competition between the state and private sectors for scarce means. The private sector was thus left untouched by the fiscal (and opposed to) monetary solution of the problem.

In fact, however, the monetary solution (using inflation or interest rates) was excluded from the outset by the fact that Egypt neither had a currency, nor an all-pervasive system of interest rates. Money is assumed to possess three basic attributes, as (1) a unit of value, (2) a store of value, and (3) an exchange value. In ancient Egypt, the copper *deben* (a weight of 91 grammes) was a unit of value and evidently a store of value, but it was not normally employed in transactions, and thus failed to meet all three criteria. The *khar* (a sack of roughly 75 litres capacity) of grain was used both as a unit of value and a unit of exchange, but storing grain is not a realistic method of keeping one's savings, so that it likewise fails to meet all three criteria.[3] Beds and other articles could be used for exchange purposes, and perhaps as stores of value, but they could not be regarded as units of value. In any case, there was no government controlled money or currency which could be used as a tool of monetary policy,[4] and thus the monetary inflationary alternative was not available.

Hypothetically, the economic significance of (1) removing workers from the land, (2) increasing the grain tax burden for the remaining farmers, and (3) paying the craftsmen and laborers with the same grain, amounts to the creation of a self-financing credit scheme since the grain that is being spent by the government would not have been available with a lower level of taxation. This taxation is therefore wealth creation, rather than the equivalent of skimming off an already existing surplus. Increasing grain production was thus inflationary, but so long as (1) the excess production could be absorbed by diverting state employment into non-agricultural sectors and (2) the resulting 'inflation' did not damage private sector entrepreneurial investment, the situation was one in which inflation played a positive rather than negative role. The existence of a grain market indicates that the state did not meet the requirements of all residents. This is crucial for the Keynesian theory as inflation in capitalist economies can have an extremely detrimental impact on both employment and investment by rendering certain industrial undertakings uneconomic. In ancient Egypt, overproduction was the equivalent of national-debt in the modern world as it increased demand. The state never ran the risk of financial bankruptcy, so overproduction was beneficial.

It is advantageous for a growing economy to have sticky wages, i.e., wages which remain stable or rising while prices rise or fall. If wages were not in money they might not remain stable in money terms, but if grain demand stays high and constant, while wages are paid in grain, taxes collected in grain, and grain serves as a medium of exchange, the threat of negative economic repercussions is avoided. It is only through increasing effective demand through high wages or income that the private sector can contribute to the economic growth stimulated by the government, as income can be absorbed through production leading to transactions and the generation and accumulation of wealth.

So long as the state was collecting grain, increasing demand was a more or less automatic process, and that demand had a positive effect on employment. The same was true on the investment side, as the employment in the temples, etc. increased both aggregate employment, and aggregate income, without taxing the capital markets, and without inflation. Without a currency, the danger of inflation was avoided, since inflation occurs when government consumption exceeds government income – and the whole basis of the program was to maximize state income. Thus, many of the basic elements of the Egyptian economy are logically ideal forms of implementing a cyclical development which would spur demand and employment, underlining the relevance of the Keynesian theory for understanding the process.

Money and investment

Of the properties of money enumerated by Keynes, the only significant aspect which did not necessarily correspond to the Egyptian reality was the condition of zero elasticity of supply as far as the private sector was concerned, in so far as private farming could conceivably have increased the supply. The failure of the state to maintain its construction projects, with the consequent decline in the collection of revenues, led to an overall decline in the economy, as the private sector was unable to actually make up for the lack in demand. This implies that grain could arguably be held to be money, and confirms that the high level of equilibrium was dependent on state intervention.

Another feature of money that has attracted a great deal of attention is the price stability of ancient Egypt. Prices changed very little over hundreds or perhaps even a thousand years. If the price of an object is considered to be merely an expression of the 'disutility of labor,' and traditional prices are the ones to which one is accustomed in a market with a limited degree of latitude in supply and demand, then price changes need not be expected. But Keynes made not only wage rates, but also interest rates a key feature in his price theory, and therefore the lack of interest in playing a key role in the economy could likewise explain the lack of price fluctuations.

Another key feature that arises from this logic is the fact that prices did not fluctuate despite enormous changes in the supply of precious metals, both between the Old Kingdom and the New Kingdom, and through the course of the New Kingdom. These variations were not reflected in prices, which indicate that the grain standard was indeed the true measure of economic activity, and that this economic activity can best be understood in terms of Keynesian theory.

The lack of a money or currency eliminated the possibility that interest rates could have a detrimental impact on investment and thus production. Investment curves in the capitalistic world are determined by interest, as the expectation of profit must exceed the anticipated interest rate, otherwise investment subsides until the interest rate has fallen. If the interest rate is zero, investment will also be zero, unless artificially stimulated. The fact that there may have been agriculturally related interest rates had the opposite effect, and was precisely the same as the state's role in skimming off agricultural production, as the exaction of interest for grain resulted in the incentive to produce more grain than was necessary for consumption. These private sector interest rates will thus (1) not have had a negative impact on the economy, actually spurring it on, and (2) the conflict between the state and the private sectors for scarce resources will have been reduced to a minimum (see Figure 8.1).

Aside from industrial investment, land ownership is one of the most enticing means of investing excess capital. The state may have been one of the major land owners in ancient Egypt, but it did not hold the greatest part of the land, and this did not seem to have increased demand for private land to the extent that the price was driven upwards. The price of land in ancient Egypt was comparatively low. This meant that capital investment would not be directed to the mere possession of land, but to using the land for productive purposes, i.e., increasing the grain supply, and thus being able to maintain a large household.

Egypt was thus basically on the grain standard, and this particular commodity was the basis on which the entire economy flourished. It was the grain which was used to pay the workers who built the monuments of the land, and by withdrawing labor from the agricultural sector, demand was actually increased, along with employment (see Figure 8.2).

Private tombs were built with private means, suggesting that the private and state sectors complemented each other. The state was also purchasing part of

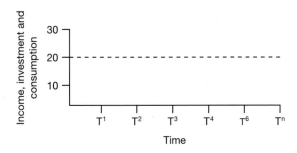

Figure 8.1 Unstimulated low investment in subsistence economy.

Note: Without growth, investment stagnates at a minimum level: an equilibrium at the poverty line. It is possible to have economic activity and even the production of luxury goods in such an economy, but prosperity is not widespread.

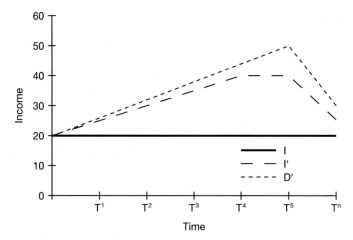

Figure 8.2 The simplified Keynesian theory applied to ancient Egypt.

Note: Investment (I) is stagnant at the subsistence level, with income stable over time. The level of investment is such that no significant changes can be achieved without substantial changes in the demand structure, i.e. artificial stimulation. This is accomplished by government artificially raising demand for grain (taxes), which is immediately paid out in wages and rations, i.e. demand (D) = investment (I), until private demand likewise increases as a result of stimulation (through new government investment (I'); creating new stimulated demand curve (D'). It is noted that with private investment, demand has risen considerably, but it is dependent upon the state investment (I') without which it falls to a little way above previously existing level because it is dependent upon the increased level of state demand. (This graph presumes that during the First Intermediate Period – right end of graph – general prosperity dropped across the country, which does not suggest that the new equilibrium eliminated wealth or the distribution of prestige goods.)

its necessities from the private sector. Some state employees spent part of their time in outside work. The economy was thus clearly mixed. Although the state probably took the lion's share of the surplus, the result cannot have been invidious to the private sector, as otherwise there would not have been so many private stele and tombs made on private contract by private craftsmen for private people. The entire economic system was thus oriented towards consumption and investment, as the potentially negative influence of interest rates and savings were effectively negated, and the 'propensity to consume' given free rein. It was merely the state fiscal system which guaranteed an equilibrium at a high level of prosperity for all.

The ideal feature of temple and tomb construction is that the demand is infinitely elastic: one can always make a larger tomb or temple, one can always employ more priests, encourage additional services, and all this without negatively effecting the rest of the economy. The state did not hamper individuals in their own investments.

An historical perspective

Theory enables us to analyze situations, compare, and distinguish the significant from the apparent. Viewing Mesopotamia, ziggurats appear to be comparable to pyramids, and thus it is tempting to equate the two systems. In Mesopotamia, however, interest rates and trade played significant roles. Price fluctuations are reflected in the documentation, and when the economy faltered, not only were tax exemptions proposed, but we also find the cancellation of debts.

In Egypt, the decline of the economy was accompanied by tax breaks, suggesting a weakening of the system, and yet the entire economy did not falter uniformly. It is clear that the masses of construction workers employed on major projects would 'go home,' but small-scale craftsmen could continue to ply their trades. The amount of grain in circulation (from the state to the workers to the market) will have fallen as the investment program slackened. Famine may have been a temporary result of the drop in state supported activity, but subsistence levels will have inevitably been maintained. The key feature is not the overall grain production, but the division of labor resulting from the state investment program. It is thus logical to view things in this perspective when Kemp suggests that:

> Any economic system that we propose for ancient Egypt has to be able to account for the apparently successful adjustments which local communities made to changes of different magnitudes within a relatively crude state system of economic direction.
>
> (Kemp 1989:240)

In view of the Keynesian theory, the economic costs in construction did not lead to the decline in the economy. It was the interruption of major construction projects that led to decline. Kemp (1983:176–7) has also pointed out that the decline in royal construction projects accompanied the decline in private undertakings, confirming that state economic activity was unable to increase general levels such that private sector demand was sufficient to release the capacities of the private sector to take responsibility for demand stimulation. Helck indicated that precisely this development took place at the end of the Old Kingdom:

> This led to a completely new development in Egypt, as the bureaucratic regimentation of the population dissolves . . . Free craftsmen appear who . . . sell their labor. Supply and demand appear in place of the planned system of labor. The power of the bureaucracy is broken . . . The planned economy is replaced by the market economy in a few areas by certain very limited groups.
>
> (Helck 1975:106, my translation)

Helck misunderstood that the collapse of the economy led to the craftsmen seeking work. The prevailing assumptions concerning the economy and the state have hitherto suggested that the private commercial sector was insignificant, and that private ownership of land was seriously restricted if it existed at all. These assumptions are not supported by evidence.

Private ownership of land was widespread from the earliest times, and private craftsmen were active before the advent of history. The state sector contributed substantially to an increase in the quality and quantity of craftsmen, and to the proportion of workers receiving rations and wages who were obliged to turn to the market to meet their non-wage requirements. This seems in turn to have spurred on the market in two ways. On the one hand, the generally prevailing level of prosperity rose with larger numbers of transactions increasing the circulation of the grain, and therefore the velocity of money. On the other hand, the state was actively involved in market trading, along with those bureaucrats trading in their own interests.

The economy began to suffer as the state reduced demand towards the end of the Old Kingdom. The dissolution of the state effected the aggregate demand structure. The key factor in the major pyramid projects of Dynasty IV was not the employment of craftsmen, but of laborers, and it was here that the economic repercussions of the demand crisis became manifest. The principle of infinitely elastic demand can explain the entire system. Whether expanding or contracting, government expenditures did not impinge on the private economy because it had a completely different base, meaning that the stimulation did not have a negative impact, as implied by Kemp's remark about the competition between private and royal tomb construction. Despite a certain limited private prosperity, and potentially production, there can be little doubt that the private economy was not up to the task of replacing royal demand. The craftsmen continued to find employment, but the toiling masses reverted to underemployment as investment declined and the economy reverted to the equilibrium at the level of poverty.

It would appear that during the first two millennia of Egyptian history, i.e. until around 1000 BC, the temples were not economically independent, but relied completely on the largesse of the ruling king for their enlargement. With the exception of crops and animals, the king seems to have held virtually all of the productive investments under his control – from mining to construction. The temples apparently maintained sufficient resources to maintain their services, but relied on the king to increase their resources. This implies not only that weakened kings might suffer diminished resources, but also that the temples were administratively unprepared to assume the role played by the king in increasing demand. Although the temples were not economically significant during the Old Kingdom, this bureaucratic obstacle may have ultimately led to the collapse of the Egyptian state at the end of the New Kingdom, because demand for grain and the management of land was neglected as the kingship weakened.

This reveals the role of demand – as opposed to redistribution – in economic stimulation, and Kemp only errs in suggesting that the finite nature of the agricultural surplus was the obstacle, as this was not the problem. The millions of cubic metres of stone involved in construction projects initiated by Cheops and Snofru indicate beyond doubt that the grain which fed Rome almost three millennia later was equivalent to the resources available, and thus that only demand was lacking. The erection of tombs in provincial areas at the end of the Old Kingdom meant that demand was present, and that the transport of grain to the center was not necessary, and yet the economy faltered because of declining state economic activity, as the private sector could not collect the revenues, i.e. stimulate demand on the same scale.

Conclusion

Payments made to the crown and the temples can be listed under the rubrics of 'corvée labor,' 'taxes,' 'administrative fees,' 'rents,' and 'trading income' (which need not necessarily be 'profit'), and the cumulative effect of all these various types of income was to spur surplus production and place it at the disposal of a powerful bureaucracy which used it for investment projects, such as temple, tomb and palace construction. This was an artificial increase in demand, which removed workers from the agricultural sector, pushing on the development of the division of labor, increasing overall employment, and spurring demand by increasing aggregate income, and thus aggregate expenditure and investment.

These seemingly simple Keynesian measures were combined in a setting which corresponded to Keynesian theory, in so far as

1   inflation was avoided by the absence of a currency which could be debased:
2   the grain standard meant that income resulted in immediate expenditure, which inevitably involved employment, and the marginalization of non-subsistence related employment; so that
3   demand was restricted only by the capacity of the state to limit it, and thus contributed to secondary and tertiary employment; while
4   interest rates failed to impede investment because of their irrelevance to the overall economy, and increasing investment and income did not negatively affect either overall investment or the interest rate structure; since
5   the possession of agricultural properties did not signify unproductive investment for prestige reasons, but actually increased income directly by
6   generating private sector employment, which benefited from state aid to training; and
7   guaranteed that the private sector could take up some slack when state demand flagged.

The most important element of the construction of temples and palaces and tombs was that demand was effectively 'infinitely elastic,' implying that this demand stimulation measure did not have an adverse effect on other economic sectors, the construction could contract, although, if state contraction was related to demand contraction, the economy suffered.

The whole system worked because Egypt was basically a closed economy, but the increased income did permit the stimulation of imports, and generated considerable wealth as far away as South Arabia, without hindering the development of local industry, as the greatest part of the local demand stimulation was spent on temples and palaces. The result was that jobs were not exported, although it was possible to spend surplus income abroad, which increased local agricultural employment, and prosperity. That the state investment policy failed to have a negative impact on the distribution of resources meant that the private sector could flourish, as far as demand would allow, which was generally at a higher level than any other country until well into the second millennium AD.

This would explain the tendency for expensive tombs and temples during periods of decline, and the presence of wealth in cemeteries of the intermediate periods, and provide the model requested by Kemp, accounting for the economy in a comprehensive fashion.

Notes

1   Additional support for these arguments may be found in my *State and Economy in Ancient Egypt: Fiscal Vocabulary of the New Kingdom*.
2   Say's law dictated that demand would rise to meet any supply, hence equilibrium was inevitable. The economics community failed to realize that Say's law required placing financial power in the hands of those seeking to acquire, and that it would only then be possible to establish a new equilibrium at a higher level.
3   It could be contended that grain was the equivalent of money, for the wealthy could afford to maintain large well-insulated silos, and the poor had few resources anyway so that the rodent problem in Egypt should not be taken so seriously. For the purposes of the Keynesian interpretation of the economy, setting grain as a true equivalent to money is not an obstacle, but actually a corollary of the argument, so that the contention that money did not exist in Egypt is intended more as a realistic appraisal of the situation than a dogmatic statement of position. Inflation through the grain standard is impossible, and increased production will only lead to economic growth and prosperity.
4   The supply of precious metals cannot have fulfilled the same investment and income roles as grain. Thus, precious metals may have performed all of the utility roles demanded of money, but they could not be employed to alter grain production, which was the basic source of wealth.

9 World systems and social change in agrarian societies, 3000 BC to AD 1500

Stephen K. Sanderson

Critique

The work of Andre Gunder Frank and Barry Gills (Frank 1990, 1991a,b, 1995; Frank and Gills 1993, and in this volume; Gills and Frank 1991, 1992) on the 5,000-year world system is, I think, of exceptional importance. Although I was initially highly skeptical of many of their claims, I have gradually come to be convinced that they have put their finger on a historical phenomenon that has been badly neglected by scholars. I have come to be convinced, that is, by their contention that the commercialization of economic life was much more significant in the early historic societies and civilizations than has generally been thought, and, moreover, that there has been a long-term process of expansion in the commercialization of economic life over the last few millennia. In this chapter I want to develop this theme of expanding world commercialization and relate it to other evolutionary processes in world history, but first let me talk about two areas concerning which I continue to disagree with Frank and Gills.

One serious disagreement concerns their argument that it makes little sense to talk of distinct modes of production – 'feudal,' 'tributary,' 'capitalist,' etc. – and of historical transitions between these modes of production, especially of a transition from feudalism to capitalism. I think this is overdoing an otherwise very important argument. The time period considered by Frank and Gills is roughly that between 3000 BC and AD 1500. I call this period the agrarian epoch, and the societies and civilizations that prevailed during it have variously been called agrarian societies (Lenski 1970), agrarian-coercive societies (Collins 1990, 1992), traditional aristocratic empires (Kautsky 1982), and by Marxist-oriented scholars the tributary mode of production (Amin 1976; Wolf 1982). It has generally been argued that the most fundamental economic relationship in such societies was that whereby landlords extracted economic surplus from peasants through rent, taxation, labor services, or some combination of these. Landlords were the dominant economic class, standing not only above peasants, but above merchants as well, at whom they looked down their noses and viewed as dirty money-grubbers who dared to dirty their hands with the soil of commerce. Despite Frank and Gills's increasingly convincing demonstration of the importance of relations of economic exchange in the long agrarian epoch, I would still hold to the traditional view that these relations were seldom dominant in that epoch. Except in a few instances, the exchange activities of merchants were strongly held in check by the dominant class, whose mode of generating wealth was quite different (i.e., it was a system of production-for-use rather than production-for-exchange). That great scholar of economic history, Max Weber (1981 [1927]), argued that various types of capitalism existed throughout world history but that they were distinct in several important ways from modern capitalism. For him, modern capitalism had six primary characteristics: (1) appropriation of the means of production as the property of autonomous private industrial enterprises; (2) the absence of irrational constraints on market exchange; (3) rational development of technology in the form of mechanization; (4) calculable law; (5) free labor; and (6) the general commercialization of economic life. I am almost certain that Frank and Gills would claim that Weber was wrong and that, indeed, all of these features were found in much earlier times. And they may be right – or at least mostly right, for I would demur with respect to Weber's sixth criterion, the general commercialization of economic life. Perhaps this is the truly critical difference between ancient and modern capitalism. Capitalist economic relations today pervade all economic and social life, but did they do so in earlier millennia? I think it would be very difficult to show that to be the case.

But there is another related point that needs to be made. Recognition of the subordination throughout the agrarian epoch of capitalist relations to tributary relations is extremely important, I think, if we are to understand a central feature of that epoch: the relatively slow rate of social evolution that occurred during it. Given the accelerating pace of social evolution between the Neolithic Revolution, which began about 10,000 years ago and introduced agriculture and settled village life, and the rise of civilization and the state, which began some 5,000 years ago and introduced a much more complex and elaborate form of social life, we should have expected such an accelerating trend to continue. At least this would be true if we were simply making a simple extrapolation from a historical trend. But such an accelerating trend did not continue, and the pace of social evolution shifted toward a much slower rhythm. And why? Because the economic and political power of agrarian ruling classes hemmed in the activities of merchants because they saw them as a threat to their own economic position and social status. The agrarian ruling classes had a vested interest in maintaining traditional economic relations. Had this not been the case – that is, had merchants been given much greater freedom of maneuver – then I think we would have seen a much more rapidly developing process of world commercialization throughout the agrarian epoch. That epoch would have come to an end much sooner, and thus we would have seen the emergence of the modern world at a much earlier point in history.

What then of Frank and Gills's claim that there was nothing especially distinctive or important about the sixteenth century – that what happened then was simply a quantitative extension of a world historical process that had been going on for millennia rather than a qualitative shift to something novel? I think it is a serious mistake to underrate what happened after the sixteenth century. There was indeed something distinctive about that period, and human society did begin to undergo a fundamental transformation at this time. There was a huge acceleration of the intensity of commercial activity and the shift to a mode of production in which capitalism became the *dominant* activity for the very first time. A truly 'world-transforming' capitalism was coming into being and it would set in motion processes never seen before in the world. There is indeed something vital about the sixteenth century that has to be explained.

Let me point to one economic phenomenon and three non-economic phenomena strongly suggestive of a major sixteenth-century social transformation. On the economic plane, perhaps the most significant event of the sixteenth century was the beginnings of European colonization, led, of course, by Portugal and Spain. Colonialism, of course, had existed at other times and places in world history, but never on quite such a scale, and the colonizers and the colonized were never quite at such a geographical distance from each other. This form of colonialism soon became by far the most important form of colonialism the world had ever seen, and involved large parts of the African continent as well. The Portuguese established plantation agriculture in what we now know as Brazil, and drew their labor supply in the form of slaves imported into Brazil from West Africa. The Spaniards made limited use of slavery, but they did reorganize the tributary forms of production found in their primary colonies (what we today call Mexico and Peru) so as to make themselves the primary beneficiaries. Clearly such a form of colonialism had to signal the beginnings of a dramatic economic shift.

But on various non-economic planes there were major shifts occurring as well. The sixteenth century marked the beginning of the first national states throughout western Europe (Tilly 1990). In the time period between AD 1000 and 1500 there was nothing even approaching a national state, a large centrally-coordinated state highly identified with a particular nationality, what today we call, for example, England, or France, or Germany. And, of course, during this period England, France, and Germany did not yet exist. These regions and many others were divided into hundreds of smaller states, and Europe was characterized by an 'enormous fragmentation of sovereignty' (Tilly 1990). There were perhaps as many as 500 states within the boundaries of Europe. In the Italian peninsula there were roughly 200 to 300 independent city-states, and in what is now southern Germany there were sixty-nine free cities and numerous bishropics, duchies, and principalities. What a contrast with the present, where there are, or at least were before the Eastern European nationalist movements of the early 1990s, only twenty-five to twenty-eight sovereign European states (Tilly 1990).

According to Tilly, the national states of Europe formed as a result of the strong concentration of both capital and military might. The new national states beginning to evolve in the sixteenth century were massive structures compared to most of their predecessors. Huge state bureaucracies were built, and these bureaucracies were devoted to both economic and military activities. They played a large role in managing and guiding the economy and making war against other national states. Large standing armies were now created to replace the relatively small private armies characteristic of feudalism. This was politics and military might on a scale never seen before in Europe, and it was clearly a product of the sixteenth century.

There was also a gigantic burst of scientific activity occurring precisely in this period (Merton 1970 [1938]; Bernal 1971; Huff 1993). The seventeenth century is usually taken as marking the European Scientific Revolution, but clearly important scientific developments were occurring in the century before the seventeenth. In 1543 Copernicus overturned the geocentric view of the universe with his heliocentric view. Copernicus's work inspired Tycho Brahe who then inspired Johannes Kepler. In the seventeenth century itself came the enormous accomplishments of Galileo and, of course, Isaac Newton. It was during this time that we find the beginnings of the institutionalization of science, as indicated by the founding of the first scientific societies, the Royal Society of London and the Royal Academy of France. Robert Wuthnow (1980) has shown that there was a very close correlation between the importance of a nation in Wallerstein's world-economy and the development of scientific activity.

Finally, let me take note of one more major social transformation that occurred in the sixteenth century, the Protestant Reformation. In a major work on the Reformation, Lewis W. Spitz (1985) dates it from 1517 to 1559. And where was the Reformation concentrated? The ideas of the leading reformers, Luther, Calvin, and Zwingli, were adopted most vigorously in regions where mercantile activity was prominent, and it was the merchant class above all others that promoted Reformationist ideas. Lutheranism was adopted in a number of German states and also in Denmark and Sweden, and Anglicanism was adopted in England (Swanson 1967). Calvinism or Zwinglianism came to be adopted in a number of Swiss cantons, in two German states, and in Bohemia, the United Provinces (Netherlands), Hungary, Transylvania, and Lowland Scotland (Swanson 1967). The social class most hostile to the Reformation was the feudal nobility, and where its power was greatest – that is, in less capitalistically advanced regions of Europe – Catholicism remained strongly entrenched. The most prominent of the states remaining Catholic were France, Spain, Portugal, Ireland, Highland Scotland, Poland, and the Italian states of Venice and Florence (Swanson 1967).

Let me now turn to Frank and Gills's claim that virtually all analyses of the development of the modern world have been crippled by a Eurocentric perspective (see, especially, Frank and Gills in this volume, and Frank 1995). The charge really consists of two parts. First, it is claimed that much of Asia was, economically speaking, at least on a par with Europe in the centuries before 1500, and in some ways even more economically advanced. Then this claim is coupled with the assertion that there was nothing especially distinctive about Europe, no particular qualities it had that distinguished it from the rest of the world, nothing that gave it some sort of special dynamic that uniquely set it apart.

The first charge, I am prepared to say, seems basically true. Frank and Gills have marshaled a great deal of evidence to show that economic commercialism was pervasive in Asia in the centuries preceeding 1500. Indeed, in a famous book Mark Elvin (1973) has shown that during the period of the Sung Dynasty

(960–1275), China had the world's most advanced economy and was possibly poised on the brink of the world's first industrial revolution, and William McNeill (1982) has shown that in the period between AD 1000 and 1500 a very high level of commercial activity had been reached on a world level. J.M. Blaut (1993), whom Frank cites copiously, has also put together a great deal of evidence to indicate the substantial amount of economic development and economic vitality of the non-European world before AD 1500. So, if we were simply to extrapolate from the economic trends of the half-millennium before 1500, there would be no overpowering reason to predict that, after 1500, Europe would undergo a massive capitalist takeoff and leave Asia and the rest of the world far behind. But that is just what it did, and this leads me to conclude that Frank and Gills's second claim, the claim that there was nothing distinctive about Europe, is false. Europe *was* distinctive; it had a number of social attributes generally not present elsewhere. Yet I must immediately qualify this point: Europe was distinctive, but it was not unique, for there was one other civilization that had the very same special qualities that Europe had. This was Japan. And we cannot fail to notice that, by the end of its Tokugawa period (1868), Japan was a society with an enormously high level of commercialism – I would call Japan at this time an essentially capitalist society – and was the most economically developed society outside of Europe. Nor can we fail to notice that Japan is today an advanced industrial capitalist society far ahead of the rest of Asia – indeed, sociological light years ahead of most of it – and soon to become the world's number one economic power. Europe and Japan were distinctive civilizations that had special qualities uniquely conducive to the development of a very advanced form of capitalism. What were these qualities? Let me suggest four.

Size Japan and two of the three leading capitalist countries of early modern Europe, England and the Netherlands, were small, and as such contrasted markedly with such Asian societies as China and India, which were large empires. Large geographical size creates problems of communication and transportation that smaller states do not have. Moreover, it is costly to maintain a large state because resources are drained away that could be used more directly for economic development. I think there is a parallel situation with large Asian societies like China and India. They were simply so big that obstacles were put in the way of economic development. In Asia Japan's much smaller size gave her a decided advantage.

Geography Japan and the leading capitalist countries of northwest Europe were located on large bodies of water that allowed them to give predominance to maritime rather than overland trade. Samir Amin (1991) has noted that the societies containing the greatest amount of protocapitalism in the long agrarian era tended to be those in which maritime trade was characteristic. It is noteworthy that the protocapitalism of China tended to be located along its southern coast, and that the great Indian Ocean trade linking the Mediterranean and East Asia between the rise of Islam in the seventh century and the beginnings of early modern Europe was indeed centered precisely there – in the Indian Ocean (Chaudhuri 1985). And where was the greatest economic development in late medieval Europe concentrated but in the city-states of Italy on the Mediterranean. The presence of maritime trade by itself determines nothing, but it is a very important precondition for capitalist development.

Climate   Europe and Japan both had temperate climates. This is important when we recognize that the bulk of the world colonized by Europe had tropical or subtropical climates. These regions were most suitable for the development of the kinds of peripheral economic activities – production of raw materials for export using forced labor – European states wanted to pursue in those zones. An important reason for the economic success of British settler colonies like the United States, Canada, and Australia was the fact that the settlers were inhabiting regions remarkably similar to western Europe (Crosby 1986). Most of North America and Australia had climates poorly suited to peripheral economic activities (the southern United States is the exception that proves the rule: its warm climate was suitable for plantation agriculture, and it was peripheralized). Japan may have escaped peripheralization by Europe at least partly because of its climate or its distant northerly location. In any event, it was not climatologically suited for peripheral development.

Political structure   Europe and Japan had the only true feudal regimes in world history. As Perry Anderson (1974a) has stressed, feudalism is a highly decentralized politico-economic system, one that rests on the 'parcellization of sovereignty.' The significance of the feudal experiences of Europe and Japan lies in the substantial freedom they gave to their merchant classes to operate economically. There is widespread agreement that large bureaucratic empires stifle mercantile activity because it is a threat to the tributary mode through which the state extracts surplus. Europe and Japan were strikingly different from the rest of the agrarian world. Their high levels of political decentralization meant that mercantile activities could not be controlled to the extent they were in large bureaucratic states. Anderson (1974a, 1974b) has called attention to the freedom of the towns in medieval Europe and Japan, and their remarkably independent role within the total economies of these societies. Likewise, Norman Jacobs (1958) has stressed the remarkable freedom and independence of Japanese merchants in contrast to the tight control of merchants in China. Indeed, it was not just that the Japanese merchants enjoyed considerable economic freedom, but that the whole conception of the importance of mercantile activity was distinctive in Europe and Japan. The freedom given to merchants may well be the most important of the four preconditions that helped push Europe and Japan forward as the first societies to undergo a capitalist revolution.

In conclusion, the development of modern capitalism in Europe and Japan cannot be attributed merely to such things as luck or geopolitical shifts within a larger world system. Europe and Japan had qualities that uniquely favored their

capitalist development. And notice how such an argument escapes the charge of
Eurocentrism. It was not a matter of Europe alone making the transition to the
modern world, for a major Asian society did the same, and largely under its own
impetus.

Reformulation

I would now like to turn my attention away from criticizing Frank and Gills and
direct the discussion toward what I regard as their extremely important positive
contributions. As indicated earlier, Frank and Gills have convinced me that economic commercialism was far more important at a far earlier date in world history
than we have usually thought. But their most important point – at least for my
main concern, which is the understanding of long-term social evolution – has to
do with their claim for the gradual expansion of the level of commercialism
throughout the world in the last five millennia. Let me add my own two cents
worth to this claim.

What I refer to as a process of expanding world commercialization can be
measured in terms of the growth of processes of economic exchange within
particular societies or civilizations, and especially in terms of growth in the size
and density of trade networks between societies. It is possible to mark off three
major stages in this process of expanding world commercialization (McNeill
1982; Curtin 1984). The first stage begins around 2000 BC and ends around
200 BC. During this phase trade was largely local or, at best, regional in scope. By
200 BC there emerged the first truly worldwide trade with the establishment of a
trade axis that ran all the way from China to the Mediterranean. After about AD
1000 there was another big leap forward in which trade networks expanded and
deepened, especially in the period between 1250 and 1350.

Philip Curtin (1984) has described some of the basic characteristics of the
worldwide trade network that was in effect between 200 BC and AD 1000 (cf.
Chaudhuri 1985). As he notes, during this period trade became regularized
between the Red Sea/Persian Gulf region and India, between India and Southeast Asia, and between Southeast Asia and both China and Japan. In the middle
Han period, Chinese merchants traveled to the west through central Asia and
established an overland trade route between East Asia and Europe. Chinese trade
with India had become extensive by the first century AD, and Chinese goods were
being sold widely in the Roman empire. During Roman times trade between
India and the Mediterranean was carried on through three different routes: an
overland route through Parthia, the Persian Gulf combined with an overland
route, and the Red Sea combined with an overland route to Egypt or some part of
the Fertile Crescent region. Maritime trade flourished in the South China Sea and
the Bay of Bengal, with Canton being an important port for trade to the south.

William McNeill (1982) has described what he regards as a new and major
burst of world commercialization beginning around AD 1000, and centering
heavily on China. It was during this time that China had by far its greatest burst
of economic activity prior to modern times, one that lags behind only late

medieval Europe and Tokugawa Japan in scale and scope. Mark Elvin (1973) has referred to this as an 'economic revolution,' most of which occurred during the period of the Sung dynasty (AD 960–1275). Elvin sees the Sung economic revolution as involving agriculture, water transport, money and credit, industry, and trade (both domestic and foreign). Elvin argues that improvements in agriculture gave China by the thirteenth century the most sophisticated agricultural system in the world, and one that provided a foundation for major thrusts forward in commercial activity. Commercial activity was also greatly aided by improvements in water transport. These improvements involved both the construction of better sailing vessels on the one hand and the building of canals and removal of natural obstacles to navigation in streams and rivers on the other. Industry flourished, especially the production of steel and iron. The economy became much more monetized. There was a much greater volume of money in circulation, and the money economy even penetrated into peasant villages. Foreign trade, especially with Southeast Asia and Japan, flourished. Markets proliferated and became hierarchically organized. At this time China was the world's most economically advanced society, and many observers have suggested that it was on the brink of the world's first industrial revolution. McNeill sees the enormous economic growth in Sung China as part of a larger picture of world commercialization. As he says, 'China's rapid evolution towards market-regulated behavior in the centuries on either side of the year 1000 tipped a critical balance in world history' (1982:25).

Janet Abu-Lughod (1989) has picked up the story where McNeill left it. She describes in great detail for the period 1250–1350 the structure and operation of a vast worldwide trade network from western Europe to East Asia. This huge network contained eight overlapping subsystems that can be categorized into three larger circuits centering on western Europe, the Middle East, and the Far East. Abu-Lughod refuses to be drawn into a discussion of whether this system was 'capitalistic' or not, but she does claim that it provided the basis for the development of modern capitalism after about 1500.

Additional corroboration for the notion of expanding world commercialization throughout the agrarian era comes from research on trends in world urbanization. Using data compiled by Tertius Chandler (1987), David Wilkinson (1992a, 1993a) has shown that urbanization is a striking trend in world history. Of course, commercialization and urbanization cannot be strictly equated, but it is likely that urbanization is more a function of increasing commercialization than of anything else. Cities may grow and expand to fulfill important political functions, of course, and certainly for various other reasons, but commercialization seems to be the main driving force behind urbanization (Bairoch 1988). It is clear that urbanization has been a striking feature of agrarian social evolution over a period of nearly 4,000 years. A particularly large leap in urbanization occurred in the period between 650 BC and 430 BC. During this period the number of cities of 30,000 or more inhabitants increased from twenty to fifty-one, and the total population represented by these cities increased from 894,000 to 2,877,000, a more than threefold increase. There was another major urbanization spurt between 430 BC and AD 100, during which the number of cities of 30,000 or more inhabitants increased from fifty-one to at least seventy-five, and also during which the total population of these cities expanded from 2,877,000 to 5,181,000, an 80 per cent increase. This period is essentially the same period that McNeill and Curtin refer to as involving the emergence of the first truly long-distance trade network between East Asia and the Mediterranean.

World urbanization suffered a setback between AD 100 and 500, but this setback was only minimal and temporary. By AD 800, the total population of the largest cities (5,237,000) had regained the level achieved in AD 100. It took longer for the number of large cities to return to the level reached in AD 100 – there were seventy such cities in AD 1000 and seventy-five or more cities in AD 1300 – but not that much longer. Moreover, after AD 1000 the scale of world urbanization was clearly very large and continuing to grow, and, as already noted, the period after AD 1000 has been seen by McNeill and Curtin as involving another major leap in world trade networks.

Wilkinson has also constructed maps that show in a very graphic way the extent of world commercialization between 2250 BC and AD 1500. These maps clearly show that not only was there a major increase in the size and number of large cities, but also that the linkages between these cities grew and deepened dramatically over this period. For the most part, these linkages would have been commercial in nature. There can be no serious doubt that the scope and density of world trade increased enormously throughout this period.

Frank and Gills see the process of expanding world commercialization – which they refer to as a process of capital accumulation – as the central developmental process of world history, and one that is needed in order to explain developments in the non-economic spheres of agrarian societies. This is my view as well. Expanding world commercialization was a world transforming phenomenon. And I would argue that it was to a large extent an autonomous process in its own right, driven by the desires of merchants for greater wealth and economic power. Moreover, I believe that this process was absolutely critical to the development of modern capitalism after the sixteenth century. Some scholars, such as Eric L. Jones (1988), speak of the rise of modern capitalism as some sort of 'miracle' or gigantic 'historical accident.' But there was nothing miraculous or accidental about it. It required a long gestation period of very slow growth over many millennia because of the peculiar position of merchants and commercialism in the social structures of agrarian societies. As we know, agrarian societies were dominated by landlords who looked down their noses at merchants. Landlords kept merchants in their place, yet merchants were useful – indeed, in many ways necessary – to landlords. They could be taxed, and they were the source of the luxury goods that landlords sought. Therefore, although they had to be controlled closely, they could not be controlled *too* closely. And this gave merchants a certain degree of leverage to expand the scale of their operations surely if slowly. And expand those operations they did, such that in time their economic power and the scale of their activity on a world level had built up to the point where it constituted a 'critical mass' responsible for triggering a massive capitalist takeoff after the sixteenth century. The birth of modern capitalism required a slow evolutionary process of the buildup of dense and extensive networks of world trade. Frank and Gills have pointed us in the direction of acknowldging this world historical process. But to acknowledge it is only a beginning. We need to study it closely with an eye to many questions. What was the extent to which earlier forms of capitalism were 'rationalized' in Max Weber's sense? Were ancient merchants profit maximizers? What was the importance of financial arrangements in earlier forms of capitalism? What was the relationship between technological advance and commercial expansion? What role did the state play in ancient capitalism? These and no doubt many other important questions remain to be answered.

Although Frank and Gills appear justified in stressing expanding world commercialization as the central developmental process of world history, they say little or nothing about how this process related to developmental processes occurring within the non-economic sectors of agrarian societies. I see four other evolutionary processes in the agrarian epoch that loom especially important. The first and perhaps most obvious of these was population growth, which I suspect played a major role in the commercial expansion of the world. As populations grew and the size and density of urban areas expanded, the size of markets increased proportionately, as did the availability of workers and of various resources necessary to industrial production. During the long agrarian epoch that we are discussing, population grew steadily, although there were periods of population decline during the time around the collapse of the Roman Empire, and again in the fourteenth century AD. Between 3000 and 1000 BC world population remained relatively small, increasing from fourteen to sixty-two million. However, after the latter date world population began to grow to considerable size, and in many areas population densities increased markedly. From sixty-two million in 1000 BC, world population increased to 110 million by 600 BC and to 257 million by AD 200. After a decline during the second half of the first millennium AD, population began to grow again, reaching 400 million by AD 1200 and 461 million by AD 1500. World population exploded after this time (Livi-Bacci 1992; Eckhardt 1992).

A second major evolutionary process was political growth. Rein Taagepera (1978) has studied changes in the size of agrarian empires over approximately the last 5,000 years. He shows that there has been a significant increase in empire size during this time and marks out three phases of empire growth. The first phase begins with the rise of the very first states around 3000 BC. Before this time there were no political units with a size greater than 0.1 square megameters (one square megameter = 386,000 square miles). During the first phase of empire building the single largest agrarian empire seemed to maintain a size of at least 0.15 square megameters and to have at least occasionally attained a size of about 1.3 square megameters. A second phase of empire building was inaugurated around 600 BC. After this time the single largest empire was never smaller than 2.3 square megameters, and the maximum imperial size attained was 24 square megameters. More detailed calculations using Taagepera's data (Eckhardt 1992) show the size of the world's largest empire for a given date, plus the total size of all the world's empires added together. In 600 BC the world's largest empire (Persia) had a size of 5.5 square megameters, and the total size of all the world's empires was 7.85 square megameters. By AD 600 the size of the world's largest empire (Mesopotamia) had increased to 9 square megameters, and the total size of all the world's empires was 18 square megameters. In AD 1200 the relevant figures are 25.2 square megameters for the world's largest empire (Central Asia), and 32.7 square megameters for all the world's empires. After the decline of the Mongols, there was a dip by AD 1500 in empire size to 12.2 for the largest empire (Europe), and to 24.2 for all the world's empires. But this was because the Mongol empire was so extraordinarily huge, and the overall trend throughout this long period was clearly toward bigger empires and more of them spread over a larger part of the globe.

Taagepera believes that the increase in empire size during the second phase of political growth (600 BC–AD 1600) probably resulted from increasing sophistication in the art of power delegation, especially through impersonal bureaucratic roles rather than personal relationships. But it is also likely that the size increase was made possible by important developments in the areas of transportation and communication, as Taagepera himself notes. Empires could not become effectively larger until the means were available for controlling and integrating much larger areas.

Taagepera sees a third phase of empire growth beginning around AD 1600 with the emergence of the modern capitalist world. However, this phase is beyond the time period considered by this paper.

It is interesting to note that Taagepera's date for a sudden surge in the size of agrarian empires (600 BC) corresponds closely to the date given earlier for the emergence of a worldwide trade axis (200 BC). The two are undoubtedly causally related, for as E.L. Jones (1988) has argued, truly long-distance trade networks only became possible with the rise of very large empires. Only empires of that size had developed the technology of communication and transportation needed to facilitate worldwide trade.

As empires have grown throughout world history there has been a corresponding increase in the amount of power available to agrarian states. Although rejecting an evolutionary view of world history, Michael Mann (1986) nonetheless notes that there has been a long-term, cumulative, and unidirectional increase in power over the past 5,000 years. Indeed, Mann argues that the increase in power capacity has been so large that it is difficult to embrace in the same category agrarian societies early in the agrarian epoch and agrarian societies late in that epoch.

Accompanying and closely intertwined with political growth was a third major evolutionary process, that of technological advance. The expansion of technological capacity has had important consequences for economic subsistence, economic exchange, and military force. Clearly one of the most important inventions during the agrarian epoch was iron smelting. Iron ore deposits were discovered by the Hittites of Asia Minor sometime around 1800 BC, and soon thereafter the Hittites invented a technique for smelting. After about 1200 BC this technique came to be widely diffused throughout the agrarian world (Lenski 1970), and iron came to be used for weapons and tools. Lenski (1970) regards its effects on tool production as so important that he distinguishes between simple agrarian societies, which have no iron tools, and advanced agrarian societies, which do. The significance of the development of iron tools has been caught by R.J. Forbes (1954:592–93), who has said that

> the effect of the introduction of iron was gradually to extend and cheapen production. Iron ores were widely distributed and readily available; iron tools were cheaper and more efficient than those made of bronze. They rendered possible the clearing of forests, the drainage of marshes, and the improvement of cultivation upon a very much wider scale. Thus iron . . . greatly reinforced man's equipment for dealing with the forces of nature.

Iron also made a major contribution to military technology in the form of the sword (Derry and Williams 1961).

There was a wide range of other important technological developments of course. Among the most important we may list the catapult, the crossbow, gunpowder, the chariot, heavy cavalries, the naval galley, irrigation systems, the spoked wheel on fixed axle, wet-soil plowing, open-sea navigation, printing, the horseshoe, a workable harness for horses, the stirrup, the wood-turning lathe, the auger, the screw, the wheelbarrow, the rotary fan for ventilation, the clock, the spinning wheel, the magnet, water-powered mills, and windmills (Lenski 1970; Mann 1986). As can be seen from the list, some of these involved military techniques, but most of them involved economic production and exchange.

Technological change during the agrarian epoch occurred in many parts of the world, and a good many things were probably invented more than once (Ronan and Needham 1978). However, much of the technological change that occurred in the West was of Eastern, especially Chinese, origin. Among the many inventions acquired by the West from China may be listed: piston bellows, the draw-loom, silk handling machinery, the wheelbarrow, an efficient harness for draft animals, the crossbow, iron casting, the segmental arch bridge, the iron-chain suspension bridge, the canal pound-lock, nautical construction principles, gunpowder, firearms, the magnetic compass, paper, printing, and porcelain (Ronan and Needham 1978). Many of these inventions were made by the Chinese a millennium or more before their acquisition by the West.

A final evolutionary process in the agrarian world occurred within the ideological realm. In the first millennium BC, and especially in the sixth century BC, we see two dramatic ideological developments: enormously important achievements in philosophy, especially among the Greeks, and the rise of most of the major world religions. This period has been called by a number of scholars the Axial Age (Jaspers 1953; Eisenstadt 1986). During it we find the emergence of Confucius and Lao-tse in China, the Upanishads and Buddha in India, Zarathustra in Iran, the Old Testament prophets in Palestine, and such Greek scholars as Homer, Plato, and Thucydides (Jaspers 1953).

Were the events of the Axial Age independent occurrences in all three regions – China, India, and the West? Jaspers argues vigorously for such a view, but with our increasing recognition of the world-systemic links between these civilizations such a view seems difficult to support. Indeed, a work of historical fiction (Vidal 1981) suggests substantial intercommunication between the Axial Age regions. And what were the causes of the Axial Age phenomena? It is impossible not to notice that the Axial Age corresponds almost exactly in time with Taagepera's date for a major leap forward in the size of political empires (600 BC), and very closely to the beginnings of a truly worldwide trade axis. Were these political and economic developments driving the ideological developments of the Axial Age? Such a view is extremely tempting.

By way of conclusion, it may be useful to consider these five historical trends in their larger context. Anthony Giddens (1984) and Michael Mann (1986), arguing against evolutionary interpretations of world history, have claimed that human history is not a 'world growth story.' But it seems to me that that is exactly what it is: a world-historical evolutionary process operating simultaneously on the economic, demographic, political, technological, and ideological planes of human society. There is no question but that the major developments on all these planes were dynamically interrelated. Are Frank and Gills right to suggest that it was the economic developments that were driving the others? I think they are. Like them, I too embrace a strongly materialist view of historical change. But the whole process cries out for much more extended study, and undoubtedly such study will reveal that all five processes were mutually interdependent even if the economic element was dominant.

Part III

Global macro-historical processes

10 Information and transportation nets in world history

William H. McNeill

Some of the leading proponents of world system history, those who are heirs to a Marxist tradition, assume that material exchanges (supplemented by flows of money and credit) were what created and sustained world systems among the people of the past. I propose to argue that paying attention to information networks offers a more promising way to understand human history. The reason is that information about material goods, business risks and potential gains was only part of what passed through such networks, and in many cases other kinds of information had far greater effect in changing the way participants in the network actually behaved. In particular, religious ideas and organizations, almost wholly overlooked by those who concentrate on material exchanges, often altered human lives profoundly, sometimes affecting economic behavior in ways that cannot be reduced to calculations of material gain. A wide range of largely or entirely secular scientific, technological and aesthetic ideas and skills also passed through information networks, and also altered human lives, in greater or lesser degree.

The simple, obvious fact is that what makes us human is participation in information networks. Only by such participation do we learn who we are and what to do in everyday life. Language is the principal medium humans use to spread information – whether practical, theoretical, or fanciful. But as I point out in *Keeping Together in Time: Dance and Drill in Human Affairs* (1995), the extraordinary success that reliance on language to direct and coordinate behavior has brought within our reach rests on top of and mingles with older, gestural forms of communication that are needed to establish and sustain emotional cooperation.

If these propositions are true, it follows that a history of the human adventure on earth ought to focus on changes in the modes of communication, taking special note of alterations in their range and carrying capacity. Technological improvements in transport and in devices for recording and retrieving information will define the major eras of such a portrait of the past. But before sketching patterns of world history so defined, let me say a few words about the patterns of human interaction that created and sustained more local communities – bands, villages, cities, territorial states, polyethnic empires, and civilizations.

All human lives begin with helpless infancy. While awake, infants engage in almost continuous communication with parents – especially the mother – and other members of the immediate family. As they grow older, this is supplemented by interaction with others in the immediate vicinity. The result of something like twenty years of messages in and messages out is an adult that resembles those around him or her closely enough to fit smoothly into the larger community, whatever its character. Gestural communication dominates at first: language takes over gradually and by about age two becomes dominant, but speech remains bedded in gestural patterns of which we become almost entirely unconscious, though they remain essential for communicating emotions.

In accordance with the biological principle 'ontogeny recapitulates phylogeny,' this presumably recapitulates the history of our species. After our ancestors learned to walk on two legs, they probably next learned to dance together, and thereby aroused shared sentiments of solidarity. This allowed bands of hunters and gatherers to smooth over personal rivalries and frictions, improve cooperation generally and in particular to keep larger bands from breaking up as they do today among our close relatives, the chimpanzees. Larger bands, in turn, had decisive advantage in defending their hunting and gathering territory against smaller bands. Hence, only dancers survive, and all humans still dance. Chalk up success number one for a (still protohuman) improvement in communication.

Complex personal interactions within such groups eventually generated language which soon began to carry new meanings, not just about material matters like where to find the best berries, or how best to kill an animal and divide its meat among members of the group, but also about the spirit world, accessible through dreams and, more predictably, through trance induced by dance. Rules for dealing with the spirits were swiftly constructed. The first specialists, almost for sure, were experts in the supernatural who guided their fellows through resulting intricacies and were accorded both gifts and deference in return. Eventually, when the first complex societies arose in Sumer, spiritual specialists managed the collective effort necessary to erect monumental buildings for housing the gods where they conducted increasingly sumptuous rituals of worship to please them, and arranged all the other cooperative activities needed to sustain the cities of the Tigris–Euphrates flood plain.

The extraordinary way Sumerian priests shaped their society along new lines illustrates the way human beings became capable of remaking themselves and the world around them in accordance with a (largely arbitrary) world of meanings created by words. Grammatically and logically structured words, linking individuals together by shared meanings, came to enjoy a quasi-independent existence of their own, evolving across time, sometimes slowly, sometimes in spurts. Each separate language became a precarious semiotic equilibrium, analogous to the local biological equilibria that together constitute the ecosystem. And, as the Sumerian priests demonstrated so unmistakably, these semiotic equilibria came to be capable of controlling collective human behavior and directing it along new lines.

The process long antedated Sumer. Unceasing interaction (and frequent friction) between the real world (where people still had to find food and other material goods after all) and the semiotic world (where they found meaning, achieved status in their own eyes and those of their fellows, and learned everything else that made life worth living) accelerated innovation of all kinds. New forms of stone tools, succeeding one another with unprecedented rapidity, beginning about 60,000 years ago, are the principal surviving evidence of this extraordinary transformation of human behavior. Presumably it arose from the way play with words can guide human hands in their play with material objects, in this case, tools.

A corollary of the spurt in human inventiveness that thus became the norm was that hunters and gatherers became more and more skillful, allowing their numbers to increase. One important response was to expand into new territories, making all necessary adjustments to thrive in differing climates and ecosystems. But eventually, soon after all the habitable earth had been occupied, in more and more locations increasing numbers made the human impact on the biosphere unsustainable. This, in turn, provoked systematic food production, starting in different parts of the earth between about 10,000 to 8,000 years ago. Food production in turn allowed still greater numbers of human beings to survive until, in specially fertile landscapes, priests began to organize the first cities – once more, in different parts of the earth at times offset from one another by no more than 2,000 years.

The lesson to draw from this thumbnail sketch of humanity's prehistory is that once human groups began to act cooperatively in accordance with more or less arbitrary meanings invented by their use of words, a new, accelerated level of evolution set in. Just as living forms of plant life once transformed the atmosphere of the earth by releasing free oxygen, thus allowing animal life to evolve across ensuing geological epochs, so also man-made semiotic equilibria began to alter the biosphere by coordinating and directing human behavior along new lines. More recently, as we all know, humans have begun to alter the physio-chemical equilibria of the atmosphere and hydrosphere as well. Perhaps the near-abroad of space will be next to be affected by this new, peculiarly human, form of evolution.

Though cities with their priests and rulers, soldiers, merchants and artisans dominate the written records we inherit from the civilized past, it is worth reminding ourselves that from the time agricultural villages started to spread across suitable landscapes until almost the present, villages were the principal social context within which human beings lived. Nearly all villages were of such a size that everyone knew everyone else by sight, and knew how to behave towards everyone else in accord with well-defined rules instilled in childhood. Strangers were few at first, and later, when they multiplied, villagers learned how to deal with them too – sometimes offering gifts, sometimes taking flight, and sometimes simply disregarding outsiders.

Even when, after the rise of cities and civilization, more and more villagers were routinely compelled to hand over rents and taxes to landlords and rulers, they retained local autonomy for everyday activity. And by nurturing the young in traditional ways villagers continued to sustain both biological and cultural continuity among humankind, despite sudden crises, ceaseless changes and occasional disasters that sometimes wiped out local communities or even entire peoples. About three-quarters of humankind lived in such communities as recently as 1850; earlier the percentage was larger. In short, village family and community life was the human norm. No stable substitute has yet been found. The success with which urban styles of life have invaded and disrupted almost all the village communities of the world since, say 1950, rests on very shaky ground. City dwellers have not yet clearly demonstrated a capacity to sustain biological and cultural continuity, as the widespread recent breakdown of family nurture shows.

When cities first appeared, they were parasitic on surrounding villagers. Not only did city dwellers import food from surrounding villages, they also failed to reproduce themselves biologically and therefore had to import a stream of villagers (freely or as slaves) to carry out all the more unattractive tasks of the urban community. This was partly because intensified infections, provoked by large numbers crowded together, commonly raised urban deaths above the number of urban births. A second, parallel factor was that many city dwellers were unable to form families and raise children because they led lives of isolated dependency as household servants, soldiers, caravan personnel or slaves of one sort or another.

Within villages, on the other hand, disease was less frequent and from age five or so, children could begin to earn their keep by helping around the house and in the fields. Doing so, they automatically acquired all the skills and knowledge needed to carry on as adults simply by associating with their parents and siblings at work, but also in play. Occasional festive dances where old and young kept time together for hours on end were the most important form of play. Such ceremonies appear to have been universal; and this, in tandem with the network of meanings expressed in words, was what made villages so resilient. Personal frictions were regularly dissipated by shared euphoria brought on by the dance. Thus, two communication networks – one linguistic, one gestural – intertwined and reinforced one another, binding villagers together into a tightly-knit group where every individual had a place and knew what he or she had to do in almost all situations.

Through most of recorded history, of course, such primary communities were embedded in a far-flung network of other sorts of communication, organized and conducted primarily by city folk. Among them, no comparably powerful, comprehensive network of shared experience prevailed. Instead cities had to struggle with diversity. Occupational, religious, ethnic and neighborhood groups jostled one another. Individuals often had multiple group affinities and, depending on circumstances, could shift loyalty and behavior patterns from one to another – or straddle conflicting duties and expectations while suffering anxious confusion. What held diverse urban groups together was their common subordination to rulers, usually a single person whose power of course depended on support and cooperation from privileged followers and agents. They in effect became one more group, perpetually jostling with other groups for position and status.

Naked force and military organization played a part in defining who commanded and who (more or less) obeyed. But legitimacy always rested on words as well, used to invest rulers with some sort of supernatural, divine sanction. Acquiescence in such claims was essential for the rulers' everyday relations with subordinated groups. Only so could tax collection become routinized, customary and more or less predictable. An alliance of throne and altar, in some form or another, thus became central in all urban societies and in all of the different civilizations as well. They were constructed on the strength of a communications network that defined norms for the behavior of ruling groups throughout broad territories where thousands of villages and scores of cities had then to adjust to their common subordination.

Each of the diverse urban groupings over which rulers presided had its own network of shared meanings and an appropriate communications net to sustain them. That, and that alone, was what made a group out of the individuals who comprised it. But such networks overlapped and made different demands, so nothing like the tight-knit whole characteristic of village life could arise. Frictions provoked by discrepancies of belief and conduct were chronic. This distressing circumstance in turn kept on generating new sorts of behavior – sometimes hostile, sometimes defensive, sometimes seeking reconciliation with others.

Cities therefore became the primary seat of innovation, and contacts among different cities became the primary pathway for spreading particularly successful or attractive inventions from their place of origin to a wider world. Resulting diffusion of new ways of doing things and of thinking about the world constitute the warp and weft of world history since that was how most historical change was generated.

To be sure, other factors were sometimes operative. The way Easter Islanders destroyed the forests they needed for making canoes and moving statues shows that an isolated population may sometimes provoke very drastic change by disrupting its relation with the natural environment. But once specialized skills and divergent outlooks established themselves in urban clusters at a few locations on the face of the earth, the most powerful current of historical change was generated by contacts between such centers and surrounding peoples.

This was so because, in general, it appears to be true that bands of hunters and gatherers as well as herdsmen and fully independent agricultural villagers soon learned how to sustain a more or less stable relation with their environment. If numbers became too great, famine could be relied on to restore the balance with local food resources. But this was not very common. Instead, local customs usually had the effect of keeping human numbers from pressing too hard on available food resources. No doubt, resulting balances were unstable, but as far as one can tell, the fate of the Easter Islanders was exceptional. Instead, it was encounters with strangers with different ideas and skills that provoked the principal changes in local custom and traditional ways of exploiting the environment from the time that important differences of skill and knowledge began to distinguish occupational specialists from one another.

The resulting pattern of change resembles the shifting highs and lows on our weather maps. Just as winds blow from areas of high pressure to areas of low pressure, so also did skills and knowledge tend to flow from populations possessing high skills and specialized knowledge toward those whose skills and knowledge were less. Deliberate imitation and borrowing sometimes took place. More often change was initiated by efforts to resist outside threats and blandishments. But success in preserving local ways of life regularly required innovation to keep strangers and their seductive ways safely at arm's length.

Not only that: effective resistance usually compelled convergence. Only independent and opposite but similar behavior was ordinarily able to meet an outside threat on even terms. And once a community or people began to interact with skilled outsiders – whether by borrowing or by rejecting their disturbing novelties – additional adjustments and alterations of customary behavior always became necessary. Self-sustaining processes of social and cultural change were thus generated across the centuries within every community and people in contact with strangers possessing different and superior skills.

Why did superiorly-skilled strangers persist in intruding? Search for precious raw materials, slaves and other goods was one motive, but only one of several. Flight from an enemy or from punishment for some crime was another common motive. Wandering off into distant parts was a risky but attractive solution for youths who confronted obstacles in assuming fully adult roles. And once the so-called higher religions arose and started to anchor the lives of believers upon new meanings, practices and truths, religious missionaries, and holy men who merely sought to escape from the corruptions of the world, had additional motives for intruding on distant peoples. Last but not least, organized armies sometimes attacked in hope of plundering neighbors, and perhaps extracting taxes afterwards, or of driving them away and settling surplus home populations on new ground.

Little is known about the resulting interactions of peoples and cultures in pre-Columbian America, and next to nothing can be said of Australia or even of the interior parts of sub-Saharan Africa before about 500 AD. I am confident however that contacts among strangers provoked historical change in those continents just as they did in Eurasia. But since differences in skill and knowledge were less pronounced in those parts of the earth than was the case in Eurasia, scrappy and inadequate archaeological remains do not show paths of diffusion very clearly. By comparison, the history of Eurasia is far more accessible, thanks both to far richer archaeology and, above all, to the mass of written records dating back almost 5,000 years. In the balance of this chapter, I will therefore only try to point out landmarks in the evolution of the Eurasian communications net, which however extended to parts of Africa from even the earliest times.

In the beginning, our ancestors walked on two legs; then they danced together; and then they learned to speak to one another. But that was only a start, for thanks to the way the semiotic equilibria created by human languages interacted with the biosphere and with the physico-chemical equilibria of the earth's surface, human communities kept on inventing new and more powerful modes of communication. This development moved along two lines. One was harnessing new sorts of energy to movement across distances, thus expanding the range and carrying capacity of human muscles. The second was inventing new ways of storing and retrieving information, thus expanding the range and carrying capacity of human memory. But each improvement in transportation and each improvement in access to information expanded the reach and intensity of interaction among individuals and groups, thus accelerating historical change as the centuries passed.

This incremental intensification fed into an already existing network of slender interaction based solely on our biological heritage of walking, gesturing and speaking. With these means, throughout the millennia required to extend human occupancy across the varied landscapes of Eurasia, encounters with neighbors sustained a net of interaction that eventually extended, however loosely, from the Atlantic to the Pacific, and from the northern forests to the central grasslands, southern deserts and beyond into the monsoon lands of India and Southeast Asia. The succession of stone tool types that diffused slowly within that network is the only surviving evidence, and no one can suppose that the sites that have been explored and analyzed yet provide anything like an accurate and full record of what actually happened. But changes did occur and did spread.

The network, obviously, became tighter and more capacious with each technical improvement. It also recurrently extended its geographic reach until in recent centuries the whole globe was caught in its meshes. Eurasian developments therefore can claim to be central to human history inasmuch as what happened there successfully intruded upon, altered and eventually engulfed all the other communications networks and lesser civilizational structures of other parts of the earth.

The major landmarks of the transport and information access stories are entirely familiar, though the way successive improvements in moving people and goods across distances, and in storing and retrieving information affected economies, polities and cultures has attracted only sporadic attention from historians. Indeed the task of writing a really plausible account of the human past boils down to recasting familiar narratives of these dimensions of our past in the light of, and in accordance with, the notion that fundamental departures from old ways were regularly stimulated by changes in transport and in access to information.

Let me sketch plausible turning points (still only surmised and inadequately tested against the variety of local histories) in these two means of communication.

The muscular strength of domesticated animals was what first allowed humankind to transcend the limitations of human muscles for carrying heavy weights from here to there. Contemporaneously with the development of grain agriculture in the Middle East, donkeys, oxen and, subsequently to about 4000 BC, horses and mules were made to carry heavier burdens than people could bear. This was important for local life. Farmers needed to carry food, fuel and other commodities to their homes from where they grew or could be found in nature. Animal portage soon became important for long distance trade as well, circulating scarce commodities far and wide – things like obsidian, metals, precious stones, rare shells, textiles, jewelry, tools and weapons. Organized into caravans, animals could carry goods across indefinite distances, wherever fodder grew wild along the way. Simply by stopping to graze for part of the day, the animals fueled the next stage of the journey.

But for millennia the capability of caravans for conveying goods and information throughout the fertile areas of Eurasia was inhibited by the problem of safeguarding precious possessions against human predators. Before caravan linkages could begin to cross the continent, states capable of monopolizing organized violence within their borders had to come into being, and their rulers had to discover that safeguarding each passing caravan in return for a modest share of the goods it carried produced a better assorted and far more assured income than unchecked predation could ever do.

A cache of Assyrian records shows that such political conditions and understandings were firmly in place across Anatolia as early as 1800 BC. They also reveal remarkably sophisticated arrangements for standardized packaging of commodities, for negotiating protection rents with local rulers and even for insurance against losses. Caravans, clearly, were nothing new in 1800 BC and in all probability dated back, in some form or other, to prehistoric times when the obsidian of Catal Huyuk (say 6000 BC) was the principal trade commodity of the region.

But Anatolia was precocious. Effective monopolization of organized violence in a few hands across the whole of Eurasia required advances in communications and transport beyond simple animal portage. Rulers had to concentrate relatively massive resources in capital cities so as to be able to support a corps of military and administrative specialists. They also had to control subordinates at a distance and keep sufficiently in touch with them to be able to enforce their will by sending an expeditionary force to the spot in case of revolt. This required new kinds of transport and communications, and not surprisingly, they came on stream before the earliest cities arose.

On suitably dry and level terrain, wheeled vehicles made concentration of goods more feasible, carrying larger loads with fewer animals than caravans could do. On water, boats were far more capacious than carts and wagons, but could only traverse relatively slow rivers and calm seas at first. Both were already familiar in Sumer when the first cities arose between 4000 and 3000 BC. Sailing in the Mediterranean probably dates back to the same period of time, when islands like Crete were occupied for the first time. Navigation along the shores of the Indian ocean (and South China Sea?) was probably older, but no one knows when sailing vessels first began to come and go across long distances by exploiting the way monsoon winds reverse direction with the seasons.

The solid-wheeled wagons of early Sumer were too clumsy to turn and suffered from too much friction to carry heavy loads very far; but shipping probably was essential for supplying the early Sumerian cities, clustered as they were near the mouths of the Tigris–Euphrates. We know that long distance voyaging was commonplace. Contacts with Egypt date back to before 3000 BC for sure; they are attested with the Indus valley only from 2500 BC but that is because ground water halted excavation at Harappa and Mohenjo Daro at about that time horizon. Important information certainly passed between Sumer and Egypt. The earliest Egyptian monumental stone structures, for example, show clear signs of borrowings from Mesopotamian mud-brick architecture; while in Mesopotamia, Naram Sin (ca. 2250 BC) may have tried to consolidate the ramshackle empire he had inherited from his grandfather, Sargon of Akkad, by importing the idea of divine kingship from Egypt.

These imports did not flourish. Egyptians swiftly developed an architecture better fitted for stone construction; and divine kingship did not suffice to hold Mesopotamia together where the swift currents in the Tigris and Euphrates prevented shipping from moving up-river as in Egypt. Nothing like the Pharonic consolidation of the Nile valley below the first cataract was possible until overland transport achieved a carrying capacity that allowed rulers to concentrate sufficient resources to sustain overwhelmingly superior armed forces around their persons and thus overawe any and all rivals.

In Sargon's time, his armies were indeed larger than anyone else's, but they lived by plundering wherever they went. Stable government required rulers to substitute taxation for plunder; but taxing was only feasible when levies in kind could be delivered to the capital or some lesser administrative seat and used to support (more or less) obedient agents of the central authority. Efficient carts and wagons, using the hub and axle design we still employ to minimize friction, were invented about 1800 BC. They allowed concentration of tax revenues from suitably dry plainlands for the first time.

Use of writing to record tax payments and transfers was equally important for effective imperial administration. In addition, writing could transmit orders from the capital to provincial authorities and frame laws to guide general policy. When laws and written instructions were further supplemented by appropriate ritual (that is, by gestural communication of emotional attitudes) the bureaucratic principle came to life and soon proved capable of governing a considerable range of human behavior across comparatively long distances even in the absence of any actual encounter with the sovereign ruler in whose name officials acted.

Efficient wheeled vehicles, the administrative use of writing, and resort to the bureaucratic principle whereby an appointed official exercised legally defined powers were all invented in Mesopotamia shortly before and after 2000 BC. These innovations overlapped with and were closely connected to a radical change in warfare that gave supremacy on Mesopotamian battlefields to compound bows shot from swift two-wheeled chariots, beginning about 1750 BC.

These new forms of power were not long confined to the region where they had been invented. Chariots spread across Eurasia very rapidly indeed, reaching Egypt with the Hyksos about 1650 BC, penetrating North China and Northwest India about 1400 BC, and filtering across the whole of Europe between 1400 and 1000 BC. The diffusion of chariots was a landmark of Eurasian history, since the new instruments of war – supplemented by carts and wagons designed on the same hub and axle lines – allowed rulers to concentrate resources more effectually then before. Writing and bureaucracy traveled less fast and far than chariots and military technology did; but with varying delay they also diffused throughout the richer agricultural regions of the continent in ensuing centuries. The historic Chinese empire descends from the arrival of chariot warfare in the Yellow River valley. Aryan India was the creation of charioteers as well. And in ancient Greece the Myceneans used chariots too, and may even have done so as absurdly as Homer says they did.

The cultural geography of Eurasia thus assumed a new shape when what we are accustomed to think of as separate civilizations took form in China, India, and Greece, each of them loosely in contact with the older center of high culture in the Middle East, but in most respects independent. Each of these new centers of high skill of course created a circle of interacting peoples around it, and across ensuing centuries resulting encounters caused civilized skills to spread onto new ground. To be sure, civilized expansion was irregular in tempo, alternating sudden spurts with recurrent collapses. But the overall trend was to expand the geographic boundaries of each Eurasian civilization. Eventually, their respective peripheral zones began to overlap and interpenetrate one another, making the Eurasian landmass into a more and more tightly interactive whole. The role of the Eurasian-wide communications net became apparent about 1000 AD, inaugurating what I would like to call the modern era of accelerated change within first a Eurasian-African and then a global theater.

Before that landmark was attained, however, and as might be expected, further improvements in transport and communication hastened and intensified the process. Simplified alphabetic writing after about 1200 BC, making literacy accessible to a far wider number of persons than before, was one such change. The skills required to ride directly on horseback, while freeing hands and arms to shoot a bow, were a second, almost equally important change that occurred after 875 BC. Let me comment briefly on both.

Alphabetic writing certainly facilitated commerce; and it is noteworthy that many of the earliest surviving shards on which such writing was inscribed were mercantile contracts of one sort or another. More important in the long run, however, was its ability to create portable religions of the book. All the so-called higher religions – Buddhism, Judaism, Christianity, Islam and (rather less clearly) even Hinduism, together with several less successful faiths like Zoroastrianism – were based on sacred scriptures. Such scriptures offered authoritative guides for everyday behavior, even, or especially, in the confusing jungle of overlapping expectations that arose where strangers came together in cities, living side by side despite innumerable differences.

Amidst the moral dissonance of urban living, portable religions of the book allowed congregations of fellow-believers to create a diluted facsimile of the sort of primary village community that sustained the rest of humanity. It was a great invention. Like the older compromise between village autonomy and the demands of outside rent and tax collectors that sustained territorial states, the establishment of religious communities used sacred scripture to recreate a tolerable moral universe for poor and unfortunate multitudes. Sometimes these same moral rules were also shared in some degree or other by the rich and powerful who ruled over them.

Political boundaries decreased in importance when millions of persons began to mold their behavior on precepts drawn from sacred books that were the same (or almost the same) everywhere. Religions transcended their initial tie to locality and gave life new meaning, anywhere and everywhere, simply by constructing an indefinitely expansible number of local primary communities. The existence of such communities stabilized city life as never before. Without this invention, it seems improbable that the Eurasian network of interacting cities and civilizations could have flourished as luxuriantly and persistently as it did. That is because life-support for common folk at the bottom of society through religious communities, like the monopolization of organized violence at the top, was probably essential for the stability and expansion of the Eurasian communications net. And they, I claim, derived directly from writing and wagons respectively.

Cavalry and horseback riding had more limited but still very far-ranging effects. Riders could travel faster than ever before, carrying messages about one hundred miles a day when relays of fresh horses could be found. This made imperial government much faster in reacting to challenges from afar. Other news also traveled faster with all the usual advantages this conferred on those with superior information. Internal social structures across most of Eurasia also changed, giving greater importance then before to mounted warriors.

But the most significant effect of the spread of horseback riding was to give the pastoral peoples of the Eurasian steppe an enduring advantage over less mobile populations of the richer, agricultural lands to their south. As a result, the frontier between steppeland and farmland became critical for Eurasian military and polit-ical history from the seventh century BC when the first large-scale cavalry raids from the steppes took place until the seventeenth century AD when improvements in Chinese and European military tactics and training put steppe cavalrymen permanently on the defensive. Between those dates, the necessity of mounting guard against raiders from the steppe continually tested the proficiency of civil-ized armed forces in Eurasia. This had the effect of raising them far above levels attained elsewhere, making global aggression comparatively easy after 1500.

Yet civilized defense was not always successful. When, for whatever reason, frontier guard against the steppe weakened, successful raids quickly built up into conquest. The political history of the agricultural peoples of Eurasia, in fact, consists of little more than alternations between cavalry conquest by outsiders, who derived directly or indirectly from the steppes, and native reactions aimed at throwing the intruders out. The Chinese revolution of 1911 was the last gasp of this long standing political pattern that had commenced in 690 BC with the sudden appearance of the Cimmerians in Anatolia.

It lasted as it did because for something like 2,300 years steppe warriors could concentrate superior force almost at will and at any given point within their horses' radius of action. Speed of march was decisive, together with even speedier com-munication by special messengers making sure that each separate detachment reached the chosen battleground as planned. By the time of Ghengis Kahn (1162–1227), steppe horsemen had attained truly remarkable proficiency in these skills, and were therefore able to conquer and administer about half of the entire Eurasian landmass.

The principal civilized riposte to the superior mobility of steppe horsemen was the building of roads to allow armies to move faster. Such roads were also used to concentrate taxes and rents where they were wanted by those who consumed them; and for facilitating peacable commerce as well. Thus wheeled transport, at first confined to use on relatively dry plains, could now cross hilly terrain as well, making far larger empires possible. The Assyrians were the first to build roads systematically; and the enlarged size of the empire they constructed – uniting Mesopotamia, Syria and Egypt for the first time – shows how effectually roads reinforced the older devices of wagons, writing, and bureaucracy, allowing them to redistribute resources across very wide territories to meet the needs of their armies and administrators. A second effect was to diminish older barriers between Egypt and Asia, so that, as contacts multiplied, what had been separate civilizations eventually merged into a cosmopolitan Middle Eastern amalgam.

A different line of development rested on improvements in Mediterranean shipping. Minoans, Phoenicians and then Greeks became expert mariners, with vessels that could sail westerly before the summer trade winds and beat their way back by hugging the coastline and exploiting the diurnal on-shore and off-shore winds created by differential heating of land and sea. From very ancient times, manufactures from Egyptian and eastern Mediterranean workshops were exchanged for raw materials, especially metal and timber; but the sea trade of the Mediterranean took on a new dimension when a few Greek cities discovered that by planting their fields with olives and grapes, they could increase their standard of living enormously by sending these rare and precious commodities overseas and exchanging them for grain, fish and other commodities collected by local potentates from coastal populations by various forms of coercion.

Middle Eastern cities got their food from peasants round about by collecting unrequited rents and taxes. Beginning in the sixth century BC a few Greek cities got their food from remote coastlands of the western Mediterranean and Black sea by trade. In effect, coercion of a rural peasantry was exported to barbarian lands along with wine and oil, while at home free and equal farmers could and did assert their right to active, participatory citizenship, thanks partly to their role in producing wine and oil for export, and partly to the prevailing tactics of phalanx and trireme warfare, which put a premium on numbers of well-armed citizen soldiers and of well-trained citizen rowers.

This is not the place to explore the peculiarities of ancient Greek history in detail. All I wish to emphasize here is that exchanges of goods of common consumption with distant coastlands provided an essential base for the efflorescence of Ionian, Corinthian and Athenian society and culture; and these exchanges in turn depended on improvements in navigational skills and ship design, permitting ships to make headway even against the wind.

Exchange of oil and wine for grain and raw materials remained central to Mediterranean society throughout classical times. Diffusion of vineyards and olive groves to suitable regions in the western Mediterranean shifted centers of prosperity westward until climatic limits were reached under the Roman Empire. Roman roads in due course supplemented seaborne exchanges; but overland transport never came close to matching the carrying capacity or social and economic importance of shipping.

Ships became more seaworthy in the Indian ocean and Southeast Asia also, but as far as I know no other part of the world came to depend on long-distance exchange of basic commodities, as some Greek cities did; and the transformative impact of folding local farmers into an urban political-economic system as respected equals was not replicated anywhere else either. Perhaps for that reason the Greek and Roman heritage retains a peculiar resonance in modern times. We, too, exchange goods of common consumption cross long distances, and aspire to participatory citizenship – and even to rationality – as well.

By the time the Romans succeeded in incorporating the coastlands of the entire Mediterranean into their empire, other imperial states had formed a slender band across the Eurasian continent, reaching all the way from China to the Roman empire. Beginning in 101 BC regular caravan connections were established throughout those imperially governed territories, since their rulers all understood that negotiated protection rents yielded them more than confiscatory force could ever do. The so-called Silk route was often interrupted by political upheavals subsequently, but never for very long since by this time the advantages of commerce were patent to all concerned.

A notable magnification of the geographic range and carrying capacity of caravan commerce came when camels displaced mules and horses as the primary beasts of burden. This occurred in the Middle East after about 300 AD and found its most conspicuous military and cultural expression in the rise of Islam after 632. Camels carried larger loads a little faster than mules liked to walk, and could also cross deserts as other animals could not. This made the desert zone of Africa and Asia far more permeable. Accordingly, West Africa, Arabia, and the desert and semi-desert lands of interior Asia were swiftly incorporated into the Eurasian commercial and informational network centering in the ancient cities of the Middle East.

But caravans could not profitably carry cheap goods of common consumption over long distances as ships could do. This inevitably limited the impact of the Eurasian caravan network since for the most part it carried luxuries which only a few could afford. Ideas could and did percolate along the trade routes, and these sometimes affected human life profoundly. The spread of Buddhism, and its multiple impacts upon steppe peoples and Far Eastern agriculturalists offers one conspicuous example; so does the parallel and even more extensive expansion of Islam. Both these faiths traveled by sea as well; and the contemporary cultural geography of Southeast Asia and its offshore islands reflects the varied reception they (along with Hinduism) met among local peoples.

The next major landmark of Eurasian history derived from the serendipitous fashion in which the construction of an elaborately reticulated network of canals in China to regulate supplies of water for rice paddies began to constitute a safe and capacious transport system for the interior of that country. After the valleys of the Yangtse and Yellow Rivers were connected by the Grand Canal (605) simple canal boats became able to carry comparatively enormous quantities of goods across vast, varied and densely populated landscapes. It took a long while for the Chinese to develop attitudes and institutions that gave scope to the commercial possibilities of such a transport system, but when in 960 the Sung dynasty began to collect taxes in money rather than in kind in more and more parts of the country, common folk found themselves compelled to enter the market to get cash to pay their taxes.

The result was a rapid intensification of market transactions. Even poor peasants began to buy and sell a large part of the produce of their fields, as Greek citizen farmers had done in the sixth and fifth centuries BC. Nothing like participatory citizenship resulted. Confucian, bureaucratic principles were far too firmly entrenched for that. But a myriad of local specializations increased economic productivity enormously. Rewards of the market propagated improved artisan skills with unprecedented rapidity, so that China's wealth and power forged far ahead of other parts of the earth, as experienced travelers like Marco Polo and Ibn Battuta both testified.

Goods of common consumption entered the trade network so that a large proportion of the entire population of China came to depend on market exchanges for necessities of life. Comparable numbers had never done so before; and when new and improved Chinese goods began to flood abroad along the caravan routes and, more significantly, throughout the coastlands of the Indian ocean by sea, the effect was to intensify commerce across all of Eurasia. Even in the remote Mediterranean, Moslem and Italian cities became marginal participants in a network of commercial exchange that had its principal center and highest intensity in China.

Resulting changes in Eurasian life were profound and multiform. I cannot explore them here, other than to point out that three innovations arriving in western Europe from China – gunpowder, printing and the compass – were fundamental in laying the ground work for the Far West's subsequent overseas expansion. That expansion, of course, depended on Europe's own transport system; navigable rivers feeding ports where all-weather ships, painfully developed to withstand Atlantic tides and storms, connected Atlantic and Mediterranean Europe into an exchange network that by 1500 approached the geographic scale and carrying capacity of the reticulated network of Chinese canals.

As in China, goods of common consumption became the staple of European interregional trade: wool, salt, wine, fish and the like. And as in China an increasing proportion of the entire population began to take part by specializing production on whatever they could do best. Western Europe, in short, was catching up with China, thanks largely to its topography and to advances in shipbuilding and navigation that accumulated rapidly from the time that Europeans began to participate actively in the China-centered trade network of Eurasia. Other factors played their part; but they operated within a framework of communication created by new technologies of transport – and printing as well.

Europe-based subsequent advances in transport and communications are entirely familiar, and I need only list landmarks around which a sensible world history of modern times might be constructed. Ocean-going sailing ships were overtaken by coal-burning steam ships and then by diesel-driven vessels; but the increases in speed, reliability and carrying capacity that these changes brought were less dramatic than the improvement in overland transportation that occurred when first canals and graveled roads, then steam-driven railroads, internal combustion motors, hard surfaced roads and airplanes overcame age-old obstacles to the long-distance transportation of people and goods.

Industrial mass production depends on such transport. Its efficiency depends also on the modern revolution in communications: telegraph, telephone, radio, TV and now digitized computer-speak. Each change of transport and communication altered everyday life for an ever increasing proportion of the world's population, and will continue to do so for a long time to come, for we are by no means yet adjusted to instantaneous global communication or to global commerce, finance and division of labor.

Old local autonomies have withered as connections with the wider world increased their impact. In particular, villages no longer stand on their own as viable moral universes. How the human need for support from fellow members of a primary community can be reconciled with global transport and communications remains to be seen. I feel sure this will be one of the pivotal issues for the twenty-first century, since as of today we seem both unable to bear the costs of global entanglement and unable to do without the gains to be had from participation in the global flow-through economy.

Whatever the upshot, it seems evident to me that the most promising way to understand what is happening around us, as well as what has happened in times past, is to focus upon the information nets created by changing communication and transport. Personal identity and social groupings arise from communication and have always done so, while at the individual level it is communication with others that makes us human. Surely, then, it is not surprising that our most distinctive characteristic offers the most appropriate key to a better understanding of the human past.

11 Neglecting Nature

World accumulation and core–periphery relations, 2500 BC to AD 1990

Sing C. Chew

From an ecological point of view, one factor that is overlooked in the study of world system history is the dynamic-exploitative relationship between the process of accumulation and Nature. In an era of increasing global concern and awareness of the finite limits of natural resources, the growing realization of the contemporary losses in plant and animal species, and the continued susceptibility of the human species to climatological changes and diseases despite various scientific and technological advances, we cannot continue to direct our efforts on understanding world system history by focusing only on the dimension of the accumulation of 'capital.' In this chapter, I will proceed by emphasizing the necessity of including the continuous exploitative relationship with Nature in our attempts to discuss 5,000 years of world system history. I will suggest that the ceaseless accumulation of capital – which is seen as the motor force of the system – is self-defeating. Nature establishes limits on this process. The question is how does this dynamic relationship between capital accumulation, core–periphery relations, and Nature play out over the long term.

The exploitation of Nature: plus ça change, plus c'est la même chose

According to Frank (1993a), the accumulation of capital has played a central role in world system history for several millennia. For Wallerstein (1992), its 'ceaseless' nature emerged only with the modern world-system in the sixteenth century. Regardless of whether this process has been the underlying feature over the last five hundred years or the last several millennia, one of its manifestations is the appearance of environmental degradation and crisis. To maintain a surplus there must be continual exploitation of the natural environment. This is played out at the system-wide structural level via core–periphery relations and power rivalries within cycles of expansion and stagnation. Nature as the underlying basis of this equation fosters, conditions and inhibits the continued reproduction of the system. *As such, the limits of Nature become also the limits of the system. The interplay between the limits of Nature and the trends and dynamics of the world system defines ultimately the historical tendencies of world system evolution.*

Given the exploitative relationship with Nature, the continuity of the systemic process of the accumulation of 'capital' over the long term becomes an important concern. Capital, in this case, is by no means what Marxists would define as wage-labor capital, but is used in a more general context to mean the accumulation of surplus dependent on the state of technology and sociocultural practices of the period in question. In this regard, as Frank and Gills stated:

> for millennia already and throughout the world (system) there has been capital accumulation through infrastructural investment in agriculture (e.g. clearing and irrigating land) and livestock (cattle, sheep, horses, camels, and pasturage for them); industry (plant and equipment as well as new technology for the same); transport (more and better ports, ships, roads, way stations, camels, carts); commerce (money capital, resident and itinerant foreign traders, and institutions for their promotion and protection); military (fortifications, weapons, warships, horses and standing armies to man them); legitimacy (temples and luxuries); and of course, the education, training, and cultural development of 'human capital.'
>
> (Frank and Gills 1992:7)

This kind of argument might be objectionable to some for it would mean that there has been no break in the systemic logic (i.e. the process of capital accumulation in the conventional sense) of the world system. However, this line of reasoning fits in with our analysis of ecological degradation and crisis over the long term of the world system.

If the accumulation of capital is one of the central dynamics of world history, the specifics by which it takes place becomes important. The dimension of trade exchange has been identified as one of the underlying processes circumscribing the accumulation of capital. Much has been written on the question of whether trade exchange constitutes and enhances the accumulation process. In the Dobb–Sweezy debate, Dobb (1952, 1976) suggested that trade was not the prime factor in the accumulation of capital at the start of 'capitalism.' Sweezy (1976), argued that medieval trade was one of the prime factors leading to the transition from 'feudalism' to 'capitalism.' In other words, trade exchanges are part of the overall process. Wallerstein (1974a: 41–2) has argued that the exchange of preciosities in Europe and Asia during the fifteenth and sixteenth centuries did not produce important impacts. Schneider (1977) challenged this position by arguing that prestige goods did generate systemic effects in premodern times by providing local elites with important sources of power and stability. Abu-Lughod (1989), Frank (1993a) and Gills (1995) also underscore the importance of prestige goods exchange. Ekholm and Friedman (1982:90) have shown that besides preciosities, trade exchanges in bulk goods such as wood and grain were undertaken by Mesopotamia around 3000 BC. What this means is that trade exchanges were part and parcel of the capital accumulation process in ancient world-systems. Chase-Dunn and Hall (1992:89–90) shared this view that trade exchanges, which can include staples or preciosities, are important aspects reflective of the interconnections of world-systems. In my own work (Chew 1992, 1993, 1995), the exchange of timber and wood products (bulk goods) between kingdoms, civilizations, and states over

5,000 years does suggest that trade exchanges help constitute the world accumulation process. The production and exchange of preciosities (such as scented woods) and bulk goods reflect the processes of the accumulation of capital on a world scale and the global exploitation of the natural environment.

Trade and commodity exchanges do play a part in the process of capital accumulation, and thus in the overall dynamics of world system/s. The issue of whether these exchanges occurred within a single overarching system as Gills and Frank (1992) have argued or whether they reflect intersocietal networks of interactions as Chase-Dunn and Hall (1992) and Curtin (1984) have stated is an issue. The discontinuity argument has been the dominant mode of analysis in contemporary historical research and world-systems analysis for a while. We have witnessed its outcomes, including the Eurocentric emphasis of world historical transformations. There is, however, less research done to date examining the possibility of a historical system that has been evolving for quite some time. In my own work, the exploitation of Nature via the production and exchange of timber and wood products suggests a continuous process for over 5,000 years. Some qualitative changes in the manner this economic production and exchange have occurred may be noted, however the exploitative manner by which human communities have related with the natural environment across spatial and temporal dimensions has not changed significantly. What qualitative and quantitative shifts have occurred are the results of technological changes in the capacity to assault the natural environment. Few forested areas of the planet have been left untouched. In reaction to this, we also find movements of resistance and philosophical challenges to the assault on Nature over world history (Chew 1995).

The accumulation of capital over the long term is characterized by core–periphery relations. In my own work, core–periphery relations contribute to the assault on Nature especially after a long cycle of intensive and extensive capital accumulation. Furthermore, this degradative activity over the long term establishes limits to the reproduction of accumulation processes (for example, requiring relocation of production depending on the exigencies of the accumulation processes), which in turn impacts on the continuation of core centers of accumulation of the world system/s.

Naturally, if cycles of expansion and stagnation punctuate the rhythms of the world system, one would expect that environmentally degradative effects would follow the patterning of the cycles of growth and stagnation. Because of their long temporality, it would be more appropriate to term the increasing appearance of environmental degradative instances as 'long swings.' My beginning and thus far limited exploration of these 'long swings' of environmental degradation seems to suggest that they correlate with population growth, at least for one country (China) over a 2,000 year period. Population growth trends have been described to fit an 's' curve (a logistic curve) whereby a period of accelerated growth is followed by a slowdown, and the limits of the curve asymptotically approaches a horizontal line that is parallel to the asymptote of origin. If this is the case, the dimension of population and its interrelations with the other features of the world system must be included in our analysis of long-term change. Especially in our case, population is a variable that determines the sustainability of Nature, which in turn is also determined by Nature.

What follows attempts to address these thematics. The information and data presented should be treated as suggestive (rather than conclusive) of the dynamics of the world system over the long term.

Forest exploitation in world history: capital accumulation, core–periphery relations and environmental limits

Wood has been exploited as a building material and a fuel for over 5,000 years (Perlin 1989; Ponting 1991). These requirements meant that forests had to be cut leading to deforestation and its associated consequences such as flooding, loss of topsoil, temperature increases and biodiversity losses (Roberts 1989). Wood has been a basic commodity underlining the reproductive aspects of societies, king-doms, states, and civilizations. As such, it facilitates the accumulation of capital or depending on cultural needs and availability, is itself a precious commodity for exchange in overall surplus generation. Deforestation to meet needs for wood is by no means the only difficulty. The clearing of land for agriculture so that grain and livestock needs could be met for local consumption or exchange has to be underscored. The advent of agriculture has been one of the main causes of deforestation and environmental degradation in early world history (Ponting 1991).

2500 BC to 500 BC: Mesopotamia, India, Crete, and Greece

If we examine the world from Mesopotamia to the Indus valley around 2500 BC we find the sustained utilization of wood products to meet various needs. In third millennium BC, the kingdom of Lagash and Ur utilized wood for buildings (including temples), ship construction and canals. Consumptive needs were high, as Lagash and Ur had populations of 37,000 and 65,000 respectively. The wide-spread use of tools requiring wooden handles, and the need for wooden furniture and utensils increased wood imports. With the increased use of bronze, wood was required as fuel for foundries. As a core center of accumulation, both local forests and imports from the Ammanus mountains (Southwest Turkey), from South-east Arabia, and as far away as the Indus region of India were exploited (Tibbetts 1956; Edens 1990; Ratnagar 1981). Wood was in such high demand that during periods of accelerated economic expansion its value was equivalent to precious stones. Some types of wood were even stored in the royal treasury (Perlin 1989:41). Expeditions were sent to seek new sources when wood supply was constricted. Luxury goods from Babylon were traded for Cretan wood. What we witness was the overall expansion of socioeconomic growth sustained through wood consumption in production, and the functioning of core–periphery relations.

In the Indus valley around mid-2500 BC, the Harappan civilization with its trade contacts with Mesopotamia was flourishing. Wood, stone, metals, cereals, oils and other items were exchanged with Mesopotamia. The Indus valley was richly forested during this period (Ponting 1991). Teak, fir, pine were extracted from the Western Ghats, the Jammu ranges, and the Panjab piedmont. Widescale building of temples and palaces required mud bricks that had to be manufactured by drying in ovens fueled by wood (Wheeler 1968; Marshall 1931). In addition, the utilization of copper and bronze for farming implements and other household items also required wood as a fuel source for their manufacture.

Bronze Age Crete, with its trade in wood products with Near Eastern Mari and Babylon, emerged as a center of accumulation. Growth was concentrated at places like Knossos (population 30,000 in 1360 BC) where an abundant supply of timber fueled transformations (Chandler 1974:79). Like Mesopotamia, massive utilization of wood was required for shipbuilding, bronze and pottery manufacturing and building construction, including palaces and administrative offices. At the height of Minoan power, there was extensive demand for wood to build merchant and warships as a consequence of the increased trade between Crete, mainland Mycenaen Greece and the eastern Mediterranean (Meiggs 1982:97).

The trade between Crete and Mycenaen Greece was facilitated by the bountiful forests on the Greek mainland. This control of abundant resources allowed the Mycenaens to demand a hefty sum for wood that the Cretans needed. As a consequence, wealth was transferred from Crete to the mainland (Perlin 1989: 54). As a center of accumulation in the Mediterranean, Mycenae by 1350 BC had a population as large as Knossos, and was in an expansionary phase building palaces and manufacturing bronze products and pottery. There were also extensive trade relations with southern Italy and the Levantine coastal areas (Chandler 1974:79; Perlin 1989). This intensive use of the environment led to major deforestation, generated severe pressure, and eventually led to decline.

Deforestation does not necessarily mean that the land is permanently devastated if the assault on the woodlands is not continuous or intensive, and ample time is provided for rejuvenation. In the case of mainland Greece, by the sixth century BC the forests had recovered. However, by this time the urban population had increased as well, and between the sixth and the fourth centuries widespread maritime trade ensued between Greece and Asia Minor. Large merchant fleets were built and colonies were established 'to ensure a flow of essential commodities and materials to the mother city' (Thirgood 1981:9). Colonization also spread with settlements in southern Italy and Sicily in the west, and around the Black Sea as well as in northern Greece (Meiggs 1982:121). These settlements became centers of commerce and manufacturing activities in addition to agriculture drawing on their hinterlands for supplies. All in all, this socioeconomic expansion facilitated the accumulation processes of the city-states of mainland Greece. In terms of timber, the trade extended to cover the central and eastern Mediterranean including the Black Sea, Asia Minor and the Caucasus (Thirgood 1981). There was also exchange of special wood products such as teak and ebony with India paid for by manufactured goods, underscoring the continuity of trading relations with India as far back as the third millennium BC. With continued economic expansion came increased urbanization, leading to pressure for increased agricultural production requiring the colonies in the outlying areas to provide food. Industrial products were manufactured to exchange for basic primary resources. Hinterland areas such as eastern Greece and western Asia Minor were subsequently depleted of forests. Other coastal regions of Phoenicia, Syria, Egypt, and Italy provided for the food needs of an urbanized Hellenistic Greece. Deforestation occurred in these areas as well.

This expansionary period generated an increase in the production of manufactured commodities requiring basic natural resources such as iron ore. Where iron was exported to mainland Greece, forests were depleted for metal smelting. A million acres of productive woodland were required to meet the needs of a single metallurgical center during the classical age (Thirgood 1989:56). With developments in the banking system from the sixth century BC there were profitable investments made in agricultural production. Rising prices for agricultural produce, and the increasing use of manures coupled with controlled times for ploughing and harvesting, made farming more profitable and thus facilitated this expansionary process. Such financial investments further spurred on deforestation.

Ecological crisis of the period

The extensive and intensive utilization of the forests led to excessive deforestation. These early social systems were dependent on the production of an agricultural surplus to reproduce their social hierarchies, with increasing numbers of priests, rulers, bureaucrats, and soldiers. In Mesopotamia, land clearings created soil erosion leading to siltation of the rivers, and making the land more waterlogged. As the land became waterlogged, the water table would rise, leading to more mineral salts being brought to the surface where the high summer temperatures (40 degrees C) produced a thick layer of salt. Perlin (1989:43) has indicated that excessive deforestation of the northern mountains of Mesopotamia around 2400 BC led to an accumulation of mineral salts in the irrigated farmlands of southern Mesopotamia which over the course of 300 years led to 42 per cent declines in crop yields. By 1800 BC, crop yields were only about a third of the Early Dynastic period, and no wheat was grown in southern Mesopotamia (Ponting 1991:72). Thus when agricultural production went down in Sumeria due to increasing salinity, 'the superstructure of administrators, traders, artisans, warriors, and priests that comprised this civilization could not survive' (Perlin 1989:43). Deforestation was one of the factors leading to the shifting of the center of accumulation from Mesopotamia to Babylonia around 1700 BC. Second millennium BC Babylon eventually suffered from the same condition. The scarcity of wood led to increasing fuel costs and prices for wooden articles.

As in Mesopotamia, the Indus Valley's complex, hierarchical social system involved intensive agricultural production to feed the ruling elite. Trees were cut down as fuel to dry bricks for their buildings and palaces. Along with deforestation, salinization also occurred in the agricultural areas leading to the further inability of the social system to support itself (Ponting 1991; Hoffman 1980:34). By 1900 BC, environmental degradation was contributing to the decline of the Indus civilization (Ponting 1991:73).

In the late Bronze Age, these conditions were repeated in Mycenaean Greece where the deforestation of the hillsides resulted in large amounts of earth and water draining from the slopes onto the Plain of Argos and filling up the streams, leading to extensive flooding. Tiryns and its agricultural lands were affected by flood waters. Pylos' harbor suffered from siltation, as did the island of Melos. With the loss of topsoil, agricultural production in areas such as Messinia diminished.

Extensive deforestation also impacted on the production processes of these social systems. Wood scarcity at Knossos forced changes in production locations or resulted in their closures. Over time, the continued reliance on imported wood from Mycenae and Pylos resulted in the transfer of wealth from Crete to the Greek mainland (Perlin 1989:54). Mycenae benefited from its abundant supply of forested areas and did not pursue a sustainable yield for its forests. By the late Bronze Age, where pasture land was cleared in Mycenae for sheep grazing, metal-lurgical production works had to be relocated to lesser populated areas where wood supplies were more available. Mycenaean prosperity built on metallurgical and pottery works suffered with the decline in fuel supplies, especially the pottery works at Berbati and Zygories. Population migration followed the closure of these manufacturing centers and the abandonment of Phylakopi coincided with the deforestation of Melos, where the town was located. The same situation occurred in Berbati, Midea, Prosymna and Zygories in 1200 BC, and there were also population losses for Mycenae, Pylos and Tiryns. Throughout Mycenaean times, towns and settlements disappeared. In Southwest Peloponnese the number dropped from 150 to fourteen. Other regions experienced similar declines (Perlin 1989:66). By the eleventh century BC, the number of inhabitants fell by 75 per cent (Perlin 1989).

400 BC to AD 500: Classical Greece and Rome

By the beginning of the fifth century BC, the ecological conditions in Athens and on mainland Greece had recovered and it was on a socioeconomic growth trajec-tory. Becoming a center of accumulation also required a strong navy to ensure control of trading routes and to thwart aggression from Persia. Because the Per-sians controlled much of northern Greece, Athens initially had to rely on local timber for shipbuilding. By 357 BC, it had an inventory of 285 triremes (Meiggs 1982:123). With the defeat of the Persians in 469 BC, Athens' position as a center of accumulation in the Mediterranean was ensured and socioeconomic expansion resulted in rapid urbanization requiring large quantities of wood for buildings and houses. By this time the city's population had grown to nearly 200,000 (Chandler 1974:79). This demographic surge, like the previous period in world history, increased the demand for wood as fuel (charcoal) and for the manufacture of commodities (Perlin 1989:86). As a consequence the price of wood rose. This prompted the Athenians to search for other sources through conquest and colonization. One such source was Amphipolis which Athens colonized in 495 BC. The extensive use of timber for shipbuilding to fight the Peloponnesian War led Athens to rely on Amphipolis (Meiggs 1982; Perlin 1989). When the latter source was cut off, Athens turned to Macedonia for wood (Meiggs 1982).

Like Hellenistic Greece, the pace of socioeconomic activity increased when Rome became a center of accumulation. Urbanization engendered deforestation. To meet its timber need, Rome subjugated its surrounding hinterland. The forests of the Po valley were also exploited. As the power of Rome grew, expansion followed into western Europe and North Africa. There was pressure to increase the food supply, and many of the outer areas of the empire were transformed into granaries, particularly after 58 BC when Roman citizens were given free grain (Ponting 1991; Thirgood 1981). The forested areas in North Africa were deforested and cultivated, and by the first century AD, the Roman province of Africa sent each year enough grain to feed a million people for eight months (Meiggs 1982:374). Besides grain, other natural resources were sought to fuel the processes of accumulation. Iberia was conquered for its silver, and copper was sought in Cyprus. Mining for these resources meant further deforestation. An extensive region-wide trade ensued, for which cheap manufactured products were produced (Thirgood 1981:29).

Like the centers of accumulation in Mesopotamia and the Indus Valley, a lavish lifestyle was established in Rome. This required the utilization of wood directly and as fuel to make bricks or concrete. By the first century AD, Rome had a population of one million people requiring substantial inputs of resources such as water. The water had to be transported via aqueducts from 700 storage basins and 130 reservoirs made out of lime-based concrete or fired clay. An oak trunk of 32 feet, one and one half feet in diameter was required to make one ton of lime (Meiggs 1982). Wood was used to heat Roman baths and villas, and to manufacture newly popular products of glass, as well as pottery, bronze, and iron. To maintain temperatures of between 130–160 degrees Fahrenheit for a single public bath, 114 tons of wood was required per year. Central heating of a Roman villa required over two cords of wood per day (Perlin 1989:112).

Ecological crisis of the period

With this scale of economic expansion, ecological degradation naturally followed. Roman forest loss was predominant by the end of the second century AD and continued to the fourth century (Shaw 1981:392; Ponting 1991:77). During the four hundred years of silver smelting in Iberia, 500 million trees were cut (Perlin 1989:125). North Africa's forests were devastated to make way for grain cultivation. Morocco lost 12.5 million acres of forests over the Roman period. Attenborough (1987) and Randsborg (1991) both note the deforestation. The Roman's view of the natural world was similar to the predominant anthropocentric viewpoint of the late twentieth century. In the words of Cicero: 'We are the absolute masters of what the earth produces. We enjoy the mountains and the plains, the rivers are ours. We sow the seed and plant the trees. We fertilize the earth . . . we stop, direct, and turn the rivers, in short by our hands we endeavor, by our various operations in this world, to make, as it were another nature' (Thirgood 1981:29–30).

With deforestation we also witnessed soil erosion and siltation of ports and low-lying areas. The port of Paestum in southern Italy silted up and the town of Ravenna lost its access to the sea (Ponting 1991). Ostia, which was the port for Rome, managed to survive after major dock reconstruction. Because of siltation, cities in Greek Asia Minor such as Priene, Myus, and Ephesus (fifth century BC to second century AD) became landlocked.

Deforestation also has the impact of forcing the relocation of industries which over time might lead to loss of commercial and productive dominance. By the fourth century BC, Athens experienced this fate and faced shortages of wood. It had to relocate its metal industries. This also occurred toward the last years of Rome when industries had to be relocated to Europe so that fuel sources were closer to production.

AD 500 to 1500: Asia

The pattern of wood resource extraction is repeated in Asia. The first assault on the forest cover in India was as early as the third millennium BC, in northern China around the Hwang Ho river basin from about the same period, and in Southeast Asia (such as the Malayan peninsula) about 2500 BC (Wheatley 1961; Tibbetts 1956). Our previous discussion underlined the trade exchange between India, Mesopotamia, and the Mediterranean zone. Tibbetts (1956:183–4) reported evidence of Indian wood in early Sumerian cities indications of wood imports as early as 2000 BC. Trade between Mesopotamia and China began as early as the seventh century BC. Wheatley (1959:19) noted that Chinese trade envoys were sent by the Han emperor Wu to explore the South Seas as far as the Bay of Bengal during his reign from 141–87 BC. Besides luxuries and spices, brazil wood, cotton cloth, swords, sandal wood, camphor, rugs, and even African slaves were traded (Wheatley 1959; Lim 1992; Lian 1988).

With the unification of China by 221 BC, expansion to the south was pursued. The classic core–periphery relationship with China as the center of accumulation and kingdoms and city-states in Southeast Asia as the periphery can be seen in the trade exchanges that occurred. China supplied the silk and manufactured com-modities while the hinterland supplied the natural resource products like wood and spices. Tribute missions from Southeast Asia and South India started arriving in China during the second century AD. Such missions, according to Wang (1958:119), paid tribute so that political and economic concessions could be obtained. The state of Lin-yi in AD 433 provided tribute to obtain territorial concessions in Chiao-chou, and the state of Funan in 484 AD demanded justice from the incursions of Lin-yi. A mission from Lin-yi brought tribute of 10,000 kati of gold, 100,000 kati of silver and 300,000 kati of copper (Wang 1958:52). Such tribute missions increased over time. By the Tang dynasty a total of sixty-four missions were recorded (Wang 1958:122–3).

By the third century AD the trade in wood products had grown. Gharu wood was imported to southern China by merchants from the Malay archipelago, Sumatra, and even Sri Lanka. City-states such as Lo-yueh (near Hanoi) were the (semiperiperal?) collection centers for forest products. Tun-sun, situated on the Malay peninsula, was a dependency of the state of Fu-nan in Indochina. Judging from the amount of tribute provided to China, these states must have been prosperous. Lo-yueh, for example, was said to have 20,000 soldiers and palaces (Wheatley 1961; Wang 1958; Dunn 1975).

The trading relationships between the kingdoms and city-states of Southeast Asia were buttressed by Persian and Arab merchants around the seventh century AD. The power and number of these merchants grew. By the mid-eighth century AD they were of such substantial strength that they settled their disagreements with the Chinese by burning buildings in Canton in 758 AD. Along with the Arabs and Persians, the kingdom of Srivijaya situated in Sumatra was developing into a regional power in Southeast Asia (Wolters 1967; Wang 1958; Wheatley 1961; Coedès 1966). Srivijaya maintained its commercial position for at least two centuries (eighth–ninth).

By the end of the ninth century AD, the zone circumscribing the Arabian Sea, the Bay of Bengal, the Straits of Malacca, and the South China Sea was one of trade and exchanges between cities and kingdoms located in southern Arabia, southern India, the Malayan archipelago, Sumatra, Java, Indochina, and southern China with the Mediterranean (Wang 1958; Wheatley 1961). The volume of trade exchange which included wood products continued and by the middle of the Tang Dynasty, the ships of Sri Lanka – over 200 feet long and carrying six to seven hundred persons – were plying the waters of the South China Sea. These ships were probably built in China because of the abundant timber resources in the coastal areas of Chang-chou and in Ch'ao-chou, Hsun-chou, Lui-chou, and Chin-chou of Kwangtung province (Wheatley 1959:109). By AD 987, during the Sung Dynasty, the southern maritime trade provided a fifth of the total cash revenue of the state. Such a high volume led the state to support missions overseas to induce foreign traders to come to trade at Chinese ports.

With its overland Central Asian trade routes cut off after 1127 AD, China proceeded to exploit the routes of the South China Sea. Ebony, gharu wood, laka wood, pandan matting, cardamons, ivory, rhinoceros horns, and bees wax were imported from Asia and India (Dunn 1975; Wheatley 1959). To illustrate the increase in trade between 1049 to 1053, the annual import of tusks, rhinoceros horns, pearls, aromatics and incense was about 53,000 units; after 1175 AD they reached 500,000 units. The increase in activity naturally led to the emergence of a powerful merchant group which gradually came to manage all the major governmental trade monopolies. With the Mongol control of South China in 1277, trade with the rest of Asia and the Middle East was further encouraged. Southern China by the end of the thirteenth century had about 85–90 per cent of the country's population. The region experienced an expansionary phase between the ninth and fourteenth centuries whereby industry intensified and agricultural production increased. This must have led to deforestation to clear land for farming and to provide wood to fuel kilns for the manufacture of pottery and metals. Metallic currency was used as payment for products of Asia and the Middle East, and along with this silk and pottery were exported. According to Wheatley (1959) and Yamamoto (1981), by the time of the Sung dynasty, there was a deficit in the Nanhai Trade which was covered by payments in bullion. During this period, China was also to experience a metallic coin shortage (Yamamoto 1981:24).

After the fall of the Yuan dynasty, the Ming dynasty proceeded to build the Nanhai Trade. China had a sizable navy; by the end of the fourteenth century, it had 3,500 ships of which over 1700 were warships and 400 were armed transports (Lo 1958). China utilized its own pine and cedar forests for shipbuilding. Between 1403 and 1433 there were seven naval expeditions comprising as many as sixty-two vessels each, and carrying 37,000 soldiers (Yamamoto 1981). Under the command of Admiral Cheng Ho, these expeditions sailed as far as Mecca, Ormuz, Aden, Mogadishu, and Juda.

The pattern of accumulation is also repeated in Japan. Forests were cleared from AD 200 onwards for fuel to produce metal implements for domestic use and for fortresses, temples, and shrines. To Totman (1989:10), 'agriculture and metallurgy were the human innovations that most dramatically affected prehistoric Japanese forests.' Forest exploitation was continuous from AD 600 to 1670. From AD 600 to 850 the ruling elites of Japan proceeded with a building boom, constructing palaces, mansions, shrines, temples, and monasteries. These buildings were erected near the capital cities of Nara and Heian (Totman 1989, 1992). By AD 628, forty-six Buddhist monasteries were built. It has been estimated that 100,000 koku of processed lumber were used to build a single monastery (Totman 1989:17). (A hundred thousand koku of processed lumber is sufficient to build 3,000 ordinary 1950s Japanese style houses.) Tokoro, as cited by Totman (1989:17), estimated that the three centuries of monastery building starting from AD 600 consumed 10,000,000 koku of processed lumber.

By AD 1000, the population of Japan had reached 6,500,000 and it was to double by 1600. Such surges meant that wood resources were required to meet the needs of the growing population. The capital city of Heian faded away by the twelfth century after its surrounding forests were cut (Totman 1992:19–20). To meet the socioeconomic expansion, Japan's old growth forests were devoured by the seventeenth century, with continued monumental construction and rising urbanization in cities like Kyoto, Osaka, and Edo, whose populations ranged from 400,000 to one million persons. By 1720, the country's population increased to thirty-one million.

Mediterranean and Europe

In the Mediterranean during this period we find Venice a center of accumulation, assuming mastery of the seas. A giant ship factory was built called the Arsenal, comprised of previously fragmented privately owned shipyards that were organized into one state operation. To satisfy the demands of this enterprise the surrounding forests provided wood and pitch for shipbuilding. The Venetian glass industry also required extensive amounts of wood that led to deforestation. To feed the growing population, pasture land had to be cleared. This led to scarcity, and by 1530 shipbuilders had to pay twice the price for wood compared to their predecessors. As a consequence, the pace of shipbuilding had to be scaled back affecting the accumulation processes. Later in the century, Venetian ships were built in northern Europe, especially in Holland, thus giving the latter the opportunities for its ascent as a center of accumulation. To Perlin (1989), this lack of access to wood further hampered Venice's position in the overall accumulation processes, and was one of the factors that led to its decline as a major trading center. Venice's decline led to the shift of commercial power to northern Europe.

By the fourteenth century the forests of southern England had regenerated from Roman era exploitation, and England was exporting wood to Holland and France. The growing rise of Holland as a center of accumulation meant that England was part of the peripheral hinterland supplying wood to fuel Holland's needs. Six hundred shiploads left England for France each year, and English wood, especially its oak, was in high demand (Perlin 1989:163). England's own consumption of wood accelerated with the development of munitions production around Sussex during the reign of Henry VIII. With the production of iron for the manufacture of canons, wood consumption rose. Production of one ton of bar iron required forty-eight cords of wood. Demand for wood also rose with increased production of copper, salt, glass, and shipbuilding for the Royal Navy and merchant marine. For the latter, a large warship required 2,000 oak trees at least a century old (Chew 1992:25). Besides utilizing its own wood resources, England also exploited the forests of Ireland.

Ecological crisis of the period

Like the ancient civilizations of Mesopotamia and the Indus Valley, rapid deforestation in early China generated the conditions of ecological crisis. With population increases requiring more arable land, and the increasing utilization of wood to provide palaces, temples, and tombs, more pressure was added to the already fragile ecological conditions. Problems emerged in the fifth century BC (Bilsky 1980).

Deforestation causes top soil loss and siltation. When forest cover is depleted flooding usually follows (Roberts 1989; Ponting, 1991). Population increases add pressure to increase agricultural production which means the clearing of land for cultivation. The statistics available for early Chinese population growth and recorded number of floods reflect a high linear correlation (0.949) (see Table 11.1). Regression analysis also shows that population increase is a good predictor of an increasing number of floods. The level of significance (r-square) is over 90 per cent. Placed within the wider context of the expansion and stagnation of growth over the long term, it is suggestive that environmental degradation also exhibits 'long swings' correlating to population growth and economic expansion. The economic growth of China from 1 AD to the present reflects successive surges (logistics) correlating with population increases. The limited data suggest

Table 11.1 Population of China by year and by number of floods, AD 1–1900

Year	Population (millions)	Number of floods
1	53.0	0
100	58.0	2
200	63.0	23
300	58.0	17
400	53.0	4
500	51.5	7
600	50.0	2
700	50.0	13
800	50.0	26
900	64.0	20
1000	66.0	42
1100	105.0	44
1200	115.0	72
1300	96.0	33
1400	81.0	81
1500	110.0	26
1600	160.0	52
1700	160.0	160
1800	330.0	172
1900	475.0	362

Source: Chu 1926; Feuerwerker 1990.

that there were four logistics in population growth: 400 BC to 200 AD, 400 AD to 1200 AD, 1550 AD to 1600 AD, and starting from 1700/1800 AD to the present. These population logistics are also repeated for Europe over the same period.

Within these long swings of population growth, the number of floods over time also exhibits increases and decreases over 200–300 years in length. Figure 11.1 and Table 11.2 outline the tempo of these long swings over the last two millennia, with the number of floods increasing and decreasing over A/B phases (following Frank 1993a,b) of the system up to 1700 AD. The limited data suggests that floods increase during A-phases and decrease during B-phases.

Conditions in China were repeated in Japan: erosion, extreme river silting, and flooding. Between 600–850 AD, the mountains adjoining the Kinai basin were deforested giving rise to fires, flooding and erosion. Deforestation was so extensive that the Emperor by 675 AD announced forest closure policies to protect the remaining stands of trees. This forest protection policy continued well into the ninth century AD, though over-cutting continued to 1678.

Besides ecological degradation, continuous assault on the landscape also engendered scarcity which, as in Hellenistic and Classical Greece, meant that production processes had to be relocated. For this period, English industrialists transported iron ore from England to Ireland for smelting because of the availability of wood. Core centers of accumulation not only had to relocate their production processes, but the lack of access to wood also engendered slippage in

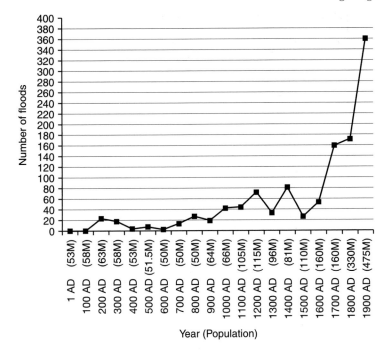

Figure 11.1 China – floods by year (population).
Source: Chu 1926; Feuerwerker 1990.

Table 11.2 Number of floods via A/B phases for China, AD 1–1700

0–200	A-phase	Increase
200–400/500	B-phase	Decrease
400/500–750/800	A-phase	Increase
750/800–950	B-phase	Decrease
950–1200	A-phase	Increase
1200–1500	B-phase	Decrease
1500–1700	A-phase	Increase

terms of their commercial and productive strengths. Venice's commercial and productive processes were affected by its lack of access to forest resources, and thus impacted on its competitive relations with the Ottoman Empire. Venetian transfer of shipbuilding to Holland facilitated Holland's rise as a commercial power in northwestern Europe.

AD 1500 to 1990: Asia

The rise of northern Europe following the fifteenth century led to increased utilization of wood for shipbuilding, construction, and manufacturing. Portuguese penetration of Asia in 1498 led to increasing needs of the Portuguese fleet (Gadgil 1988:49). The Dutch colonization of Java in the seventeenth century engendered the cutting of teak wood for the Dutch East India Company, and imperial Holland. Further consumption is revealed by the construction of shipyards, where we find by 1675, one employing over 250 persons and the presence of wind powered sawmills. In concert with local rulers and middlemen traders, the Dutch East India Company harvested the teak trees which occupied about 6 per cent of the total surface area of Java. Other trees that covered approximately 17 per cent of Java were deemed junglewood and treated as worthless, suitable for destruction 'of which nobody suffers' (Boomgaard 1988:61). When the Dutch East India Company ceased to exist in 1800, control of the forests was turned over to the Dutch Republic. In later years, the degradation of the forests was exacerbated by the production of sugar, coffee, indigo, and tobacco. This cash-crop production required the increased felling of trees to generate arable land, building construction, and fuel to process the sugar, tobacco, and coffee. Annual production of teak logs grew from an average of 16,700 logs from 1733–1765 to 145,000 logs from 1837–1865 (Boomgaard 1988:66, 77).

Such practices occurred in other parts of Southeast Asia where Great Britain was the colonial power. Malaya, Burma, and British Borneo witnessed the exploitation of their tropical forests by the British colonial administration. British companies searched for teak wood in Burma, and according to Rush (1991:41) such quests 'would play a part in Britain's annexation of Burma.' British companies also cleared lands surrounding the Irrawaddy River for rice cultivation (Adas 1983). In Malaya, the forests were cut to grow rubber and to open up areas to mine tin. To facilitate the establishment of a rubber plantation economy, the British Government encouraged the local rulers to sell their land and provided tax incentives to the new owners to plant rubber for export. As in Java, local Malay rulers and merchants were intimately involved in the extraction of forest products. Borneo was administered by a chartered company, the British North Borneo Company. The forest and forest products were, in many cases, the company's main source of revenue (Lian 1988). In Thailand, British timber companies also penetrated teak forests in the nineteenth century. In the early twentieth century, Thai forests were granted as concessions to foreign companies from Great Britain, France, and Denmark.

Such penetration also occurred in the Philippines. Spanish colonization saw the island of Cebu stripped of its hardwood to build Spanish galleons (Tadem 1990:15). Under US rule, the Forest Law of 1904 formed the blueprint for the modernization of the logging industry and cemented the close relationship between the Bureau of Forestry and large foreign and domestic timber companies. A number of other laws such as the Public Lands Act of 1902, the Mining Law of 1905, and Executive Order No.27 of 1929 opened up the forests for private commercial exploitation. Huge profits were made from the harvest of the tropical forests (Tucker 1988:223). As with other parts of Southeast Asia, the local elites were active participants in this accumulation process. The exploitation of the country's natural resources by foreign concerns transformed the economy to one dependent on natural resource exports to the United States (Bellow *et al.*

1982). Deforestation rates were about 140,600 hectares per year during the 1920s and 1930s. This increased by another 30,000 hectares per annum in the post-independence era (Bautista 1990:69).

Europe and North America

Back in Europe, English merchants and the state sought to replenish England's wood supply which was running low by the mid-seventeenth century (Chew 1992). This condition had been reached as a result of the previous century of growth. It was as some would say an 'age of wood' (Lower 1973). Tanners, soap boilers, gunpowder manufacturers, and glass makers all required wood products, such as oak bark and potash, for their operations. The mining industry needed sturdy timber for its mine shafts. Brick manufacturers, sugar refiners, and salt producers used wood. Fifty cubic feet of hardwood was required to produce 2,000 bricks, and more than a load (50 cubic feet) of hardwood was needed to produce 2 hundredweight of salt (Chew 1992:23). Such intensive utilization was exacerbated by the enclosure movements and the intensive growth in farming prior to the mid-seventeenth century which led to an extensive cutting of trees. We find England seeking out wood resources in northeastern Europe and North America. The fir forests of the Baltic shores and the oak belt found to the south and west, along with the forests of New England, became important regions for exploitation. The Baltic area was preferred because of its proximity. However, with Napoleon's blockade of 1807, British timber interests shifted operations to North America. The pace of operations continued throughout the nineteenth century, and along with indigenous American operations, the forests on the eastern seaboard of North America continued to be assaulted until the early parts of the twentieth century. Deforestation occurred, though these areas had lower population densities, and thus were less impacted in terms of floods and other consequences. After the turn of the twentieth century, the exploitation of the forests of North America progressively moved to the mid-west and the west coast. Douglas fir and coastal redwoods were shipped from the Pacific Northwest.

In the late-twentieth century, the exploitation of the forests continues to be a global process. In Latin America and Asia, the tropical rainforests have been systematically cut to meet accumulation and consumption needs which are both local and global in nature. Either operating independently or in collaboration with local concerns, multinational companies based in Japan, Canada, and the United States have been active in harvesting the forests (Petesch 1990). In India, the forests of the Himalayas are being assaulted (Guha 1989). In Southeast Asia, Japanese timber operations have managed to penetrate the tropical rainforests (Chew 1993). In Latin America, debt servicing, multinational activities, ranching and international organizations have been responsible for the destruction of the rainforests (Barbosa 1993; Hecht and Cockburn 1990). With mounting environmental group pressures in North America the search for wood has moved to Siberia, and to Canada's boreal forests (Goto 1993:6, Chew 1993).

In the late-twentieth century, the United States and Japan have replaced

England and France as the two main centers of accumulation, and consequently wood consumption. At this stage, the dynamics of wood exploitation occur in parts of the world system that are the most amenable to the accumulation of capital. Consequently we find extensive wood operations by American and Japanese multinationals in North America, Latin America, Asia, Siberia, and West Africa. For Japan, whose wood resources were severely exploited in the past, global efforts are made to maintain a constant supply from foreign sources (Nectoux and Kuroda 1990:27). Japanese dependency on imported wood has risen from 5.5 per cent in 1955 to 55 per cent in 1970 and 66.5 per cent in 1986 (Nectoux and Kuroda 1990:27). For nearly two decades, Japan has been the world's major tropical timber hardwood importer. Total volume of tropical wood imports into Japan amounted to 29 per cent of the world total in 1986 (Nectoux and Kuroda 1990:5). The high level of consumption reflects an age of exuberance much like what the United States experienced in the postwar era (Devall 1993). In the paper products area, Japan has emerged as the world's largest importer of forest products, second largest producer of paper and paperboard, the third largest producer of pulp, and the second largest consumer of paper after the United States (Penna 1992:1). Total consumption of paper and paperboard has increased over 548 per cent during the last thirty years (Penna 1992:3).

Over the last decade, Japan has been importing unfinished logs from Southeast Asia on an average of 11 million cubic meters, or about 38 per cent of its total volume of log imports (Kato 1992:95). Malaysia, Indonesia and Papua New Guinea were the main contributors (Mori no Koe, April/June 1993:8). By the end of the 1980s this slowed not because of a drop in consumption, but because of a diminishing resource and bans on the export of raw logs. Tadem (1990:23) has indicated that Japan has been labeled an economic imperialist by some of the Southeast Asian wood producers, for it levies higher import taxes on finished wood products than on logs. For example, a 20 per cent import tax is levied on plywood imports against 0 per cent for unprocessed logs. It has been suggested that this measure protects Japan's labor intensive wood manufacturing industry (Tadem 1990:24). Attempts by Southeast Asian producers (Council of Southeast Asian Lumber Producers Association) to control supply has been met with Japan slashing prices of logs and lumber 'to break up any wood and forest product cartel in the region' (Tadem 1990:25). Such actions are hardly unique in the history of the world system.

Ecological crisis of the period

If we move forward to the late twentieth century, with deforestation quickening as a result of improvement in timber harvesting technology, disastrous effects can be seen throughout the whole of North America, Latin America, and Asia (Devall 1994; Chew 1993; Mendez 1990). The consequences of this deforestation should be familiar to us: river siltation, soil erosion, flooding, and certain animal, insect, and plant species extinction. In the Pacific Northwest, several ecosystems are being threatened (Grumbine 1992). In Asia the most dramatic deforestation occurred between 1950 to 1976 according to the United Nations Economic and Social Commission for Asia and the Pacific (1980), when 4 million hectares were cleared per annum. Soil loss, erosion, and intermittent flooding of lowland areas during the monsoon season have been consequently experienced by Malaysia, Indonesia, Thailand, the Philippines, India, and in the Himalayas. Soil loss is followed by sedimentation problems in harbors and rivers. This has often led to flooding as in West Malaysia, and harbor dredging in Sarawak in East Malaysia. Indonesia, the Philippines and Thailand have also experienced these conditions. Concomitant are the effects on fish stocks either in the mangrove areas of Malaysia, Indonesia, Philippines or in the Gulf of Thailand. The sedimentation issue has also affected the ph levels of the rivers, and in turn, this has affected aquaculture and fishery stocks in the coastal zones.

Besides erosion, another consequent threat to the environment is the loss of biodiversity. The tropical rainforests of Southeast Asia have one of the greatest diversity of plant and animal species on this planet. The loss to date has been drastic. In West Malaysia logging has placed almost sixty-one species of mammals and sixteen species of birds on the verge of extinction, with a further 130 species of mammals and 148 species of birds on the vulnerability threshold. Hurst (1990:121) indicates that some primate species like the Siamang, the White-Handed Gibbon, and the Dusky leaf-monkey suffered population losses of over 50 per cent between 1958 and 1975. No doubt these losses have increased. The threat to wildlife diversity also occurs in Indonesia, Thailand, and the Philippines. Some species like the Philippine Monkey-Eating Eagle have been reduced to only 600 pairs, and the elephant population in Thailand, and the orangutan and the Java rhino in Indonesia, are being threatened.

Conclusion

This historical journey has provided some suggestive accounts of the continuity and the self-defeating nature of the accumulation process. Ecological degradation has been a continuous process. With the rise and fall of centers of accumulation, environmental degradation shifts from one region to another. Some regions never fully recover.

The devastation of the environment is prompted further by core–periphery relations. Those states/kingdoms in more advantageous positions in the accumulation process can extract either through tribute, conquest or trading relations, the wood products to meet their socioeconomic transformative needs. Yet it is Nature which in the long run still defines the parameters of world system expansion and conditions of production and accumulation. Lack of access to natural resources such as wood has reduced the competitiveness of some centers of accumulation. Kingdoms and civilizations have collapsed due to their extreme degradation of the environment. Environmental degradation must be considered as one of a set of factors contributing to this demise. Nature, and the limits it sets for global transformations, should be recognized in materialist analyses.

As the accumulation process intensifies, environmental degradation increases exponentially. The limited long-term data on environmental degradation in China (using flooding as an example) suggest that there might be 'long swings' in environmental degradation correlating with the long-trend logistic of population and economic growth over world history, and also with A/B phases of long economic cycles. Further investigation might help to clarify this relationship.

Environmental crisis-like conditions also spark societal ecological consciousness and conservation practices (Chew 1995). The current concern and debate over environmental crises reflect similar practices of prior historical periods. The question is whether our current environmental crisis is one which is qualitatively different from prior periods of world history. The answer cannot be easily provided due to the limited materials we currently possess. It does however appear that with the 'cumulation of accumulation' the global reach of capital has rendered the possibility of *global* environmental devastation more likely.

12 Accumulation based on symbolic versus intrinsic 'productivity'

Conceptualizing unequal exchange from Spondylus shells to fossil fuels

Alf Hornborg

For many years I have been working on aspects of indigenous South American social organization, and scrutinizing data on the pre-Columbian Andes. Meanwhile, I have been trying to reconceptualize precisely in which respects modern industrial technology represents a historical discontinuity or new mode of accumulation (Hornborg 1992). This chapter articulates both projects by comparing ancient Andean mechanisms of accumulation with those prevalent in the modern world. My basic question is how to define 'capital accumulation,' a central concept in world systems discourse.

Towards a transdisciplinary understanding of accumulation

Considering how liberally the concept of 'accumulation' is applied, it is remarkable to find so little discussion of how it is to be defined. There is a wide consensus that the cycles and shifts of world system history best can be understood in terms of accumulation, but very little explicit agreement on what accumulation is, how it is achieved in different historical contexts, and whether historical discontinuities are at all significant.

So as not to risk committing it to the historical specificities of any single kind of material logic, the concept might be defined in a deliberately vacuous manner, such as by equating it with any strategy, material or other, yielding an increment in abstract purchasing power. Cumulative, infrastructural growth (of e.g. irrigation systems, armies, industrial technology) could then be viewed as a manifestation of, or strategy for, growth in purchasing power. Yet purchasing power may increase with but a minimal mediation of infrastructure (e.g. on the stock exchange), and material infrastructure may be accumulated with but a minimal mediation of abstract wealth (e.g. through coercion). Though closely connected to both, then, the concept of accumulation does not seem to be completely congruent with either. We are left with a residual and even more abstract formulation: capital accumulation as a self-reinforcing, symbolic and/or material expansion of the capacity to command various kinds of resources. Both 'capacity' and 'resources' would here have to encompass the symbolic and social as well as material dimensions, and the concept of capital would be very close to collapsing into the concept of power.

I think it is essential that capital accumulation continues to be understood as a phenomenon of human exchange. This is not to say that it can be understood within the framework of existing economic theory. Economics and economic history have not been able to clarify the nature of either the continuities or the discontinuities between preindustrial and industrial accumulation. The reason is that accumulation is a phenomenon at the interface of the social sciences, the humanities and the natural sciences. An explanation of any historical process of accumulation will need to take into account: (a) the social institutions which regulate exchange, (b) the symbolic systems which ultimately define exchange values and rates, and (c) the thermodynamic and other physical circumstances which permit us to determine the direction of net flows of energy and materials. Only by juxtaposing the operation of these different factors can we come to a full understanding of the continuities and discontinuities represented by modern industrial capitalism.

Such a transdisciplinary understanding of accumulation requires broadening of economic thought in three directions. First, it implies familiarity with the relativization of market institutions accomplished long ago in economic anthropology (Polanyi 1958). Second, it means acknowledging the cultural dimension underlying definitions of value or rationality (Sahlins 1976). Third, and most difficult, it requires consideration of how physical factors such as thermodynamics impinge on the development and maintenance of socially constituted infrastructures (Georgescu-Roegen 1971; Odum 1988; Martinez-Alier 1987). Unfortunately, the people who read Polanyi or Sahlins are generally not the same as those who read Georgescu-Roegen or Odum. It is towards a confluence of these considerations that this argument is directed.

There have been attempts to include 'nature' in the world system model (cf. Chew in this volume), and it is indeed imperative that ecological considerations are incorporated into theories of accumulation over time. If we are going to include nature, we will need some conceptual tools from the natural sciences. Civilizations are 'dissipative structures' in the sense defined by Prigogine. They are maintained only through the continuous degradation of imported order. Physicists speak of exergy (with an X) as the inverse of entropy, the 'quality' or 'potential work' embodied in the energy resources that are being dissipated in the production process.[1] The global technomass of industrial society is such a dissipative structure, although conventional economic thought assumes that it is generative. The commonsensical logic of the market is that the center is to be paid more (i.e., be rewarded with more resources) the more resources it has already dissipated. If market-organized center-periphery structures are typically founded on the exchange of manufactured goods for those required for their production (including fuels and food), the general implication is that price and exergy content are inversely related (see below). An industrial market economy operating in a universe obeying the Second Law of Thermodynamics inexorably accelerates the social transfer of exergy resources and the human production of entropy.

Social transfers of exergy, invisible to economists, are fundamental to capital accumulation. To conceptualize the successive modes of accumulation in world history, a crucial question is the scale of exergy appropriation. Whose exergy resources are being exploited by whom? This is the question that will illuminate both the significant discontinuities and the role of technology in the history of accumulation. In order to clarify these issues, we have to pay more attention to the properties of key trade goods. It will not be enough to consider relative price and profit accruing to various kinds of trade. We also have to consider the exergy content of the traded products and the net transfer of exergy between different zones of the world system. Only then can we appreciate the extent to which the feasibility of infrastructural accumulation is confined to a restricted social space.

Modes of conversion and modes of accumulation

Human economies rely on three kinds of socially organized conversion. First, there is the application of labor, draught animals, tools and machines to the appropriation of crops and natural resources. Second, there is the transformation of food into labor and draught animals, and of labor, fuels and materials into tools, machines and finished consumption goods. Finally, there is the social conversion of any of these things to any other through exchange.

The first two modes (let us call them appropriative and transformative) are subsumed in conventional terminology under the concept of 'production.' The third mode of conversion (exchange) is unique in being completely social in nature and obeying no immediate material constraints. Precisely because it is not subject to any immediate physical constraints, commercial or other social modes of conversion introduce an illusion of reversibility into the system. The first two types of conversion constitute an asymmetric, linear process: fuels are burnt, materials transformed, exergy is degraded, labor expended, technology worn out. Yet in conventional images of the economy, no distinction is made between what is *physically* convertible (through production) and what is *socially* convertible (through exchange). Consequently, irreversible conversions are constructed as reversible, and cycles of production-and-exchange generate linear processes of accumulation (in the center) and impoverishment (in the periphery). We must develop a more differentiated approach to what we recognize as 'production' or 'accumulation,' with particular attention to the kinds of goods traded and the relationship between their exchange value and their physical, productive potential.

The different modes of economic conversion allow us to construct a simple typology of goods according to the uses to which they may be put. We may speak of transformable goods such as food, raw materials and fuels, appropriative goods such as tools and machines, and items which are simply convertible, such as valuables and consumption goods. Labor can serve as a transformable good (in relation to tools or machines), an appropriative good (in relation to crops or minerals) and as a socially convertible good (in relation to products bought with wages). As accumulation is always founded on some kind of conversion, these categories help us generate a typology of modes of accumulation. The basic conceivable strategies are:

1   Mercantile exploitation of intercultural discrepancies in the evaluation of socially convertible goods.
2   Undercompensation of labor relative to its products, through:

    a   barter implying an unequal exchange of labor time,
    b   redistribution,
    c   market wages, or
    d   coercion, e.g. slavery.

3   Underpayment for the productive potential of energy and raw materials relative to the products into which they are transformed, e.g. for

    a   food relative to labor and/or the products of labor,
    b   fodder relative to draught animals and/or their contribution to transport or agriculture,
    c   draught animals relative to their contribution to transport or agriculture, or
    d   fuels and raw materials relative to manufactured products.

Which of these modes are to be characterized as 'capital accumulation' or 'capitalism'? Strategy one is founded on social convertibility, symbolic exchange value and the appropriation of abstract purchasing power. Strategies two and three are founded on physical convertibility, productive potential and the concrete logic of material transfers. Although more or less 'pure' forms are conceivable, most processes of accumulation involve both strategies. Though analytically distinguishable, they tend to be inextricably intertwined. As food and fuels usually have exchange values as well as productive potential, they can be exploited for purely mercantile as well as thermodynamic profit by different parties in the same system.

There are several different modes of accumulation employed by different actors and achieving predominance in successive historical systems. In what sense does industrial technology represent a discontinuity? For comparison I offer a condensed interpretation of accumulative processes in the prehistoric Andes. Pre-Columbian Nuclear America is especially interesting. If the Afro-Eurasian world system was basically one single system (Frank and Gills 1993), then the New World system (and there are reasons to believe that it, too, should be phrased in singular) is the only one we have for comparison. It has been suggested that it was precisely the historical articulation of the Afro-Eurasian with the American system in the sixteenth century that, through the injection of bullion, created the preconditions for the new modes of accumulation which were to spark the Industrial Revolution. Against this background, it was indeed one of those momentous occasions in world history when in 1525 Pizarro's pilot Bartolomé Ruiz, heading south in the pursuit of gold and silver, encountered Peruvian merchants heading north in search of Spondylus shells.

Modes of accumulation in the pre-Columbian Andes

A growing body of data suggests a framework for interpreting Andean history that focuses on the struggle of local elites to control long-distance trade in items essential to their redistributive political economy. Yet archaeologists working in the Andes have been hesitant to use long-distance exchange to account for early stratification. Rarely do they address standard Mesoamericanist topics such as the localization of sites on strategic trade routes, urbanism as a reflection of specialized export production, and other subsystem responses to the articulation (or disarticulation) of wider interaction spheres. The models employed by Andeanists have been concerned with cooperation or conflict relating to local subsistence. This may be due to the conspicuous role of hydraulic agriculture and topographical circumscription imposed by Andean geography, or to our spotty view of Andean history. Even as new indications of long-distance contacts are accumulating, a reluctance to treat these contacts as crucial lingers.

This is a paradox. Few regions of the world are more conducive to trade than the Andes. We would expect the diversity of zones, from coastal desert to Amazonian rainforest, to have generated bilateral demands for trans-Andean products and facilitated strategic 'middleman' control of supplies. However, existing ethnohistory and ethnography suggest that the flow of goods up and down the Andean slopes was regulated by institutions granting each local group direct access to several zones (Murra 1972/1975). These 'vertical' economic systems have dominated Andean studies to the point where at least one leading Andeanist would deny that there was *any* 'trade between the highlands and the forest' (Murra, personal communication 1981). Murra's 'vertical archipelagos' have generated a rather parochial discourse that subsumes any new evidence of exchange under the functionalist category of 'ecological complementarity' (cf. Masuda, Shimada and Morris 1985).

'Trade,' as opposed to 'verticality,' is probably best defined as a relationship of indirect access, based on the mediation of specialized middlemen pursuing goals of their own. In periods of political fragmentation (e.g. the Early and Late Intermediate Periods), evidence of long-distance exchange reflects mercantile 'trade' to an extent unfeasible during the 'horizons.' Though embedded in social ties and obligations to local elites, it would be unjustified to assume that Andean traders were always as 'administered' as the Inca *camayoc* serving Cuzco.[2]

The evidence for 'vertical archipelago' economies certainly abounds. The question is whether direct access has always been the Andean rule, or whether its pervasive distribution derives from the impact of large-scale, pre-Columbian political schemes to convert trade into tribute. In areas such as the Titicaca Basin (Pease 1982; Wachtel 1982), 'vertical archipelagos' and *mitimas* colonists predate Inca expansion, but even in these areas did not preclude specialized trans-Andean exchange activities. Wassén (1972) shows that Callawaya herbalists traded tropical plants in the southern highlands at least as early as the Middle Horizon. In the south Peruvian valley of Chincha, Rostworowski (1977) has adduced documentary evidence for the existence of specialized merchants dealing in copper,

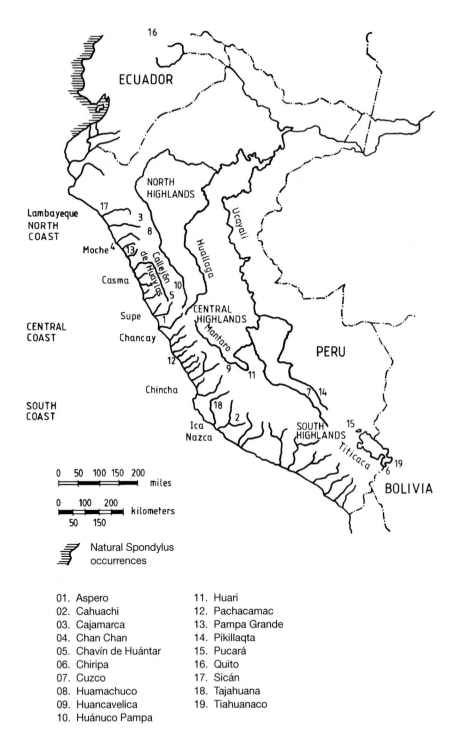

ECUADOR

NORTH
HIGHLANDS

Lambayeque
NORTH
COAST

Moche

Casma

CENTRAL
COAST

Chancay

Chincha

SOUTH
COAST

Ica
Nazca

CENTRAL
HIGHLANDS

Ucayali

Huallaga

Callejón de Huaylas

Mantaro

PERU

SOUTH
HIGHLANDS

Titicaca

BOLIVIA

0 50 100 150 200
                    miles

0   100   200
              kilometers
  50   150

Natural Spondylus
occurrences

01. Aspero	11. Huari
02. Cahuachi	12. Pachacamac
03. Cajamarca	13. Pampa Grande
04. Chan Chan	14. Pikillaqta
05. Chavín de Huántar	15. Pucará
06. Chiripa	16. Quito
07. Cuzco	17. Sicán
08. Huamachuco	18. Tajahuana
09. Huancavelica	19. Tiahuanaco
10. Huánuco Pampa	

Map 12.1 The Andes.

Ecuadorian Spondylus shell, and other items along the coast at the time of the Spanish conquest, and suggests that their activity would have been more intensive prior to the Incas. Similarly, Salomon's (1986) archival research on the archaic highlands of Ecuador reveals that specialized long-distance merchants (*mindalá*), by providing their highland allies with exotic goods for local redistribution, were of key political importance prior to Inca dominance. These goods included Spondylus shell beads (*mullu*), gold nuggets, copper hatchets, coca, salt, red pepper, and cotton cloth. Salomon (1986) shows that advantage in procuring such wealth objects 'amounted to leverage on the reproduction of society itself.' Copper hatchets and 'hatchet-coins' served as bridewealth and grave goods in pre-Columbian Ecuador (ibid.). Shimada (1985, 1987) found that hatchet-shaped copper currency was produced in large quantities on the north coast of Peru in the Middle Horizon, presumably as a means of obtaining valuables from Ecuador. It has been suggested that trade in Spondylus was the basis of a maritime exchange system stretching from southernmost Peru to the west coast of Mexico (Murra 1971/1975; Paulsen 1974, 1977; Marcos 1977/78; Salomon 1986:92).[3]

In the Andes the prospects for more profound understanding of the local cultural incentives of this early exchange are unusually bright thanks to the rich ethnohistoric record. Studies summarized by Murra (1971/1975), Paulsen (1974) and Marcos (1977/78) reveal some of the symbolic significance of the Spondylus shell, a major trade commodity already in Early Horizon Chavín culture (Keatinge 1981:183–4). In the Inca empire, Spondylus represented rain and fertility and was considered the principal food of the gods. Besides being used for ritual offerings, Spondylus ornaments have been found in elite burials in various parts of Peru from around 1000 BC. Access to Spondylus for ritual and redistribution appears to have been a major basis of political power. We may suspect that it was one of the crucial factors determining the shifting course of political evolution in the pre-Hispanic Andes.

Inca domination was achieved by establishing an atmosphere of reciprocity between Cuzco and the various local elites and on strategic deployment of valuables such as *mullu* and cloth (Murra 1962). Morris (1978, 1979, 1982) has demonstrated that impressive 'administrative' centers such as Huánuco Pampa were primarily designed for hosting the large-scale, ceremonial consumption of maize beer (*chicha*). The rationale of Inca expansion was Cuzco's unwillingness to let its position as 'middleman' of the empire depend on the vicissitudes of market exchange. Products from coast, highland and jungle were redistributed according to patterns which probably reflected preincaic demand, but trade was replaced by other institutions, primarily various forms of labor-service (Rowe 1982; Murra 1982). The South Andean 'vertical archipelago' model was used as the blueprint for a successful imperial institution, whereby Cuzco everywhere could lay claims to lands and set up colonies to supervise their management. Mercantile activities survived at the fringes, as Cuzco's link to not yet conquered territories.[4] The Callawaya, the *mindalá*, and the maritime merchants of Chincha thus represent the expanding frontier of Tawantinsuyu,[5] but they undoubtedly had predecessors throughout the preincaic Andes (cf. Carrasco 1982:38; Shimada 1987).

The Middle Horizon expansion of Wari and Late Intermediate Period expansion of the Chimú capital of Chan Chan appear to have built on strategies of institutionalized generosity to which Cuzco was merely an heir. Sites designed for *chicha* consumption and other redistributive activities seem diagnostic of all three periods (Morris 1982; Isbell 1987; Klymyshyn 1987; Mackey 1987), and the rationale for expansion was probably similar. The Wari, Chimú and Inca empires represent attempts to consolidate preexistent interaction spheres into corporate polities in order to guarantee the supply of exotic goods crucial to the redistributive maintenance of power. The allocation of valuables provided access to the labor of dependent subsystems, a part of which was invested in infrastructure for agriculture and manufacture (e.g. maize, textiles, metallurgy, shell ornaments) further enhancing elite redistributive potential.

The long-term continuities in Andean culture are striking. Colonies of *mitimas* (relocated ethnic groups), redistributive *chicha* drinking bouts, elite accumulation of cloth, and specialized trade in tropical plants and Spondylus can all be traced at least to the Middle Horizon. On the north coast of Peru, the same system of fortifications was used repeatedly in the Early Intermediate Period, Middle Horizon and Late Intermediate Period (Topic and Topic 1987:55). Similarly, Inca roads were built on the main arteries of earlier Andean exchange (cf. Salomon 1986:151, 158; Schreiber 1987:92; Shimada 1987:132; Raymond 1988:297–8). Traditional, Late Intermediate Period ethnic boundaries, manifested in costume, were largely intact through the Late Horizon (Rowe 1982:110; Hastings 1987). Cosmology seems similarly timeless. Symbols and iconographic patterns can be traced from Early Horizon Chavín culture through two and a half millennia to the Spanish conquest.

These many continuities suggest that while the fortunes of imperial politics were fluctuating in the pre-Columbian Andes, the local building-blocks (ethnic groups, cultural traditions, communication routes) were surprisingly constant (Carrasco 1982:34–5; Pease 1982:173–98). In light of this, a summary of Andean prehistory might view the various regional populations as nodes in a network more permanent than the recurrent political attempts to encompass it. The dynamic of expansion and decline lends itself to topological approaches, such as tracing the 'implosion' of peripheries into centers (Gills and Frank 1993:96) in ways similar to those of Mesoamerica (e.g. Rathje 1973; Jones 1979; Millon 1988) and the Old World. The various archaeological indications of Andean trade and accumulation certainly deserve such treatment. Though obviously beyond the scope of this chapter, a tentative outline based on published data, may nonetheless be offered (Haas, Pozorski and Pozorski 1987; Keatinge 1988).

Andean cultural history as shifts in center–periphery relationships: outlines of a topological interpretation

By the late Preceramic Period (ending 1800 BC), a number of small, intercommunicating chiefdoms along the north and central coasts of Peru were linked to a second interaction sphere in the north central highlands and adjacent montaña (Callejón de Huaylas–Upper Huallaga). Finds of Spondylus at Aspero suggest maritime trade with coastal Ecuador. Both long-distance connections may have provided coastal elites with valuables crucial to the redistributive political economy.

The Initial Period (1800–900 BC) saw the expansion of a powerful coastal polity based in the Casma Valley and the intensification of trans-Andean exchange linking the coast with the north central highlands and tropical forest areas. Towards the end of the Initial Period the Casma polity collapses and the valley is invaded by its former highland trading-partners. The invaders introduce camelids, guinea pigs, and redistributive *chicha*-drinking on the north coast. In southern Peru, trans-Andean trade networks were already conveying obsidian from Huancavelica, copper from Chiripa in the Titicaca Basin, and tropical plants from the Bolivian montaña.

Having engulfed the Casma area, the north central highland Chavín polity in the Early Horizon (900–200 BC) continued to threaten neighbors on the north coast, who responded by fortifying their settlements. Conflicts seem to have focused on the access of coastal polities to the coca-producing *chaupiyunga* zone (between coast and sierra) and to highland trade routes. The Chavín elite may also have sought to control the import of goldwork from the Lambayeque Valley in the north and of Spondylus from Ecuador. Chavín was also connected, probably through maritime trade, with the Paracas area on the south coast of Peru, where access would have been gained to obsidian and cinnabar from Huancavelica, copper from the Titicaca area, and local cotton cloth. In exchange, Paracas may have been offered goldwork and Spondylus from the north. Towards the end of the Early Horizon, the entire exchange network was rearranged. The south coast connections with the Casma area seem to have been broken, whereas contacts with the south central highlands and the Titicaca Basin were intensified. The expansive north coast Moche polity, which had escaped Chavín dominance, may have come to control critical goldwork and Spondylus imports, and established direct llama caravan trade with the north highlands and the montaña beyond. This may have undermined Chavín's 'middleman' position between montaña and coast.

These two shifts encouraged colonization of the montaña in both areas in the Early Intermediate Period (200 BC – 600 AD), a major focus of which may have been the cultivation of coca and other tropical plants for trans-Andean trade. Moche developed an intensive production of cloth and metals and seems to have founded colonies for controlling metal production on the far north coast, textile production on the central coast, and guano exploitation off the south coast. The production of Spondylus artifacts at the last Moche capital, Pampa Grande, indicates intensive maritime connections with Ecuador. The threat of an expanding Cajamarca polity in the north highlands prompted heavy Moche fortification and may, perhaps by impeding trade routes, have been partly responsible for its eventual demise. Meanwhile, the south central highland Wari polity in the Mantaro Basin established colonies in the Nazca Valley on the south coast. Nazca textile production relied increasingly on alpaca wool from the adjacent highlands. In the Titicaca Basin, emerging urban centers like Tiwanaku and Pucará intensified the production of metal objects used in trade with the Bolivian montaña, the Mantaro Basin, and the south coast. Direct, maritime contact between the north and south coasts seems to have been reestablished towards the end of the period.

In the Middle Horizon (600–1000 AD), the Titicaca metal industry began producing bronze, which should have been in high demand throughout this trade network. Tiwanakoid iconography was diffused by means of textiles and narcotic and medicinal plant paraphernalia conveyed by herbalists. Travelling herbalists stimulated the demand for tropical plants in the Mantaro Basin, and Wari intensified the colonization of its adjacent montaña. Wari's manipulation of local labor was based on the redistribution of valuables and *chicha* beer, which stimulated trade, craft production and maize agriculture. In addition to trade goods from Titicaca and the montaña, Wari would have obtained Spondylus and cotton cloth via Cawachi (only ten days by foot) and Pachacamac on the central coast. Obsidian and turquoise were also widely exchanged. In struggling to control these vital flows, the expanding Wari polity finally embraced the entire south and central coasts and the highlands from Pikillaqta in the south almost as far north as Cajamarca. Urbanism in the incorporated central coast polities of Supe and Chancay-Pachacamac reflects intensive craft production. Unconquered by Wari, the urbanized north coast Sicán polity imported copper ore from the north highlands in order to produce hatchet-shaped copper currency (today referred to as *naipes*) for importing Spondylus, gold nuggets and gems from Ecuador. Sicán also maintained contact with emerging Chan Chan in the Moche Valley, Pachacamac on the central coast, and Wari itself. The expansion of Chan Chan seems correlated with the demise of Wari at the close of the Middle Horizon, perhaps by undermining its monopoly on copper and Spondylus.

In the Late Intermediate Period (1000–1476 AD), a reincarnated Moche (Chimú) polity based at Chan Chan reconquered the adjacent Sicán and Casma polities and dominated the central coast. Only Pachacamac was able to preserve its identity. An alliance with the urbanized, north highland Cajamarca polity was probably crucial to the Chimú expansion. Like Wari, Chimú control was based on the redistribution of valuables and *chicha* beer. The metal industry of Sicán was the main target of conquest. Control over the massive trade in Spondylus was probably also a major incentive. Compared to Sicán, the Casma polity maintained a relatively autonomous status within the Chimú kingdom. Chimú agriculture was largely devoted to the production of cotton for textiles. There is documentary evidence of conflict with a north highland Huamachuco polity over coca-producing *chaupiyunga* lands. The same type of coast–highland conflict is documented on the central coast. Throughout southern and central Peru, the collapse of Wari left fragmented polities warring with their neighbors. The urban craft centers of the south coast and Titicaca Basin were abandoned, but a trade-oriented Chincha polity on the south coast continued to convey Spondylus into the southern highlands. One of Chincha's primary trade connections was Cuzco, only kilometers from the ruined Wari outpost of Pikillaqta, where it helped control southern trade routes into the montaña and the Titicaca Basin. Predictably, Cuzco's first step toward the Late Horizon empire of Tawantinsuyu was to subdue the Chanca, heirs of the Wari heartland, who blocked what was to become the Inca highway to Chinchasuyu. The rest, as they say, is history.

This admittedly speculative interpretation of the dynamics of Andean accumulation points to some ways in which political consolidation would leave traces in the archaeological record. An obvious difference between politically unified regions and non-political interaction spheres is the capacity for militarism (Webb 1987). Second, previously united regions are more easily annexed to other, expanding polities (Pease 1982; Rosaldo 1982:463; Salomon 1986:134). On the other hand, like those ethnic groups which allied themselves with the Spaniards against Cuzco, they may also more easily be lost in times of crisis. A third aspect is thus the tendency of long-standing political unification to produce ethnicity and regional resiliency. Fourth, there is a difference in the scale of vulnerability. The impact of disturbances in crucial exchange flows will have wider repercussions if what is threatened is not a few local elites but the entire imperial superstructure. The abruptly truncated 'horizons' testify to this. Finally, as indicated by Gills and Frank (1993:96), the emergence of new centers of accumulation will tend to occur on trade routes just beyond the established political reach of antecedent polities. This pattern seems to be applicable to a long series of Andean centers including Chavín de Huántar, Moche, Nazca, Wari, Cajamarca, Chan Chan, and Cuzco, each of which emerges on the periphery of earlier centers. Significantly, the Inca civil war which met the Spaniards suggests that Quito was about to be added to this list.

I foresee the objection that this way of accounting for Andean history is monocausal. It may be useful to recall, however, that to recognize how 'primitive valuables' may have guided the political and economic history of the pre-Columbian Andes is simply to acknowledge that Spondylus shell ornaments may be no less desirable than the yellow and gray metals which lured the Spaniards and transformed two worlds.

Accumulation based on symbolic versus intrinsic 'productivity'

Several interrelated modes of accumulation appear to have been in operation in the pre-Columbian civilizations of the Andes. With reference to the typology previously suggested, long-distance exchange in Spondylus and copper would have provided opportunities for strategy 1: the exploitation by merchant groups of intercultural discrepancies in evaluation. Locally, however, such items were used at various levels of leadership according to mode 2b: redistribution and ritual to gain access to corvée labor. Much of the labor was invested in infrastructure (e.g. terraces) and the production of other goods for redistribution. It is fair to say that the rationale of such redistributive cycles required that labor was 'undercompensated' relative to its products. By way of a simplified example, the *chicha* with which to appease laborers on the maize fields could only have represented a fraction of the harvest.

The local, evaluative mechanisms which determined what we might call the 'productive potential' of redistributed products hinged on symbolic systems and social conventions of reciprocity. In addition to local standards, which organized exchange between elites and their subordinates, the rates organizing long-distance exchange represent another mechanism, partially geared to local evaluations but subject as well to its own, supra-local logic. It represents the supra-cultural and socially disembedded sphere of conversion that we have come to know as the world market. The total conjuncture of prerequisites for ancient Peruvian accumulation thus included, schematically, (a) the rate at which Spondylus could be locally converted into corvée labor, (b) the rate at which copper could be converted into affinal obligations in coastal Ecuador, and (c) the rate at which long-distance merchants could convert copper into Spondylus.

All three points of conversion, though ultimately subject to material constraints, are dependent on value systems and social negotiations. To the extent that we can speak of the ancient Peruvian civilizations as 'centers' in relation to an Ecuadorian 'periphery,' this is a consequence of differences in local, symbolic determinations of the productive potential of the items traded, rather than of differences in 'intrinsic' potential. In relation to the ratio at which copper was exchanged for Spondylus, the capacity of Spondylus to mobilize Peruvian labor was obviously vastly greater than the capacity of copper to mobilize Ecuadorians.

Turning to the modern world system, we begin with the observation that Peru has been transformed into a peripheral sector in relation to a world economy dominated by the United States. A major export to the US is oil, while a major import from the US is arms. What are the local, evaluative mechanisms which determine the 'productive potential' of these products? In Peru, investment in

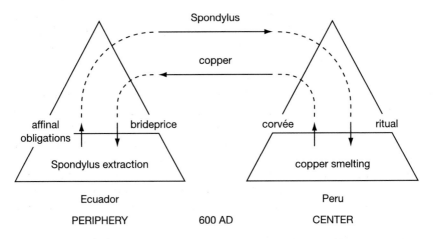

Figure 12.1 Conjuncture of evaluative mechanisms in the exchange of copper for Spondylus in the pre-Columbian Andes.

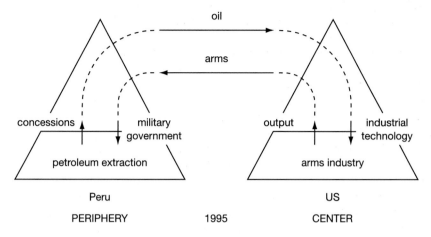

Figure 12.2 Conjuncture of evaluative mechanisms in the exchange of arms for oil in the modern world system.

arms is an effective elite strategy for guaranteeing continued extraction of natural resources at minimum costs. The military government represents a mechanism for converting arms into oil. In the US, the productive potential of oil (including the rate at which it can be converted into arms) is determined by its access to industrial technology. This technology represents an evaluative mechanism analytically comparable to the various theocratic-redistributive, kinship-organized and politico-military structures we have identified as elsewhere serving such functions of conversion. The conjuncture of prerequisites for accumulation in the US includes (a) its technological infrastructure, (b) the capacity of peripheral governments such as the one in Peru to guarantee the extraction of natural resources, and (c) world market prices of oil vis-à-vis arms.

One implication of this analysis is that industrial technology represents an *objectification* of the local determination of an item's productive potential. We have seen that in societies where production is based exclusively on human labor, productive potential is defined by the local, symbolic context. The ratio by which labor was exchanged for maize beer, for instance, was defined by local cosmology and social institutions. In the case of industrial technology, on the other hand, the productive potential of various imports such as oil is locally objectified so as to appear independent of human evaluation, relying instead on the thermodynamic properties of the articulated substances. The conventional, objectifying view of technology, however, neglects the fact that this articulation itself relies on the supra-local, evaluative mechanism we know as the world market (e.g. oil prices). I refer to this as 'machine fetishism' (Hornborg 1992). Once again, following Marx, we can discover how relations between people masquerade as relations between things.

A significant difference between the two modes of accumulation we have considered is that the roles of 'center' versus 'periphery' in the former instance hinge exclusively on the relative potential for conversion inherent in the local value systems, whereas in the latter they hinge at least in part on the intrinsic, thermodynamic properties of the traded items themselves. In the former case, imports to the center operate as catalysts unleashing the productivity of local labor, while in the latter case it is the productive potential itself that is imported. In terms of our typology of modes of accumulation, the former belongs to category 2b, the latter to 3d: the underpayment for fuels and raw materials in relation to manufactured products. The distinction between symbolic and intrinsic 'productivity' should be seen as an analytical polarity with several conceivable, intermediate instances. The large-scale import of food, fodder, draught animals or wood fuels to early centers of civilization all represent strategy 3: the underpayment for the intrinsic, productive potential of energy and raw materials in relation to the products into which they are transformed. Another intermediate instance is the slave trade (mode 2d), also a matter of importing the productive potential itself, which, in its ambiguous position somewhere between strategies 2 and 3, illustrates the continuity between the two modes of exploitation. Labor is also a potentially underpaid source of energy, but a very special one since, except for slavery, it requires some form of symbolically mediated coaxing. Strategies 2a, 2b and 2c represent three major forms of coaxing, corresponding to Polanyi's categories of reciprocity, redistribution and market.

Is 'capitalism' or 'capital accumulation' to be equated with modern industrialism and dated to the eighteenth century? Eric Wolf's answer is yes, because this was the point at which 'the rate of profit was no longer determined solely by regional discrepancies in price (which allowed merchants to buy cheap and sell dear), but by the process of production itself' (Wolf 1982:353). This distinction between two analytically separate principles of accumulation is commendable (and corresponds to my distinction between modes 1 and 2/3), but in suggesting that the latter mode appears for the first time in eighteenth century England, Wolf ignores all those earlier social systems in which mercantile profits were interwoven with systematic undercompensation of labour and underpayment for energy and materials. These latter versions of unequal exchange, in which the rate of profit and capital accumulation is partly determined by 'the process of production itself,' have in one form or another been a part of human history for thousands of years. The specific and novel form which this mode of accumulation assumed in eighteenth-century England was primarily a matter of adopting a technology based on fossil fuels. It can be said to represent the advent of 'industrial capitalism,' but not the advent of 'capital accumulation.' Industrial technomass is only the latest in a series of socially constituted infrastructures, in which productive capacity is accumulated through unequal exchange.

Modern industrialism based on fossil fuels introduces a new possibility for unequal exchange and accumulation, but with antecedents in earlier civilizations founded on large-scale imports of energy. This mode of accumulation (strategy 3) can be contrasted with other strategies such as (1) the mercantile exploitation of inter-cultural discrepancies (cf. Adams 1974), and (2) the undercompensation of labor relative to its products. Whereas unequal exchange founded on strategy 1 could theoretically be checked by an implementation of the perfect neoclassical market, that founded on strategy 3 could not be checked in this way, for its inequality is not primarily geared to the conjunctures of human demand but to the thermodynamic properties of the traded products, and, as we shall see, the concomitant, inexorable underpayment for energy and raw materials. In this system, where the discrepancy between exchange value (price) and productive potential is crucial, the neoclassical conflation of exchange value and use value is of supreme ideological significance. It leaves no room for the *idea* of unequal exchange. What could be more ideologically instrumental than to equate all forms of 'utility,' declaring that the value of a product basically corresponds to its price? As in the case of the Inca laborer praising the hospitality of his host, this is another illustration of how unequal relations will 'in one way or other – by means of some mysterious process that we must analyze – present themselves as a reciprocal exchange of services' (Godelier 1986).

On the social prerequisites of industrialism: the inverse relationship of exchange value and productive potential

Accumulation is the common denominator underlying the major threats to global human survival, including resource depletion, environmental destruction, world poverty and armament. I began by arguing that it is a problem at the very interface of natural and social science. If industrial technomass is a dissipative structure, but the logic of its operation largely rests on specific cultural categories and social institutions, then neither natural nor social scientists can hope to grasp its essence alone. I advance an alternative understanding of economic 'growth' and technological 'development' that demonstrates the logic by which historically specific, sociocultural concepts and institutions interact with natural law (thermo-dynamics) in generating an inequitable world order (Hornborg 1992). A crucial element in this understanding is the relativization or 'defamiliarization' (Marcus and Fischer 1986) of cultural categories (e.g. 'market,' 'prices') which to most of us are as natural and unquestionable as water is to fish. Achieving epistemological distance from such categories is essential to any prospect for ever transcending them. The transdisciplinary challenge is to develop a perspective on industrial technomass as a dissipative structure that also accounts for the specific socio-cultural conditions for its reproduction. Some of the foundations of such a perspective are as follows:

1   Industrial production entails a generalized center–periphery structure of world trade, where industrial centers trade finished products for fuels and raw materials from peripheral areas.
2   In accordance with the Second Law of Thermodynamics, the sum of fuels and materials imported to industrial centers (I) must contain more thermo-dynamic potential (exergy) than the sum of exported products and waste (E).

3   The driving force of industrial expansion is the expectation of monetary gain, which implies that the sum of exports and waste (E) is priced higher than the sum of imports (I).

4   It is thus inherent in the logic of market-organized industrialism that there is an inverse relationship between the price of a commodity and the proportion of its original exergy content (i.e. fuels and other materials spent in producing it) that is still intact. The more of its exergy content that has been dissipated, the higher the price, which means that the more new resources can be procured in the next round of 'production.'

5   Since the sale of a product will always enable the industrialist to purchase more (I) than is required for producing (E), industrial centers will be able to (a) continuously increase their claims on the resources in their periphery, and (b) invest a continuous net gain in exergy in their expanding technomass. These processes recursively increase the total rate of throughput, global exploitation, resource depletion and waste production. In other words, this system will inexorably reward an accelerating transfer of resources from peripheral to central areas, where a buildup of infrastructure thus becomes feasible, and an accelerating dissipation of these resources. Global inequality and biospheric degradation are two sides of the same coin. The inverse relationship between exergy content and price is the driving force of industrial expansion and explains why 'growth' remains a socially restricted phenomenon. The global agglomeration of technomass is an index of net import of exergy, and presupposes peripheral sectors with a net export of thermodynamic potential. The logic by which market mechanisms interact with the Second Law of Thermodynamics defines the conditions for the historically specific mode of accumulation we know as industrialism.

Someone might object that exergy content is not what makes industrial products valuable. This is true. Nor am I saying that exergy is a 'value.' We must recognize thermodynamics and cultural evaluations as distinct in order to grasp the logic of their interaction. We can completely disregard the subjective 'utility' of the products, which is arbitrary because it is culturally defined (cf. Sahlins 1976) and ephemeral because it diminishes rapidly with use, and observe that if a finished product is priced higher than the resources required to produce it, those dissipating resources will continuously be rewarded with even more resources to dissipate.

I am not offering an 'exergy theory of value.' On the contrary, we must view the human inclination to value products higher than raw materials (irrespective of cultural context) as a level of reality analytically distinct from (though functionally articulated with) thermodynamics. Our concern is with the logic by which the phenomenon of evaluation is connected to its ecological consequences. Only then can we see how the blind logic of general-purpose money operates in world systems as well as ecosystems. Most attempts at achieving a rapprochement of ecology and economics are deeply entrenched in the ambition to envisage principles for 'correct' pricing that will guarantee long-term sustainability. But since evaluation is an altogether cultural phenomenon, a discussion of objective aspects of industrial resource management that does not problematize the assumption that finished products have a 'higher value' than raw materials suffers from a confusion of logical types. As 'prices' are socially negotiated exchange relationships between human beings, it is useless to search for their correlates in the material world. Only when we stop looking for a 'real' measure of value, which should correlate with price, and recognize the impossibility of such a congruity, can we appreciate the profundity of the problem and perhaps begin to envisage ways of transcending it. Like other modes of accumulation, industry subsists on *not* compensating its environment for the social and ecological disorder it generates.[6]

Conclusion

Both industrial technology and theocratic ritual are 'machinations' dependent on evaluative mechanisms. The difference is that, in industrialism, the evaluative mechanism has been locally objectified (into technology) so as to seem entirely 'material' and non-social. But what has happened is really that the most significant, evaluative moment has been shifted from the local to the global level. Locally, it has been delegated to the non-negotiable, kinematic logic of machines, but these are in themselves manifestations of global exchange rates.

In ancient Peru imported symbols were *socially* convertible into manual labor. The productive potential in the system was local labor, and the rate at which prestige goods were converted into labor was negotiable. In modern industrial centers, it is increasingly the productive potential itself that is imported, which means (a) that the imports are *physically* convertible into work, (b) that it is the global rather than the local conversion rates which ultimately determine the feasibility of accumulation, and (c) that asymmetric, social transfers of exergy are increasingly global in scale. Increasingly, the productive potential that is being underpaid is resources in the periphery rather than labor in the center. Machines cannot be negotiated with. No less than ritual, they mystify us, now by pretending to be 'productive' independently of global exchange rates. Apparently, it will take more than the traumatic 'oil crises' of the 1970s to shake us out of that illusion.

Acknowledgment

Portions of this text appeared in 'Stratification and Exchange in the Pre-Columbian Andes' (*Ethnos* 54:217–28). I wish to thank the Swedish Council for Planning and Coordination of Research (FRN) for their support.

Notes

1 I have assumed exergy to be close to the concept of 'negative entropy' (cf. Schrödinger 1944/1967; Georgescu-Roegen 1971) and to denote the thermodynamic potential located in any physically manifest information or contrast which, when neutralized,

can unleash 'work' (see e.g. Wall 1986; Kåberger 1991). I have suggested an extension, from biomass to 'technomass,' of Schrödinger's (1944/1967:79) classic observation that 'the device by which an organism maintains itself stationary at a fairly high level of orderliness (= fairly low level of entropy) really consists in continually sucking orderliness from its environment.'

2   This assumption seems also to have been the point of departure for Murra's early discussion of trade and merchants in the Inca empire (Murra 1956/1980, ch. 7), which remains an essential source on the historical evidence of indigenous Andean commerce.

3   Some of the more striking similarities between Mesoamerican and Andean cultures, e.g. ceramic jars with stirrup spout (Paulsen 1977:146) or shaped like acrobats (Lathrap, Collier and Chandra 1975:60), suggest that the two areas were integrated into a common 'world system' by about 1000 BC.

4   This pattern conforms with Sahlins' (1972) structural account of the relegation of balanced reciprocity, money and market exchange to peripheral social sectors.

5   With the exception of modern place names like Huaylas and Huallaga, I use 'wa' for the phoneme traditionally spelled 'hua.'

6   This is not the place for visions of remedies, but in a very general sense the core of the problem is perhaps to find other ways of compensating manufacturers for the value they have added to the raw materials than to give them access to increasing volumes of the same materials, which tends to generate an accelerating destruction of resources. The fundamental problem is the logic of general-purpose money itself.

13 War and warfare

Scales of conflict in long-range analysis

Claudio Cioffi-Revilla

A variety of scholarly approaches and methods of investigation have been used by social scientists and historians to discover and analyze long-range patterns of international conflict. By 'long-range' I mean both long-term (diachronic) and worldwide (synchronic) comparative analysis. Origins, cycles, transformations, fusions, collapses, and fluctuations are some of the social patterns that are analyzed on a large array of long-range analysis, covering thousands of years and all regions of world politics, from local to global. In spite of the acknowledged complexity of these processes and systems, however, little attention has focused on critical conceptual, empirical, and theoretical distinctions that are crucial to establish, as between different scales of conflict in long-range analysis. Conflicts that occur on different scales (e.g. the French and Indian War versus the French–British War; the Six Day War versus the Arab–Israeli War; or the Korean War versus the Soviet–American Cold War) are generally assumed to obey different causal mechanisms, unless proven otherwise (scale invariance). From an applied policy perspective, the scale of conflict also matters, often critically so, for purposes of early warning, intervention, or resolution. The Vietnam War affected an entire generation; but the Soviet–American Cold War affected several generations. Scale matters in international conflict, just as it does in all complex phenomena.

In this chapter I discuss and propose some solutions to the puzzle of scales in the long-range analysis of war. The thrust of my approach centers on several key distinctions regarding two critical scales of conflict: the behavioral scale of violent belligerence and the chronological scale of historical processes. These distinctions and some of the concepts that accompany them are new and they may help clarify not only the nature of the long-range approach to conflict, but also – more importantly – shed some light on the character of war. The main implications of these ideas are (i) new methods for systematically recording the empirical long-range incidence of war, essential for constructing more insightful theoretical explanations, and (ii) a more precise framework for developing causal explanations and a better understanding of long-range patterns. Preliminary application of these ideas already suggests that the approach is feasible and insightful, both cross-sectionally (synchronically) and cross-temporally (diachronically).

Scales in long-range analysis

Premises   The occurrence of war in human history is an ancient, complex, and on-going phenomenon, particularly when the topic is approached from a long-range comparative perspective, meaning both cross-culturally and cross-temporally. By way of measurement and conceptual background, the operational definition of war used in the Long-Range Analysis of War (LORANOW) Project is as follows:

Definition: A war (a 'war event') is an occurrence of purposive and lethal violence between two or more social groups pursuing conflicting political goals that results in fatalities, with at least one belligerent group organized under the command of authoritative leadership.

This definition satisfies several important criteria for conducting comparative analysis – e.g. cross-temporal and cross-cultural applicability (Bartolini 1993) – as I have discussed elsewhere in detail (Cioffi-Revilla 1991; 1996). Such a definition and others with similar empirical resolution (Levy 1983; Richardson 1960; Small and Singer 1982; Wright 1942) can record conflict events such as the First Punic War, World War I, and the Korean War. However, it fails to record similarly significant conflict events such as the Arab–Israeli War, or the Soviet–American Cold War. Why? Why cannot the latter class be measured in the same way as the former? How does the measurement instrument fail to record the latter events? More precisely, what are some of the behavioral characteristics of the latter set of conflicts that make them difficult or impossible to detect by the standard definitions of war? How can long-range analysis contribute toward the solution of this problem? Answers to these questions can provide insights for designing better measurement instruments capable of detecting and measuring the class of larger-scale conflicts exemplified by the Arab–Israeli War and the Soviet–American Cold War. For example, improved detection and measurement could have anticipated the surprising end of the Cold War.

A long-range theory of war should be based on a distinction between inter-related but different dimensions or *scales* of conflict phenomenon:

1   the *scale of belligerence* with respect to the behavior under investigation (the subject matter), and
2   the *scale of process* chosen as a temporal framework for the investigation (the analytical focus).

From a theoretical perspective, these scales are used to distinguish 'the trees' from 'the forest.' The first dimension of war phenomenon, what I call 'the scale of belligerence,' refers to the nature or *type of conflict* that is manifested by the actors within a broader system of social interactions. To define the scale of belligerence one must first answer a set of substantive questions, such as: What constitutes belligerence? Which kinds of events are to be considered and what are to be excluded? Is it possible to avoid the traps of nominalism or common language conventions used in historiography and move beyond uninformative designations such as 'the War of X against Y,' 'the X–Y Crisis,' 'X's Conquest of Y,' or 'the War of Y's Disintegration'? As I explain in greater detail below, defining the appropriate scale of belligerence in a systematic fashion is essential for a rigorous treatment and theoretical explanations of the long-range dynamics of war.

The second dimension of the war phenomenon, what I call 'the scale of process,' refers to the chronological *focus* or degree of temporal resolution that one wishes to have on the sequential detail of history. This is important to define because historically some events of belligerence take place over the relatively short time span of months or even (e.g. the Franco-German War, World War I, the Korean War), even with high magnitude, whereas others can last decades (e.g. the Great Peloponnesian War, the Punic Wars, the Thirty Years War, the Soviet–American Cold War). Does the endurance characteristic of some wars make any difference for understanding their causes and properties? Theoretically, we know that duration alone affects the set of opportunities available to belligerents in carrying out repeated engagements (Cioffi-Revilla and Starr 1995). Defining the appropriate scale of process is therefore just as important for conducting a valid and systematic long-range analysis of war.

Given these premises, I propose to differentiate between two distinct phenomena on the scale of belligerence – 'war' and 'warfare' – and two distinct phenomena on the scale of process – 'macroprocesses' and 'microprocesses.' The differences between these phenomena in each scale, as well as their corresponding theoretical implications, are both qualitative (structural) and quantitative (measurable). Accordingly, as detailed in the next sections, *macroprocesses* cover the universal history of organized lethal belligerence, from origins to the present, whereas *microprocesses* cover particular or detailed histories of warfare, from one war to the next.[1] These relative differences in analytical scales are analogous to the differences that exist in the following disciplines and phenomena:

Macro-scale	*Micro-scale*
Cosmology	Astronomy
Galactic motion	Planetary motion
Geology	Seismology and vulcanology
Climatology	Meteorology
Motion of objects	Brownian motion
Evolution of species	Life of organisms
Symphony	Movement
'The forest'	'The trees'

The hierarchical nature of macro and microprocesses is obvious and familiar. What may not be so obvious is that – unfortunately – the social science of international relations (or social science in general for that matter) lacks what cosmology and climatology provide for astronomy and meteorology: long-range context to understand basic principles and system change. This is the central scientific objective of the long-range analysis of war: to discover and understand diachronic and synchronic patterns of war through comparative analysis. As with all real world complex phenomena that evolve in historical time, the long-range analysis of war must account for phenomena in both macroprocesses and microprocesses, the latter embedded within the former.

Scale of belligerence: war and warfare

In common language there is no well-established distinction between the terms 'war' and 'warfare'; they are synonyms. In long-range analysis, however, the scale of belligerence matters and refers to theoretical and empirical aspects of violent social conflict having to do with a set of key dimensions, such as: (1) behavioral units of analysis, (2) type or degree of organization of the conflict, (3) complexity or size, (4) chronological duration, and (5) multidimensional consequences of belligerence (political, economic, cultural). Table 13.1 illustrates the defining features of these two types of belligerence along the common set of characteristic dimensions just described, distinguishing between 'war' and 'warfare.' As a taxonomy, the distinction is admittedly idealized and the comparative dimensions (i.e. units of behavior, organization, complexity, and so on) are complementary, not mutually exclusive. This theoretical and empirical classification of violent conflicts by scale of belligerence (i.e. war versus warfare) is intended to be taxonomic; the various characteristic dimensions are not.

In terms of scale of belligerence, and consistent with the definition given earlier, a *war* (as opposed to 'warfare') is therefore conceptualized as a relatively disaggregated and simple event that generally lasts no longer than some years ($10^2 - 10^3$ days). Wars are commonly classified as either civil (internal), interstate, or internationalized conflict (e.g. Small and Singer 1982; Geller and Singer 1998), as well as other types discussed later. Most social science and historical research on violent social conflict has focused on this type of belligerence – wars.[2]

Warfare, on the other hand, is an aggregate, relatively more complex process that generally lasts at least decades and is far less systematized than wars (10^3–10^4 days). Social scientists and historians have focused relatively less attention on this larger scale belligerence – 'warfare' – although arguably this is the scale that has greater impact on the long-range development of societies and civilizations. *If war is what 'forges' a state, warfare is what forges an entire civilization.*

War and warfare differ along the following dimensions of scale of belligerence:

Unit of behavior   War and warfare differ by the referent analytical unit of behavior being investigated. As suggested by the historical examples in Table 13.1, a war is

Table 13.1   Scale of belligerence – war and warfare

	War ('the trees')	Warfare ('the forest')
Historical examples:	• Spanish–Aztec War • Conquest of Tayasal • French and Indian War • French–Russian War • Korean War • Six Day War	• Spanish Conquest of the New World • French–British War • Napoleonic Wars • Cold War • Arab–Israeli Conflict
Unit of behavior:	Event-like	Process-like
Organization:	Disaggregated	Aggregated
Complexity:	Relatively simple	Relatively complex
Duration:	Years 10^2–10^3 days	Decades 10^3–10^4 days
Typology:	Civil, interstate, hegemonic, global, world wars	Protracted, integrative, disintegrative, sporadic

Source: Prepared by the author.

more like an *event* that occurs over a relatively short term (e.g. the French and Indian War or the Korean War). By contrast, warfare is a *process* that tends to involve a long-term interaction, as an enduring conflict or rivalry (e.g. the French–British war or the Soviet–American Cold War). Since several events constitute a process, it can therefore be said that several wars can constitute warfare. Thus, in the examples given in Table 13.1, the Spanish–Aztec War was part of a larger process of warfare called the Spanish Conquest of the New World. Similarly, the Korean War was part of the Cold War, the latter viewed as a case of warfare that also involved several other wars (e.g. the Angolan War, the Vietnam War), and even sub-war events (e.g. the 1948 Berlin Crisis, the 1962 Cuban Missile Crisis, the 1973 Alert Crisis, etc.) and civil wars (Cuban Revolution, Hungarian Revolt, Czech Uprising, Angolan Civil War). Wars are to warfare as events are to a process; the former composes the latter. Warfare can assume the form of a rivalry (Diehl 1998), when wars and disputes, occur over time among the same belligerents. However, as I discuss later, not all forms of warfare are rivalries (e.g. a succession of wars of expansion or conquests that produce an empire).

Organization   Wars and warfare also differ by degree of organization. Compared to warfare, a war is a more disaggregated conflict, consisting of battles or engagements and usually involving fewer belligerents. By contrast, warfare has *aggregate* organization, sometimes involving numerous belligerents. Thus, the Maya–Spanish War, the Aztec–Spanish War, the Inca–Spanish War, and other separate wars fought between Spain and the various Indian belligerents aggregate to form the warfare known as the Spanish Conquest of the New World. Each of the New World wars had separate termination. The aggregate warfare, however, ended when Spain finally conquered the last sovereign Indian enclave – at the Battle of Tayasal, Guatemala, in AD 1697, marking the end of the Maya–Spanish War. Similarly, England, France, Portugal and – later – the United States also carried out warfare for conquest or expansion in the New World. The recent Cold War was also a case of warfare involving the aggregate belligerence between Western allies, the Soviet allies, and sometimes Third World 'neutrals.' A war constitutes a relatively disaggregated form of belligerence, while warfare is relatively more aggregated, with a conceptual relation similar to that between trees and forests, such that

Wars : warfare : : trees : forest.

Complexity   War and warfare also differ by degree of complexity. A war is relatively simple, compared to warfare, because a war is most frequently organized as a two-sided conflict (Richardson 1960; Wilkinson 1980), whereas in warfare the conflict commonly involves many sides, not just two, and sometimes involves alliances (Neilson and Prete 1983; Starr 1972). Spain's New World belligerence between the late fifteenth century and the late seventeenth century was a far more complex, many-sided conflict than any of the individual wars between Spain and the Indians. Similarly, Franco-German warfare (and rivalry) during the past two centuries has involved many complex interactions, including shifting systems of alliance, territorial changes, repeated crises, and repeated European and colonial wars. Empirically, the greater complexity of warfare can be recorded by appropriately designed graph-theoretic parameters capable of measuring adjacency, centrality, thickness, connectivity, vertex-degree and other significant dimensions.

Duration   The preceding differences imply that wars and warfare must necessarily also differ in terms of their duration. The duration of a war is most frequently measured in months or years. In antiquity many wars consisted of single-battle engagements (Ferrill 1985/1997; Gabriel and Metz 1991; Hackett 1989; Hassig 1992; Humble 1980; Keeley 1996; Marcus 1995; Montgomery 1968). In more recent modern times few wars have lasted longer than a few years (Beer 1983; Cioffi-Revilla 1995; Levy 1983; Small and Singer 1982).

By contrast, warfare generally lasts decades and sometimes can endure for centuries. The following are some well-established cases of multi-century warfare in antiquity: Sumerian–Elamite, Egyptian–Hittite, Egyptian–Israelite, Assyrian–Elamite, Chinese–Xiong Nu, Japanese–Korean, Greek city-states, Roman–Carthagenian, Maya city-states, Maya–Toltec, Aztec and Peruvian Coastal and Highland warfare. For modern times, cases of long-duration warfare include the following: Franco-German, Anglo-German, Russo-German, Sino-Russian, Russo-Japanese, and Iranian–Iraqi warfare. Were it not for several fundamental changes in the national identity of the belligerents, the following are perhaps some of the closest parallels that can be traced between antiquity and modernity in terms of protracted or long-range warfare:

Antiquity	*Modernity*
Egyptian–Israelite	Arab–Israeli
Mesopotamian–Elamite	Iraqi–Iranian
Chinese–Rong	Sino-Russian
Japanese–Korean	Japanese–Korean
Toltec–Maya	Mexican–Guatemalan
Peruvian–Chavín	Peruvian–Ecuadorian

The purpose of the above comparison is not to draw any premature inferences, but simply to suggest that warfare – not just isolated wars – has a long-range record in human history, even if the nature or official institutional name of some belligerents has undergone considerable change (e.g. from archaic states with primitive economies to industrialized states with modernized economies). Warfare is also quite often a multigenerational phenomenon, thereby engaging a larger population of belligerents for a much longer period of time and social mechanisms for reproducing belligerence. Wars often have only a transitional impact on a society; whereas warfare usually shapes a society, affecting its basic political culture, defining friends and enemies through cognitive schema, and not merely affecting the polity and economy.

Typology   Finally, given the preceding theoretical and empirical distinctions, wars and warfare also differ by their typology. Wars are most often classified into civil wars and interstate wars. In turn, civil wars include purely domestic wars and internationalized wars, whereas interstate wars include major–major power wars, minor–minor wars, and major–minor wars. Other categories of wars are also used, such as great power wars, hegemonic wars, world wars, colonial wars, and others (Cioffi-Revilla 1995; Levy 1990; Midlarsky 1988; Thompson 1988). Warfare, on the other hand, is not as systematized and – regrettably – typologies of warfare have not yet attracted the same amount of attention as typologies of war. A typology of warfare is long overdue, given the emerging long-range record of warfare in history (Cioffi-Revilla and Lai 1995). A typology of warfare is also necessary for measurement and modeling purposes.

I propose the following typology of warfare based on the measurement and analysis experience thus far developed at the Long-Range Analysis of War (LORANOW) Project: (1) *protracted* warfare, (2) *integrative* warfare, (3) *disintegrative* warfare, and (4) *sporadic* warfare. Each pattern of warfare is illustrated by the graphic models in Figure 13.1.

Protracted warfare is defined as a sequence of recurring wars between the same belligerents fighting for similar objectives (same ostensible causes) (e.g. Mesopotamian–Elamite warfare, Greek–Persian warfare, Punic Wars, Chinese–Xiong Nu warfare, Franco-German warfare, Arab–Israeli warfare, Iran–Iraq warfare). Interstate rivalries (Diehl 1998; Thompson, 1999) often consist of this

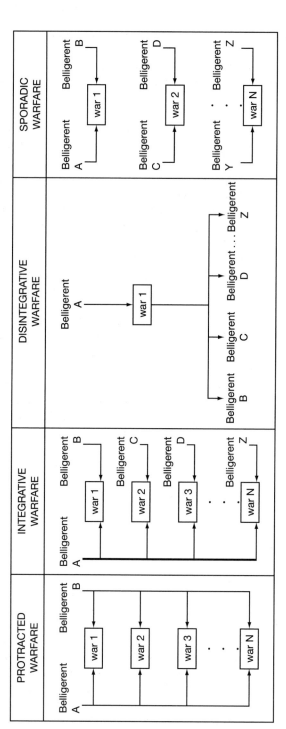

Figure 13.1 Typology of warfare.

Note:

PROTRACTED WARFARE: The same belligerents (A and B) engage in repeated wars over a period of time.

INTEGRATIVE WARFARE: One belligerent (A) engages a set of other belligerents (B, C, D, . . . , Z) and wins a series of wars that result in some form of political control over the formerly autonomous belligerents. Warfare by fusion.

DISINTEGRATIVE WARFARE: One belligerent actor (A) experiences a war that results in a set of autonomous belligerents (B, C, D, . . . , Z). Warfare by fission.

SPORADIC WARFARE: Different sets of belligerents (A-B, C-D, . . . Y-Z) engage in different wars over a period of time.

type of warfare – when they manifest not just disputes but actual combat as well.

Integrative warfare – a violent conflict process that begins with several belligerents and eventually ends with one victor – is a sequence of wars in which the same belligerent wins in repeated wars with different belligerents, annexing or conquering the territory of the vanquished side (e.g. Alexander's campaigns, wars of Roman expansion, Aztec warfare, Spanish Conquest of the New World, American–Indian wars, War of Italian Unification). Many states and perhaps all empires (Taagepera 1968) have been forged by this type of warfare.

Disintegrative warfare – the reverse process of integrative warfare, beginning with one belligerent actor and ending with many – is a sequence of wars in which the original unitary belligerent becomes increasingly fragmented by secessions (e.g. warfare of Roman imperial disintegration, wars of Spanish, British, and French imperial disintegration, warfare of Yugoslavian fragmentation). Integrative and disintegrative types of warfare involve opposite processes of political consolidation (fusion) and dispersion (fission), respectively – a complex dual process that remains poorly understood but can be readily identified through long-range analysis.

Sporadic warfare is a series of unrelated wars fought among different belligerents for a period of time, typically over different objectives. The 1991 Gulf War may represent a case of sporadic warfare (assuming it ended with the 1991 cease-fire agreements), although as long as relations between Iraq and the UN allies remain hostile it may be considered part of an ongoing protracted conflict with fluctuating hostility and occasional outbreaks of violence (cruise missile attacks, punitive bombings, economic warfare, etc.). Until extensive long-range measurement is undertaken we will not know the composition of total warfare in terms of sporadic or related types (protracted, integrative, disintegrative).

Note that the graphic structure of each pattern of warfare is distinct. This property – the characteristic graphic signature of warfare – is important because it means that the graphic structure itself can be used to identify and classify the appropriate pattern regardless of conventional or nominal historical designations (nominalism), as shown below.

Figures 13.2 and 13.3 illustrate the use of this typology for systematically describing warfare in ancient China and Mesoamerica using long-range analysis. Figure 13.2 describes the observed patterns of Chinese warfare in the East Asian system, from the Legendary period to the end of the Western Zhou dynasty, a period of two millennia, from 2700 BCE to 722 BCE (Cioffi-Revilla and Lai 1995). Figure 13.3 describes the observed patterns of Maya warfare in the Mesoamerican system, based on a preliminary data set used here only for illustrative purposes (Cioffi-Revilla, Chupik and Resnick 1998). This type of graphic representation is called a chronographic model and it can be used for representing a variety of long-range conflict patterns extending over millennia and including many (or all) belligerents in a given system. A chronograph can also be derived from a geographic information system (GIS) containing time-dependent war data (Jones 1997; Starr 1998).

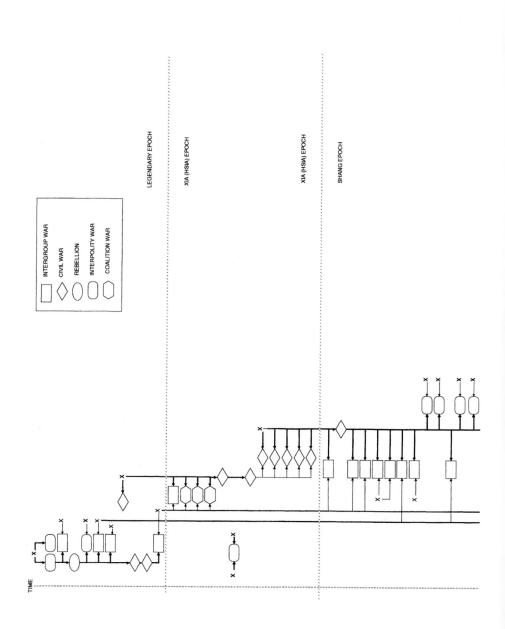

TIME

LEGENDARY EPOCH

XIA (HSIA) EPOCH

XIA (HSIA) EPOCH

SHANG EPOCH

INTERGROUP WAR
CIVIL WAR
REBELLION
INTERPOLITY WAR
COALITION WAR

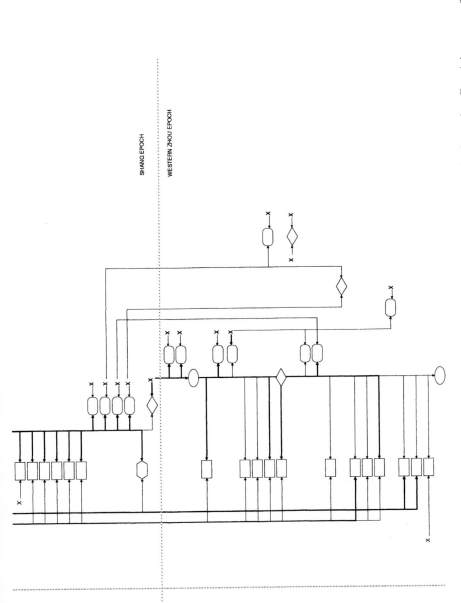

SHANG EPOCH

WESTERN ZHOU EPOCH

Figure 13.2 Chronograph of Chinese wars and emergent long-range patterns of warfare in the ancient East Asian system, 2700–722 BC.

TIME

Early Pre-Classic: 2000 B.C. to 800 B.C.

Middle Pre-Classic: 800 B.C. to 300 B.C.

Late Pre-Classic: 300 B.C. to 250 A.D.

Early Classic: 250 A.D. to 600 A.D.

Early Classic: 250 A.D. to 600 A.D.

Late Classic: 600 A.D. to 900 A.D.

INTRAGROUP WAR

INTERGROUP WAR

EXTRAGROUP WAR

WAR BETWEEN UNKNOWN GROUPS

NON-WAR POLITICAL EVENT

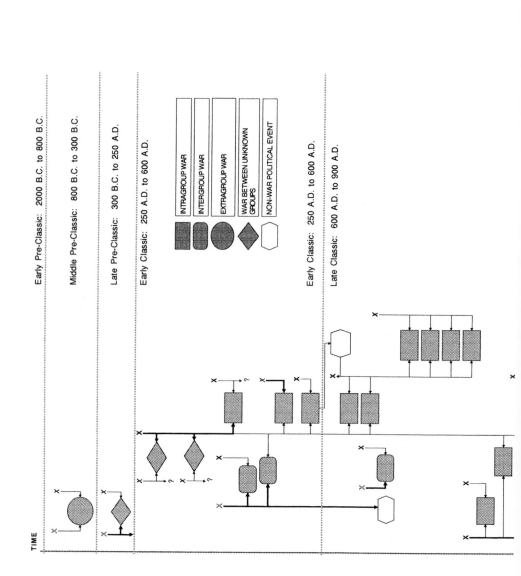

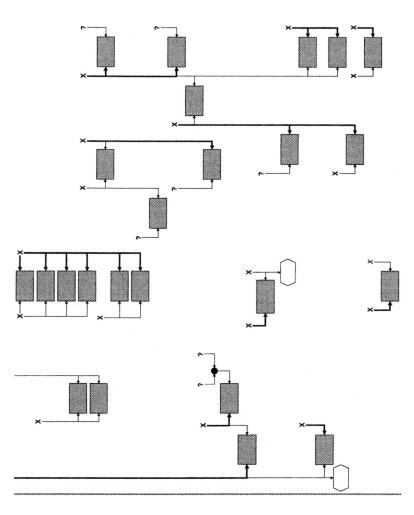

Figure 13.3 Chronograph of Maya wars and emergent long-range patterns of warfare in the ancient Mesoamerican system ca. 800 BC–AD 700.
Source: Cioffi-Revilla, Chupik and Resnick (1997). Copyright © 1998 Claudio Cioffi-Revilla. All rights reserved.

Although vastly different in their cultural context and civilizations character-istics, some long-range patterns of warfare in these ancient systems are strikingly comparable in several significant respects – an empirical property that cannot be easily detected without appropriate conceptual categories and measurement instruments that help distinguish 'the forest' from 'the trees.' As shown in Figure 13.2, the Chinese patterns for the eastern Asian system exhibits several cases of protracted warfare (the Chinese fighting against the barbarian Xiong Nu), inte-grative warfare (conflicts that unified China under the Xia, the Shang, and the Zhou), and cases of sporadic warfare (Yin-Pi Shi War of 1945 BCE, Xu–Jing War of 966 BCE). In Figure 13.3, the Maya pattern for the Mesoamerican system also shows cases of protracted warfare (several Maya states engaging in repeated wars), little if any integrative warfare (unlike the Chinese, the Maya never attained a unified political system), and several cases of sporadic warfare.

Similar charts describing the long-range structure of war and warfare – parallel regional chronographs – are being developed for other space-time regions of the world historical system. Additional recurring types of warfare beyond the above four elementary types may be discovered in the future, and such a set of patterns may eventually constitute a true taxonomy (exhaustive and mutually exclusive), as opposed to just a typology (as is now for interstate wars). A scale of such types (minimally nominal in level of precision) can then be used in long-range analysis to measure and model warfare in new ways that would advance our understanding.

Scale of process: macroprocesses and microprocesses

Beyond its intrinsic importance for developing a long-range theory of war, the preceding discussion of the scale of belligerence – viz., the distinction between war and warfare – also provides an essential premise for discussing the other conceptual dimension of conflict, the scale of process. From a theoretical perspec-tive, here again I distinguish between two different phenomena that are distinct in terms of several key dimensions, such as (1) analytical focus, (2) referent systems of actors, (3) historical process, (4) time scale, and (5) coevolutionary mechanisms. Table 13.2 uses this set of dimensions to define the two types of processes accord-ing to their scale, distinguishing between 'microprocesses' and 'macroprocesses.'

Macroprocesses have a universal or global focus on the world system, or largest regional system, examining the history of polities from their earliest known origins to the present. The time scale of a macroprocess is marked by centuries and millennia. On such a scale, theoretical attention must focus on the origins and subsequent development of warfare, with less emphasis on individual wars. The original areas of warfare correspond to the Fertile Crescent (Palestine, Mesopo-tamia, and Egypt), East Asia (Yellow River and Blue River basins), Mesoamerica (Gulf of Mexico Coast and Oaxaca Valley), and South America (Peruvian Coast and Highlands).[3] In the scale of macroprocesses it is large-scale social entities such as civilizations (Quigley 1979; Wilkinson 1991), international or regional systems (Scott 1967), peer–polity interactions systems (Renfrew 1986), macro social

Table 13.2 Scale of process – macroprocesses and microprocesses

	Macroprocesses	Microprocesses
Focus, granularity:	Universal, global, coarse-grained	Detailed, local, fine-grained
System:	Whole world or large regions	Several belligerents
History:	Origins to present	War to war
Time scale:	Centuries to millennia (10^2–10^3 years), eras, multigenerational	Months to years (10^0–10^1 years), epochs
Rise and fall:	Macro social systems, civilizations, culture areas, horizons	Tribes, chiefdoms, states, empires, alliances
Belligerence:	Warfare	War
Graphic structural representation:	Pleogenic model 	Chronographic model
Puzzles:	Multiple origins (pleogenesis), parallel evolution, fusion points, durations between fusions, post-fusion turbulence (effects on politics, economics, culture, etc.), hegemonies, cycles, pulsations; warfare and system structure.	War onset, magnitude, duration processes; sequence of wars (e.g, among different types); effect of the war-to-war process on the rise, evolution, and fall of actors in the system (polities); war contagion and diffusion.
Coevolution:	Parallel subsystems, sometimes with cultural, commercial or ideational contact, which consolidate at a small number of fusion points.	War process and political process are not independent of one another, nor of other social processes (economic, technological, climatological, etc.).

Source: Prepared by the author.

systems (Cioffi-Revilla 1998a), world-systems (Chase-Dunn and Hall 1997), and supraregional groupings of cultural horizons (Willey 1991), or archaeological traditions (Peregrine 1998) that undergo the developmental processes of 'rise and fall,' accompanied by warfare and other defining processes. The pleogenic model – human history experienced multiple pristine origins in terms of the rise of polities and warfare – provides a paradigm for understanding macroprocesses of conflict and political development (Cioffi-Revilla 1991, 1996, 1998b). The principal puzzles in long-range macroprocesses concern the antiquity of the processes themselves (when did they begin?), multiple origins (pleogenesis: where did they begin?), and the understanding of parallel evolution, coevolution, fusion points, post-fusion turbulence, dynamics of political dominance, and similar topics. To date, relatively few social scientists and historians have examined this macro scale, given the challenging empirical and theoretical difficulties.

By contrast, *microprocesses* are more detailed or localized, focusing on systems with fewer belligerents, examining history from one war to the next, and using a shorter time scale. Here the social entities involved are mostly tribes, chiefdoms, states, alliances, empires, and other similar ('sovereign') belligerents that rise, fall, and are affected by wars. The detailed chronographic models used in Figure 13.2 and 13.3 earlier (Chinese and Maya wars in East Asian and Mesoamerican systems, respectively) provide graphic representations of microprocesses. The main puzzles concerning microprocesses are patterns of war escalation, onset, magnitude, duration, contagion, diffusion, and other similar phenomena. A relatively large community of social scientists has focused many investigations on these microprocesses, producing a growing corpus of new scientific knowledge (Bremmer and Cusack 1994; Cioffi-Revilla 1995; Diehl 1998; Geller and Singer 1998; Midlarsky 1989, 1998; and Vasquez 1993).

Macroprocesses and microprocesses of conflict differ along the following dimensions:

Focus   Macroprocesses and microprocesses of conflict are phenomena that differ primarily by their theoretical and empirical focus. The focus of macroprocesses is on the universal or global history of social systems on the largest possible scale, including their belligerence. The macro-level focus is sometimes – not always – identified with a primarily diachronic perspective. By contrast, the focus of microprocesses is far more detailed and is sometimes identified with a primarily synchronic perspective. Numerous investigations exemplify the micro-level focus, such as individual works on the Persian wars, the Punic wars, the Napoleonic wars, or the wars of the French Revolution. Note that both levels – macro and micro – can take a long-range approach, but the details of the referent process will vary with the focus. In terms of relative historical granularity, the macro-level is coarse-grained whereas the micro-level is fine-grained.

System   Macroprocesses and microprocesses also differ by the kind of referent system that is the object of long-range investigation. The type of system examined in macroprocesses refers to the entire world or at least its major regions or macro social systems (e.g. Fertile Crescent, East Asia, Europe, America, Polynesia). The 'world historical system' approach is also in this macro-level tradition (chapters in this volume; Chase-Dunn and Hall 1997; Dark 1998; Frank and Gills 1993; Thompson 1983), following earlier landmark work by historians and social scientists that provided foundations for long-range analysis (Braudel 1987; Dawson 1958; McNeill 1993; Sorokin 1937; Toynbee 1934–61; and Wright 1942). By contrast, microprocesses examine smaller systems of belligerents that experience wars and other events during their history (e.g. Chinese warring states, Rome and Carthage, Classic Maya Lowlands, Soviet–American Cold War system). The identification of the referent system is essential for defining the appropriate scale of process.

History Macroprocesses and microprocesses differ by the relative length of the historical process being examined. In the case of a macroprocess, the time domain covers from the earliest origins of warfare to its present state. In terms of individually identifiable historical events, this is a process with a history of at least 6,000 years, beginning with the earliest Sumerian wars (Cioffi-Revilla and Sommer 1993). Considering the first evidence of warfare (Jericho pre-pottery B level) the process would extend back at least another 5,000 years (Kenyon 1979; Roper 1975). By contrast, in a microprocess the time scale is such that the process ranges from one war to the next and is therefore much more fine-grained (Cioffi-Revilla 1997; Vasquez 1987).

Time scale Because of the preceding differences in scale, macroprocesses and microprocesses are also measured according to different clocks or time scales. In general, macroprocesses are marked by events that are spaced apart by centuries or millennia (e.g. the 'ages' of human history associated with stone, copper, iron, industry, and information). By contrast, microprocesses use a time scale that is marked by more discrete events (wars, political transitions, etc.) that are usually spaced apart by years or decades (e.g. the 'epochs' of human history marked by various dynasties and regimes). These different time scales make a great difference in terms of the conflict process being considered.

Rise and fall Keeping in mind the relative nature of macroprocesses and microprocesses, the nature of the social units that evolve through the process of rise, development, and fall represents another major difference. In macroprocesses what rise and fall are the largest identifiable social units that have ever existed in human history: civilizations, cultures, international systems and other macro social systems identified earlier. By contrast, what rise and fall in a microprocess are much smaller social units, although sometimes they can define a larger area as a dominant center: tribes, chiefdoms, states, alliances, federations, empires, and other components of the larger macro social systems within which these entities interact. Clearly, the types of social units that are involved in conflict – rising, enduring, and eventually declining – make a significant difference in terms of the scale of process being examined.

Belligerence   Significantly, macroprocesses and microprocesses also differ in terms of the scale of belligerence examined in each process. Macroprocesses provide a more appropriate framework for the investigation of warfare, given the coarser focus, the broader system of belligerents, and the longer chronological timeline. Most individual wars can look like minute events in the context of a macroprocess, except for those that have large system-transforming effect (e.g. some world wars). By contrast, microprocesses focus more effectively on wars, given the more detailed focus, the relatively smaller sets of belligerents, and the shorter chronological timeline. Considering the two scales combined, macroprocesses are to warfare as microprocesses are to war.

Graphics   Given these differences in scales, different descriptive approaches are required for graphically modeling the two types of processes (Tufte 1983, 1990, 1997). Macroprocesses may be best represented by the pleogenic model containing multiple warfare origins (pleogenesis), parallel lines of development, several points of fusion, fissions and other developmental characteristics of warfare, as discussed earlier (see Table 13.2; also Cioffi-Revilla 1998b: Figure 1). Microprocesses are best represented by a chronographic model containing the set of belligerents, alliances, different types of wars, and other defining characteristics of microevolution (see Figures 13.2 and 13.3 and Table 13.2). Unfortunately, effective graphic methods for scientific investigation are still notoriously lacking in social science in general, and in fields like international relations in particular. Long-range analysis can contribute significantly toward developing such new tools.

Puzzles   Logically, macroprocesses and microprocesses must differ by the kind of research puzzles being addressed. Macro-level puzzles include the following: how ancient is warfare? When, how, and why did warfare first occur in human history? Did warfare first occur in one location and subsequently diffuse to others, or did warfare initiate spontaneously (ex novo) in several pristine areas (pleogenesis)? Why did political complexity arise sooner but slower in the Old World, as opposed to later but faster in the New World? When and how does fusion between two or more systems occur? What determines one belligerent dominating others at a fusion point? How do various segments or subsystems (Mesopotamia, China, Mesoamerica) compare in terms of their patterns of war and political change? From an interdisciplinary perspective, these puzzles are similar to those raised in fields like cosmology or climatology, as opposed to the puzzles raised in astronomy or meteorology, respectively. Puzzles are scale-specific. By contrast, micro-level puzzles are more synchronically focused and include the following: How can we account for patterns of war onset, magnitude, or duration? What are the correlates of war? What makes some disputes escalate to war and others not? How can we account for the war-to-war process? Conversely, from an interdisciplinary perspective, these puzzles are like those raised in astronomy and meteorology, as opposed to cosmology and climatology. These and other puzzles depend on the scale being considered.

Coevolution Finally, macroprocesses and microprocesses differ by the type of coevolutionary mechanisms that may operate within each process. At the macro-level the main coevolutionary process of warfare consists of (a) parallel systems undergoing their own history elsewhere in the world (literally, 'parallel worlds') and (b) other macro-level processes within each evolving area (e.g. changes and trans-formation in the economic system or in political culture). Some parallel worlds of the ancient past (e.g. West Asia and East Asia at 3000 BCE) may have had weak and remote ideational contact by means of a diffused long-distance 'information net' (McNeill, this volume). However, such systems were otherwise disconnected in terms of any significant political, economic, or military interactions. Other parallel worlds in the Old World and the New World did not even share such weak inter-actions (e.g. Mesoamerica and Mesopotamia). Parallel worlds merged occasionally – thereby ending their separation – at a small number of fusion points.

By contrast, in the scale of microprocesses that which coevolves with warfare are the associated political, economic, cultural, and demographic processes that are defined within a referent system of belligerents. For instance, in a process of integrative warfare (Figure 13.1, column 2), the political system grows, as does the economy and – usually but not always – the territorial reach of the expanding polity. Warfare and politics also coevolve at this level, producing the first complex forms of political development and organized warfare (Brumfiel and Earle 1987; Brumfiel and Fox 1994; Cioffi-Revilla 1998b; Marcus and Flannery 1996).

Conclusion

In this chapter I identified the puzzle of scales in the long-range analysis of conflict in world historical systems and proposed some solutions. To address the puzzle, I focused on the critical distinction between different levels of belligerence (scale of belligerence) and the different levels of historical evolution (scale of process). Different scales of belligerence – the 'war' versus 'warfare' distinction – not only highlight the significance of these different phenomena but also offer a systematic typology for empirical classification, measurement, and modeling of conflict. The value of this approach is enhanced in the area of comparative analysis, both cross-culturally and cross-temporally, an area that is essential in any truly long-range investigation.

Similarly, different scales of process – the 'macro' versus 'micro' distinction – focus attention on significantly different historical mechanisms that must also obey different principles because their scale is so different. Moreover, the two scales of process – different clocks of human history – also present vastly different sets of research puzzles. For instance, whereas traditionally political scientists have been more interested in the microprocesses of wars, archaeologists, anthropologists, and world historians have dedicated more attention to the macroprocesses of warfare. The approach I propose in this chapter may also contribute to the type of interdisciplinary collaboration that is becoming increasingly necessary to achieve real scientific advances in our understanding of the long-range evolution of war, its causes and effects on human history.

Acknowledgement

I am grateful to Jacek Kugler and William R. Thompson for their comments on an earlier version of this chapter.

Notes

1   Military historians and military operations research analysts often examine the next, lower level of detail in terms of scales of analysis, given by campaigns or field operations (Battilega and Granger 1984; Dockery and Woodcock 1993; Ferrill 1985/1997; Hughes 1984; Jones 1987; Margiotta 1984). Thus, consistent with the scales of long-range analysis: (i) several battles or engagements compose a campaign; (ii) several campaigns compose a war; and (iii) several wars compose warfare.
2   See, e.g., Blainey (1975), Bremer and Cusack (1994), Cioffi-Revilla (1995), Dupuy and Dupuy (1993), Eckhardt (1992), Geller and Singer (1998), Keegan (1993), Levy (1983), Margiotta (1984), Midlarsky (1988), Richardson (1960), Small and Singer (1982), Vasquez (1993), and Wright (1942).
3   For recent authoritative works on these pleogenic regions see Burger (1995), Chang (1980), Frangipane (1996), Haas *et al.* (1987), Keightley (1983), Liverani (1988), Marcos and Flannery (1996), Rothman (1999), Sharer (1994), and Willey (1991).

14 The evolution of the world-city system, 3000 BCE to AD 2000

Andrew Bosworth

Civilization is a recent phenomenon, arising 5,000 years ago in Mesopotamia. Indeed, only about 5 per cent of human history has been characterized by irrigated agriculture, political administration, writing, calendars, institutionalized long-distance and other civic technologies. Yet, during this brief period, world population has grown from about 20 million to 5.7 billion people, an increase of staggering proportions. This expansive process merits analysis. What are the organizing structures of civilization? How can we measure long-term, large-scale change? What does it mean for civilization to 'evolve'?

Cities and the world-city system

As building-blocks of civilization, cities become the most vital units of analysis for long-term study. Economically, cities represent markets and production centers in their most concentrated form; as such, they are vital to growth and innovation. Pendulum-like cycles of economic expansion and contraction – such as the 250-year A and B phases described by Barry Gills and Andre Gunder Frank (1992) – find support in rates of urban population growth (Bosworth 1995a,b). Politically, cities embody the very essence of politics, 'polis' being Greek for 'city' but also for 'politics.' Socially, cities are microcosms of regional populations and centers for education and religion. And culturally, cities reflect a relationship between humans and the earth dependent on large-scale agriculture and expanding markets. In sum, cities reflect the four interrelated dimensions of human experience: economic, political, social and cultural.

More crucially, cities presuppose connections. In 1891, a German geographer, F. Ratzel, argued that cities develop wherever one or more of three conditions exist: (1) the end of a transport route; (2) the junction of two transport routes of the same kind; or (3), the junction of two transport routes of different kinds. Indeed, no city is an island; each is part of a larger network, a 'world-city system' that provides the circuitry for civilization. This world-city system exhibits a structural order, or 'architectonics,' defined primarily by vital connections (rather than cities, which rise and fall in more rapid succession than the trade routes of which they are a part). As Janet Abu-Lughod argues: 'In a system it is the connections between parts that must be studied. When these strengthen and reticulate, the system may be said to 'rise'; when they fray, the system declines, although it may later undergo reorganization and revitalization' (1989:367). The world-city system's connections have clearly undergone reorganization from the dawn of civilization to today, and, broadly speaking, there have been six successive yet overlapping 'architectonic orders.'

The 'Fertile Crescent' period extends from approximately 3000 BCE to 1500 BCE, which for some represents the Bronze Age. First, there was a breakthrough to civilization in Mesopotamia, specifically in Sumeria. Second, there was a similiar breakthrough in Egypt along the Nile, where there emerged a unified kingdom in contrast to the more complex array of Mesopotamian city-states. During this time, Mesopotamia and Egyptian civilizations, inherently expansive, fused, creating what might be called 'Central Civilization.' And third, there was the emergence of civilization in Syria, Palestine, the Levant and even parts of Asia Minor – largely sparked by the original riverine civilizations.

The 'Regional Eurasian' period extends from about 1500 BCE–1 AD and approximates what many have called the Iron Age. This was a time when western Asian, Mediterranean, Chinese and Indian societies developed along relatively independent lines. Regional transportation arteries emerged: The Royal Road of Persia, the Grand Trunk Road of India, the Ambassador Road and Yellow River system of China, the Incense Road of Arabia and, adjacent to it, the Phoenician sea lanes of the Mediterranean. Regional constellations of cities sharpened in resolution; a world galaxy of cities was still embryonic. This regional Eurasian order no longer reflected Middle Eastern dominance but rather a fourfold cultural balance among the regions of high culture. By 200 BCE, China, India, the Middle East and the Mediterranean had robust populations, each with between 30–45 million people.

The 'Silk Road' period begins about 200 BCE when Chinese crossed Central Asia to obtain horses, jade, fur and gold (and to sell silk). The road soon linked the powerful Han dynasty of China with the Romans. The period ends around 1350 AD when bubonic plague gutted Silk Road cities and eroded the Mongol Empire

Table 14.1 Architectonic orders

Approx. time frame	Architectonic order	Vital cities
3000–1500 BC	Fertile Crescent	Ur, Babylon, Mari, Memphis, Thebes
1500 BC–1 AD	Regional Eurasian	Loyang, Patna, Nineveh, Susa, Sardis, Marib, Knossos, Carthage
200 BC–1350 AD	Silk Roads	Rome, Changan, Bactra, Constantinople, Baghdad
50 BC–1750 AD	Spice Routes	Alexandria, Anuradhapura, Broach, Canton, Cairo, Calicutt
1500–1950	Atlantic	Lisbon, Seville, Bahia, Havana, Mexico City, Amsterdam, Le Havre, London, New York
1900–	Pacific-Global	San Francisco, Sydney, Shanghai, Los Angeles, Hong Kong, Vancouver, Tokyo

that had linked them together from the Mediterranean to the Pacific. Few merchants ever traversed the entire length of the Silk Roads; instead, a city-to-city relay system arose that detoured according to climate, plagues, civil wars, bandits, taxes and tolls. There were two main southern branches and a northern steppe route, each with its own variations. Ideas as well as goods coursed from one end to the other. Religious pilgrims and wayfarers diffused Nestorian Christianity, Buddhism, Zoroastrianism and other faiths.

The Spice Routes period, which can be broken down into four phases, largely overlaps with the Silk Road period because these maritime routes, which emerged around 50 BCE, represented alternate linkages between East and West. The Spice Routes began, in their first phase, as a relay system between three circuits (Arabian Sea, Bay of Bengal and South China Sea) overlapping in Ceylon and the Malaccan Straits, where cargoes would be exchanged. The circuits were marked by quarterly shifts of monsoon winds that imparted cyclical rhythms to maritime trade, in effect stranding Muslim and Buddhist merchants in foreign ports for months at a time and allowing for religious diffusion. During the Spice Routes's second phase, a single circuit emerged as Abbasid trading colonies were founded in China. In the third phase the relay system was restored, partly because of xenophobic massacres of Muslims in China. In its fourth phase Portugal, the Netherlands, France and Britain founded colonies in Arabian, Indian and Malaccan ports. Over the course of the entire Spice Routes period there was a great increase in the bulk of traded goods but also in its diversity: carpets, wine, sugar, salted fish, fruits and, in the sixteenth century, American tobacco and silver. Coffee was also widely distributed for the first time, diffusing from Mocha and Aden in Arabia. Despite the bulk and dynamism of Spice Route trade, this system was eclipsed by the Atlantic, when, by at least 1750, European expansion turned the Indian Ocean into a backwater.

The 'Atlantic System' begins after 1492 with the European discovery of the Americas. There arose an amalgam of Spanish, Portuguese, Dutch, French, British and North American city systems, each with its own patterned flow of traders, soldiers, missionaries, colonizers and slaves. There was a historical momentum that began with an Iberian system anchored in Lisbon and Seville and ended in the twentieth century, in a reversal of polarity, with a North American system anchored in New York. This Atlantic period of the world-city system is striking. The world's largest migration occurred as over fifty million people entered the Americas. The Industrial Revolution, with colonial trade at its base, evolved out of this Atlantic matrix and concentrated world economic and military power in northern Europe for 300 years. Technology revolutionized medicine, and the world's population exploded. Today the Atlantic system declines in importance as civilization's center-of-gravity continues its westward trajectory and shifts to the Pacific, the new Mare Nostrum.

The 'Pacific-Global' period is so named because unlike the dominance of the Atlantic system in its day, the Pacific system is merely 'prominent' within a truly global civilization that is likely half-a-century away from being orbital as well. This Pacific-Global order has its origins in the annual Spanish Manila Galleon trade between 1565 and 1810 that exported Mexican silver, gold and cacao from Acapulco and imported Asian silk, spices and porcelain from Manila. A more clear beginning can be traced to the 1890s and early twentieth century: US troops occupied the Philippines and were deployed in China; the US absorbed Hawaii; a diaspora of Chinese labor continued to reach California and Peru; and, in 1914, the Panama Canal linked the Atlantic and Pacific oceans. After World War II, the first war to define the Pacific as a military theatre, the growth of East Asian economies – of Japan, then of the 'Four Tigers' (South Korea, Taiwan, Hong Kong and Singapore) and now coastal China – has created a third industrial core in addition to Europe and North America. Today, trans-Pacific trade exceeds trans-Atlantic trade, and in North America, innovations in aviation, bioengineering, and computer technologies are clustering around Los Angeles, San Francisco and Seattle.

These successive architectonic orders do not appear out of thin air; restructuring, rather than substitution, is the operative principle. This restructuring often emerges out of challenges or crises that can take the form of trade blockages. (Of all connections, trade routes are the most visible, and although long-distance trade was not immense in ancient times it had enormous political and ideological consequences.) The process of restructuring is one of transcendence and inclusion; each order contains its own logic but also those of the previous orders, however decayed. Architectonic orders reflect routes of trade, invasion, migration and colonization, and although not explored here, they also reflect intellectual and spiritual world-views. This is most apparent in the maturation of the Atlantic system, one so influenced by industrial, rational and secular paradigms. For some observers, it is also evident in the shift to the Pacific-Global order, one increasingly shaped by a synthesis of East and West.

An evolving world-city system

Evolutionary theory represents a broad research program in which disagreement abounds, particularly in regard to the relative importance of selection, adaptation and chance. Yet, minimally defined, we can define 'evolution' as a process of change in which forms, driven by pressures of survival and the capacity or will to change, tend toward greater structure, connectivity and differentiation. Thus, evolution can provide direction; it does not necessarily provide, in a teleological sense, destination.

The direction toward greater structure, connectivity and differentiation – or from simplicity to complexity – is significant in terms of evolution. (Movements from complexity to simplicity do happen, such as the cave crayfish that loses its eyes, but they are far more rare.) Clearly, systems of a higher order are advantageous: 'It is a fundamental characteristic of the material world,' observes Peter Corning (1994:3), 'that things in various combinations, sometimes with others of like kind and sometimes with very different kinds of things, are prodigious generators of novelty'. Generators of novelty, he adds, are 'extravagantly favored' by natural selection. This principle of evolution – that evolution engenders complexity – can in fact be applied to the world-city system, which, like any complex system, is a product of three factors: (1) the number and size of parts included in the system; (2) the connectivity and integration among the parts; and (3) the differentiation, diversity, division of labor, or degree of hierarchy among the parts. For the world-city system, it is possible to evaluate and even measure change in each of these dimensions (supporting the claim that evolutionary theory can produce testable hypotheses).

The world-city system's movement toward greater structure is virtually self-evident. Around 3000 BCE this system rested on the riverine civilizations of the Fertile Crescent and contained no more than five million people. Today the system is global in scope, and about half of the world's 6 billion people are urban. The largest twenty-five cities alone contain over 350 million people, more than 5 per cent of world population. Geographically, the world-city system has enveloped ever-larger regions (the Middle East, Eurasia, and the Americas) and ever-larger bodies of water (the Aegean Sea, the Mediterranean Sea, and the Indian, Atlantic and Pacific oceans, in that order). This structural expansion was not gradual or continuous. Centuries of stagnation were followed by decades of accelerated, quantum change – punctuated evolution.

The world-city system has also moved toward further connectivity and integration. Economically, there has been a historic and well-documented shift in trade from low-weight, high-priced goods to heavy-weight, low-priced ones. There has also been a general expansion and diversification of all trade goods to the point where today 'information' is added to the world's commodity pool. This integration is even visible at the household level. A century ago household items were of local and regional origin, with a few treasured valuables like porcelain (from China) or lace (from Britain) representing imports. Today, a much higher portion of household items are imported, and they come from all over the world.

Political integration, furthered in ancient times by the expanding average size of empires, was more recently furthered by colonial empires and their transformation into a global nation-state system. Within this expanding community of nations, democratization integrates populations into an alliance structure and encourages the emergence of common norms and values. The process of democratization, which depends on diffusion, can be viewed as a self-reinforcing learning process whose rewards include peace: history demonstrates that democratic societies do not make war against one another. With about half of the world's population now living in democratic polities (a percentage that has steadily increased in modern times exept for the 1930s and 1940s), it is entirely possible that, with more complete democratization, war can be made extinct.

Social integration is also notable, especially the diffusion of English as the world's *lingua franca*. More deplorable to some is the rise of a consumerist monoculture sustained by multinational corporations. More tragic signs of integration are global epidemics. Just as increased movement across Eurasia made possible the fourteenth-century bubonic plague, and just as the expansion of Europe in the sixteenth century brought smallpox and influenza to Mexico and Peru, contemporary migration from developing to developed regions, travel, tourism and the rise of a global sex industry have helped AIDS reach intercontinental proportions. The world has indeed become smaller, often with tremendous costs.

The third major criterion of evolution considered here is differentiation. A system under evolutionary pressure tends to become internally complex, specialized and hierarchic. There arises a greater division of labor among the parts. This is also true for the world-city system whose functional hierarchy increased with the Industrial Revolution and the emergence of manufacturing cities of unprecedented size. The Information Revolution of the last few decades has further complexified the world-city system. The largest cities of the developed world are no longer industrial; they are 'postindustrial' centers of banking, education and service.

Another dimension of differentiation is cyclical: 'world urban hierarchy.' In this study, this hierarchy is defined by the ratio between the population of the world's largest city and its twenty-fifth largest (whose population is usually similar to all cities in the fifteenth to fiftieth range). High ratios of this indicator, produced when the largest city in the world surges in population, can be associated with economic growth and political concentration – at least until the late twentieth century. Figure 14.1 measures the changing ratio of the world's largest city to the twenty-fifth largest from about 500 BCE to AD 2000. Adapted from urban population estimates, this figure is compatible with the historical record. Each of these cities is widely recognized as having been the world's largest for a considerable period of time.

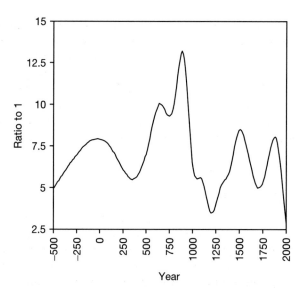

Figure 14.1 World urban hierarchy between 500 BCE and AD 2000.

Source: Based on data from Chandler (1987).

Note: This figure displays the ratio of size difference between the world's largest and twenty-fifth largest cities. Increases of this ratio are produced by the pulling with periods of general economic and political expansion (and decreases with contraction).

This figure, which exhibits a harmonious wave-like pattern (supporting, incidentally, the existence of fluctuation at the world level), shows the first major wave produced by Rome, which integrated the Mediterranean basin and exerted a pull of attraction on the world economy; the second by Baghdad, the center of an Abbassid Muslim commercial and intellectual movement; the third by Peking, which, although more isolated than Hangchow, was Asia's largest city when the world's center-of-gravity still rested in that continent; and the fourth by London, capital for a network of cities that unleashed the explosive Industrial Revolution.

Fluctuations play a role in evolution. As Ilya Prigogine (1984) argues, when fluctuations are of greatest amplitude a complex system is at a 'bifurcation point' and able to 'choose' among varying regimes of order. If true for the world-city system, fluctuations of urban hierarchy represent opportunities for structural metamorphosis. Indeed, each fluctuation of urban hierarchy coincides with the transition to a new architectonic order; in other words, each peak of urban hierarchy matches one turning point in the evolution of the world-city system. The first wave coincides with the development of the Silk Roads as the most prominent (if not dominant) mode of cross-cultural transmission. The wave of AD 900 coincides with the mid-point in the 'struggle' between Silk Roads and Spice Routes leading to the eventual primacy of the latter. The wave of AD 1600 coincides with the rise of an Atlantic network and its rapid eclipse of its Indian Ocean counterpart. Finally, the last wave of AD 1900 coincides with the modern development of a Pacific-Global system.

These synchronicities – between ratios of world urban hierarchy and architectonic change – raise interesting questions: are transitions from one architectonic order to another dependent on fluctuations in the system? Do these fluctuations represent 'structural instability' and therefore 'bifurcation points'? Do great concentrations of economic and political power precipitate shifts of world connections? It is a tantalizing possibility. A final question emerges: why does each fluctuation contract in time span from about 1,000 to 800 to 500 to 300 years? Are world-level processes accelerating as communication networks tighten?

Adaptation in the world-city system

Another realm of concern is adaptation, an important hallmark of evolution. For the world-city system, the capacity to respond to a changing environment is of course the product of local adaptive behavior trickling-up to effect systemic change. At this local level, adaptive behavior emerges in the face of 'blockages' brought about by military and political choke-holds on world trade: taxes, tolls and other obstacles. (Some blockages, particularly for the Silk Roads, were induced by epidemics and desertification.) Thus, blockages represent a form of 'selection' and circumventions a form of 'adaptation,' with the cities forging new connections becoming, if not more powerful and prosperous, at least more secure. Indeed, the two most important transitions of the world-city system – from an overland Silk Road to a maritime Spice Route system, and then from a pre-industrial Spice Route to an industrial Atlantic system – were each induced by a series of blockage-circumvention sequences. Table 14.2 lists important blockage-circumvention sequences and the rise of associated cities.

The first blockage was caused by the loss of Chinese control over the western Tarim Basin. According to Franck and Brownstone (1986), the Parthian empire capitalized on these developments:

> In the absence of secure passage, much was lost en route to raiders who had no taste for the longer-term rewards of trading. And in the absence of a central power favorable to merchants, traders had to pay high taxes and duties to every petty state along the way west. The result was a diminution of the flow of silks from the East, just as Rome was developing a powerful appetite for them. And Parthia took advantage of the 'buyer's market' to make the highest profits it could.
>
> (Franck and Brownstone 1986:118)

In response, Augustus Caesar (who ruled from 27 BCE to AD 14) tried to find another route to the East. The route north of the Caspian Sea was afflicted by similar problems, so he turned to the Red Sea. The Romans were aware that Arabs and Greeks had been sailing from Egypt to India for about a century, and Caesar hoped to tap this connection. His first military expedition to the region, as large as eighty warships and 10,000 men, was a fiasco, with thousands succumbing to heat and exhaustion. The second expedition was successful. The Romans sacked the major port of the Incense region, Arabia Eudaemon (Aden), forcing traffic up to Roman ports such as Aela. Nearby Alexandria became the western anchor for the Spice Routes and a distribution center for the entire Mediterranean. Of the Roman effort John Firth (1902:281) writes: 'Certainly the Red Sea became a Roman water and the trade of the Far East was largely diverted from the old caravan ports through Arabia into the Egyptian ports and the Nile Route, to the great profit of Egyptian revenue.' By the beginning of the first century AD trade along the Silk Roads had been reduced to a 'trickle,'

Table 14.2 World-city system blockages and circumventions

Blockage	Circumvention	City rise
I. Parthia blocks Silk Roads c. 25 BC	Romans develop Red Sea route	Rome, Alexandria, Anuradhapura
II. Persia blocks Byzantium c. 550 AD	Byzantium develops northern steppe route	Constantinople, Changan
III. Northern tribes in China, c. 800–1100 AD	Sung dynasty expands maritime trade	Hangchow, Canton, Cairo
IV. Muslim powers block Europe c. 1400–1500 AD	Europeans find Cape route, Atlantic crossings	Lisbon, Seville, Amsterdam, London

having given way to the 'larger flow' of the Spice Routes (Franck and Brownstone 1986).

The second blockage also happened along the Silk Roads. Because Silk Roads remained the most direct link between the Mediterranean and China, and because China's population was still largely northwestern, Constantinople restored the overland route but soon found it hindered by the Persian empire. Thus, Emperor Justinian (who ruled from AD 527 to 565) tried to forge an alliance with the Ethiopian kingdom of Axum (connected to Ceylonese trade) by appealing to their common religion, Christianity. The Axumites, however, putting profit before principle, declined Justinian's overtures. Constantinople then looked to the northern Eurasian steppe. From the northeast shores of the Black Sea, the city's merchants allied themselves with the Jews of Khazaria and the Turkish tribes to link up, once again, with China. This opened up a new Silk Road, a more northerly track around the top of the Caspian Sea that would be inherited centuries later by the Mongols.

The third blockage considered here was a series of barbarian invasions plaguing China from the ninth through the eleventh centuries and disrupting continental trade. The Khitai, an early tribe of Mongols, initiated this disruption and paved the way for other tribes as Franck and Brownstone argue:

> In about 840 the Uighur Turks, defeated and pushed south by the Kirghiz Turks, forced the Tibetans out of the Kansu marshes and ruled there on China's border until the 11th century. Trade continued to struggle on over the northern Tarim route of the Silk Road and over the steppe route of the T'ien Shan. But, after China's loss of hegemony, it was never the same and dwindled, with more and more of the east west trade traveling by the Spice Routes.
>
> (Franck and Brownstone 1986:206)

Ironically, many of these tribes intended to facilitate Silk Road trade and even established bureaucracies to this end. The disruption was largely due to the unpredictable coming and going of short-lived empires.

Other trends conspired to weaken the Silk Roads. In 960 a new Chinese dynasty, the Sung, took the throne in Kaifeng, a city integrated into the canal and coastal trade. In 1126 war with the northern Chin forced the Sung to relocate their capital further south to Hangchow, the bustling port of the Spice Routes Marco Polo would visit. China's center of population, reflecting these developments, became coastal.

The last case of blockage considered here precipitated oceanic expansion and led to a global system. Clearly, Muslim powers in the Middle East hindered European access to the Black Sea and the Red Sea, gateways to the East – a hindrance that stemmed less from the seldom-enforced ban on trading with infidels and more from regulations designed to favor Muslim traders. This was one reason for Portuguese exploration of the West African coast in the fifteenth century, a drive that culminated with Vasco de Gama's 1497 rounding of Africa's

Cape of Good Hope. On repeat voyages, the Portuguese blocked the Red Sea to Muslim shipping. Cairo declined as a direct result and its Mamluke Slave Sultanate was conquered by Ottoman Turks in 1516. Lisbon rose in size and importance along with its trading partners: Antwerp and, later, Amsterdam.

Unlike many schoolbook stories, it is in fact correct that Muslim blockages of trade contributed to the European discovery of the Americas. After all, Christopher Columbus expressed his determination to find a shorter and unfettered route to 'Cathay' (China) and the islands of 'Cipangu' (Japan), and he mistook Caribbean islands for the Indies. (It would be only after Columbus died that Amerigo Vespucci concluded otherwise.) Columbus's 'circumvention' led to commercial expansion and cultural conquest.

These cycles of Silk Road and Spice Route alternation lead to a compelling proposition: the world-city system, as civilization's highest level of organization, reflected a tension between continental and maritime systems, each a strategy for building systemic structure, connectivity and differentiation – for moving the system toward complexity. By implication, the rise and fall of cities and empires is deeply embedded in the survival contest between Silk Roads and Spice Routes.

During this survival contest, a higher proportion of the world's largest twenty-five cities became, as the centuries wore on, oceanic ports. This 'maritime shift' of the world-city system, compatible with a historical record that has long recognized a shift from land-based to sea-based empires, is further evidence for the existence of evolutionary processes. Interestingly, Figure 14.2, which displays this maritime shift, can be compared to a 'learning curve' in that initial progress levels off before resuming.

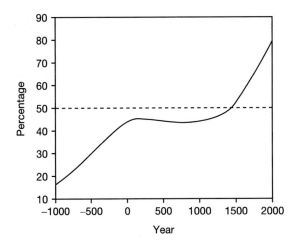

Figure 14.2 Maritime shift of the world-city system between 1000 BCE and AD 2000, as a percentage.

Source: Based on data from Chandler (1987) and McEvedy and Jones (1978).

Note: This figure demonstrates that a significant percentage of the world's largest twenty-five cities have become oceanic ports.

Ports have a clear advantage: less dependent on the viability of one or few connections, they are less vulnerable to blockages. Ports, especially oceanic ports, are better able to forge linkages with other parts of the system, and over time this creates a self-reinforcing trend: the maritime shift. Cooperation, as the maritime shift suggests, is as important in evolution as competition. More precisely, the world-city system reveals cooperation to be the dominant principle within trade routes and competition to be the dominant principle among trade routes. Pulses of local cooperation and competition translate into systemic adaptation.

Conclusion

This study demonstrates that the world-city system's structure, connectivity and degree of differentiation have all increased. The system has cycled its way to a maritime orientation. It has evolved. Hopefully, this study also suggests the merits of evolutionary theory for formulating and testing hypotheses of long-term, large-scale change. This approach can bridge the gap between social and biological analysis, with the former emphasizing qualitative change in structures and the latter quantitative change in populations. Indeed, through this prism civilization appears to be a technology (economic, political, social and cultural) of species survival and reproduction – the ultimate imperative for all life.

The evolutionary approach is capable of moving beyond the nineteenth century Social Darwinist focus on competition (an oversimplification of Darwin). Cooperation is an ingredient as important as competition in the evolutionary cauldron. Ironically, it is the 'realist' school, with its Machiavellian emphasis on state struggle amid perpetual anarchy, that unwittingly adopts, wholesale, the calculus of Social Darwinism.

Finally, there are advantages in retiring nations as primary units of analysis in favor of species-wide structures like the world-city system. One advantage is that such structures are better windows into the diversity of human experience. Cities are simultaneously local and global agents in economic, political, social and cultural processes. Another advantage is that our research program is brought into line with the borderless challenges facing our civilization.

Part IV

Comparison, cumulation, cooperation

15 Comparing approaches to the social science history of the world system

William R. Thompson

Studying thousands of years of world system history is an ambitious undertaking. Attempting to explain what happened over the long term in a non-descriptive fashion is even more ambitious. For that matter, 'merely' describing what took place in recorded history is no simple feat. Thus, it is fortunate that a number of social scientists have begun to tackle such projects. The undertaking will no doubt require a small army with each platoon chipping away at their version of history's reality. The armies are necessary because the task is imposing. It is also important. For, fundamentally, what each perspective on world system history shares is a commitment to the idea that contemporary structures and processes are embedded in a long-term, historically contingent context. To make sense of these contemporary structures and processes, it is necessary to appreciate how and why they have assumed their present form. In many cases, the present forms may not be much different from older forms. Indeed, a central question is to what extent have major structures and processes been characterized by continuity – and how far back in time does that continuity extend? Social science students of world system history are betting that the continuity extends back much farther than most people realize. In the 1970s, world system analysis was provocative and revolutionary because the argument was that we needed to encompass the last five hundred years in our models of socioeconomic and political behavior, and to do so from a systemic perspective. In the 1990s, the new assertion is that hundreds of years are no longer sufficient. Now, it is thousands of years that must be accommodated in our theories and analyses of systemic change.

But how should we best go about accommodating thousands of years? How many thousands of years are really necessary? How much difference is there in the different approaches that are currently available? The first question (how should we interpret world system history) ultimately requires a subjective answer, although it is certainly not beyond the reach of empirical testing. The second question (how many years) hinges on the answer to the first question. The appropriate temporal span of one's inquiry depends on what is thought to be important. The third question (how much difference is there among approaches) requires neither a subjective response nor is it a derivative of a set of assumptions. Moreover, it is important to pause from time to time in order to evaluate the distances separating approaches to similar phenomena. Are we converging or diverging on our answers to what makes the world tick? To what extent may this convergence or divergence be attributed to a priori assumptions and analytical preferences?

A basic divide currently separates analytical approaches to world system history into two basic camps: either 1500 is a cardinal watershed or it is not. To make the comparison easier, I will focus here only on the schools of thought for whom 1500 is not *a* or *the* basic watershed. While more approaches are sure to develop or are being developed, there currently appear to be four major paths to explaining the very long-term development of the world system. To avoid overly personalizing the work going on in the various schools of thought, I assign relatively neutral labels based on some distinctive aspect of what they emphasize. The four approaches are: the continuing world system (Frank and Gills), the comparative study of world systems (Chase-Dunn and Hall, the engulfing world system (Wilkinson), and the evolving world system (Modelski and Thompson).[1] Each approach deserves a brief overview prior to any attempt to compare the four. To facilitate comparison, the overviews focus selectively on ideas about systemic origins, division of labor, hegemony/leadership, long-term economic foci, and affinities for evidence and data analysis.

The continuing world system

System origins   The world system originated in the overlapping intersection of the spheres of influence of Sumer, Egypt, and northern India (2700–2400 BC). None of the early agrarian states were self sufficient. In order to acquire resources that were not available locally, a combination of division of labor subordination and participation in long-distance trade was necessary. The expansion of several states simultaneously increased their tendencies toward competition and conflict over control of the sources of supply, and the routes used to deliver desired commodities. The basic political dynamic thus was one of perpetual rivalry among competitive units interested in safeguarding their individual abilities to accumulate surplus.

Division of labor   Center–periphery–hinterland – the center extracts surplus from a subordinated periphery and a less subordinated hinterland.

Hegemony/leadership   Hegemony involves the concentration of privilege in one or more center predicated on the ability to accumulate surplus more effectively and at the expense of other zones of the world system. A condition of *super-hegemony* prevails to the extent that one center establishes itself at the apex of an overarching hierarchy of smaller-scale hierarchies. Possible candidates include India, China and the Abbasids before 1500. Post-1500 candidates are 'Iberia,' the Netherlands, Britain, the United States and perhaps Japan (in the twenty-first century). However, the idea of *intersecting hegemonies* (as in the sixteenth century case of Portugal, the Habsburgs, Ottomans, Mughals, and Ming China) seems to be preferred to the concept of a sequence of singular hegemons. Similarly, the idea of hegemonic transition is seen as occurring in several places at about the same time.

Long-term economic foci Capital accumulation has been a constant concern of world system actors. However, accumulation activities are characterized by A (expansion) and B (contraction) phases lasting roughly two hundred or so years, at least prior to the modern period. Evidently, these phases gradually became shorter and took the more familiar form of Kondratieff waves. Hegemonies form in A phases and decline in B phases. B phases are also characterized by decreased trade, increased conflict and war, and intensified intra-elite and class struggle.

Evidence advanced The continuing school has yet to emphasize the need to advance explicit evidence for their assertions however they have encouraged others to explore the accuracy of their generalizations.

The comparative study of world-systems

System origins The basic driving forces behind the development of world-systems are multiple and interactive. Population growth leads to environmental degradation and increased demand for food and raw materials. One response is migration until or unless this becomes too costly due to resistance from environmental and human barriers (*circumscription*). Two alternatives to migration are conflict over scarce resources and/or intensified production based on technological development, that may be accompanied by a more hierarchical organizational structure in order to reduce internal conflict. However, since technological development tends to create new types of scarcities that can be rectified by trade and/or conquest, the second alternative is unlikely to be conflict-free. Technological development may also encourage greater rates of population growth and consequent pressures for greater resources.

World-systems come in four types – kin-based, tributary, capitalist, and socialist or some other future organizational principle. Each type of system operates on a different accumulation logic but each generates four types of interaction networks through which the accumulation logics are pursued: bulk goods, prestige goods, political-military, and information. Whether a world-system can be said to exist depends on the extent to which its key reproduction and transformation processes are relatively autonomous. Kin-based world systems can be traced back 10–12,000 years but have gradually been absorbed by tributary and capitalist systems. While bulk-goods networks (BGN) have tended to be 'down-the-line' interactions, an Afro-Eurasian prestige-goods network (PGN) or super-system first came into existence with the interactions between the Roman and Han Chinese tributary systems (circa 200 BC). Since that point in time, the central super-system has expanded and contracted (a *pulsation-decoupling* process). It has also gradually changed, especially after the seventeenth century, from a tributary mode type of system in which state coercion was dominant in surplus extraction to a capitalist mode system in which private entrepreneurs manage surplus extraction, assisted by their control of 'weak' capitalist city and national states.

Division of labor   Core–semiperiphery–periphery – The core–periphery differentiation is a function of interaction between groups characterized by greater complexity and population density and lesser complexity/density. Whether the differentiation also develops into a hierarchical relationship in which the core dominates the periphery is an open question. The semiperiphery is an intermediate zone in terms of location and characteristics, combining features of the core and the periphery without assuming all of their liabilities. As a consequence, the semiperiphery has an unusually good structural position to exploit opportunities for upward mobility opened up by core decline and uneven development.

Hegemony/leadership   Any hierarchical system will have dominant powers (hegemons) by definition that rise and fall without exception. However, the manner in which hegemons rise and fall apparently varies with the type of world-system and its predominant accumulation mode. The Netherlands, Britain, and the United States are considered successive hegemons in the central super-system after the seventeenth century.

Long-term economic foci   Different accumulation modes characterize different eras at the super-system level. Within any given era, multiple world-systems coexisting more or less autonomously may exhibit a variety of accumulation modes. Capitalistic practices have been around for a long time but only became prevalent in the seventeenth century. Emphasis is placed on the transition between modes. The spread of capitalism is attributed in part to the weakness of the tributary mode in Europe and the vigorous existence there of semiperipheral, capitalist city-states.

Evidence advanced   The comparative school has so far emphasized the advancement of framework construction over the analysis of evidence although some examination of city size data has been conducted.

The engulfing world system

System origins   Mesopotamia and Egypt formed a 'central civilization' around 1500 BC. A civilization or world system is an urban network that is militarily, politically, and geotechnically isolated from significant outsiders (who invade, conquer, or make alliances). The historical dynamic is basically one of a central civilization located where Asia and Africa come together gradually engulfing twelve other autonomous societies. However, coexisting with the engulfment process is a multicivilizational macroeconomy (the Old World oikumene) that is predicated on long-distance trade linkages. The origins of this world economy predate the creation of the central civilization by two millennia. Mesopotamia and Egypt were linked by trade by the fourth millennia BC. India was linked after 200 BC. East Asia was linked after the early seventh century AD. Throughout most of recorded history, the scope of the world economy remains more spatially extensive than the boundaries of the central civilization until the twentieth century AD. In fact, an important dynamic is civilizational expansion in pursuit of greater control over the world economy.

Division of labor   Core, semiperiphery, and periphery – the core of a civilization is its most powerful and wealthy center. The semiperiphery is poorer and weaker than the core but strongly connected to it. The periphery is only weakly connected to the core through trade. Core domination and exploitation of the semiperiphery is more likely to be attributable to politico-military coercion than to an economic division of labor.

Hegemony / leadership   While the location of military, political, economic and cultural domination, and the identity of *dominant powers* may shift from one zone in the central civilization to another (or within civilizations), parahegemony has been virtually absent. *Parahegemony* is a situation in which one state within the world economy derives extraordinary economic benefits and privileges as a function of its leadership in invention, investment, or entrepreneurship. It must also be able to defend its advantageous position and/or outside the striking range of its rivals. Only nineteenth-century Britain and the United States for a brief period of time after World War II satisfy the criteria.

Long-term economic foci   Economic organization fluctuates toward and away from capitalism/statism according to whether the system is characterized by many states that are relatively weak and small (toward capitalism) or by few states that are strong and large (toward statism). The world economy is always characterized by a mix of production modes.

Evidence advanced   Arguments about assertions in the engulfing approach have so far relied heavily on city size data, measurements of polarity, and taxonomies of categories.

The evolving world system

System origin   The world system is conceptualized as a set of four, nested structures or networks of city-based interactions: economic, political, social, and cultural. Each network experiences structural evolution but not necessarily at the same time. Yet because the networks are nested, the pace of change is synchronized. In general, the world system has moved through three historical phases. An initial Bronze/Middle Eastern phase (3500 BC to 1000 BC) was followed by an Iron/Eurasian phase (1000 BC to AD 1000), which, in turn was superseded by a western/global phase (AD 1000 to 3000). A fourth, 'post-modern' phase is predicted to begin around AD 3000.

Division of labor   Center-hinterland – centers are created by their lead in, and monopoly of, innovation. Hinterlands are alternatively passive and assertive and can conceivably reverse their variable dependency on the center. To what extent the center–hinterland differentiation leads to a dependency relationship must remain an open question. Note, however, that this differentiation need not be restricted to a material distinction. The conceptualization also emphasizes a dynamic of center concentration and deconcentration brought about by the periodic leveling activities of populations resident in the hinterland.

Hegemony/leadership   Economic leadership is predicated on constituting the primary source of innovation in the system (the active zone). A continuous transition of economic active zones began after 1000 AD with sequential locations in Sung China, Genoa, Venice, Portugal, the Netherlands, Britain, and the United States. The evidence examined to date suggests that earlier economic active zones existed but not in a continuous sequence. Economic leadership, especially after 1000 AD, leads to leadership in naval power in order to protect maritime routes for long distance trade. To what extent economic and naval leadership leads to hierarchy and subordination outside the world economy remains an open question.

Long-term economic foci   The Eurasian world economy has been characterized by long pulses of concentration and dispersal. Innovation, urbanization, and economic growth are initially highly concentrated activities that are diffused. Diffusion, in turn, facilitates the growth of trade. After the tenth century AD, successive Kondratieff waves (viewed as radical innovations in commerce and production) drive the evolution of the world system. Kondratieffs come in paired surges with a period of systemic crisis separating the first and second wave. The first wave tends to be located in a new zone and signals new economic leadership. The consequent conflict of a destabilized status quo in the systemic crisis period increases the probability of a second wave in the same active zone although not necessarily associated with the same leading sectors.

Evidence advanced   Leading sectors have been measured more or less from the tenth century on. Naval concentration data have been generated for the post-1494 period. Population and city size data have been examined over a four to five thousand year range. Migration data have been used to periodize the center/hinterland process.

Comparison

The four schools of thought converge on the need to examine structures and processes prior to 1500. They agree more or less on specifying the origins of the central world system around Mesopotamian – Egyptian activity in the fourth and third millennia BC. They also agree on the general significance and early emergence of an Afro-Eurasian trading network, specializing initially in the exchange of 'luxury' commodities over long distances. If pressed, analysts associated with most if not all of the perspectives would probably accept the idea of nested political, economic, military, and cultural networks. All four perspectives do emphasize the idea of urban networks as providing armatures for the world system's structure(s). Once we move beyond these basic appreciations, however, disagreements become more noticeable.

The division of labor question   All four schools use similar vocabulary but the similar-sounding concepts do not always mean the same thing. The center/core distinctions are relatively convergent as long as one does not pursue very far the source of the center–periphery–hinterland differentiation. Yet, because the differentiation processes are not the same, it is unlikely that each school of thought would place the same parts of the world into the same categories at the same time. And even if considerable overlap did occur, it would not be entirely meaningful because the categories do not have the same meanings. Once one moves beyond the center/core, the potential for categorical confusion increases exponentially. For instance, the continuing school's hinterland seems similar to the engulfing school's periphery while the comparative school's periphery seems to approximate the engulfing school's semiperiphery. The evolutionary school's hinterland presumably encompasses everybody else's semiperiphery, periphery, and hinterland, in addition to some of their core/center.

Perhaps even more important than the disarray of the labeling is the disagreement on whether the differentiation implies unidirectional exploitation and subordination. The continuing school assumes that this is the case. The comparative

Table 15.1 Schools of thought

	Perpetual	*Comparative*	*Evolutionary*	*Engulfing*
Systemic origins	2700–2400 BC	c. 10,000 BC (for kin-based systems)	3500 BC	1500 BC
Division of labour	center periphery hinterland	core semiperiphery periphery	center hinterland	core semiperiphery periphery
Hegemony/ leader	intersecting hegemonies super-hegemony	hegemons vary by predominant accumulation mode	economic active zone leaders	dominant powers parahegemons
Long-term economic foci	constant capital accumulation A/B phases	accumulation modes transitions	radical innovation waves	not particularly applicable
Types of evidence advanced	not particularly applicable	some data analysis of city sizes	leading sectors; naval concentration; city and population sizes	strong reliance on city size and polarity data

and evolutionary schools regard it as an open question. However, one gathers that the comparative school would expect differentiation and hierarchy in most cases involving actors of unequal capability. Innovation in the evolutionary school's center is likely to create technological and commercial gradients that imply some type of dependency arrangement. Contrastingly, the engulfing school views center–semiperiphery subordination from a military coercion angle. Yet, to date, little work has been attempted on this question of variable subordination, dependency, and dependency reversal. One exception to this generalization is the agreement suggested by arguments associated with the comparative and evolutionary perspectives on the rise of Europe to centrality within the world economy – one of the more spectacular cases of dependency reversal. Both perspectives stress the significance of autonomous merchant republics surviving and thriving in circumstances that would have been difficult to replicate outside Europe.

The hegemony/leadership question   Fundamental disagreements about the nature of politico-military, economic, and cultural power concentration and its implications have long plagued the analysis of world systems. All analysts converge on the analytical centrality of something like power concentration but there is far less convergence on how best to conceptualize it. The continuing school makes little distinction between land and maritime-based dominant powers. Thus Safavid Persia and Portugal can be hegemonic simultaneously but with different (yet over-lapping?) domains. Concurrently, this school's ultimate position vis-à-vis 'super-hegemony' is ambiguous suggesting that a consistent preference for 'intersecting hegemonies' versus super-hegemons has yet to be worked out.

In contrast, the evolutionary school makes clearcut distinctions between land and seapowers but not solely because of their varying strategic orientations. Sea-power is both a key ingredient and byproduct of active zone dynamics and the concentration of innovation after the tenth century AD. As a consequence, the Sung dynasties were not fully comparable to the Ming dynasty in this sense, any more than the Ming dynasty was comparable to Venice, Portugal, or the Nether-lands. Venice, Portugal, and the Netherlands were at the center of the active zones of their times. The Ming dynasty was not. On the other hand, the comparative school stresses the transition of capitalist logics over tributary logics in the seven-teenth century. Thus each stage is characterized by a different set and type of dominant powers. Dominant powers in the tributary stage do not behave exactly as dominant powers in the capitalist stage.

The engulfing school's conceptualization of 'parahegemons' overlaps con-ceptually with the comparative school's emphasis on capitalist hegemons and the evolutionary school's stress on innovation leaders. The problem is that only two parahegemons can be found while three capitalist hegemons and eight or nine innovation leaders (depending on whether one counts Britain twice) are advanced.

The resulting problem is that any effort at generalization about hegemony/leadership in the world system must be confined to one school of thought. Each school of thought identifies a different population, summarized in Table 15.2, because each school of thought operates with a different conceptualization of what constitutes dominance/hegemony/leadership. There is overlap but probably not enough for cumulative, cross-school understandings.

The long-term economic foci question   Disagreement on economic foci is particularly marked. In fact, several questions can be subsumed under this heading. One has to do with the question of capitalism. The continuing school of thought has it as continual. The comparative school of thought stresses that capitalistic practices only became predominant about 300 years ago. The other two approaches do not view this dispute as one of major interest.

The evolutionary school instead stresses the AD 1000 break-point which marked a shift toward the continuous sequence of innovation surge-systemic crisis-innovation surge. The continuing school sees no meaningful breakpoints. Behavior before AD 1000 and after are thought to be inherently similar. Breakpoints in the comparative school hinge on transitions to new production modes. The functional equivalent of breakpoints in the engulfing perspective may revolve around the appropriate dates for incorporating previously autonomous civilizations into the central civilization. For instance, the Far East is not seen as becoming significantly linked to the Afro-Eurasian world economy until the early seventh century AD while the other three perspectives argue for much earlier incorporation dates.

A third area of dispute concerns the centrality of economic expansion/stagnation rhythms. They are part of the continuing school's conceptual triad

Table 15.2 Dominant powers/hegemons/leader foci

Super-hegemon candidates (continuing school)	Capitalist hegemons (comparative school)	Active zone leaders (evolutionary school)	Dominant powers (engulfing school)
India		N. Sung	Byzantine E.
China		S. Sung	Arab Caliphate
(pre-1500)		Genoa	Frankish E.
Abassids		Venice	Holy Roman E.
Iberia		Portugal	Mongol Khanate
Netherlands	Netherlands	Netherlands	Ottoman Sultanate
Britain		Britain	Spanish E.
	Britain		Austrian Hapsburg E.
United States	United States	United States	French Monarchy
Japan?			French Rev./Nap. E.
			British E.
			German E.
			German Third Reich
			Japanese E.
			American E.
			Soviet Russian E.

(hegemony/rivalry, core–periphery, and A/B phases) and are seen to extend far back in antiquity. Economic fluctuations are critical to the evolutionary school too but with the emphasis placed primarily on the nineteen K-waves of the past millennium. The continuing school's emphasis appears to be more focused on fluctuations in prices and trade while the evolutionary school's focus is on commercial and technological innovation. Economic rhythms of this sort are not particularly prominent in the work of the comparative and engulfing approaches.

Evidence advanced   There can be no question that the types of questions that are being raised by very long-term foci on world system history do not lend themselves readily to operationalization. The data are simply hard to find. Nevertheless, the willingess to develop explicit empirical evidence for the assertions that are being made is highly variable. That is unfortunate inasmuch as the assertions that are made are often controversial. They also concern phenomena with which many social scientists are unfamiliar. How many readers are equally familiar with such topics as the development of language in the Bronze Age, the diffusion of metallurgical technology in the early Iron Age, the differences between Han, T'ang, and Sung trade routes, and the strategic preferences of the Portuguese, Ottomans, and Ming? Generalizing about these topics is an uphill battle. Not only are there extraordinary start-up costs in developing familiarity with these activities, there is very little about them that it is safe to assume that readers are already familiar. Therefore, an important part of the process of persuading audiences of the accuracy of one's generalizations must be placed on generating convincing evidence that can be summarized and presented in compressed form. The presentation of evidence alone will not suffice to convince skeptical audiences but without evidence, it is only too easy to dismiss generalizations about long-term history as esoteric figments of our collective imaginations. It should go without saying that we also need data to test our theories, not merely to persuade skeptics, but also to be able to assess to what degree the various theoretical arguments have explanatory utility.

Conclusion

In general, then, there are some important similarities among the four social science approaches to the history of the world system. Yet the deeper one probes, the more superficial the similarities begin to appear. When one looks at the processes we choose to emphasize or ignore, the dissimilarities begin to appear more impressive than the elements on which some convergence is registered.

To some considerable extent the divergences reflect the authors' path dependencies in analytical preferences. Two of the schools – the continuing and comparative approaches – 'betray' their roots in the world-systems movement. Some of the questions emphasized are identical as are some of the answers. The engulfing perspective emerged from a comparative civilizations background and may, for that reason, find it difficult to move beyond charting the incorporation process. Nor is it a coincidence that the evolutionary perspective 'evolved' from a long-cycle interpretation of the past 500 years to a perspective that highlighted long cycles over the past 1,000 years, and, most recently, to a five thousand year plus perspective. As in the case of the world system, we are what we once were (and not that long ago) to some extent, with some room permitted for progressive development of our individual research programs.

What would it take to bring about greater convergence? Unfortunately, greater convergence may only be possible through a process of analytical conversion. By conversion, I do not mean the wholesale adoption of a new set of assumptions and an abandonment of current commitments. It is unlikely that analysts associated with one school of thought will abandon their own research program for another. Rather, the best that we may be able to hope for would be the adoption/ cooptation of elements of one research program into others. An example is the strong reliance on urbanization data in the engulfing school. Not only have the urbanization data been employed to examine propositions from the continuing school, the utilization of urbanization data has been emulated to different extents by the comparative and evolutionary schools.

Alternatively, we may find increasing elements of overlap through a form of serendipity. The strong emphasis on the early emergence of an Afro-Eurasian trading network is an important example because it constitutes the fundamental context within which world system development has taken place. Continued participation in the trading network imparts synchronicities to other important activities just as a common emphasis on the influence of this central trading network should work toward synchronizing some of the outcomes of our research into how the processes work, and at what pace they work. For instance, once one accepts the premise of an old, central trading network, it is difficult to escape an improved appreciation for the historical and pivotal role(s) of Central Asia. All four schools share this appreciation and an interest in mapping the historical fluctuations in the interdependence of Afro-Eurasia.

Another type of convergence may come through partial overlaps between two schools of thought. For instance, the comparative and engulfing schools share an interest in how multiple world systems move toward one central system that is not equally prominent in the other two schools that prefer to stress the unity of the world system. As a consequence, comparative and engulfing generalizations and conclusions about the process of incorporation have some greater probability of converging.

But partial overlaps need not be made more likely only through the agency of similar starting assumptions. A case in point are the similarities in the comparative and evolutionary school's explanation of the rise of the West. The explanations are not identical but they are strikingly compatible. Both accounts attribute the 'missing link' to the relatively novel emergence of the European merchant republics, the regional environment which facilitated the survival of these capitalist niches, and the connections of the trading city-states to the larger, Afro-Eurasian trading system.

Nonetheless, what amounts to a moderately pessimistic evaluation of the chances for increased convergence through the explicit cooptation of some findings from other schools, through serendipity, or through coincidence needs to be tempered by the fact that we have not been doing this type of research for very long. We do not yet have a number of detailed examinations to review. We do not yet have a number of well-specified theories to evaluate. We do not yet have a critical mass of scholars engaged in analyzing the history of the development of the world system from social scientific points of view. In other words, we have only just begun to crawl out of the primordial analytical mud. The prospect of considerable evolution to come awaits us.

More specifically, the continuing school's arguments about continuity have not yet been subjected to close scrutiny. The comparative school's arguments about the value of comparing different types of world systems have not yet been demonstrated by compelling analytical demonstrations. The engulfing school's fixation on the incorporation process has yet to move much beyond its taxonomical interests in, and descriptive observations about, multiple civilizations. The evolutionary school's long attachment to the post-1494 era, and more recently the last millennia, leaves a great deal to be done in integrating its 'modern' findings with 'premodern' history.

Perhaps, then, it would be naive to expect much convergence so early in the game. Premature convergence may also prove to be undesirable. It may not take a hundred blooming flowers to bring some order to the complexities of world system development but, evolutionarily speaking, variety is more desirable than uniformity. All four of the main schools of thought currently available appear to be undergoing evolutionary processes of their own as they engage in a trial-and-error confrontation with the enormity of world system developments. Other perspectives are sure to emerge and evolve as well. Selection processes, ideally, will ensure the survival of the optimal explanations until somebody comes up with something better.

Note

1   The choice of labels is not meant to imply that any one approach monopolizes an evolutionary stance. The comparative study of world systems school claims to be studying systemic evolution as well. Equally, that school has no monopoly on a comparative stance. The choice of labels hinged on explicit emphases. It should also be noted that these schools of thought or approaches are hardly static monoliths. Changes in assumptions and arguments should be anticipated. My comparative comments are based on a reading of the following works: for the continuing school, see Frank 1993b; Frank and Gills 1993; Sanderson 1995b; for the comparative school, see Chase-Dunn and Hall, 1991, 1997; for the evolutionary school, see Modelski 1994, this volume; Modelski and Thompson 1988, 1996a, 1996b; Rasler and Thompson 1994; Thompson 1988, 1995; for the engulfing school, see Wilkinson 1992a, 1993a; Frank and Gills 1993, and Sanderson 1995b.

16 Cumulation and direction in world system history

Robert A. Denemark

Students of world system history are seeking to shed light on long-term global processes, in great part through the reintegration of the fractured social sciences. This chapter considers intellectual cumulation, problems of method, and questions of academic praxis faced by this group. Important elements of cumulation are identified. These elements are not of a sort likely to generate lock-step interaction, and this is to be considered a strength and not a weakness. World system history also eschews the individual level of analysis and so finds itself out of step with contemporary methodological currents. Though the system level is defended, possible gains from seeking to provide microfoundational linkages are suggested. Finally we turn to the question of academic praxis. The ability of world system history to explain important social phenomena is not sufficient to ensure its survival, let alone its popularity. Specific strategies are suggested.

Cumulation

Are students of world system history, born of different fields and backgrounds, creating a coherent body of knowledge to which they and subsequent students may add? There are reasons for concern. We are separated by our disciplinary backgrounds, assumptions and commitments. Terminological differences abound, sometimes highlighting conceptual disagreements. Some have been disheartened by our inability to agree on what data would be most important to gather, or to see clear evidence of cross-fertilization. Lack of resources and a tendency toward the development of individual research programs exacerbate these difficulties.

I contend that such pessimism is unwarranted. The intellectual conformity that is apparently missing is not necessarily what we should expect or desire. Some critics point to methodological conformity in the hard sciences as the model to be followed. Contrary to general wisdom, lock-step conceptual and methodological convergence is not the model presented us by the successful hard sciences. Cumulation may instead be disaggregated into six different processes, many of which we already appear to be engaging in quite successfully. We may also note significant instances of 'analytical conversion.' Finally, our terminological problems may be more apparent than real, while our different methodologies, concepts, and processes may actually be a source of strength.

Does convergence spell success?

How central is broad-based agreement on critical issues to the success of an analytical endeavor? Coming from the social sciences, where there is generally little agreement, it is easy to romanticize both the unity allegedly inherent in the hard sciences, as well as its value. Histories of the unraveling of the structure of DNA and the mathematics of quantum mechanics offer a very different picture.

The fundamental structure of DNA was uncovered by a Ph.D. candidate and a postdoctoral fellow in their spare time. The first was a refugee from biology who wanted to study chemistry. The second was a refugee from physics doing the same. There existed no consensus regarding the importance of DNA in the field of biology, in the relevant sub-fields of genetics or biochemistry, in the various more specific areas of study within which Watson and Crick worked, or even in the lab where the discovery was made. Even the biologists involved in the hunt for DNA's structure did not agree on its significance, what empirical or theoretical methods should be used to explore it, or about the processes that might distinguish DNA's function from those of other proteins. Watson and Crick were nonetheless able to draw upon insights from a wide array of work best characterized by its lack of agreement, methodological coherence, and direction. Watson and Crick each brought to the hunt very different sets of analytical tools and interests. They agreed to work together in the search for the solution to a common interesting problem. There is little evidence that they spent much time on the development of a common outlook beyond their immediate interaction (Watson 1968).

A similar picture emerges in the study of quantum physics. Werner Heisenberg's search for a form of mathematics that would be adequate to model the quantum wave function led him to matrix mechanics. While the quantum interpretation of physics was dominant, there was little if any agreement over how to conceive of the relevant forces. Heisenberg was basically a mathematician, having nearly failed his physics orals because he could not explain the principles behind the functioning of a common battery. His methods were so complex and arcane that only a very few of his colleagues understood his work (Cassidy 1992). Heisenberg's mathematics also required a radical decontextualization of the physical nature of matter, which was contrary to the main methodological currents of the day (Baggott 1992:28–33). Heisenberg's insight was soon to be matched by Erwin Schrödinger and his wave equation (Wessels 1983:259). Schrödinger was working on a quantum theory of gas, and came from the explicitly descriptive tradition of Mach whose proponents abhorred decontextualization (Moore 1989:ch. 6). Schrödinger's work was easier to understand and conceptualize in physical terms, and for that reason even the likes of Einstein preferred it. Niels Bohr created the synthesis in which the incompatible elements of the two interpretations were identified, some ideas as to why they were incompatible were forwarded, and the entire field was simply asked to understand that proponents of the various interpretations would all simply have to agree to disagree if progress was to be made possible (Baggott 1992:81–8). Lack of lock-step conformity allowed for the development of various potentially useful approaches.

The manner in which what Kuhn calls 'normal science' or Lakatos a 'fruitful research program' promotes advancement is clear. General agreement allows a significant portion of the appropriate research community to engage in the solving of relevant puzzles. Scholars no longer need to start from first principles or justify the use of each concept. When a group of scholars are dedicated to producing knowledge relevant to a single area it is far easier to advance. But this condition may be quite rare. Kuhn argues that 'History suggests the road to a firm research consensus is extraordinarily arduous' (Kuhn 1970:15). More prevalent is science lacking a strong paradigm. When this happens all facts look equally relevant, fact gathering is unstructured, the output is an incoherent morass, and descriptions often miss critical details necessary to later theoretical development (Kuhn 1970:14–17). This is a more apt description of my native field of international politics than of the nascent study of world system history. Where has world system history gone right?

The elements of cumulation

Cumulation might be considered in terms of six elements. These include the questions asked, the methods utilized, the terms adopted, the concepts developed, the processes that are hypothesized, and finally the disciplinary strategy most generally employed. How much cumulation does the world system history school manifest?

This group is characterized by little other than the fact that we ask the same general questions. Our collective interest is in the long-term development of the global system. It is all the more notable that the four principal papers in this volume were written by scholars from three fields, and scholars from five fields responded. It is rare enough that scholars from two fields agree to deal with similar subjects. It is rarer still that five fields would be represented. This diversity is destined to make convergence more difficult, and increase the already significant intellectual start-up and keep-up costs required. On the plus side, it will increase the scope of the substantive, theoretical, and methodological knowledge at our disposal.

The focusing by scholars of world system history on 'the questions' is important. It underscores the fact that this set of questions is far broader than any single discipline, and that our responses must be as well. This escape from disciplinarity is a difficult and an important one. The university system, with independent departments for the study of various fields, confers legitimacy on those who can separate their subject matter from that of others. The specialized knowledge that results constitutes a formidable achievement, but falls short of providing broad insights exactly because it was acquired at the cost of possible synthesis.

There are three alternatives to disciplinarity. Multidisciplinary work includes those from different fields applying their unique lenses to a problem. While useful, positive effects of cross-fertilization end with the collaboration. Another option is interdisciplinarity, where scholars learn and use a second set of analytical tools in considering an issue. Such work is rewarding, but still treats a phenomenon as having separate facets that need to be considered as interactive. World system history is, instead, transdisciplinary. The approach to a complex question is viewed as requiring the simultaneous use of several sets of analytical tools. The focus is not on the 'interaction' of separate analytics, but on their integration in the pursuit of understanding. This is a powerful form of cumulation.

Students of world system history also identify many of the same processes as critical. Cycles or pulses, concentration and deconcentration, historical symmetries, and core/periphery relations sit near the heart of each perspective. We create concepts (e.g. innovation, evolution, accumulation) of joint interest, and gather data (as on city systems, wars, or upswings/downswings) that we each acknowledge as relevant.

We can therefore question the degree to which we are atomistic scholars building independent programs immune to significant change. A number of important conversions have already taken place. Modelski now rejects 1500 as a starting date. Chase-Dunn (1989) considered core/periphery relationships universal. Chase-Dunn and Hall (1997) do not. Thompson's (1995) work on the shifting of dominance from Asia to Europe is an important alteration, as is Frank and Gills' new reticence about hegemony, likely the result of long-standing arguments by Wilkinson. This group of scholars has remained remarkably open to one another and to those in other areas. This is a significant strength.

Contrast the significance of these and other alterations with the relatively simple problem of non-standard terminology. While it would certainly be nice to have all the scholars in the area adopt a single nomenclature, it is not necessary. We have better things to do than deal with such nuisances until and unless they become real impediments to the creation of further knowledge.

We show very few of the tendencies identified by Kuhn as the telltale signs of paradigmlessness. We have also avoided what Lakatos called the 'degeneration' of our research program into *ad hoc* debates in defense of core hypotheses (Bohman 1991:3). There are still significant areas where agreement does not exist. We do not agree on terms or methods, significant conceptual and processual disagreement remains, and the question of strategy remains open. But methodological, processual and conceptual agreement was also lacking among the major students of biology and physics involved in some of the most important physical research of our time. The lessons to be learned in the history of science and in reflecting on our own interaction are several:

1   'Cumulation' is better understood and more effective if it is defined in terms of the asking of like questions, and not the creation of unified methods and concepts with which to attack those questions.

2   The asking of similar questions drives us to search for similar information. We do this more efficiently as a group, even if we do not all agree on what information would be best to consider. Given the breadth of our topic area,

this rather requires that we remain as open as possible to transdisciplinary interactions.

3   Though the gulf that separates the four principal perspectives remains wide, some significant convergence has already taken place. These changes have not always been minor in nature, nor have they been coerced in any way. This is evidence that our interactions have been effective and that the process of cumulation is ongoing.

On the meaning of our method

While methodological diversity was not a significant impediment to major work in the hard sciences, there was probably more agreement among biologists and physicists over the critical questions of why one would select, how one would pursue, and by what criteria one should evaluate research. Students of social phenomena are more vulnerable to methodological traps and difficulties. In this section I argue that while the adoption of the individual as the sole legitimate unit of analysis is gaining ground in the social sciences, it is an error. While its champions often justify this method by expressing the desire to emulate the success of the hard sciences, the *a priori* identification of a unit of analysis is contrary to the model adopted there. Individual level analyses are also narrow, internally inconsistent and biased. These difficulties notwithstanding, I argue that we ought still pay some attention to the manner in which various 'structural' logics can be linked to individual action.

The ills of the individual level of analysis

It is ironic that the current methodological trend in areas as diverse as neoclassical liberal microeconomics, analytical Marxism, and some of postmodernism, is to call for a grounding of one's work in an analysis that must begin with the preferences, beliefs and decision processes of 'individual' human beings. Such a strategy can be seen as harmful from several perspectives. First, use of the 'individual' may actually constitute another, albeit less obvious form of 'structuralism.' Second, though the prespecification of units of analysis is often touted as the model of the hard sciences, it is not. Such prespecification is quite the opposite of successful methodological models in fields like physics. Third, exclusive focus on the individual, and particularly on individual behavior as the phenomena to be explained and/or understood, is destructive of broader understanding in the social sciences. Finally, we have good reason to believe that radical adherence to the individual level of analysis is nothing more than the expression of a particular ideological predisposition.

How unitary is the individual? In a novel attack upon rational choice analysis, McKeown (1986) argued that the assumption that individuals constitute coherent units may be unwarranted. Individuals have highly complex sets of desires and interests that vary over time, across contexts, and can be notoriously inconsistent. The 'individual' may be no more than a convenient form of social aggregation.

Those who privilege the individual in their analyses may therefore be just as guilty of illegitimate reification as those they accuse of 'other' forms of structuralism.

Neoclassical liberal economics is often touted as the closest of the social sciences to the hard science model. But the prespecification of a fundamental unit is inconsistent with the models offered us by the hard sciences. The terrain of physics, for example, is littered with the corpses of assertions as to the primacy of one physical entity or another. 'Atoms', and later 'protons, neutrons and electrons' proved no more useful than 'earth, wind and fire' in the search for fundamental physical units. The model that has instead developed deals directly with phenomena in their relevant contexts. Physicists find a phenomenon they cannot readily explain. They set to work on an explanation. If the phenomenon is pernicious enough to appear insoluble by means of the extension of known forces or relationships, new ones are hypothesized. Both theoretical and experimental processes allow for a full range of assertion about the nature of the phenomena and their components. The search for physical knowledge is not constrained by debates about what forces are or are not *a priori* legitimate foci of attention. As a result we have added various quarks, other leptons, and even anti-matter to the list of those particles we recognize, and the level of sophistication of physical explanation has been enhanced. To prespecify the fundamental units involved would narrow the search for understanding, and possibly doom it to failure. It would halt progress in the field. It is a bad idea.

Prespecification of fundamental units is not much more helpful with regard to social phenomena. If individuals are the sole legitimate focus of our attention, then individual behavior becomes the obvious candidate for explanation. Rational choice models, for example, take opportunities and preferences as givens and 'generate from them a stream of intended outcomes' (Modelski in this volume). Many forms of microfoundational analysis stress that individuals are 'rational actors,' meaning they take careful note of and respond in a calculated manner to the incentives with which the *environment* presents them. Nonetheless it remains the behavior, and not the *environment*, that serves as the focus of attention. This emphasis on immediate behavioral outcomes casts a necessarily static and ahistorical pall. Action is assumed to emerge from incentives, but the creation, maintenance, and alteration of incentive structures are off limits to analysis. Some studies assume them to be static, or to change only in response to some form of exogenous (hence untheorized) modification. Liberal economics is fond of using 'ideas' as the prime exogenous variable, as if nothing could possibly explain the emergence of ideas at certain times, much less their successful adoption. Hence a recent nobel laureate in economics parrots the old refrain that religious beliefs explain the variables that ultimately lead to the 'rise of the west' (North 1993). From this perspective the world is viewed as being reducible to inherently simple tendencies where trajectories and relationships are reversible, where lawful and deterministic behavior reigns, where generalizations may be universal in scope and where the operation of systemic wholes are unaffected by the movement of the constituent parts (Thompson 1994). This 'mechanical' model of the world saw its heyday in the eighteenth and nineteenth centuries, but has proven less useful across a range of disciplines since.

In the end much of the radical individualism we find appears to be little more than ideological window dressing. Whether in the hands of microeconomists seeking to justify some politically charged principal, or in the hands of post-modernists struggling against what they see as the tyranny of all metasociological projects, the individual level of analysis is touted for essentially instrumental purposes.

The individual level of analysis suffers from any number of important ills. It is for that reason that calls for a 'grounding' of world system history in the logic of individual action have been ignored. But the structural approaches of world system history do not lack the potential for microfoundational grounding, and may well benefit from it.

Strengths and weaknesses of structuralism

The four major perspectives represented here all assume that individuals can only be understood when considered in their social contexts. Social contexts constrain the beliefs and actions of individuals, though without completely determining them. Replication is not seamless. Changes emerge that may be traced to the interaction of individuals *and* their social contexts. But it is the social structure, viewed as a set of incentive *systems*, that needs to be explained and/or understood. Individual behavior is more determined than determinative of those incentives, and is usually organized in such a way as to reproduce the system. Systemic behavior will likely exhibit characteristic chains of responses. Fundamental alterations, if they occur, will be rare. Does such a perspective allow our work to successfully explain both systemic replication and change?

There is little agreement among the major perspectives over the mechanisms by which these incentive systems emerge or play themselves out. Worse yet, all of the perspectives contain anomalies or lacuna that raise critical questions as to their validity. This is to be expected in a field so young and brash. It is nonetheless a problem.

Wilkinson's 'engulfing' perspective considers the rise and functioning of 'central civilization.' It envisions population growth driving urbanization, enhancing the division of labor, hence increasing demand to mobilize new resources, and driving production which supports the larger population (Wilkinson 1993c: 235–6). An uneven distribution of resources and technology provides another incentive for civilizations to couple or engulf. When they do, peripheral areas are formed.

Is population increase a truly independent variable? Could the drive for wealth and the uneven distribution of resources and technology suffice to drive civilizational interaction in the absence of population increase? Did production gains in Europe out-pace production losses in places like India during central civilization's late eighteenth and early nineteenth century? Why might technology be unevenly distributed? A 'pulse' is noted in the expansion process. Why does it exist? What explains it?

Chase-Dunn and Hall's 'comparative' perspective also seeks to explain the consolidation of social units. Population pressure leads to hierarchies and eventually expansion. Increased competition, new resource scarcities, risks of failure, and collective needs for savings and investment are the new problem areas created. A set of four types of systems may be identified that covary, expand and contract. There are both pulsations and fundamental transformations. Semiperipheries are formed within which the dynamics of change and transformation are easiest to find. Peripheries are also formed most of the time.

Again we must ask whether population increase is a truly independent variable? There are numerous forms by which to deal with all the changes and challenges posed by the system. Chase-Dunn and Hall (1997), acknowledge that actual outcomes can be situationally specific. Specific to what? How do we know when we have identified all the relevant forms in which 'systems' might exist? Each system has a pulse in that it expands and contracts. Why? How do these iterations lead to systemic transformations? How do we know when such a thing has occurred?

Gunder Frank and Gills' 'continuity' perspective stresses the development of a single social system over the last 5,000 years and seeks to understand its functioning. Trade and the world economy are its centerpieces. Capital accumulation is the motor force of this world system. The system is characterized by a core/ periphery hierarchy, cycles of hegemony and rivalry, and economic long cycles. It is not punctuated by any fundamental alterations, though it is characterized by long cycles throughout its history.

Why is there a drive for ceaseless accumulation? Why is the drive for ceaseless accumulation ceaseless? What drives those long cycles?

Modelski and Thompson's 'evolutionary' perspective posits a symmetrical set of sociopolitical layers that undergo change on a variety of schedules. The master processes are those of evolutionary learning. Initial variety, cooperation, a process of selection, and finally consolidation (preservation and transmission) are reproduced in hypothesized global processes that aggregate from twenty-five to 8,000 years duration. The shorter cycles hypothesized are more carefully explained than any processes in any of the other perspectives. Problems nonetheless emerge.

The evolutionary perspective offers a model with a frightening symmetry. As carefully explained as the first 1,000 years appear, the evolutionary learning model itself seems inadequate to account for the symmetry. Innovation drives the initial level of the model. What drives innovation? Why is it so regular?

Evolutionary and/or learning processes are models designed to facilitate survival and progress. War emerges as the primary selection process in this model, but can our ability to destroy, progressing steadily over the years until we now possess the ability to end all human life on the planet, be an effective adaptation? It has not increased the chances for species survival. The chances for accidents, imprudent use, and the debilitating costs involved, increase the likelihood of catastrophe. Can we conclude that the resources needed to win a war are similar to those necessary to progress within the system? The USSR took a prominent place among the victors of the last systemic war. Germany and Japan were the losers.

How are we to understand what appears to be a cumulative learning process that spans some 8,000 years in the context of the periodic rise and decline of civilizations? Abu Lughod (1989, introduction) suggests that what might be termed 'civilizational knowledge' is lost or discarded during crises and must later be replicated. How then does it aggregate?

Finally, what drives the frighteningly uniform regularities across spatial and temporal contexts of dizzying proportions? Can we hope to address such an issue when the reasons for and the periodization of innovation, the lowest level fundamental process, remain unclear?

Back to the individual?

Each of the perspectives forwarded suffers from three difficulties. First, they do not yield unique predictions. Their very different logics allow for a variety of nonetheless similar predictions. Many agree on the existence of cycles or pulses, the centrality of central Asia, and the development of exploitative core/periphery relations, though for different reasons. Second, they each undertake issues relevant to the thorny question of determinism. A variety of anomalies and agency effects are identified as sufficient to alter the predictions that would otherwise emerge from a more linear analysis. Can we further specify where they come from and when they might emerge? (See Denemark 1999 on the methodological challenges involved here.) Finally, we have the substantive questions above. What leads to population increase? Why is there innovation? Why is there 'ceaseless' accumulation? Why do all these things appear to cycle?

Unfortunately the problems of indeterminacy, determinism, and the failure to theorize initial processes cannot be dealt with at the structural level alone. They do not concern the extension of our knowledge, but the establishment and consideration of the link between the macro-level phenomena that constitute the critical incentive structures, and the behaviors that these then elicit. These are the behaviors that define the actual functioning of the system, its replication or its alteration.

The solutions to these problems require some consideration of the individual actions that emerge in the context of ongoing world system relations. We need not fall into the trap of the 'rationalists' and consider behavior itself (as opposed to the dynamic link between structure and behavior) the issue to be explained. We also need not fall into the trap of assuming that behaviors and outcomes must be intentional. Instead our consideration of behavioral outputs should focus on why different relevant behaviors emerge as they do, and what the various impacts on the dominant incentive structure might then be.

James Bohman (1991) uses Marx to illustrate the power of the integration of the micro– and the macro– levels. In *Capital*, Marx establishes why accumulation is necessary in capitalist systems, and goes on to show that technical innovation contributes to crisis tendencies. Bohman suggests that for many Marxists:

> this tendency operates 'independently of our will,' entirely at the macro-level as a consequence of systemic relationships in the mode of production. But

technical innovation is pursued by the capitalist to increase productivity and reduce wages; at the same time, other capitalists are pursuing the same innovation, resulting in a drop in the price of a commodity along with wages, leading to a new round of innovations. Thus, Marx seems to be providing a 'micro-analysis of macro-patterns,' rather than simply explaining one macro pattern (technical innovation) by another (increase in average profit).

(Bohman 1991:172)

Is Marx simply aggregating micro behavior into macro structure? Bohman argues to the contrary:

Marx is also not simply reducing such macro-patterns to micro-motives, as rational choice Marxists assert. Certainly, part of the explanation relies on the maximizing behavior of individual capitalists. However, the explanation ultimately rests on institutional facts about the interdependency of such choices in market situations and shows the systemic consequences of individual strategies; without such interrelated consequences, no downward spiral is created. Hence such micro-analyses require that there exist a stable set of institutions which aggregate choices and interrelate actions. Those institutions cannot themselves be explained by the choices and actions of individuals within them, since their structures create consequences that undermine many of these same goals and objectives.

(Bohman 1991:172–3)

Bohman (p. 173) illustrates a three level Marxist model. There exists (1) a large-scale social system (capitalism) with (2) its attendant structuring institutions (state and market) and the actions of (3) individuals (in this case grouped as classes) making choices defined within the system.

There is also a three-step form to this analysis. First, relationships within a social structure are described or modeled as accurately as possible. Second, the conditions of action and agency in the social system are specified, including the goals that actors pursue and the knowledge necessary for participation. Finally, the description of the social institutions and practices analyze those recurrent processes or practices that link the system to the agents.

The most interesting part of this particular illustration is the ability of the analysis to avoid the traps into which studies generally adopting individual levels of analysis fall. There are no atomistic value maximizers wandering vacuously through ahistory. Action may be purposeful, but intentionality is not assumed. Indeed the contradictory elements of the social interactions emerge as a specifically unintended consequence of short-term rationality. The overall scale is by no means short term. Feedback, both reinforcing and destructive, can be found and analyzed in the dynamic elements that are readily identified in the mixture of systemic, institutional, and individual action. Adoption of this form by all concerned would make it easier to compare perspectives, to merge coincident analyses, and to search for non-obvious conclusions or potential volatilities. (A review of some of the difficulties in creating micro-macro linkages is also provided in Denemark 1999.)

How large a leap?

How close do the four perspectives come to following the steps Bohman suggests are necessary to 'ground' their work? All are adept at the first, the specification of relationships within the social structure. They are weaker in step two. Agents are only rarely theorized, and their motives or capacities are usually simply assumed. But models which carefully link structures to outcomes via the review of sets of resulting incentives and behaviors are prevalent. Note, for example, Gunder Frank (1978a) and Chase-Dunn (1989) on the nature of relationships in the periphery, Hall (1989) on the effects of regional incorporation on individuals. And this linkage is certainly no more than a breadth away in the work of Gills (1993) on state domination of economic planning in parts of Asia; Modelski and Thompson (1996a) on innovation; and Chase-Dunn and Hall (1997) on the potential for change in the semiperiphery.

There is no necessary contradiction between 'structural' and 'individualist' analyses. They each make assumptions and they each have shortcomings. Studies produced by 'individualists,' particularly of the more virulent sort, are vapid and sterile. But there is nothing inherent in the methodology that renders it useless to those with a greater sense of the context within which social action must be ultimately situated.

Academic praxis: a note on strategy

World system history emerges as a school with much to recommend it. It invests serious scholarship in non-trivial questions. It is open, takes transdisciplinary cooperation seriously, and continues to grow. It is capable of shedding significant light on long-standing puzzles. Without extraordinary care, however, its prospects may not be particularly bright. World system history exists in tandem with a variety of perspectives with which it has little in common, and relative to which it exists at a significant disadvantage. We are small and new. Our ideological roots are highly suspect in this age of neo-liberal orthodoxy. Likewise our methodology. We have adopted a position that requires significant transdisciplinary work, making the way forward much more complex. World system history requires far greater than average intellectual start-up costs. This slows our progress and reduces the number of potential students. Our analyses are not state or policy centric. They only rarely and indirectly address the question of 'what we should do' in any given situation. This makes us less potentially 'relevant' than other perspectives, and affects our ability to garner research funds. Being more accurate than others in our understandings of social reality is not enough.

I offer four palliatives. First, we ought work to generate more light than heat. There are a series of questions in a large number of other fields and subfields that the world system history can shed significant light upon (Chase-Dunn 1981; Frank and Gills 1992; Frank 1993a,b; Modelski and Thompson 1996a; Wilkinson 1987). We ought to work to highlight these explanations.

Second, where insights are particularly significant, we ought not to shy away from creating heat. There are few clear, concise, contemporary statements in support of world system history, its structure and its methods. Some ought to be forwarded. In international relations the myths of anarchy, of the predominance of military power as revealed in the parable of the Peloponnesian War, and of the birth of both the form and the relevant dynamics of the European state system at Westphalia, are all directly challenged by this literature. Other myths, like the logic of comparative advantage or European exceptionalism are likewise vulnerable. Given the need to attract students and attention, and the huge tasks world system history sets for itself, the generation of a little well directed heat will be worth the time required.

Third, students of world system history might pursue some important joint projects. This does not imply an expectation of unity, only a collective effort to focus intellectual energies on an important topic. An obvious and strategically important choice would be cycles. The possibility that cycles exist in human affairs is intoxicating. Students in a variety of fields have mentioned the existence of regularities, but given the complexities involved they can usually neither confirm nor explain them. Should these regularities be more real than apparent a number of important implications would follow. It would be clear that critical social processes are at work that we have yet to define or come to understand. Apprehension of these processes would provide significant, possibly unparalleled insights into human society.

Least enamored with the idea of cycles or pulsations is Wilkinson's engulfing perspective, though he identifies any number of potential cycles in his listing of those processes which might someday be sufficient to provide a process-based definition of the world system (Wilkinson in this volume). He hypothesizes a general war/general peace cycle, a rise and decline of core powers cycle, polycultural fluctuations, and a cycle that drives large scale social units to come into and go out of existence.

More important for Wilkinson are the fluctuations between state systems and world state/universal empires (within which there may also be a polarity fluctuation), and an economic/demographic growth and decline cycle, as revealed by city-size data. Decline in the first is at least in part a function of exhaustion, as taxes designed to allow for expansion sap the strength of the society and lead to upheaval (Wilkinson 1991:155–60 citing Quigley favorably in this regard).

The problem with fluctuations of growth and stagnation (identified primarily in city-size data), is that trends are hidden against the backdrop of a strong secular upswing, are irregular, and are convoluted by a series of interactional variables. Lacking evidence of any truly global downturn, Wilkinson suggests that the dynamic underpinning of any pulse must be located at the local or national level.

The comparative perspective is motivated primarily by the search for a logic of macro-transitions. The move from kin-based to state based or tributary modes was followed by the transition to capitalism in this more traditional interpretation. A move to some future, potentially socialist world system might be facilitated by an understanding of previous systemic transformations. Along the way, however, Chase-Dunn and Hall (this volume:108) discover another set of cycles. 'Iterations of population pressure, intensification and hierarchy-formation provided the engines of development and the dynamics of political rise and fall that are visible in all systems.' Cycles of rise and decline, waves of territorial expansion followed by slower expansion or contraction (pulsation), and processes of internal differentiation and similarity are all in evidence. Pulsations cross all temporal, spatial and organization boundaries, and are associated with trade expansion (Chase-Dunn and Hall 1997:234). These pulsations also appear to be a local or national level phenomena as opposed to a global one. Chase-Dunn and Hall (1997:ch. 6) suggest that a fundamental element of historical evolution rests with the interaction between their various iterations and transformations. Even if our goal is to understand transitions, one has to also, or perhaps first, understand iterations.

It was a recognition of the regularity with which these iterations emerge that drove the continuity school to turn away from the study of both epochal characterizations (e.g. feudalism, capitalism, socialism) and 'transitions.' Gunder Frank and Gills assert a unity and essential consistency across 5,000 years of human interaction. They have gathered extensive information on cycles within what they believe to be a single world system of considerable duration. It would therefore be most reasonable to compare the processes which propagate upturns and downturns across these contexts. The continuity school is also unique in suggesting that the generative processes of these cycles are global, and not national. This also alters the nature of the comparisons to be made. Instead of searching for internally generated processes in areas we assume to be otherwise similar, we must look to the position of each area in the overall system to understand its functioning.

While the continuity perspective has gone the farthest in charting long cycles, the nature of cyclical *interactions* are most carefully explicated by Modelski and Thompson. Though a variety of cycles are nested in a learning/evolutionary model, the basic 100-year dynamic features a paired K-wave nested within a single political leadership cycle. Innovation driving an upswing leads to war. War produces a downswing, which after victory is achieved turns again to expansion. These paired K-waves coevolve with a political process of agenda setting, coalition building, macro decision (usually a war) and execution. Innovation initiates the cycle, war provides its pulse. 'Leaders' are usually only good for one round. Then the focal point of the process moves along. Further iterations produce other macro-level evolutionary alterations. These cumulate into a hypothesized 8,000 year civilizational evolutionary circuit.

All four perspectives consider the issue of cycles or pulses. Each identifies different forms of cyclical behavior, and each attributes it to different phenomena. Once again we are asking similar questions and applying a variety of methods, data sets, and hypotheses to its explication. Given the central nature of the question of cycles or pulses, this would be an excellent topic for joint consideration.

Finally, it would be nice if we could somehow lower the barriers to entry to this field. This, however, may simply not be possible. The nature of the tasks of reintegrating the social sciences and history, and of using that synthesis to elucidate social processes over the longest term, may not be amenable to many short-cuts. At least not at this time. Perhaps the best strategy remains the production of clear statements for important journals in as many fields as possible. Sharp analyses of difficult problems, coupled with concise statements of the logic underlying their solutions, could capture the imaginations of both students and colleagues and inspire them to dig deeper. In the meantime the projects represented in this volume will provide the next critical steps for those who wish to help us undertake this exciting intellectual journey.

Bibliography

Abler, T.S. (1992) 'Beavers and Muskets: Iroquois Military Fortunes in the Face of European Colonization,' in R. Ferguson and N. Whitehead (eds) *War in the Tribal Zone: Expanding States and Indigenous Warfare*, Sante Fe NM: School of American Research Press.

Abu-Lughod, J. (1989) *Before European Hegemony: The World System AD 1250–1350*, New York: Oxford University Press.

Adas, M. (1983) 'Colonization, Commercial Agriculture and Destruction of the Deltaic Rainforests of British Burma in the Late 19th Century,' in R. Tucker and J. Richards (eds) *Global Deforestation and the 19th Century World Economy*, Durham NC: Duke University Press.

Adams, R. (1966) *The Evolution of Urban Society*, Chicago: Aldine.

—— (1974) 'Anthropological Perspectives on Ancient Trade,' *Current Anthropology* 15, 3:239–58.

—— (1981) *Heartland of Cities*, Chicago: University of Chicago Press.

Adams, R. and Nissen, H. (1972) *The Uruk Countryside: The Natural Setting of Urban Societies*, Chicago: University of Chicago Press.

Aguirre Beltran, G. (1979) *Regions of Refuge*, Washington DC: Society for Applied Anthropology, Monograph No. 12.

Akkermans, P. (1989) 'Tradition and Social Change in Northern Mesopotamia During the Later Fifth and Fourth Millennium B.C.,' in E. Henrickson and I. Thuesen (eds) *Upon this Foundation: The 'Ubaid Reconsidered*, Copenhagen: Museum Tusculanum Press.

Algaze, G. (1993) *The Uruk World System: The Dynamics of Expansion of Early Mesopotamian Civilization*, Chicago: University of Chicago Press.

Allen, M. (1997) 'Contested Peripheries: Philistia in the Neo-Assyrian World-System,' unpublished Ph.D. dissertation, University of California at Los Angeles.

Amin, S. (1976) *Unequal Development: An Essay on the Social Formations of Peripheral Capitalism*, trans. B. Pearce, New York: Monthly Review Press.

—— (1980) *Class and Nation, Historically and in the Current Crisis*, New York: Monthly Review Press.

—— (1989) *Eurocentrism*, London: Zed Press.

—— (1991) 'The Ancient World-Systems versus the Modern Capitalist World-System,' *Review* 14, 3:349–85.

Andersen, E.S. (1994) *Evolutionary Economics: Post-Schumpeterian Contributions*, New York: Pinter Publishers.

Anderson, D.G. (1994) *The Savannah River Chiefdoms: Political Change in the Late Prehistoric Southeast*, Tuscaloosa: University of Alabama Press.

Anderson, P. (1974a) *Passages from Antiquity to Feudalism*, London: New Left Books.

—— (1974b) *Lineages of the Absolutist State*, London: New Left Books.

Arrighi, G. (1979) 'Peripheralization of Southern Africa, I: Changes in Production Processes,' *Review* 3, 2:161–91.

—— (1994) *The Long Twentieth Century: Money, Power and the Origins of Our Times*, London: Verso.

Aston, T. and Philpin, C. (eds) (1985) *The Brenner Debate: Agrarian Class Structure and Economic Development in Pre-Industrial Europe*, Cambridge: Cambridge University Press.

Attenborough, D. (1987) *The First Eden: The Mediterranean World and Man*, Boston: Little Brown.

Axelrod, R. (1984) *The Evolution of Cooperation*, New York: Basic Books.

Azevedo, J. (1997) *Mapping Reality: Evolutionary Realist Epistemology for the Natural and Social Sciences*, Albany NY: SUNY Press.

Baechler, J., Hall, J. and Mann, M. (eds) (1988) *Europe and the Rise of Capitalism*, Oxford: Basil Blackwell.

Baggott, J. (1992) *The Meaning of Quantum Theory*, Oxford: Oxford University Press.

Bairoch, P. (1988) *Cities and Economic Development: From the Dawn of History to the Present*, Chicago: University of Chicago Press.

Barbosa, L. (1993) 'The World-System and the Destruction of the Brazilian Amazon Rainforest,' *Review* 16, 2:215–40.

Barel, Y. (1973) *La Reproduction Sociale*, Paris: Antropos.

Barfield, T.J. (1989) *The Perilous Frontier: Nomadic Empires and China*, Cambridge MA: Basil Blackwell.

—— (1991) 'Inner Asia and Cycles of Power in China's Imperial Dynastic History,' in G. Seaman and D. Marks (eds) *Rulers from the Steppe: State Formation on the Eurasian Periphery*, Los Angeles: Ethnographics Press.

Bartolini, S. (1993) 'On Time and Comparative Research,' *Journal of Theoretical Politics* 5:131–67.

Battilega, J. and Granger, J. (1984) *The Military Applications of Modeling*, Ohio: Air Force Institute of Technology Press.

Bautista, G. (1990) 'The Forestry Crisis in the Philippines: Nature, Causes and Issues,' *The Developing Economies* 27, 1:67–94.

Beer, F. (1983) *Peace Against War*, San Francisco: W.H. Freeman.

Bell, B. (1971) 'The First Dark Age in Egypt,' *American Journal of Archaeology* 75, 1:1–26.

Bellow, W., Kinley, D. and Elinson, E. (eds) (1982) *Development Debacle, the World Bank in the Philippines*, San Francisco: Institute for Food and Development Policy.

Bentley, J.H. (1993) *Old World Encounters: Cross-Cultural Contacts and Exchanges in Pre-Modern Times*, Oxford: Oxford University Press.

Bernal, J.D. (1971) *Science in History*, four volumes, Cambridge MA: MIT Press.

Bernal, M. (1987) *Black Athena: The Afroasiatic Roots of Classical Civilization*, two volumes, New Brunswick NJ: Rutgers University Press.

Berquist, J. (1995) 'The Shifting Frontier: The Achaemenid Empire's Treatment of Western Colonies,' *Journal of World-Systems Research* 1:17. Available on-line at http://csf.colorado.edu/wsystems/jwsr/vol1_nh.htm

Bilsky, L. (1980) 'Ecological Crisis and Response in Ancient China,' in L. Bilsky (ed.) *Historical Ecology*, New York: Kennikat Press.

Blainey, G. (1975) *The Causes of War*, New York: Free Press.

Blaut, J.M. (ed.) (1992) *1492: The Debate on Colonialism, Eurocentrism and History*, Trenton NJ: Africa World Press.

—— (1993) *The Colonizer's Model of the World: Geographical Diffusionism and Eurocentric History*, New York: Guilford Press.

Bohman, J. (1991) *New Philosophy of Social Science: Problems of Indeterminacy*, Cambridge MA: MIT Press.

Boomgaard, P. (1988) 'Forests and Forestry in Colonial Java,' in J. Dargavel, K. Dixon and N. Semple (eds) *Changing Tropical Forests*, Canberra: Centre for Resource and Environment Studies.

Boswell, T. and Chase-Dunn, C. (2000) *The Spiral of Capitalism and Socialism*, Boulder CO: Lynne Rienner Press.

Bosworth, A. (1995a) 'The March of Cities: The Evolution of the World-City System from 3000 BC to 2000 AD,' unpublished Ph.D. dissertation, University of Washington.

—— (1995b) 'World Cities and World Economic Cycles,' in S. Sanderson (ed.) *Civilizations and World-Systems*, Walnut Creek CA: AltaMira.

Bozeman, A.B. (1994) *Politics and Culture in International History: From the Ancient Near East to the Opening of the Modern Age*, New Brunswick NJ: Transaction Press.

Braudel, F. (1984) *The Perspective of the World*, New York: Harper and Row.

—— (1987) *A History of Civilizations*, New York: Penguin.

Bremmer, S. and Cusack, T. (1994) *Advancing the Scientific Study of War*, London: Gordon and Breach.

Brumfiel, E. and Earle, T. (eds) (1987) *Specialization, Exchange, and Complex Societies*, Cambridge: Cambridge University Press.

Brumfiel, E. and Fox, J. (eds) (1994) *Factional Competition and Political Development in the New World*, Cambridge: Cambridge University Press.

Bücher, K. (1893) *Die entstehung der volkswirtschaft*, Tubingen: Verlag der H. Laupp'shen buchhandlung.

Burger, R. (1995) *Chavin and the Origins of Andean Civilization*, London: Thames and Hudson.

Cady, J.F. (1966) *Thailand, Burma, Laos, and Cambodia*, Englewood Cliffs NJ: Prentice-Hall.

Carneiro, R.L. (1970) 'A Theory of the Origin of the State,' *Science* 169:733–8.

Carrasco, P. (1982) 'The Political Economy of the Aztec and Inca States,' in G. Collier, R. Rosaldo and J. Wirth (eds) *The Inca and Aztec States 1400–1800: Anthropology and History*, New York: Academic Press.

Cassidy, D. (1992) *Uncertainty: The Life and Science of Werner Heisenberg*, New York: Freeman and Company.

Cavalli-Sforza, L., Menozzi, P. and Piazza, A. (1994) *The History and Geography of Human Genes*, Princeton: Princeton University Press.

Chandler, T. (1974) *Three Thousand Years of Urban Growth*, New York: Academic Press.

—— (1987) *Four Thousand Years of Urban Growth: An Historical Census*, Lewiston NJ: St. David's University Press.

Chang, K. (1980) *Archaeology of Ancient China*, New Haven CT: Yale University Press.

Chase-Dunn, C. (1981) 'Interstate System and Capitalist World-Economy: One Logic or Two?,' *International Studies Quarterly* 25, 1:19–42.

—— (1989) *Global Formation: Structures of the World-Economy*, Cambridge MA: Basil Blackwell.

—— (1992) 'The Comparative Study of World-Systems,' *Review* 15, 3:313–33.

—— (1994) 'Hegemony and Social Change', *Mershon International Studies Review* 38, 2:361–3.

—— (1996) 'Agency, Structure and the World-System: Systemic Transformation,' *Humboldt Journal of Social Relations* 22, 2:85–96.

—— (1998) *Global Formation: Structures of the World-Economy*, revised edition, Lanham MD: Rowman and Littlefield.

Chase-Dunn, C. and Hall, T. (eds) (1991) *Core/Periphery Relations in Pre-Capitalist Worlds*, Boulder CO: Westview Press.

—— (1992) 'World-Systems and Modes of Production: Toward the Comparative Study of Transformations,' *Humboldt Journal of Social Relations* 18, 1:81–118.

—— (1994) 'The Historical Evolution of World-Systems,' *Sociological Inquiry* 64, 3:257–80.

—— (1995) 'Cross-World-System Comparisons: Similarities and Differences,' in S. Sanderson (ed.) *Civilizations and World-Systems*, Walnut Creek CA: AltaMira Press.

—— (1997) *Rise and Demise: Comparing World-Systems*, Boulder CO: Westview Press.

Chase-Dunn, C., Manning, S. and Hall, T. (forthcoming) 'Rise and Fall: East-West Synchronicity and Indic Exceptionalism Reexamined,' *Social Science History*.

Chase-Dunn, C. and Podobnik, B. (1995) 'The Next World War: World-System Cycles and Trends,' *Journal of World-Systems Research* 1:6. Available on-line at http://csf.colorado.edu/wsystems/jwsr.vol/1/v1.n6.htm

Chase-Dunn, C. and Willard, A. (1993) 'Systems of Cities and World-Systems: Settlement Size Hierarchies and Cycles of Political Centralization, 2000 BC–1988 AD,' paper presented at International Studies Association, Alcapulco, Mexico.

Chaudhuri, K. (1985) *Trade and Civilization in the Indian Ocean: An Economic History from the Rise of Islam to 1750*, Cambridge: Cambridge University Press.

—— (1990) *Asia Before Europe: Economy and Civilization of the Indian Ocean from the Rise of Islam to 1750*, Cambridge: Cambridge University Press.

Chernykh, E. (1993) *Ancient Metallurgy in the USSR: The Early Metal Age*, Cambridge: Cambridge University Press.

Chew, S.C. (1992) *Logs for Capital: The Timber Industry and Capitalist Enterprise in the 19th Century*, Westport CT: Greenwood Press.

—— (1993) 'Environmental Imperatives and Development Strategies: Challenges for Southeast Asia,' *Studies in National and International Development Working Paper*, Kingston, Canada: Queen's University.

—— (1995) 'Environmental Transformations: Accumulation, Ecological Crisis, and Social Movements,' in D. Smith and J. Borocz (eds) *A New World Order? Global Transformation in the Late Twentieth Century*, Westport CT: Greenwood Press.

Chu, C. (1926) 'Climatic Pulsations During Historic Time in China,' *Geographical Review* 16, 2:274–82.

Cioffi-Revilla, C. (1991) 'The Long-Range Analysis of War,' *Journal of Interdisciplinary History* 21, 4:603–29.

—— (1995) *The Scientific Measurement of International Conflict: Handbook of Datasets on Crises and Wars, 1495–1988 AD*, Boulder CO: Lynne Rienner.

—— (1996) 'Origins and Evolution of War and Politics,' *International Studies Quarterly* 40, 1:1–22.

—— (1997) 'The Road to War,' paper presented at the IMA Conference on Mathematical Models of International Conflict, Wadham College, Oxford.

—— (1998a) 'Origins, Evolution and Complexity in Macro Social Systems,' unpublished manuscript.

—— (1998b) 'Ancient Warfare,' in M. Midlarsky (ed.) *Handbook of War Studies II*, Ann Arbor: University of Michigan Press.

Cioffi-Revilla, C., Chupik, C. and Resnick, A. (1998) 'Maya Warfare,' working paper, Long-Range Analysis of War Project, University of Colorado, Boulder.

Cioffi-Revilla, C. and Lai, D. (1995) 'War and Politics in Ancient China, 2700 BC to 722

BC: Measurement and Comparative Analysis,' *Journal of Conflict Resolution* 39, 3:467–94.

Cioffi-Revilla, C. and Sommer, H. (1993) 'War and Politics in Ancient Mesopotamia: A Tri-Force Theory of War,' paper presented at the annual meeting of the American Political Science Association, Washington D.C.

Cioffi-Revilla, C. and Starr, H. (1995) 'Opportunity, Willingness and Political Uncertainty: Theoretical Foundations of Politics,' *Journal of Theoretical Politics* 7:447–76.

Clastres, P. (1974) *La Société contre l'état*, Paris: Les Editions de minuit.

Coedès, G. (1966) *The Making of South East Asia*, trans. H.M. Wright, London: Routledge & Kegan Paul. [Original (1962) *Les Peuples de la Peninsule Indoshinoise*, Paris: Dumond.]

—— (1968) 'The Indianized States of Southeast Asia,' edited by W. Vella, trans. S. Cowing, Honolulu: East-West Center Press.

Cohen, M. (1977) *The Food Crisis in Prehistory*, New Haven CT: Yale University Press.

Collier, G.A., Rosaldo, R.I. and Wirth, J.D. (eds) (1982) *The Inca and Aztec States 1400–1800: Anthropology and History*, New York: Academic Press.

Collins, R. (1978) 'Some Principles of Long-Term Social Change: The Territorial Power of States,' in L. Kriesberg (ed.) *Research in Social Movements, Conflicts and Change*, Volume 1, Greenwich CT: JAI Press.

—— (1981) 'Long-Term Social Change and the Territorial Power of States,' in R. Collins (ed.) *Sociology Since Midcentury*, New York: Academic Press.

—— (1986) *Weberian Sociological Theory*, Cambridge: Cambridge University Press.

—— (1990) 'Market Dynamics as the Engine of Historical Change,' *Sociological Theory* 8, 111:35.

—— (1992) 'The Geopolitical and Economic World-Systems of Kinship-Based and Agrarian-Coercive Societies,' *Review* 15, 3:373–88.

Cooper, J. (1973) 'Sumerian and Akkadian in Sumer and Akkad,' *Orientalia* 42:239–46.

Corning, P. (1994) 'Synergy and Self-Organization in Human Evolution,' paper presented at the 38th Annual Meeting of the International Society for the Systems Sciences, Pacific Grove CA.

Crawford, H.E.W. (1973) 'Mesopotamia's Invisible Exports in the Third Millennium B.C.,' *World Archaeology* 5, 2:232–41.

—— (1991/1997) *Sumer and the Sumerians*, Cambridge: Cambridge University Press.

Crosby, A.W. (1972) *The Columbian Exchange: Biological and Cultural Consequences of 1492*, Westport CT: Greenwood Press.

—— (1986) *Ecological Imperialism: The Biological Expansion of Europe, 900–1900*, New York: Cambridge University Press.

Curtin, P.D. (1984) *Cross-Cultural Trade in World History*, New York: Cambridge University Press.

—— (1990) *The Rise and Fall of the Plantation Complex*, Cambridge: Cambridge University Press.

Dales, G. (1976) 'Shifting Trade Patterns between the Iranian Plateau and the Indus Valley in the Third Millennium B.C.,' in J. Deshayes (ed.) *Le Plateau Iranien et l'Asie Centrale des Origines à la Conquête Islamique*, Paris: CNRS.

Dark, K. (1998) *The Waves of Time: Long-Term Change and International Relations*, London: Pinter.

Dawson, C. (1958) *The Dynamics of World History*, LaSalle IL: Sherwood Sugden.

Denemark, R. (1999) 'World System History: From Traditional International Politics to the Study of Global Relations', *International Studies Review* 1, 2:43–75.

Derry, T.K. and Williams, T.I. (1961) *A Short History of Technology: From the Earliest Times to AD 1900*, New York: Oxford University Press.

Descat, R. (1995) 'L'economie', in R. Briant and P. Lévêque *et al.* (eds) *Le monde grecaux temps classiques*, volume one, Paris: Presses Universitaires France.

Devall, B. (1993) *Living Richly in an Age of Limits*, Salt Lake City UT: Peregrine Smith.

—— (1994) *Clear Cut: The Tragedy of Industrial Forestry*, San Francisco: Sierra Club Books.

De Vries, J. (1984) *European Urbanization, 1500–1800*, Cambridge MA: Harvard University Press.

Diakonoff, I.M. (1973) 'The Rise of the Despotic State in Ancient Mesopotamia,' in I. Diakonoff (ed.) *Ancient Mesopotamia: Socio-Economic History*, Wiesbaden: Martin Sändig oHG.

Diehl, P. (ed.) (1998) *The Dynamics of Enduring Rivalries*, Urbana: University of Illinois Press.

Dobb, M. (1952) *Studies in the Development of Capitalism*, New York: International Publishers.

—— (1976) 'A Reply,' in R. Hilton (ed.) *The Transition from Feudalism to Capitalism*, London: New Left Books.

Dockery, J. and Woodcock, A. (eds) (1993) *The Military Landscape: Mathematical Models of Combat*, Cambridge: Woodhead Publishing.

Dogan, M. and Pahre, R. (1990) *Creative Marginality: Innovation at the Intersections of Social Sciences*, Boulder CO: Westview.

Dunaway, W. (1994) 'The Southern Fur Trade and the Incorporation of Southern Appalachia into the World-Economy, 1690–1763,' *Review* 18, 2:215–42.

—— (1996a) *The First American Frontier: Transition to Capitalism in Southern Appalachia, 1700–1860*, Chapel Hill: University of North Carolina Press.

—— (1996b) 'Incorporation as an Interactive Process: Cherokee Resistance to Expansion of the Capitalist World-System, 1560–1763,' *Sociological Inquiry* 66, 4:455–70.

Dunn, F.L. (1975) *Rain Forest Collectors and Traders: A Study of Resource Utilization in Modern and Ancient Malaya*, Kuala Lumpur: Malayan Branch of the Royal Asiatic Society.

Dupuy, R. and Dupuy, T. (eds) (1993) *The Harper Encyclopedia of Military History*, fourth edition, New York: HarperCollins.

Eckhardt, W. (1992) *Civilizations, Empires and Wars: A Quantitative History of War*, Jefferson NC: McFarland.

Edens, C. (1990) 'Indus-Arabian Interaction During the Bronze Age,' in G. Possehl (ed.) *Harappan Civilization and Rajdi New Delhi*, New York: Oxford University Press.

Eisenstadt, S.N. (ed.) (1986) *The Origin and Diversity of Axial Age Civilizations*, Albany: State University of New York Press.

Ekholm-Friedman, K. (1972) 'Power and Prestige: The Rise and Fall of the Kongo Kingdom,' unpublished Ph.D. dissertation, Uppsala.

—— (1975) 'System av sociala system och determinanterna i den sociala evolutionen,' *Antropologiska studier* 14, 1:15–23.

—— (1977) 'External Exchange and the Transformation of Central African Social Systems,' in J. Friedman and M. Rowlands (eds) *The Evolution of Social Systems*, Gloucester UK: Duckworth.

—— (1985) ' "Sad Stories About the Death of Kings": The Involution of Divine Kingship,' *Ethnos* 50, 3–4:248–72.

—— (1991) *Catastrophe and Creation: The Transformation of an African Culture*, London: Harwood.

Ekholm, K. and Friedman, J. (1982) '"Capital" Imperialism and Exploitation in Ancient World-Systems,' *Review* 6, 1:87–110.

Elster, J. (1989) *Nuts and Bolts for the Social Sciences*, Cambridge: Cambridge University Press.

Elvin, M. (1973) *The Pattern of the Chinese Past*, Stanford: Stanford University Press.

Esman, M. (ed.) (1977) *Ethnic Conflict in the Western World*, Ithaca NY: Cornell University Press.

Ferguson, R. and Whitehead N. (eds) (1992) *War in the Tribal Zone: Expanding States and Indigenous Warfare*, Santa Fe NM: School of American Research Press.

Ferrill, A. (1985/1997) *The Origins of War*, London: Thames and Hudson, second edition, Boulder CO: Westview.

Feuerwerker, A. (1990) 'Chinese Economic History in Comparative Perspective,' in P. Ropp (ed.) *Heritage of China: Contemporary Perspective on Chinese Civilization*, Berkeley: University of California Press.

Finley, M.I. (1973) *The Ancient Economy*, Berkeley: University of California Press.

Firth, J. (1902) *Augustus Caesar and the Organization of the Empire of Rome*, New York: G. Putnam and Sons.

Forbes, R.J. (1954) 'Extracting, Smelting, and Alloying,' in C. Singer, E. Holmyard and A. Hall (eds) *A History of Technology*, volume 1, Oxford: Oxford University Press (Clarendon Press).

Franck, I. and Brownstone, D. (1986) *The Silk Road: A History*, Oxford: Facts on File.

Frangipane, M. (1996) *La nascita dello Stato nel Vicino Oriente*, Bari, Italy: Editori Laterza.

Frank, A.G. (1966) 'The Development of Underdevelopment,' *Monthly Review* 18, 4:17–31.

—— (1978a) *World Accumulation 1492–1789*, New York: Monthly Review Press.

—— (1978b) *Dependent Accumulation and Underdevelopment*, New York: Monthly Review Press.

—— (1990) 'A Theoretical Introduction to 5,000 Years of World System History,' *Review* 13, 2:155–248.

—— (1991a) 'A Plea for World System History,' *Journal of World History* 2, l:1–28.

—— (1991b) 'Transitional Ideological Modes: Feudalism, Capitalism, Socialism,' *Critique of Anthropology* 11, 2:171–88.

—— (1992) 'The Centrality of Central Asia,' *Comparative Asian Studies Series*, No. 8, Center for Asian Studies Amsterdam (CASA).

—— (1993a) 'Bronze Age World System Cycles,' *Current Anthropology* 34, 4:383–429.

—— (1993b) '1492 and Latin America at the Margin of World History: East-West Hegemonial Shifts (992–1492–1992),' *Comparative Civilizations Review* 28, 1:1–40.

—— (1994a) 'The World Economic System in Asia Before European Hegemony,' *The Historian* 56, 4:259–76.

—— (1994b) 'Hegemony and Social Change,' *Mershon International Studies Review* 38, 2:371–2.

—— (1995) 'The Modern World-System Revisited: Rereading Braudel and Wallerstein,' in S. Sanderson (ed.) *Civilizations and World Systems*, Walnut Creek CA: AltaMira Press.

—— (1998) *ReOrient: Global Economy in the Asian Age*, Berkeley: University of California Press.

Frank, A.G. and Gills, B.K. (1992) 'The Five Thousand Year World System: An Interdisciplinary Introduction,' *Humboldt Journal of Social Relations* 18, 2:1–80.

—— (eds) (1993) *The World System: Five Hundred Years or Five Thousand?*, London: Routledge.

Frank, T. (1916/1992) 'Race Mixture in the Roman Empire,' in D. Kagan (ed.) *The Decline of the Roman Empire*, third edition, Boston: D.C. Heath.

Frankenstein, S. (1979) 'The Phoenicians in the Far West: A Function of Neo-Assyrian Imperialism,' in M.T. Larsen (ed.) *Power and Propaganda: A Symposium on Ancient Empires*, Copenhagen: Akademisk Forlag.

Frankfort, H. (1971) 'The Last Predynastic Period in Babylonia,' in L. Davies (ed.) *The Cambridge Ancient History*, volume one, part two, Cambridge: Cambridge University Press.

French, A.A. (1964) *The Growth of the Athenian Economy*, New York: Barnes and Noble.

Friedman, J. (1979/1998) *System, Structure, and Contradiction: The Evolution of Asiatic Social Formations*, second edition, Walnut Creek CA: AltaMira.

—— (1994) *Consumption and Identity*, Chur, Switzerland: Harwood Academic.

Friedman, J. and Rowlands, M. (1977) 'Notes Toward an Epigenetic Model of the Evolution of "Civilization",' in J. Friedman and M.J. Rowlands (eds) *The Evolution of Social Systems*, London: Duckworth.

Gabriel, R. and Metz, K. (1991) *From Sumer to Rome: The Military Capabilities of Ancient Armies*, Newport CT: Greenwood.

Gadgil, M. (1988) 'On the History of the Kannada Forests,' in J. Dargavel, K. Dixon and N. Semple (eds) *Changing Tropical Forests*, Canberra: Centre for Resource and Environmental Studies.

García Canclini, N. (1995) *Hybrid Cultures: Strategies for Entering and Leaving Modernity*, Minneapolis: University of Minnesota Press.

Gauchet, M. (1977) *Dette du sens et racines de l'état*, Paris: Libre 2.

Gelb, I. (1973) 'Prisoners of War in Early Mesopotamia,' *Journal of Near Eastern Studies* 32, 1:70–98.

Geller, D. and Singer, J. (1998) *Nations at War: A Scientific Study of International Conflict*, Cambridge: Cambridge University Press.

Georgescu-Roegen, N. (1971) *The Entropy Law and the Economic Process*, Cambridge MA: Harvard University Press.

Giddens, A. (1984) *The Constitution of Society*, Cambridge: Polity Press.

Gills, B.K. (1992) 'The International Origins of South Korea's Export Orientation,' in R. Palan and B. Gills (eds) *Transcending the State-Global Divide: The Neo-Structuralist Agenda in International Relations*, Boulder CO: Lynne Rienner Press.

—— (1993) 'Hegemonic Transitions in the World System,' in A. Frank and B. Gills (eds) *The World System: Five Hundred Years or Five Thousand?*, London: Routledge.

—— (1994) 'Hegemony and Social Change,' *Mershon International Studies Review* 38, 2:369–71.

—— (1995) 'Capital and Power in the Processes of World History,' in S. Sanderson (ed.) *Civilizations and World Systems*, Walnut Creek CA: AltaMira Press.

Gills, B.K. and Frank, A.G. (1990/1) 'The Cumulation of Accumulation: Theses and Research Agenda for 5000 Years of World System History,' *Dialectical Anthropology* 15, 1:19–42.

—— (1991) '5000 Years of World System History: The Cumulation of Accumulation,' in C. Chase-Dunn and T. Hall (eds) *Core/Periphery Relations in Precapitalist Worlds*, Boulder CO: Westview Press.

—— (1992) 'World System Cycles, Crises, and Hegemonial Shifts 1700 BC to 1700 AD,' *Review* 15, 4:621–87.

—— (1993) 'The 5,000-Year World System: An Interdisciplinary Introduction,' in A.G. Frank and B.K. Gills (eds) *The World System: Five Hundred Years or Five Thousand?*, London: Routledge.

Gills, B., Rocamora, J. and Wilson, R. (eds) (1993) *Low Intensity Democracy: Political Power in the New World Order*, London: Pluto Press.

Gilroy, P. (1993) *Small Acts: Thoughts on the Politics of Black Cultures*, London: Serpent's Tail.

Gleick, J. (1987) *Chaos: The Making of a New Science*, New York: Penguin.

Glover, I., Suchitta, P. and Villiers, J. (eds) (1992) *Early Metallurgy, Trade and Urban Centers in Thailand and Southeast Asia: 13 Archaeological Essays*, Bangkok: White Lotus.

Godelier, M. (1986) *The Mental and the Material*, London: Verso.

Goldstone, J. (1991) *Revolutions and Rebellions in the Early Modern World*, Berkeley: University of California Press.

Goto, D. (1993) 'Logging in Siberia: Japan's Involvement,' *Japan Environmental Exchange Newsletter*, Tokyo: July.

Grumbine, E. (1992) *Ghost Bears*, Covelo: Island Press.

Guha, R. (1989) *The Unquiet Woods*, Berkeley: University of California Press.

Gurr, T.R. (1994) 'People Against States: Ethnopolitical Conflict and the Changing World System,' *International Studies Quarterly* 38, 3:347–77

Haas, J., Pozorski, S. and Pozorski, T. (eds) (1987) *The Origins and Development of the Andean State*, Cambridge: Cambridge University Press.

Hackett, J. (1989) *Warfare in the Ancient World*, New York: Facts on File.

Hall, J. (1985) *Powers and Liberties: The Causes and Consequences of the Rise of the West*, London: Penguin.

Hall, S. (1996) 'When was the Postcolonial?' in L. Curti and I. Chambers (eds) *The Post Colonial in Question*, London: Routledge.

Hall, T. (1986) 'Incorporation into the World-System: Toward a Critique,' *American Sociological Review* 51, 3:390–402.

—— (1989) *Social Change in the Southwest, 1350–1880*, Lawrence: University of Kansas Press.

—— (1996) 'World-Systems and Evolution: An Appraisal,' *Journal of World-Systems Research* 2, 2:1–43. Available on-line at http://csf.colorado.edu/wsystems/jwsr/vol 2/v2-n4.htm

—— (1998) 'The Effects of Incorporation into World-Systems on Ethnic Processes: Lessons from the Ancient World for the Contemporary World,' *International Political Science Review* 19, 3:251–67.

—— (1999) 'World-Systems and Evolution: An Appraisal,' in P.N. Kardulias (ed.) *Leadership, Production, and Exchange: World-Systems Theory in Practice*, Lanham MD: Rowman and Littlefield.

—— (2000) 'Frontiers, Ethnogenesis and World-Systems: Rethinking the Theories,' in T. Hall (ed.) *A World-Systems Reader: New Perspectives on Gender, Urbanism, Cultures, Indigenous Peoples, and Ecology*, Lanham MD: Rowman and Littlefield.

Hall, T. and Chase-Dunn, C. (1993) 'The World-Systems Perspective and Archaeology: Forward into the Past,' *Journal of Archaeological Research* 1, 2:121–43.

—— (1994) 'Forward into the Past: World-Systems Before 1500,' *Sociological Forum* 9, 2:295–306.

Hamashita, T. (1988) 'The Tribute Trade System and Modern Asia,' *The Toyo Bunko: Memoirs of the Research Department of the Toyo Bunko* 46:1–28.

—— (1994) 'Japan and China in the 19th and 20th Centuries,' unpublished manuscript presented at Cornell University, Ithaca, NY.

Harris, M. (1977) *Cannibals and Kings: The Origins of Cultures*, New York: Random House.

—— (1979) *Cultural Materialism: The Struggle for a Science of Culture*, New York: Random House.

Harte, N. (1971) *The Study of Economic History: Collected Innaugural Lectures 1893–1970*, Ilford UK: Frank Cass.

Hassig, R. (1992) *War and Society in Ancient Mesoamerica*, Berkeley: University of California Press.

Hastings, C.M. (1987) 'Implications of Andean Verticality in the Evolution of Political Complexity: A View from the Margins,' in J. Haas, S. Pozorski and T. Pozorski *(eds) The Origins and Development of the Andean State*, Cambridge: Cambridge University Press.

Heichelheim, F.M. (1958) *An Economic History, from the Palaeolithic Age to the Migrations of the Germanic, Slavic, and Arabic Nations*, Leiden: A.W. Sijthoff.

Hecht, S. and Cockburn, A. (1990) *The Fate of the Forest*, New York: Harper.

Helck, W. (1975) *Wirtschaftsgeschichte des Alten Ägypten im 3. und 2. Jahrtausend vor. Chr.*, Leiden: Brill.

Herz, J. (1951) *Political Realism and Political Idealism*, Chicago: University of Chicago Press.

Hilton, R. (ed.) (1976) *The Transition from Feudalism to Capitalism*, London: New Left Books.

Hodgson, M. (1974) *The Venture of Islam*, three volumes, Chicago: University of Chicago Press.

—— (1993) *Rethinking World History: Essays on Europe, Islam and World History*, Cambridge: Cambridge University Press.

Hoffman, M. (1980) 'Pre-Historic Ecological Crises,' in L. Bilsky (ed.) *Historical Ecology*, New York: Kennikat Press.

Hole, F. (1989) 'Patterns and Burial in the Fifth Millennium,' in E. Henrickson and I. Thuesen (eds) *Upon this Foundation: The 'Ubaid Reconsidered*, Copenhagen: Museum Tusculanum Press.

Holland, J. (1992) 'Complex Adaptive Systems,' *Daedalus* 121, 1:17–30.

Hopkins, T., Wallerstein, I. *et al.* (1982a) 'Patterns of Development in the Modern World-System,' in T. Hopkins, I. Wallerstein *et al.*, *World-Systems Analysis: Theory and Methodology*, Beverly Hills CA: Sage.

—— (1982b) 'Cyclical Rhythms and Secular Trends of the Capitalist World-Economy: Some Premises, Hypotheses, and Questions,' in T. Hopkins, I. Wallerstein *et al.*, *World-Systems Analysis: Theory and Methodology*, Beverly Hills CA: Sage.

Hornborg, A. (1992) 'Machine Fetishism, Value and the Image of Unlimited Good: Towards a Thermodynamics of Imperialism,' *Man* 27:1–18.

Horowitz, D. (1985) *Ethnic Groups in Conflict*, Berkeley CA: University of California Press.

Huff, T.E. (1993) *The Rise of Early Modern Science: Islam, China, and the West*, New York: Cambridge University Press.

Hughes, W. (1984) *Military Modeling*, Washington DC: Military Operations Research Society.

Humble, R. (1980) *Warfare in the Ancient World*, London: Cassell.

Huntington, S. (1996) *The Clash of Civilizations and Remaking the World Order*, New York: Simon and Schuster.

Huot, J. (1989) 'Ubaidian Villages of Lower Mesopotamia,' in E. Henrickson and I. Thuesen (eds) *Upon this Foundation: The 'Ubaid Reconsidered*, Copenhagen: Museum Tusculanum Press.

Hurst, P. (1990) *Rainforest Politics*, London: Zed Press.

Iberall, A. and Wilkinson, D. (1984a) 'Human Sociogeophysics – Phase I: Explaining the Macroscopic Patterns of Man on Earth,' *GeoJournal* 8, 2:171–9.

—— (1984b) 'Human Sociogeophysics – Phase II: The Diffusion of Human Ethnicity by Remixing,' *GeoJournal* 9, 4:387–91.

—— (1986) 'Human Sociogeophysics – Phase II (Continued): Criticality in the Diffusion of Ethnicity Produces Civil Society,' *GeoJournal* 11, 2:153–8.

—— (1987) 'Dynamic Foundations for Complex Systems,' in G. Modelski (ed.) *Exploring Long Cycles*, Boulder CO: Lynne Rienner.

—— (1993) '"Polycultures" and "Culture-Civilizations": Forms and Processes in the Evolution of Civilizations,' *Comparative Civilizations Review* 28:73–9.

Isbell, W.H. (1987) 'State Origins in the Ayacucho Valley, Central Highlands, Peru,' in J. Haas, S. Pozorski and T. Pozorski (eds) *The Origins and Development of the Andean State*, Cambridge: Cambridge University Press.

Jacobs, J. (1969/1984) *Cities and the Wealth of Nations*, New York: Random House.

Jacobs, N. (1958) *The Origin of Modern Capitalism and Eastern Asia*, Hong Kong: Hong Kong University Press.

Jacobsen, T. (1957) 'Early Political Development in Mesopotamia,' *Zeitschrift für Assyriologie* 52:91–140.

Janssen, J. (1975) *Commodity Prices from the Ramessid Period: An Economic Study of the Village of Necropolis Workmen at Thebes*, Leiden: Brill.

Jasim, S.A. (1989) 'Structure and Function in an 'Ubaid Village,' in E. Henrickson and I. Thuesen (eds) *Upon this Foundation: The 'Ubaid Reconsidered*, Copenhagen: Museum Tusculanum Press.

Jaspers, K. (1953) *The Origin and Goal of History*, New Haven CT: Yale University Press.

Johnson, G. (1975) 'Locational Analysis and the Investigation of Uruk Local Exchange Systems,' in J. Sabloff and C. Lamborg-Karlovsky (eds) *Ancient Civilization and Trade*, Albuquerque: University of New Mexico Press.

Jones, A. (1987) *The Art of War in the Western World*, Urbana: University of Illinois Press.

Jones, C. (1979) 'Tikal as a Trading Center: Why it Rose and Fell,' paper presented at the XLIII International Congress of Americanists, Vancouver BC, Canada.

Jones, C. (1997) *Geographical Information Systems and Computer Cartography*, Harlow UK: Longman.

Jones, E. (1981) *The European Miracle: Environments, Economies and Geopolitics in the History of Europe and Asia*, Cambridge: Cambridge University Press.

—— (1988) *Growth Recurring: Economic Change in World History*, Oxford: Oxford University Press.

Kåberger, T. (1991) 'Measuring Instrumental Value in Energy Terms,' in C. Folke and T. Kåberger (eds) *Linking the Natural Environment and the Economy: Essays from the Eco-Eco Group*, Boston: Kluwer Academic

Kant, I. (1784/1991) 'Idea for a Universal History with a Cosmopolitan Purpose,' in H. Reiss (ed.) *Kant: Political Writings*, second edition, Cambridge: Cambridge University Press.

Kardulias, N. (1990) 'Fur Production as a Specialized Activity in a World System: Indians in the North American Fur Trade,' *American Indian Culture and Research Journal* 14, 1:25–60.

Kato, T. (1992) 'Structural Changes in Japanese Forest Product Imports During the 1980s,' in *The Current State of Japanese Forestry*, Tokyo: Japanese Forest Economic Society.

Kautsky, J. (1982) *The Politics of Aristocratic Empires*, Chapel Hill: University of North Carolina Press.

Keatinge, R.W. (1981) 'The Nature and Role of Religious Diffusion in the Early Stages of State Formation: An Example from Peruvian Prehistory,' in G.D. Jones and R.R. Kautz (eds) *The Transition to Statehood in the New World*, Cambridge: Cambridge University Press.

—— (ed.) (1988) *Peruvian Prehistory: An Overview of Pre-Inca and Inca Society*, Cambridge: Cambridge University Press.

Keegan, J. (1993) *A History of Warfare*, New York: Knopf.

Keeley, L. (1996) *War Before Civilization*, Oxford: Oxford University Press.

Keightley, D. (1983) *The Origins of Chinese Civilization*, Berkeley: University of California Press.

Kemp, B. (1983) 'Old Kingdom, Middle Kingdom and Second Intermediate Period,' in B. G. Trigger *et al.*, *Ancient Egypt: A Social History*, Cambridge: Cambridge University Press.

—— (1989) *Ancient Egypt: Anatomy of a Civilization*, London: Routledge.

Kenyon, K. (1979) *Archaeology in the Holy Land*, London: Benn Norton.

Keynes, J.M. (1936) *The General Theory of Employment, Interest and Money*, London: Macmillan.

Kirch, P. (1984) *The Evolution of Polynesian Chiefdoms*, Cambridge: Cambridge University Press.

Klymyshyn, A. (1987) 'The Development of Chimu Administration in Chan Chan,' in J. Haas, S. Pozorski and T. Pozorski (eds) *The Origins and Development of the Andean State*, Cambridge: Cambridge University Press.

Knapp, A.B. (1988) *The History and Culture of Ancient Western Asia and Egypt*, Chicago: Dorsey.

Knight, S. (1985) *The Brotherhood*, London: Grafton.

Kohl, P. (1987a) 'The Use and Abuse of World Systems Theory: The Case of the "Pristine" West Asian State,' in M. Schiffer (ed.) *Advances in Archaeological Methods and Theory*, volume 11, New York: Academic Press.

—— (1987b) 'The Ancient Economy, Transferable Technologies and the Bronze Age World-System: A View from the Northeastern Frontier of the Ancient Near East,' in M. Rowlands, M. Larsen and K. Kristiansen (eds) *Centre and Periphery in the Ancient World*, Cambridge: Cambridge University Press.

Kramer, S.N. (1963) *The Sumerians: Their History, Culture, and Character*, Chicago: University of Chicago Press.

Kristiansen, K. (1991) 'Chiefdoms, States and Systems of Social Evolution,' in T. Earle (ed.) *Chiefdoms: Power, Economy and Ideology*, Cambridge: Cambridge University Press.

—— (1992) 'The Emergence of the European World System in the Bronze Age: Divergence, Convergence and Social Evolution during the First and Second Millennium B.C. in Europe,' in K. Kristiansen and J. Jensen (eds) *Europe in the First Millennium B.C.*, Sheffield UK: University of Sheffield Press.

Kuhn, T. (1970) *The Structure of Scientific Revolutions*, second edition, enlarged, Chicago: University of Chicago Press.

Lamborg-Karlovsky, C. and Beale, T. (1986) *Excavations at Tehpe Yahya, Iran 1967–1975*, Cambridge MA: Peabody Museum.

Larsen, M. (1967) *Old Assyrian Caravan Procedures*, Istanbul: Netherlands Historish Arceologisch Instituut te Istanbul.

—— (1976) *The Old Assyrian City-State and its Colonies*, Copenhagen: Akademisk Forlag.

—— (1979) 'The Tradition of Empire in Mesopotamia,' in M. Larsen (ed.) *Power and Propaganda*, Copenhagen: Akademisk Forlag.

Lasch, C. (1995) *Revolt of the Elite and the Betrayal of Democracy*, New York: W.W. Norton.

Lathrap, D.W., Collier, D. and Chandra, H. (1975) *Ancient Ecuador: Culture, Clay and Creativity 3000–300 B.C.*, Chicago: Field Museum of Natural History.

Lattimore, O. (1940/1951) *Inner Asian Frontiers of China*, New York: American Geographical Society.

—— (1962) *Studies in Frontier History: Collected Papers, 1928–58*, London: Oxford University Press.

Leemans, W. (1960) *Foreign Trade in the Old Babylonian Period*, Leiden: E.J. Brill.

Lenski, G. (1970) *Human Societies: A Macro-Level Introduction to Sociology*, New York: McGraw-Hill.

Lévi-Strauss, C. (1952) *Race et historie*, Paris: UNESCO.

Levy, J. (1983) *War in the Modern Great Power System, 1475–1975*, Lexington: University of Kentucky Press.

—— (1990) 'Big Wars, Little Wars, and Theory Construction,' *International Interactions* 16, 3:215–24.

Lian, F. (1988) 'The Economies and Ecology of the Production of the Tropical Rainforest

Resources by Tribal Groups of Sarawak, Borneo,' in J. Dargavel, K. Dixon and N. Semple (eds) *Changing Tropical Forests*, Canberra: Centre for Resource and Environmental Studies.

Lim, H.F. (1992) 'Aboriginal Communities and the International Trade in Non-Timber Forest Products: The Case of Peninsular Malaysia,' in J. Dargavel and R. Tucker (eds) *Changing Pacific Forests*, Durham: Forest History Society.

Little, D. (1991) *Varieties of Social Explanation*, Boulder CO: Westview Press.

Liverani, M. (1988) *Antico Oriente: Storia, societá, economia*, Rome: Editori Laterza.

Livi-Bacci, M. (1992) *A Concise History of World Population*, trans. C. Ipsen, Oxford: Blackwell.

Lo, J. (1958) 'The Decline of the Ming Navy,' *Oriens Extremus* 5: 149–68.

Lombard, M. (1975) *The Golden Age of Islam* , Amsterdam: North-Holland.

Love, J.R. (1991) *Antiquity and Capitalism*, London: Routledge.

Lower, A. (1973) *Great Britain's Woodyard*, Kingston: Queen's University Press.

Lumsden, C. and Wilson, E. (1981) *Genes, Mind, and Culture: The Coevolutionary Process*, Cambridge MA: Harvard University Press.

Mackey, C.J. (1987) 'Chimu Administration in the Provinces,' in J. Haas, S. Pozorski and T. Pozorski (eds) *The Origins and Development of the Andean State*, Cambridge: Cambridge University Press.

Mann, M. (1986) *The Sources of Social Power: A History of Power from the Beginning to A.D. 1760*, Cambridge: Cambridge University Press.

Marcos, J.G. (1977/1978) 'Cruising to Acapulco and Back with the Thorny Oyster Set: A Model for a Lineal Exchange System,' *Journal of the Steward Anthropological Society* 9:99–132.

Marcus, G. and Fischer, M. (1986) *Anthropology as Cultural Critique: An Experimental Moment in the Human Sciences*, Chicago: University of Chicago Press.

Marcus, J. (1995) 'Cinco mitos sobre la guerra Maya,' paper presented at the Mesa Redonda de Palenque, Pelenque, Mexico.

Marcus, J. and Flannery, K. (1996) *Zapotec Civilization: How Urban Society Evolved in Mexico's Oaxaca Valley*, London: Thames and Hudson.

Margiotta, F. (ed.) (1984) *Brassey's Encyclopedia of Military History and Biography*, London: Brassey's.

Margueron, J. (1989) 'Architecture et société a l'époche d'Obeid,' in E. Henrickson and I. Thuesen (eds.) *Upon this Foundation: The 'Ubaid Reconsidered*, Copenhagen: Museum Tusculanum Press.

Marr, D. and Milner, A. (eds) (1986) *Southeast Asia in the 9th to 14th Centuries*, Singapore: Institute of Southeast Asian Studies & Research School of Pacific Studies, Australian National University.

Marshall, J. (1931) *Mohenjo-daro and the Indus Civilization*, three volumes, Cambridge: Cambridge University Press.

Martin, W. (1994) 'The World-Systems Perspective in Perspective: Assessing the Attempt to Move Beyond Nineteenth Century Eurocentric Conceptions,' *Review* 18, 2:145–85.

Martinez-Alier, J. (1987) *Ecological Economics: Energy, Environment and Society*, New York: Blackwell.

Masuda, S., Shimada, I. and Morris, C. (eds) (1985) *Andean Ecology and Civilization: An Interdisciplinary Perspective on Andean Ecological Complementarity*, Tokyo: University of Tokyo Press.

McEvedy, C. (1961) *The Penguin Atlas of Medieval History*, New York: Penguin.

—— (1967) *The Penguin Atlas of Ancient History*, New York: Penguin.

—— (1972) *The Penguin Atlas of Modern History (to 1815)*, New York: Penguin.

—— (1980) *The Penguin Atlas of African History*, New York: Penguin.

—— (1982) *The Penguin Atlas of Recent History (Europe since 1815)*, New York: Penguin.

McEvedy, C. and Jones, R. (1978) *Atlas of World Population History*, New York: Penguin.

McKeown, T. (1986) 'The Limitations of Structural Theories of Commercial Policy,' *International Organization* 40, 1:43–64.

McNeill, W. (1963/1991) *The Rise of the West*, Chicago: University of Chicago.

—— (1976) *Plagues and Peoples*, Garden City NY: Doubleday.

—— (1982) *The Pursuit of Power: Technology, Armed Force and Society since AD 1000*, Oxford: Blackwell.

—— (1986) *Polyethnicity and National Unity in World History*, Toronto: University of Toronto Press.

—— (1993) *A History of the Human Community*, fourth edition, New York: Prentice Hall.

—— (1995) *Keeping Together in Time: Dance and Drill in Human History*, Cambridge MA: Harvard University Press.

Meadows, D., Meadows, D.L. and Randers, J. (1992) *Beyond the Limits: Confronting Global Collapse, Envisioning a Sustainable Future*, White River Junction VT: Chelsea Green Publishing.

Meiggs, R. (1982) *Trees and Timber of the Ancient Mediterranean World*, Oxford: Clarendon Press.

Melko, M. (1995) 'The Nature of Civilizations,' in S. Sanderson (ed.) *Civilizations and World-Systems*, Walnut Creek CA: AltaMira Press.

Mendels, D. (1992) *The Rise and Fall of Jewish Nationalism*, New York: Doubleday.

Mendez, C. (1990) *Fight for the Forest*, London: Latin American Bureau.

Merton, R. (1938/1970) *Science, Technology, and Society in Seventeenth Century England*, New York: Howard Fertig.

Metzler, M. (1994) 'Capitalist Boom, Feudal Bust: Long Waves in Economy and Politics in Pre-industrial Japan,' *Review* 17, 1:57–119.

Meyer, E. (1910) *Kleine Schriften zur gleschichtstheorie und zur Wirtschaftlichen und Politischen Geschichte des Altertums, von Eduard Meyer*, Halle a.S.: M. Niemeyer.

Midlarsky, M. (1988) *The Onset of World War*, Boston: Unwin Hyman.

—— (ed.) (1989) *Handbook of War Studies*, Boston: Unwin Hyman.

—— (ed.) (1998) *Handbook of War Studies II*, Ann Arbor: University of Michigan Press.

Millett, P. (1990) 'Sale, Credit and Exchange in Athenian Law and Society,' in P. Cartledge, P. Millett and S. Todd (eds) *Nomos: Essays in Athenian Law, Politics and Society*, New York: Cambridge University Press.

Millon, R. (1988) 'The Last Years of Teotihuacan Dominance,' in N. Yoffee and G. Cowgill (eds) *The Collapse of Ancient States and Civilizations*, Tucson: University of Arizona Press.

Mishkin, B. (1992/1940) *Rank and Warfare among the Plains Indians*, monograph No. 3 of the American Ethnological Society, Seattle: University of Washington Press, reprinted Lincoln: University of Nebraska Press.

Modelski, G. (1987) *Long Cycles in World Politics*, London: Macmillan.

—— (1991) 'Is World Politics Evolutionary Learning?,' *International Organization* 44, 3:1–24.

—— (1994) 'Evolutionary Paradigm for World Politics,' paper presented at the Workshop on Evolutionary Paradigms in the Social Sciences, Seattle WA.

—— (1996) 'An Evolutionary Paradigm for Global Politics,' *International Studies Quarterly* 40, 3:321–42.

—— (1999a) 'From Leadership to Organization: The Evolution of Global Politics,' in V. Bornschier and C. Chase-Dunn (eds) *The Future of Global Conflict*, London: Sage.

—— (1999b) 'Ancient World cities 4000–1000 BC: Center/Hinterland in the World System,' *Global Society* 13, 4:383–92.

—— (1999c) 'Classical World Cities 1200 BC to 1000 AD: Facets of World System Evolution,' *Encyclopedia of Human Ecology*, San Diego CA: Academic Press.

—— (1999d) 'Enduring Rivalry in the Democratic Lineage: The Venice-Portugal Case', in W.R. Thompson (ed.) *Great Power Rivalries*, Columbia SC: University of South Carolina Press.

Modelski, G. and Modelski, S. (1988) *Documenting Global Leadership*, London: Macmillan.

Modelski, G. and Thompson, W.R. (1988) *Sea Power in Global Politics, 1494–1993*, London: Macmillan.

—— (1996a) *Leading Sectors and World Powers: The Coevolution of Global Politics and Economics*, Columbia: University of South Carolina Press.

—— (1996b) 'The Evolutionary Pulse of the World Economy,' paper presented at the annual meeting of the International Studies Association, San Diego, California.

—— (1999) 'The Evolutionary Pulse of the World System: Hinterland Incursions and Migrations 4000 BC to 1500 AD,' in P.N. Kardulias (ed.) *Leadership, Production and Exchange: World-Systems Theory in Practice*, Landham MD: Rowman and Littlefield.

Mommsen, T. (1911) *The History of Rome*, New York: Everyman.

Montgomery, B. (1968) *A History of Warfare*, Cleveland OH: World Publishing Company.

Moore, W. (1989) *Schrödinger: Life and Thought*, Cambridge: Cambridge University Press.

Moseley, K. and Wallerstein, I. (1978) 'Precapitalist Social Structures,' *Annual Review of Sociology* 4:259–90.

Morris, C. (1978) 'The Archaeological Study of Andean Exchange Systems,' in C. Redman (ed.) *Social Archaeology: Beyond Subsistence and Dating*, New York: Academic Press.

—— (1979) 'Maize Beer in the Economics, Politics and Religion of the Inca Empire,' in C. Gastineau, W. Darby and T. Turner (eds) *Fermented Food Beverages in Nutrition*, New York: Academic Press.

—— (1982) 'The Infrastructure of Inka Control in the Peruvian Central Highlands,' in G. Collier, R. Rosaldo and J. Wirth (eds) *The Inca and Aztec States 1400–1800: Anthropology and History*, New York: Academic Press.

Murra, J. (1956/1980) 'The Economic Organization of the Inka State,' Supplement 1 to *Research in Economic Anthropology*, Stamford CT: JAI Press.

—— (1962) 'Cloth and its Functions in the Inca State,' *American Anthropologist*, 64:710–28.

—— (1971/1975) 'El tr fico de mullu en la costa del Pacfico,' in *Formaciones económicas y polítcas del mundo andino*, Lima: Instituto de Estudios Peruanos.

—— (1972/1975) 'El control vertical de un máximo de pisos ecológicos en la economía de las sociedades andinas,' in O. de Zúñiga (ed.) *Vista de la provencia de Léon de Huánuco, 1562, volume 2*, Huánuca Universidad: Nacional Hermilio Valdizán.

—— (1982) 'The Mit Obligations of Ethnic Groups to the Inka State,' in G. Collier, R. Rosaldo and J. Wirth (eds) *The Inca and Aztec States 1400–1800: Anthropology and History*, New York: Academic Press.

Myrdal, G. (1971) *Economic Theory and Underdeveloped Regions*, New York: Harper and Row.

Nectoux, F. and Kuroda, Y. (1990) *Timber from the South Seas*, Geneva: World Wildlife Fund.

Neilson, K. and Prete, R. (1983) *Coalition Warfare: An Uneasy Accord*, Waterloo, Ontario: Wilfrid Laurier University Press.

Nissen, H. (1986) 'The Archaic Texts from Uruk,' *World Archaeology* 17, 3:317–34.

—— (1990) *Protostoria del Vicino Oriente*, Bari, Italy: Laterza.

Nitz, H. (1993) ' Introduction,' in H. Nitz (ed.) *The Early-Modern World-System in Geographical Perspective* , Stuttgart: Steiner Verlag.

Nix, H. (1985) 'Agriculture,' in R. Kages, J. Ausubel and M. Berberian (eds) *Climate Impact Assessment: Studies of the Interaction of Climate and Society*, New York: John Wiley.

North, D. (1993) 'Competition and Values in the Rise of the West,' *Swiss Review of World Affairs* November:23–4.

North, D. and Thomas R. (1973) *The Rise of the Western World: A New Economic History*, Cambridge: Cambridge University Press.

Oates, D. and Oates, J. (1976) *The Rise of Civilization*, Oxford: Elsevier-Phaidon.

Oates, J. (1977) 'Mesopotamian Social Organization: Archaeological and Philological Evidence,' in J. Friedman and M. Rowlands (eds) *The Evolution of Social Systems*, Gloucester UK: Duckworth.

—— (1979) *Babylon*, London: Thames and Hudson.

Odum, H.T. (1988) 'Self-Organization, Transformity, and Information,' *Science* 242:1132–9.

Oppenheim, A.L. (1954) 'Sea-faring Merchants of Ur,' *Journal of the American Oriental Society* 74:6–17.

Palat, R. and Wallerstein I. (1990) 'Of What World System was pre-1500 "India" a Part?,' paper presented at the Internatioanl Colloquium on Merchants, Companies and Trade, Paris, France.

Parsons, T. (1966) *Societies: Comparative and Evolutionary Perspectives*, Englewood NJ: Prentice Hall.

Paulsen, A. (1974) 'The Thorny Oyster and the Voice of God: Spondylus and Strombus in Andean Prehistory,' *American Antiquity* 39, 4:597–607.

—— (1977) 'Patterns of Maritime Trade between South Coastal Ecuador and Western Mesoamerica, 1500 B.C.–A.D. 600,' in E. Benson (ed.) *The Sea in the Pre-Columbian World*, Washington DC: Dumbarton Oaks Research Library and Collection.

Pease G. (1982) 'The Formation of Tawantinsuyu: Mechanisms of Colonization and Relationship with Ethnic Groups,' in G. Collier, R. Rosaldo and J. Wirth (eds) *The Inca and Aztec States 1400–1800: Anthropology and History*, New York: Academic Press.

Penna, I. (1992) *Japan's Paper Industry*, Tokyo: Chikyu no Tomo.

Peregrine, P. (1996) 'Archaeology and World-Systems Theory,' *Sociological Inquiry* 65, 4:486–95.

—— (1998) *Outline of Archaeological Traditions*, New Haven CT: Human Relations Area File.

Perlin, J. (1989) *A Forest Journey: The Role of Wood in the Development of Civilization*, Cambridge MA: Harvard University Press.

Petesch, P. (1990) *Tropical Forests: Conservation with Development*, Washington DC: Overseas Development Council.

Piccone, P. (1994) 'Confronting the French New Right,' *Telos:* 98–9.

Pijl, K. van der (1998) *Transnational Classes and International Relations*, London: Routledge.

Polanyi, K. (1944/1957) *The Great Transformation: The Political and Economic Origins of Our Time*, Boston: Beacon Press.

—— (1958) 'The Economy as Instituted Process,' K. Polanyi, C. Arensberg and H.W. Pearson (eds) *Trade and Markets in the Early Empires*, Chicago: The Free Press.

—— (1977) *The Livelihood of Man* edited by H. Pearson, New York: Academic Press.

Ponting, C. (1991) *A Green History of the World*, London: Penguin.

Postgate, J.N. (1994) *Early Mesopotamia: Society and Economy at the Dawn of History*, London: Routledge.

Prigogine, I. (1984) *Order Out of Chaos*, New York: Bantam Books.

Quigley, C. (1979) *The Evolution of Civilizations*, Indianapolis IN: Liberty Fund.

Rand, E.K. (1975) 'The Latin Literature of the West from Antonies to Constantine,' in *The Cambridge Ancient History*, volume 12, Cambridge: Cambridge University Press.

Randsborg, K. (1991) *The First Millennium A.D. in Europe and the Mediterranean*, Cambridge: Cambridge University Press.

Rasler, K. and Thompson, W.R. (1994) *The Great Powers and Global Struggle, 1490–1990*, Lexington KY: University of Kentucky Press.

Rathje, W. (1973) 'Classic Maya Development and Denouement: A Research Design,' in T. Culbert (ed.) *The Classic Maya Collapse*, Albuquerque: University of New Mexico Press.

Ratnagar, S. (1981) *Encounters: The Westerly Trade of the Harappan Civilization*, New Delhi: Oxford University Press.

Ratzel, F. (1896) *The History of Mankind*, London: Macmillan and Co.

Raymond, J. (1988) 'A View from the Tropical Forest,' in R. Keatinge (ed.) *Peruvian Prehistory: An Overview of Pre-Inca and Inca Society*, Cambridge: Cambridge University Press.

Reich, R. (1992) *The Work of Nations: Preparing Ourselves for 21st Century Capitalism*, New York: Vintage Books.

Renfrew, C. (1975) 'Trade as Action at a Distance: Questions of Integration and Communication,' in J. Sabloff and C. Lamborg-Karlovsky (eds) *Ancient Civilization and Trade*, Albuquerque: University of New Mexico Press.

—— (1977) 'Alternative Models for Exchange and Spatial Distribution,' in T. Earle and T. Ericson (eds) *Exchange Systems in Prehistory*, New York: Academic Press.

—— (1986) 'Introduction,' in C. Renfrew and J. Cherry (eds) *Peer Polity Interaction and Socio-Political Change*, Cambridge: Cambridge University Press.

Richardson, L. (1960) *Statistics of Deadly Quarrels*, Pittsburgh PN: Boxwood Press.

Roberts, J. (1993) *History of the World*, Oxford: Oxford University Press.

Roberts, N. (1989) *The Holocene: An Environmental History*, Oxford: Basil Blackwell.

Ronan, C. and Needham, J. (1978/1981) *The Shorter Science and Civilisation in China*, two volumes, Cambridge: Cambridge University Press.

Roper, M. (1975) 'Evidence of Warfare in the Near East from 10,000–4,300 BC,' in M. Nettleship, R. Givens and A. Nettleship (eds) *War: Its Causes and Correlates*, The Hague: Mouton.

Rosaldo, R. (1982) 'Afterword,' in G. Collier, R. Rosaldo and J. Wirth (eds) *The Inca and Aztec States 1400–1800: Anthropology and History*, New York: Academic Press.

Rostovtzeff, M.I. (1926) *The Social and Economic History of the Roman Empire*, Oxford: Clarendon Press.

—— (1941) *The Social and Economic History of the Hellenistic World*, Oxford: Clarendon Press.

Rostow, W. (1960) *The Stages of Economic Growth: A Non-Communist Manifesto*, Cambridge: Cambridge University Press.

Rostworowski de Diez Canseco, M. (1977) 'Coastal Fishermen, Merchants, and Artisans in Pre-Hispanic Peru,' in E. Benson (ed.) *The Sea in the Pre-Columbian World*, Washington DC: Dumbarton Oaks Research Library and Collection.

Rothman, M. (ed.) (1999) *Mesopotamia in the Era of State Formation*, Santa Fe NM: School of American Research Press.

Rowe, J. (1982) 'Inca Policies and Institutions Relating to the Cultural Unification of the Empire,' in G. Collier, R. Rosaldo and J. Wirth (eds) *The Inca and Aztec States 1400–1800: Anthropology and History*, New York: Academic Press.

Rowlands, M., Larsen, M. and Kristiansen, K. (eds) (1987) *Centre and Periphery in the Ancient World*, Cambridge: Cambridge University Press.

Rush, J. (1991) *The Last Tree: Reclaiming the Environment in Tropical Asia*, New York: Asia Society.

Sahlins, M. (1972) 'On the Sociology of Primitive Exchange,' in M. Sahlins (ed.) *Stone Age Economics*, Chicago: Aldine-Atherton.

—— (1976) *Culture and Practical Reason*, Chicago: University of Chicago Press.

Sallnow, M. (1989) 'Precious Metals in the Andean Moral Economy,' in J. Parry and M. Bloch (eds) *Money and the Morality of Exchange*, Cambridge: Cambridge University Press.

Salomon, F. (1986) *Native Lords of Quito in the Age of the Incas: The Political Economy of North Andean Chiefdoms*, Cambridge: Cambridge University Press.

Sanderson, S.K. (1990) *Social Evolutionism: A Critical History*, Cambridge MA: Blackwell.

—— (1991) *The Evolution of Societies and World-Systems*, Boulder CO: Westview Press.

—— (1992) 'The Transition from Feudalism to Capitalism: The Theoretical Significance of the Japanese Case,' *Review* 17, 1:15–55.

—— (1995a) *Social Transformations: A General Theory of Historical Development*, London: Basil Blackwell.

—— (ed.) (1995b) *Civilizations and World Systems: Studying World-Historical Change*, Walnut Creek CA: AltaMira Press.

—— (1999) *Social Transformations: A General Theory of Historical Development*, expanded edition, Lanham MD: Rowman and Littlefield.

Sarawak Campaign Committee (1993) 'Japan and the World's Forests,' *Mori No Koe* (Voice of the Forest), December. Available on line at http://forests.org/gopher/aisa/tokyo.txt

Schneider, J. (1977/1991) 'Was There A Pre-capitalist World-System?,' *Peasant Studies* 6, 1:20–9, reprinted in C. Chase-Dunn and T. Hall (eds) *Core/Periphery Relations in Precapitalist Worlds*, Boulder CO: Westview Press.

Schortman, E. and Urban, P. (1987) 'Modeling Interregional Interaction in Prehistory,' in M. Schiffer (ed.) *Advances in Archaeological Methods and Theory*, volume 11, New York: Academic Press.

Schreiber, K. (1987) 'From State to Empire: The Expansion of Wari Outside the Ayacucho Basin,' in J. Haas, S. Pozorski and T. Pozorski (eds) *The Origins and Development of the Andean State*, Cambridge: Cambridge University Press.

Schrödinger, E. (1944/1967) *What is Life? Mind and Matter*, Cambridge: Cambridge University Press.

Scott, A. (1967) *The Functioning of the International Political System*, New York: Macmillan.

Secoy, F. (1953/1992) *Changing Military Patterns of the Great Plains Indians (17th Century Through Early 19th Century)*, Monographs of the American Ethnological Society, 21, Locust Valley NY: J.J. Augustin, reprinted Lincoln: University of Nebraska Press.

Sennett, R. (1970) *The Uses of Disorder: Personal Identity and City Life*, New York: W.W. Norton.

Sharer, R. (1994) *The Ancient Maya*, Stanford CA: Stanford University Press.

Shaw, B. (1981) 'Climate, Environment, and History: The Case of Roman North Africa,' in T. Wrigley, M. Ingram and G. Farmer (eds) *Climate and History*, Cambridge: Cambridge University Press.

Sherratt, A. (1992) 'The Relativity of Theory,' in N. Yoffee and A. Sherratt (eds) *Archaeological Theory – Who sets the Agenda?* Cambridge: Cambridge University Press.

—— (1993a) 'What Would a Bronze-Age World System Look Like? Relations Between Temperate Europe and the Mediterranean in Later Prehistory,' *Journal of European Archaeology* 1, 2:1–57.

—— (1993b) 'Core, Periphery and Margin: Perspectives on the Bronze Age,' in C. Mathers and S. Stoddart (eds) *Development and Decline in the Mediterranean Bronze Age*, Sheffield: Sheffield Academic Press.

—— (1993c) 'Who are You Calling Peripheral? Dependence and Independence in

European Prehistory,' in C. Scarre and F. Healy (eds) *Trade and Exchange in Prehistoric Europe*, Prehistoric Society Monograph, Oxford: Oxbow.

—— (1995) 'Fata Morgana: Illusion and Reality in Greek-Barbarian Relations,' *Cambridge Archaeological Journal* 3,1: 139–53.

—— (1997) *Economy and Society in Prehistoric Europe: Changing Perspectives* , Princeton: Princeton University Press.

Sherratt, A. and Sherratt, E. S. (1991) 'From Luxuries to Commodities: The Nature of Mediterranean Bronze Age Trading Systems,' in N. Gale (ed.) *Bronze Age Trade in the Mediterranean*, Jonsered: SIMA.

Sherratt, E. S. (1994) 'Commerce, Iron and Ideology: Metallurgical Innovation in 12th–11th Century Cyprus,' in V. Karageorghis (ed.) *Cyprus in the 11th Century B.C.*, Nicosia: A.G. Leventis Foundation/University of Cyprus.

Sherratt, E. S. and Sherratt, A. (1993) 'The Growth of the Mediterranean Economy in the Early 1st Millennium BC,' *World Archaeology* 24, 3:361–78.

Shimada, I. (1985) 'Perception, Procurement, and Management of Resources: Archaeological Perspective,' in S. Masuda, I. Shimada and C. Morris (eds) *Andean Ecology and Civilization: An Interdisciplinary Perspective on Andean Ecological Complementarity*, Tokyo: University of Tokyo Press.

—— (1987) 'Horizontal and Vertical Dimensions of Prehistoric States in North Peru,' in J. Haas, S. Pozorski and T. Pozorski (eds) *The Origins and Development of the Andean State*, Cambridge: Cambridge University Press.

Silver, M. (1985) *Economic Structures of the Ancient Near East*, London: Croom Helm.

Simon, H. (1965) 'The Architecture of Complexity,' *General Systems* 10:63–76.

Small, M. and Singer, J. (1982) *Resort to Arms*, Beverly Hills CA: Sage.

Sorokin, P. (1937) *Fluctuations of Social Relationships, War, and Revolution*, volume three, New York: American Book Company.

Spitz, L. (1985) *The Protestant Reformation, 1517–1559*, New York: Harper & Row.

Starr, H. (1972) *War Coalitions: The Distribution of Payoffs and Losses*, Lexington MA: D.C. Heath.

—— (1998) 'Geographic Information Systems (GIS) and the Study of Borders in International Relations,' paper presented to the International Studies Association, Minneapolis.

Swadesh, M. (1971) *The Origin and Diversification of Language*, Chicago: Aldine.

Swanson, G. (1967) *Religion and Regime: A Sociological Account of the Reformation*, Ann Arbor: University of Michigan Press.

Sweezy, P. (1976) 'A Critique,' in R. Hilton (ed.) *The Transition from Feudalism to Capitalism*, London: New Left Books.

Taagepera, R. (1968) 'Growth Curves of Empires,' *General Systems* 13:171–5.

—— (1978a) 'Size and Duration of Empires: Systematics of Size,' *Social Science Research* 7:108–27.

—— (1978b) 'Size and Duration of Empires: Growth-Decline Curves, 3000 to 600 B.C.,' *Social Science Research* 7: 180–96.

Tadem, E. (1990) 'Conflict over Land Based Natural Resources in the ASEAN Countries,' in T. Lim and M. Valencia (eds) *Conflict over Natural Resources in S.E. Asia and the Pacific*, Singapore: Oxford University Press.

Teggart, F. (1925/1960) *Theory of History*, New Haven CT: Yale University Press, reprinted Berkeley: University of California Press.

—— (1939) *Rome and China: A Study of Correlations in Historical Events*, Berkeley CA: University of California Press.

Thirgood, J. (1981) *Man and the Mediterranean Forest: A History of Resource Depletion*, London: Academic Press.

Thompson, W.R. (1983) *Contending Approaches to World Systems Analysis*, Beverly Hills CA: Sage.

—— (1988) *On Global War: Historical-Structural Approaches to World Politics*, Columbia: University of South Carolina Press.

—— (1994) 'Ten Centuries of Global Political-Economic Coevolution,' paper presented at the Workshop on Evolutionary Paradigms in the Social Sciences, Seattle, Washington.

—— (1995) 'The 1490s: A Question of (Dis)Continuity?,' paper presented at the annual meeting of the International Studies Association, Chicago, Illinois.

—— (1999) *Great Power Rivalries*, Columbia: University of South Carolina Press.

Thornton, R. (1987) *American Indian Holocaust and Survival*, Norman: University of Oklahoma Press.

Tibbetts, G. (1956) 'Pre-Islamic Arabia and Southeast Asia,' *Journal of the Malayan Branch of the Royal Asiatic Society* 29, 3:182–208.

Tibebu, T. (1990) 'On the Question of Feudalism, Absolutism, and the Bourgeois Revolution,' *Review* 13, 1:49–152.

Tilly, C. (1984) *Big Structures, Large Processes, Huge Comparisons*, New York: Russell Sage.

—— (1990) *Coercion, Capital, and European States, AD 990–1990*, Cambridge MA: Basil Blackwell.

Topic, J. and Topic, T. (1987) 'The Archaeological Investigation of Andean Militarism: Some Cautionary Observations,' in J. Haas, S. Pozorski and T. Pozorski (eds) *The Origins and Development of the Andean State*, Cambridge: Cambridge University Press.

Totman, C. (1989) *The Green Archipelago*, Berkeley CA: University of California Press.

—— (1992) 'Forest Products Trade in Pre-Industrial Japan,' in J. Dargavel (ed.) *Changing Pacific Forests*, Durham: Forest History Society.

Toynbee, A. (1934–1962) *A Study of History*, volumes 1–12, London: Oxford University Press.

Tucker, R. (1988) 'The Commercial Timber Economy under Two Colonial Regimes in Asia', in J. Dargavel, K. Dixon and N. Semple. (eds) *Changing Tropical Forests*, Canberra: Centre for Resources and Environmental Studies.

Tufte, E. (1983) *The Visual Display of Quantitative Information*, Cheshire CT: Graphics Press.

—— (1990) *Envisioning Information*, Cheshire CT: Graphics Press.

—— (1997) *Visual Explanations: Images and Quantities, Evidence and Narrative*, Cheshire CT: Graphics Press.

Tyumenev, A.I. (1973a) 'The State Economy of Ancient Sumer,' in I. Diakonoff (ed.) *Ancient Mesopotamia*, Wiesbaden: Martin Sändig oHG.

—— (1973b) 'The Working Personnel on the Estate of the Temple of Ba-U in Lagash During the Period of Lugalanda and Urakagina (25th–24th Century B.C.),' in I. Diakonoff (ed.) *Ancient Mesopotamia*, Wiesbaden: Märtin Sandig oHG.

United Nations Economic and Social Commission for Asia and the Pacific (1980) *State of the Environment for Asia and the Pacific*, Bangkok: United Nations.

UNRISD (1995) *States of Disarray: The Social Effects of Globalization*, Geneva: United Nations.

Vasquez, J. (1987) 'The Steps to War: Toward a Scientific Explanation of Correlates of War Findings,' *World Politics* 40, 1:108–45.

—— (1993) *The War Puzzle*, Cambridge: Cambridge University Press.

Vidal, G. (1981) *Creation: A Novel*, New York: Random House.

Voll, J. (1994) 'Islam as a Special World-System,' *Journal of World History* 5, 2:213–26.

Wachtel, N. (1982) 'The Mitimas of the Cochabamba Valley: The Colonization Policy of Huayna Capac,' in G. Collier, R. Rosaldo and J. Wirth (eds) *The Inca and Aztec States 1400–1800: Anthropology and History*, New York: Academic Press.

Waines, D. (1987) 'Cereals, Bread and Society,' *Journal of the Economic and Social History of the Orient*, 30.

Wall, G. (1986) 'Exergy: A Useful Concept,' Unpublished thesis, Chalmers Tekniska Hgskola, Gothenburg.

Wallerstein, I. (1974a) *The Modern World-System I: Capitalist Agriculture and the Origins of the European World-Economy in the Sixteenth Century*, New York: Academic Press.

—— (1974b) 'The Rise and Future Demise of the World Capitalist System: Concepts for Comparative Analysis,' *Comparative Studies in Society and History* 16, 4:387–415.

—— (1975) 'The Present State of the Debate on World Inequality,' in I. Wallerstein (ed.) *World Inequality: Origins and Perspectives on the World-System*, Montreal: Black Rose Books.

—— (1979a) *The Capitalist World-Economy*, Cambridge: Cambridge University Press.

—— (1979b) 'Underdevelopment and Phase-B: Effect of the Seventeenth-Century Stagnation on Core and Periphery of the European World-Economy', in W. Goldfrank (ed.) *The World-System of Capitalism: Past and Present*, Beverly Hills CA: Sage.

—— (1980) *The Modern World-System II: Mercantilism and the Consolidation of the European World-Economy, 1600–1750*, New York: Academic Press.

—— (1982) 'World-Systems Analysis: Theoretical and Interpretative Issues,' in T. Hopkins, I. Wallerstein *et al.* (eds) *World-Systems Analysis: Theory and Methodology*, Beverly Hills CA: Sage.

—— (1983) *Historical Capitalism*, London: Verso.

—— (1984) *The Politics of the World-Economy*, Cambridge: Cambridge University Press.

—— (1989) *The Modern World-System III: The Second Era of Great Expansion of the Capitalist World-Economy, 1730–1840s*, San Diego CA: Academic Press.

—— (1991) 'World System Versus World-Systems: A Critique,' *Critique of Anthropology* 11, 2:189–94.

—— (1992) 'The West, Capitalism, and the Modern World-System,' *Review* 15, 4:561–620.

Wang, G. (1958) 'The Ninhai Trade: A Study of the Early History of Chinese Trade in Southeast Asia,' *Journal of the Malayan Branch of the Royal Asiatic Society* 31, 2:1–135.

Warburton, D. (1997) *State and Economy in Ancient Egypt: Fiscal Vocabulary of the New Kingdom*, Fribourg: Göttingen, Vendenhoeck and Rupprecht.

Wassén, S.H. (1972) 'A Medicine-man's Implements and Plants in a Tiahuanacoid Tomb in Highland Bolivia,' *Etnologiska studier* 32:8–114.

Watson, A. (1983) *Agricultural Innovations in the Early Islamic World: The Diffusion of Crops and Farming Techniques* , 700–1100, Cambridge: Cambridge University Press.

Watson, J. (1968) *The Double Helix*, New York: Signet Books.

Webb, M. (1987) 'Broader Perspectives on Andean State Origins,' in J. Haas, S. Pozorski and T. Pozorski (eds) *The Origins and Development of the Andean State*, Cambridge: Cambridge University Press.

Weber, M. (1927/1981) *General Economic History*, trans. F. Knight, New Brunswick NJ: Transaction Books.

Weiss, H., Courty, M., Wetterstron, W., Guichard, F., Senior, L. and Curnow, A. (1993) 'The Genesis and Collapse of Third Millennium North Mesopotamian Civilization,' *Science* 261:995–1004.

Wessels, L. (1983) 'Erwin Schrödinger and the Descriptive Tradition,' in R. Aris, H. Davis and R. Stuewer (eds) *Springs of Scientific Creativity: Essays on Founders of Modern Science*, Minneapolis: University of Minnesota Press.

Westenholz, A. (1979) 'The Old Addadian Empire in Contemporary Opinion,' in M. Larsen (ed.) *Power and Propaganda*, Copenhagen: Akademisk Forlag.

Wheatley, P. (1959) 'Geographical Notes on Some Commodities Involved in the Sung Maritime Trade', *Journal of the Malayan Branch of the Royal Asiatic Society* 32, 2:1–140.

—— (1961) *The Golden Khersonese*, Kuala Lumpur: University of Malaya Press.

Wheeler, R. (1968) *The Indus Civilization*, Cambridge: Cambridge University Press.

White, L. (1962) *Medieval Technology and Social Change*, Oxford: Clarendon Press.

Wight, M. (1977) 'De systematibus civitatum,' in M. Wight, *Systems of States* edited with an introduction by Hedley Bull, Leicester: Leicester University Press.

Wilkinson, D. (1980) *Deadly Quarrels: Lewis Fry Richardson and the Statistical Study of War*, Berkeley: University of California Press.

—— (1982) 'A Definition, Roster and Classification of Civilizations,' paper presented to the International Society for the Comparative Study of Civilizations,' Pittsburgh PN.

—— (1983) 'Civilizations, States Systems and Universal Empires,' paper presented to the International Society for the Comparative Study of Civilizations, Buffalo NY.

—— (1985) 'Spykman and Geopolitics,' in C. Zoppo and C. Zorgbibe (eds) *On Geopolitics: Classical and Nuclear*, Dordrecht: Martinus Nijhoff.

—— (1986) 'Kinematics of World Systems,' *Dialectics and Humanism* 1:21–35.

—— (1987a) 'Central Civilization,' *Comparative Civilizations Review* 17:31–59.

—— (1987b) 'The Connectedness Criterion and Central Civilization,' in M. Melko and L. Scott (eds) *The Boundaries of Civilizations in Space and Time*, Lanham MD: University Press of America.

—— (1988) 'Universal Empires: Pathos and Engineering,' *Comparative Civilizations Review* 18:22–44.

—— (1989) 'The Future of the World State: From Civilization Theory to World Politics,' paper presented at the Annual Meeting of the International Studies Association, London.

—— (1991) 'Cores, Peripheries, and Civilizations,' in C. Chase-Dunn and T. Hall (eds) *Core/Periphery Relations in Precapitalist Worlds*, Boulder CO: Westview Press.

—— (1992a) 'Cities, Civilizations and Oikumenes: I,' *Comparative Civilizations Review* 27:51–87.

—— (1992b) 'Decline Phases in Civilizations, Regions and Oikumenes,' paper presented at the Annual Meeting of the International Studies Association, Atlanta GA.

—— (1993a) 'Cities, Civilizations and Oikumenes: II,' *Comparative Civilizations Review* 28:41–72.

—— (1993b) 'Cities, States, and States-Systems: The Indic Case,' paper presented at the annual meeting of the International Studies Association, Acapulco, Mexico.

—— (1993c) 'Civilizations, Cores, World Economies, and Oikumenes,' in A.G. Frank and B.K. Gills (eds) *The World System: Five Hundred Years or Five Thousand?*, London: Routledge.

—— (1993/1994) 'Spatio-Temporal Boundaries of African Civilizations Reconsidered,' Part I, *Comparative Civilizations Review* 29:52–90; Part II, 31:46–105.

—— (1994a) 'Hegemony and Social Change,' *Mershon International Studies Review* 38, 2:374–6.

—— (1994b) 'Reconceiving Hegemony,' paper presented at the annual meeting of the International Studies Association, Washington DC.

—— (1995a) 'Civilizations *Are* World Systems,' in S. Sanderson (ed.) *Civilizations and World Systems*, Walnut Creek CA: AltaMira.

—— (1995b) 'Decline Phases in Civilizations, Regions and Oikumenes,' *Comparative Civilizations Review* 30:33–78.

—— (1995c) 'From Mesopotamia through Carroll Quigley to Bill Clinton: World Historical Systems, the Civilizationist, and the President,' *Journal of World-Systems Research* 1:1. Available on line at http://csf.colorado.edu/wsystems/jwsr/vol1/v1_n1.htm.

—— (1995d) 'Sorokin vs. Toynbee on Congeries and Civilizations,' in J. Ford, P. Talbutt and M. Richard (eds) *Sorokin: A Centennial Assessment*, New Brunswick NJ: Transaction Books.

Wilkinson, D. and Iberall, A.S. (1986) 'From Systems Physics to World Politics: Invitation to an Enterprise,' in M. Karns (ed.) *Persistent Patterns and Emergent Structures in a Waning Century*, New York: Praeger.

—— (1994) 'Missing Civilizations?,' paper presented at the International Society for the Comparative Study of Civilizations, Dublin, Ireland.

Will, E., Mosse, E. and Goukovsky, P. (eds) (1961) *Le Monde grec et l'orient*, vol. 2, Paris: Presses Universitaires de France.

Willard, A. (1993) 'Gold, Islam and Camels: The Transformative Effects of Trade and Ideology,' *Comparative Civilizations Review* 29:80–105.

Willey, G. (1991) 'Horizontal Integration and Regional Diversity: An Alternating Process in the Rise of Civilizations,' *American Antiquity* 56, 2:197–215.

Wilmer, F. (1993) *The Indigenous Voice in World Politics: Since Time Immemorial*, Newbury Park CA: Sage.

Wolf, E. (1982) *Europe and the People Without History*, Berkeley CA: University of California Press.

Wolters, O. (1967) *Early Indonesian Commerce*, Ithaca NY: Cornell University Press.

Woolf, G. (1990) 'World-Systems Analysis and the Roman Empire,' *Journal of Roman Archaeology* 3:44–58.

Wright, H. (1969) *The Administration of Rural Production in an Early Mesopotamian Town*, Museum of Anthropology Anthropological Papers No. 38, Ann Arbor: University of Michigan.

Wright, H. and Johnson, G. (1975) 'Population, Exchange and Early State Formation in Southwestern Iran,' *American Anthropologist* 77, 2:267–89.

Wright, Q. (1942) *Study of War*, Chicago: University of Chicago Press.

Wuthnow, R. (1980) 'The World-Economy and the Institutionalization of Science in Seventeenth-Century Europe,' in A. Bergesen (ed.) *Studies of the Modern World-System*, New York: Academic Press.

Wyatt, D. (1984) *Thailand: A Short History*, New Haven CT: Yale University Press.

—— (1994) *Studies in Thai History*, Chiang Mai, Thailand: Silkworm Books.

Yamamoto, T. (1981) 'Chinese Activities in the Indian Ocean Before the Coming of the Portuguese,' *Diogenes* 111:19–34.

Name index

Abu-Lughod, Janet xx, 11, 13, 15, 16, 107, 192, 217, 307, 373
Adams, R. McC. 5, 9, 156, 157, 158, 162, 167, 248
Algaze, G. 157, 158, 166
Amir, S. xix, 3, 8, 13, 14, 15, 87, 185, 189
Andersen, E.S. 29
Anderson, P. 2, 9, 102, 190
Arrighi, G. 94, 95, 133
Aston, T. 16
Augustus Caesar 151, 280
Axelrod, R. 40, 43
Azevedo, J. 53

Barfield, T.J. 96, 105, 107
Beer, F. 258
Bernal, M. 16
Blaney, G. 272
Blaut, J. 6, 15, 16, 126, 189
Bohman, J. 307, 308
Bosworth, A. 11, 42, 125, 373
Bozeman, A.D. 143, 150, 151
Braudel, F. 3, 13, 14, 16, 17, 48, 53n, 269
Bremer, S. 268, 272
Brownstone, D. 125, 280, 281

Caracalla 151
Cavalli-Sforza, L. 25, 27, 29
Chandler, T. 11, 12, 21, 55–6, 81, 192, 220, 222, 278, 282
Chang, K.C. 272
Chase-Dunn, C. 13, 17, 18, 19, 20, 22, 80, 81, 83, 85, 86, 87, 100, 217, 218, 268, 269, 302, 306, 309, 310, 311
Chaudhuri, K. 16, 17, 107, 126, 190, 191
Chernykh, E.N. 6
Chew, S. 104, 217, 234
Childe, G. 118

Chupik, P. 261, 265
Cimon 141
Cioffi-Revilla, C. 106, 254, 255, 258, 259, 261, 265, 268, 269, 270, 271, 272
Clinton, Bill 77–8
Collins, R. 89, 96, 185
Corning, P. 276
Crick, F. 300
Curtin, P. 191, 193, 218

Darwin, C. 31; neo-Darwinian focus on competition 283
Demosthenes 141
Denemark, R.A. 307, 309
Diehl, P.F. 259, 268
Dupuy, R.E. and Trevor, N. 272

Eisenstadt, S.N. 196
Ekholm-Friedman, K. 100, 134, 144, 154, 155, 217
Elster, J. 31
Elvin, M. 17, 188

Ferrill, A. 258, 272
Finlay, M. 5, 118, 134, 135
Flannery, K. 271, 272
Forbes, R.J. 196
Franck, I. 125, 280, 281
Frank, A.G. 4, 9, 12, 14, 17, 18, 22, 27, 79, 80, 63, 100, 101, 103, 105, 133, 185, 186, 193, 194, 195, 217, 218, 242, 269, 288, 298, 302, 306, 309, 310, 311
Friedman, J. 89, 134, 142, 144, 154, 155, 217

Geller, D.A. 256, 268, 272
Genghis Khan 48, 211

Wilkinson, D. 4, 11, 13, 18, 18, 24, 53, 57, 59, 60, 61, 67, 77, 79, 82, 86, 100, 192, 258, 266, 288, 298, 302, 206, 302, 305, 309, 310, 311

Willey, G. 268, 272
Wolf, E. 8, 9, 14, 87, 95, 116, 131, 185, 248
Wright, Q. 254, 269, 272
Wuthnow, R. 188

Subject index